1995-1996 Edition

Mc[illegible]om's Camera Bluebook

A complete, up-to-date ***price & buyers guide*** *for* ***new & used*** *cameras, lenses, & accessories*

Over 200 Photos!

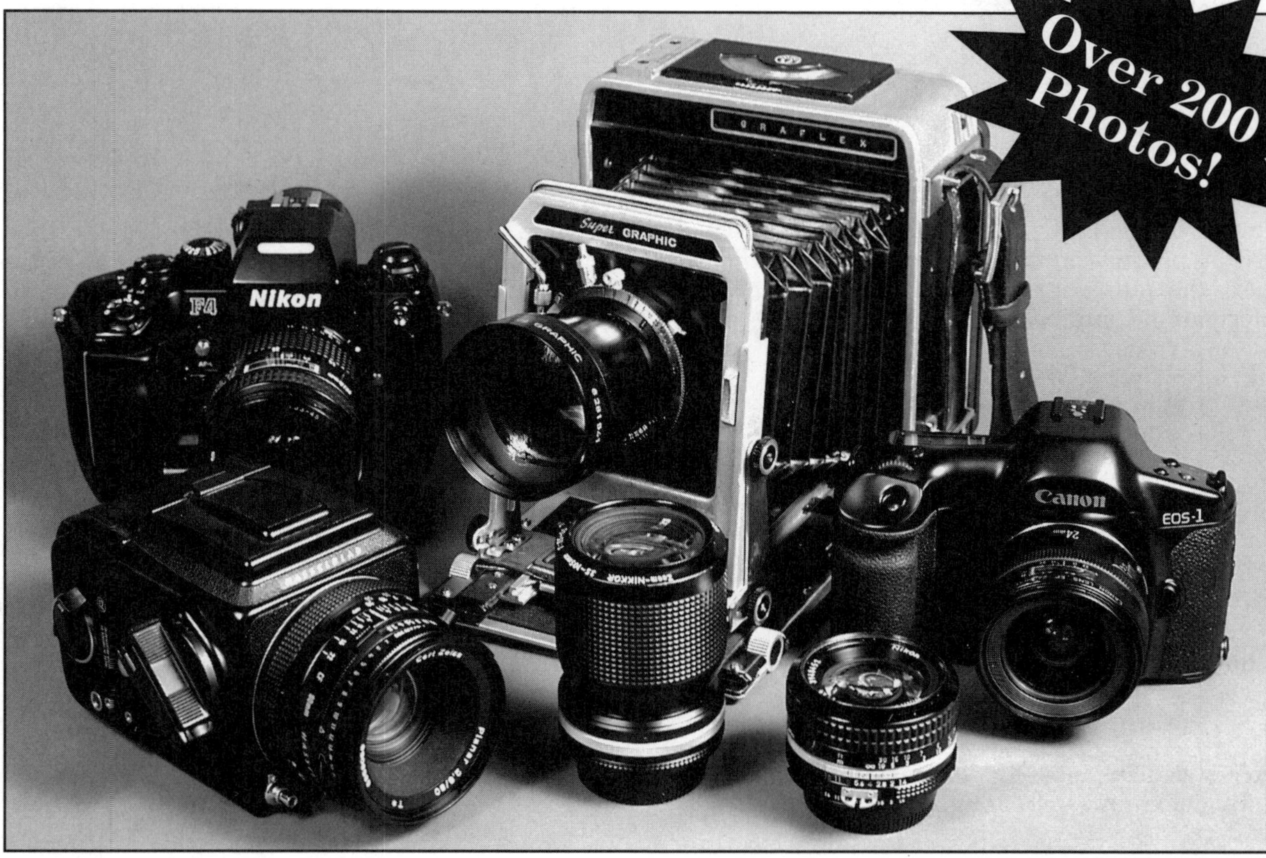

Published by:
Amherst Media, Inc.
PO Box 586
Amherst, NY 14226
Fax: 716-874-4508

ISBN: 0-936262-35-4
Library of Congress Number: 95-79714

Publisher: Craig Alesse

Editors: Michael McBroom &
Robert Roberge

Research Assistant: Robert Roberge

Layout & Cover Design: Richard Lynch

Printed in the United States of America

10 9 8 7 6 5 4 3 2 1

Exclusive distributor for Germany, Switzerland, Austria, and the Netherlands:
H. Lindemanns Buchhanlung
Nadlerstrasse 10
Postfach 10 31 51
D-70173 Stuttgart
tel (0711) 23 34 99
fax (0711) 236 96 72

Acknowledgements

Anyone who takes on the task of writing a comprehensive book soon realizes that it cannot be created in a vacuum. Such is especially the case here. I have many people to thank for their unflagging support, encouragement and advice. I would like to thank them all personally, although I know I will leave someone out, so I apologize in advance for any omissions.

Special thanks go out to Silvio Bello of Silvio's Photoworks in Torrance, California, for providing many of the cameras used for illustrations, and for his help with tracking down answers to a host of questions; to Tod Maltby of Alpha Photo-Technical in Salt Lake City, Utah, for providing me with hundreds of listings, especially those in the large format section; to Charles Duckworth of Sierra Camera in Reno, Nevada, for his help with the Leica, Zeiss and large format sections; to Roger Adams, for his tutelage on the Graflex system; to Bob and Laura Greenberg and the courteous crew at Alhambra Camera in Alhambra, California, for providing information on many recent camera models; to James Spencer of James Spencer Photography in Phoenix, Arizona for his coaching and insight with the large format arcana; and especially to Craig Alesse at Amherst Media, whose unsinkable optimism, cajoling and support kept me going, even when I was convinced I couldn't possibly write another word.

Others who have passed on valuable advice, or provided cameras for illustrations, must be mentioned also, although I know I'll be leaving many out. Thanks to Peter Ashworth, Mark Baehr, Bill Bagnall, Tom Bates, Don E. Brown, Jack Chalais, Bill Carrol, Bill and Cecilia Cox, Imre de Pozgay, Keith Fornof, Jim and Mike Frizle, Bill Gabb, Eric Gilbert, Richard Griffin, Murray Gutman, Les Hobbs, Manfred Kallweit, Reza Kami, Gigi Lash, Filippo Laveneziana, Gene Lester, Phil Lohman, Greg Locke, Chuck Mahan, Rob McBerge, Joe McGerald, Steve Molitor at Long Beach Camera, Roger Newsham, Grant Perkins, Bill Rogers, Gene Taylor, Raja Vejendla, Ricky Yen, and the rest. Simply put, this book would not have been possible without you.

Table of Contents

Introduction

The intent of this book is to provide the reader with a comprehensive listing of prices and descriptions for popular photo equipment. This is not a collector's price guide, although there is some inevitable overlap with a few makes, such as Leica and Rollei. In such cases, only models still bought and sold as user cameras are included. I have intentionally omitted all special and limited edition models, since these were intended as collectibles. Also omitted are certain rare makes and models that, while not originally intended as collectibles, have become such.

The cameras you will find in this book are the ones people buy to use. All the popular camera brands are listed, while a number of border-line and lesser-known makes haven't been included. From a purely logistical standpoint, the line had to drawn somewhere simply because of the law of diminishing returns. It takes much more time to compile information and prices on a Konica, for example, than it does for a Nikon. Yet, in terms of sales, there are probably a hundred Nikons sold for every Konica.

The *McBroom's Camera Bluebook* Condition Rating System

I've adopted a simplified version of the system popularized by *Shutterbug* magazine for describing equipment condition. Price ranges are broken down into four categories: New, Mint, Excellent and User. Using the Excellent range as an example, a price on the high end of the range usually represents an item whose condition is known in *Shutterbug* parlance as "Excellent Plus" (often abbreviated as Exc+), while the low price represents "Excellent Minus" (Exc-).

Yes, but what does this mean, you ask? Well, since you asked, here it is in a nutshell: New is self-explanatory. Mint = new condition, but previously sold. Mint minus (the lower end of the Mint range) = a minor mark or two. Excellent = light signs of use, minor brassing or bright marks on corners (less wear for the high end of the range, more for the lower end). User = noticeable signs of use, pronounced brassing or bright marks on corners, expect to find a ding or two. An item whose price is listed in the lower end of the User range won't be pretty.

The ratings reflect an item's cosmetic condition only. An item's mechanical, electrical or optical condition is always assumed to be in good working order unless specifically stated otherwise.

Prices

Although a few price-guide pretenders would have you believe otherwise, *McBroom's Camera Bluebook* is still the only book available that provides the reader with a comprehensive listing of current, real-world prices for popular photo equipment. You'll find no photocopies of manufacturers' price lists here. Nor will you find sliding-scale pricing strategies based on list prices. The prices for new and used equipment shown in the following pages were obtained from a variety of sources, ranging from businesses who advertise in national photo-oriented publications, such as *Shutterbug*, *Popular Photography*, and *Petersen's*

Photographic, to camera swap meets. Be aware that the prices shown are *asking prices* and much of the time an item can be obtained for less if you're willing to haggle. Also, if you attend camera swap meets, you'll generally see lower prices than those shown here. The reasons are simple: dealers at camera shows often have less overhead than advertisers in national magazines and pass their savings to their customers, and the competition at these shows drives prices down.

All prices are grouped within ranges and rounded off to the nearest five dollars. The range of new prices usually reflects the differences found between the large East Coast mail order retailers (lower), and most other discount retailers (higher). List prices are given only when the items are sold at list, even by discount retailers.

New prices were included for a few reasons:

1. This book can serve as a quick reference when shopping for new camera equipment.

2. For many items, especially newer ones, used prices were unavailable. Having a price range for an item in new condition allows the buyer to make an informed judgement when buying that item in used condition. It's a little like the transitive property in algebra: If a=b and b=c, then a=c. If Knowledge = Power and Power = Money, then Knowledge = Money. In this case it means money saved, which is still money in your pocket that may not have been there otherwise.

3. To put used prices in perspective. In some instances prices for used equipment are higher than new. Some mail order retailers have been known to advertise new equipment for cheap prices when it's not readily available or not even in stock. However, another factor is more often the case: If a dealer's price for a new item falls around the high end of the "New" range, he or she may price a used item based on a discount of his or her own new price. This is usually why you will see frequent overlaps in prices between the New and the Mint ranges.

PRICE VOLATILITY

The slide of the U.S. dollar on international money markets has severely affected the photographic equipment market. As the dollar falls, the prices of imports rise, which, in turn, causes a great deal of price volatility with new photo equipment, since virtually all of it is imported. This volatility trickles down to used prices, as well. So, keep in mind that though the prices here are current, there's a good chance that when this book reaches the bookshelves they won't be. My advice to you is to keep a pencil handy and update the book as you come across new, higher prices (that's what I do) — and hope the dollar firms up soon.

Buying Pointers

New Photo Equipment

There are essentially three ways to buy a new item:

1. **Your local camera shop.** If you value service both before and after the sale, there is no better way to go. Your local camera shop will take the time to point out an item's features, demonstrate it, and compare it with similar items. Their prices are usually higher than those of the other alternatives, but you're getting personalized service. Plus, you've established a rapport that may well prove invaluable as years go by, especially if you're a pro or a serious amateur. In this day and age, the local camera shop has become an endangered species. If you can afford it, support your local camera shop. You'll be glad you did.
2. **Your local discount retailer.** Usually a discount department store that carries photo equipment in addition to clothing, major and minor appliances, recliners, sporting goods, hardware and tires, has better prices than your local camera shop, since they buy in large quantities. But there are trade-offs. You'll more often than not be discussing an item's features with someone who knows next to nothing about it and the selection may be limited. In other words, if you want cheap prices, you take what they give you and don't count on service after the sale.
3. **A mail-order photo equipment house.** Buying from a mail-order photo retailer is usually the best way to save money, but it has risks. Mail-order houses buy in tremendous quantities compared to your local camera shop. When a mail-order house sells tens of thousands of dollars of a single manufacturer's merchandise each week, as opposed to that much per year from a small retailer, it only stands to reason that these large retailers will receive more favorable price breaks from a manufacturer than small retailers will. However, there are trade-offs to buying by mail and they are several: No personalized service; you can't see the item before you buy it; it may not have a U.S. warranty; it may not be complete as supplied by the manufacturer; it may have been sold before. You should consider buying an item via mail order only if you are already familiar with its features and capabilities.

Horror stories abound about buying photo equipment through the mail. Some mail-order dealers are more reputable than others. If you're unsure, ask around. Your local camera club might be a good place to start.

In all fairness, I must tell you that my good experiences outweigh the bad. In large part my good fortune is due to being selective. My success has also been due to the way I have ordered. What follows is a list of some practices I've employed to help me decide when to purchase by mail, and how to minimize problems:

1. *Read the ad thoroughly before calling, especially the fine print.* Is there a disclaimer stating that "some" merchandise may be "parallel imports" (aka gray market)? Be aware that gray market merchandise will not have a U.S. warrantee. In the aftermarket lens listings, are all lens mounts offered at the same price? If words such as "other mounts may vary [in price]" are used, you can count on the fact that any mount other than the one for which their prices apply will be higher.

If no price is listed for an item and the advertizement says "Call" instead, call their toll-free number. This number is usually reserved for credit card orders only, but if they won't (or can't) print an item's price, why should you have to pay for the call? With very new items, a store's ad for an item may list "Call" instead of a price, because they may only know that it will be available soon, but do not know what it's selling price will be. This is usually due to publication deadlines. A lead time of up to three months may be required to place an ad. Obviously, a store doesn't want to miss out on any sales, even though it may not yet know what it will sell for, so its ad will say "Call." In other cases, stores may choose to print "Call" if an item is new, but is also in very short supply. Stores will then charge whatever price they feel the market will bear. Beware. Sometimes you're paying for availability.

But in other instances, a store can't print the price without being subjected to a significant penalty. Why can't a store print a price? It has to do with something called shared-cost advertising. Manufacturers frequently help stores defray the cost of advertising by sharing in the cost of these ads. In their efforts to protect smaller dealers, some manufacturers set prices below which their products cannot be advertised. If a store advertises an item below these set prices, it runs the risk of losing a manufacturer's ad contributions. In a national publication, the cost of one, full-page ad can run into thousands of dollars, so it behooves the store to do what it can to lower this cost.

2. *Does the store offer a 30-day money-back guarantee?* Is there a restocking fee? If the answers are No and Yes (in that order), take your business somewhere else.

3. *When you call, ask if the advertised price includes a U.S. warranty.* If the item comes with an "international warranty," be aware that an international warranty is valid only if the item is purchased *outside* the U.S. Some mail-order houses offer warranties on their gray market merchandise, but they may not be as comprehensive as those offered by the manufacturers. Be advised that with many of the latest computerized cameras, only the manufacturer's factory-trained service personnel know how to repair them.

   Ask what the item's price will be with a U.S. warranty. You can bet it will be higher. Armed with this knowledge, you can make an informed decision as to which way you want to go.

4. *Ask what the shipping and handling charge will be.* This single item on the invoice often contains most of the store's profit from a sale. Don't be surprised if the shipping and handling charge for even a small, inexpensive accessory is in the neighborhood of $10.

5. *Make sure the item comes complete with all accessories as supplied by the manufacturer.* Some unscrupulous dealers remove accessories from camera boxes, such as straps, eyecups, batteries, or separate lenses from factory-supplied lens cases, then sell them back to the customers at inflated prices. This practice, called stripping, isn't nearly as big a problem as it used to be, but it still happens occasionally.

6. *To minimize the possibility that the seller will back-order your merchandise, use a credit card or send COD, shipped UPS second-day air and ask them to check stock.* You'll have to pay a few extra dollars for second-day service, but it may remove the temptation for them to tell you they have it in stock when they really don't. If they don't have an item in stock, by law they have up to 30 days before they must notify you that the item has been back ordered. Meanwhile, they have the use of your money and you don't.

   If you order by anything other than a credit card, send a money order, or have it shipped COD. If you send a personal check, the order may be held until the check clears. If you plan to send a money order, you should still ask them to check stock. The chances that the item won't be back-ordered are at least reduced. Another downside to ordering by mail is that you can't use these stores' toll-free numbers. They're for credit card orders only.

7. *Be patient.* If you plan to order several items, start by ordering one item from one store. See what sort of service you get. If it's not to your liking, take your business elsewhere.

If all this seems to be too much trouble, remember why you were ordering the item through the mail in the first place — to save money. If it still seems like too much trouble, do what most professionals do and patronize your local camera shop.

Used Photo Equipment

Before buying any piece of used equipment, check it thoroughly. It's always a good idea to get some sort of assurance from the seller that a piece of photo equipment is working properly. Many camera dealers will supply their used equipment with warranties, typically from 30 to 60 days. Others offer a 10 to 15 day return privilege, which gives the buyer ample time to try it out. If the dealer is unwilling to offer a warranty or return privilege, take your business somewhere else.

Camera Buying Pointers

1. *If the camera has a meter, does it work?* Is it accurate? Compare its readings with another camera or hand-held meter of known accuracy. To avoid metering errors due to different metering patterns, these tests should be conducted by using lenses of the same focal length, *both set at infinity* (if you're comparing two cameras' meters), and by metering a blank, evenly lit surface. A 50mm lens is best for this, especially if you're comparing the camera with a hand-held light meter. If the readings are within ½ stop of each other, chances are it's close to factory specifications. Different camera manufacturers have different philosophies about what correct exposure is. A manufacturer may incorporate an *exposure factor* into a camera's meter. This is why you should allow up to ½ stop latitude between readings from two different cameras.
2. *Do the other features of the camera work properly?* Check them all. If you don't know how, have the seller demonstrate them.
3. *Set the camera on its slowest shutter speed (other than B or T) and trip the shutter.* The slowest speeds are seldom used and sometimes become sluggish because the lubricant in the timing mechanism may have become gummy. If the slowest speed times out reasonably well, then all the other slow speeds should be close. If the camera has an electronically-controlled shutter, still check the one or two second setting. I rarely check shutter speeds that extend to 30 seconds or more. With an electronic shutter, if one second works, chances are the slowest speed will work as well.
4. *Check the inside of the camera, especially the film transport areas.* Look for abrasions, corrosion, excessive amounts of dust, and make sure that somebody hasn't tried to put a finger through the shutter. Examine the film pressure plate for wear or scratches. It should be smooth. Cameras that have seen lots of use will often show some wear on the pressure plate, but it should still be smooth. To look for pinholes in a focal plane shutter, gently raise the mirror (if possible), and, with the shutter closed and the back open, point the camera toward a light source. Examine the shutter. There should be absolutely no light leaks. Because focal plane shutters have two shutter curtains, this procedure should be performed twice: with the shutter cocked and uncocked.
5. *Look into the viewfinder.* Is it dirty? One or two specks is nothing to worry about; dirt in the viewfinder can in no way affect the quality of your photos. But if the finder is really dirty, chances are pretty good that the rest of the camera's interior is, too, and that it wasn't well cared for by its previous owner. At the very least, it will need a cleaning.
6. *Check around the metal joints and screws for any evidence of corrosion.* Most cameras will tolerate a little moisture without showing any effects. However, lots of people take their cameras to the beach and then forget to clean them off afterward. Salt air may be invigorating to humans, but it is death to metal. If a camera has been in contact with salt water, forget it. It's junk.

Lens Buying Pointers

1. *Check that the aperture iris blades move freely.* If the lens has been stored on its side for a long time, or if it has seen the inside of a hot car once too often, the lubricant for the focusing helical may have oozed out and coated the aperture blades. If this happened, the lens must be dismantled and cleaned.
2. *Check the focusing ring.* Does it move freely? If it's stiff, the lubricant has begun to coagulate. To remedy this, the lens must be dismantled, the old lubricant removed and replaced with fresh lubricant. Does the focusing ring move freely, but bind noticeably in one spot? If it's a very slight sluggishness, this could be caused by a patch of the lubricant that's begun to coagulate, which can often be

worked out by turning the ring back and forth. But if there is a noticeable drag in one spot, chances are the lens has been dropped and the focusing ring was bent, in which case the ring must be replaced. If the focusing ring moves with almost no resistance, the lens has probably been used a lot. This does not necessarily indicate a problem; in fact lots of folks prefer their lenses this way.

3. *If the lens is a one-touch zoom lens, check for wobble.* Zoom the lens out to its maximum extension and, holding an end in each hand, *gently* flex the lens. Cheap zooms, even when new, often show significant amounts of wobble. Good quality zooms should not.

   Does the zoom collar slip? Some folks mind this, others don't. Nikon makes some of the finest zoom lenses money can buy, but many Nikkor zooms are particularly prone to this problem. In fact, of all the zoom lenses that usually exhibit collar-slippage, the worst is the Nikkor 80-200 f/4.5, but optically it's one of the best 80-200's that has ever been made. Nevertheless, this can be annoying, especially when the camera is mounted on a tripod and inclined away from horizontal. Short of having the lens dismantled and re-lubricated, there are a couple of other solutions. The first is to place a wide rubber band on the barrel behind the collar. This will prevent the collar from slipping toward the camera. To prevent it from slipping forward, the rubber band can be positioned so its width overlaps the rear edge of the collar. The other solution is simpler: use a piece of tape.

4. *Make sure the lens focuses at infinity.* Try to focus on something as far away as possible. Distant mountains or the moon are best, if available. Many telephotos with focal lengths of 300 millimeters or longer will actually focus past infinity. They are designed in this way to counter the expansion experienced in hot weather, which can affect infinity focus.

5. *With the lens off the camera, look through it at a strong light source* (not the sun!). A mini penlight works great for this. Is there dust inside? If there is, don't worry. Even a moderate amount of dust inside a lens will not affect your photographs, but it can be used as a negotiating point.

   Check for element separation and for imperfections or scratches in the coating or surface of both front and rear lens elements. Much misconception exists about the effect scratches have on photographs. Generally, a scratch on the rear element of a lens — especially a wide-angle lens — will have a greater effect on photographs than a scratch on the front element. But, in all except the most severe instances, the only effect a scratch will have is on a lens' resale value.

   Try this: take a piece of string and hold it to the front of your mounted camera lens. Look through the viewfinder and focus on whatever you want. Can't see the string, can you? Neither will the photograph. Now, imagine how ugly the front element of that lens would look if it had a scratch the same size as that piece of string.

   In the worst of instances, a scratch may cause a loss of contrast because extraneous light rays are being refracted from the scratch and are bouncing around inside the lens. But even this isn't incurable. An old optician's trick is to fill scratches with india ink. Astronomers and telescope makers have known about this for years and it works beautifully.

   Although lenses with scratches are often priced far cheaper than those in equivalent condition without scratches, many uninformed buyers will reject them out-of-hand. But for you, the knowledgeable lens buyer, those scratches have become transformed from a detriment into a negotiating tool.

   Far worse than a scratch is fungus. In severe cases, fungus will cause noticeable degradation in contrast and will kill the resale value of a lens. Fungus results when equipment has been stored for years in a dark, moist place, or when stored for years in a dark place with a sufficient amount of moisture for it to propagate, or when stored for shorter periods in a hot and humid environment. Fungus attacks the coating and sometimes even the cement that may hold elements together. If caught early, the fungus can be removed without having caused any noticeable damage. If it has been eating away at the coating for some time, however, it's very likely that it will have actually etched the glass. In any case, the lens must be entirely dismantled, cleaned, then recollimated and reassembled.

Remember, when shopping for used equipment, if it's priced too low, there's usually a reason. As always, caveat emptor — and happy hunting!

Canon

Canon manual-focus systems are listed first, followed by EOS SLRs and lenses. Camera descriptions appear in the approximate order of their introduction. Canon rangefinder cameras, which use the Leica thread lens mount, are listed in the Screw-Mount Leica section.

Following is a brief overview of Canon FL and FD SLRs. Excluded are the R-series Canons, such as the Canonflex and Canon R2000, which were the predecessors to the FL-series, and a few other Canon SLRs contemporary to FL cameras that, while having generally rendered photos of excellent quality, have become somewhat obscure. One other Canon SLR that is not listed is the Canon Pellix. Its popularity has always been due to its novelty instead of its picture-taking ability. Pellixes in very clean condition are still popular on the used market, but only for their collectible value.

Canon FL-Mount Cameras

The following cameras were designed to accept Canon's FL-style breech lock lenses. The most significant difference between these cameras and later models designed to accept FD-style lenses is that the subject must be metered at taking apertures. But, so as not to render FL-mount cameras obsolete, Canon designed the FD lens line to be backward-compatible, hence FD lenses work well with these older cameras.

Canon FT-QL

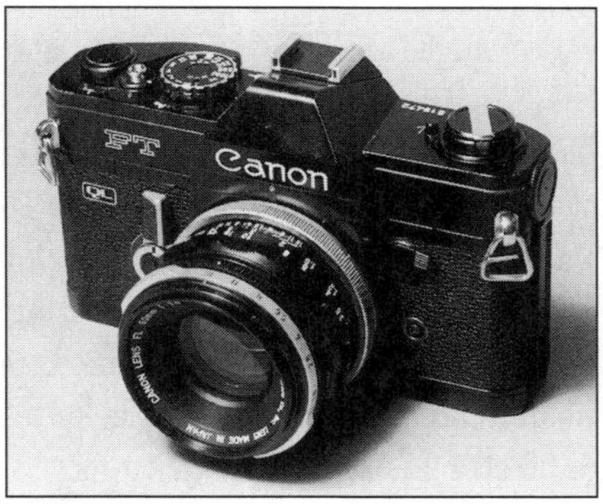

Canon FT-QL

This was Canon's first model with through the lens (TTL) metering and, perhaps more importantly, was the first Canon that let the photo world know Canon was serious about building quality 35mm SLR cameras.

The FT-QL's meter is activated by pushing the large, contoured lever (which doubles as a self-timer) toward the lens mount. This same motion stops the lens down and provides a depth-of-field check. Moving the lever in the opposite direction charges the self timer. Metering occurs only within a central rectangle, which encompasses about 12% of the image area. This metering rectangle is easily noticeable, being slightly darker than the surrounding viewing area.

Shutter speeds range from 1 second to 1/1000, plus B. X-sync occurs at 1/60. The camera has a "cold shoe," that is, an accessory shoe without a flash contact, and a PC socket. Other handy features are mirror lock-up, a self-timer, and Canon's unique-at-the-time QL (Quick Load) feature.

Canon FX & FP

The FX is a well-made, solid picture taker, even if it appears to be rather antiquated by today's standards. An external CdS exposure meter is located on the front of the camera, just below the film rewind crank. The meter readout scale is on the top left of the camera body. There is no meter information inside the viewfinder.

Shutter speeds cover the standard range, from 1 second to 1/1000, plus B. X sync is at 1/60. Other features are a self timer, mirror lock-up, an accessory shoe and a PC socket.

The FP is identical to the FX, except it lacks a meter.

Canon TL-QL

The TL-QL is a simplified FT-QL with a top shutter speed of 1/500 second, no mirror lock-up, no battery check and no shutter-release lock.

Canon FD-Mount Cameras

Canon's design work for FD-mount cameras and lenses began in the mid-1960's, although the first examples weren't released until 1971. FD-mount Canon cameras were an enormous success during the 1970's and 1980's. Since the advent of the EOS line, however, Canon's interest in FD-mount cameras has plummeted despite the fact that there are millions of dedicated users of the older, manual-focus system. Canon pledged in 1990 that it would continue to support the FD line for another ten years, but this statement may be deceptive. "Support" may mean nothing more than a pledge to provide technical support, service and repairs on FD lenses and the more recent FD-mount cameras until this ten-year period ends. Currently, the only FD-mount camera still being produced by Canon is the New F-1. The T-60 is made by Cosina.

Canon FTb & FTbn

The FTb was Canon's first SLR designed specifically for use with FD lenses to reach the retail market. As one might expect by the model designation, the FTb closely resembles the FT. Most notable among the similarities to its predecessor, the FTb retains Canon's QL feature, its full range of shutter speeds, and employs the same selective-area metering design used with the FT.

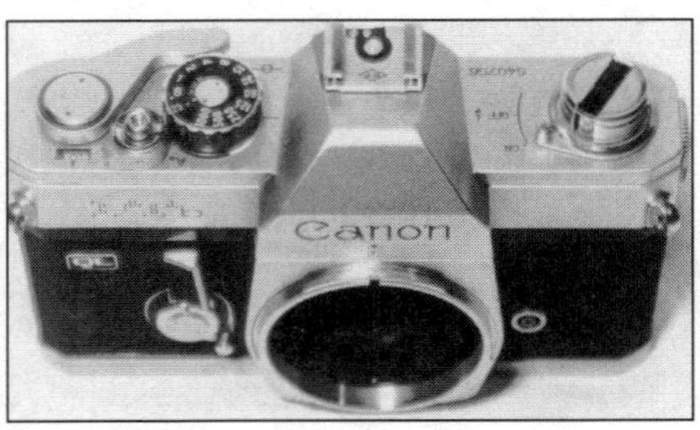

Canon FTb

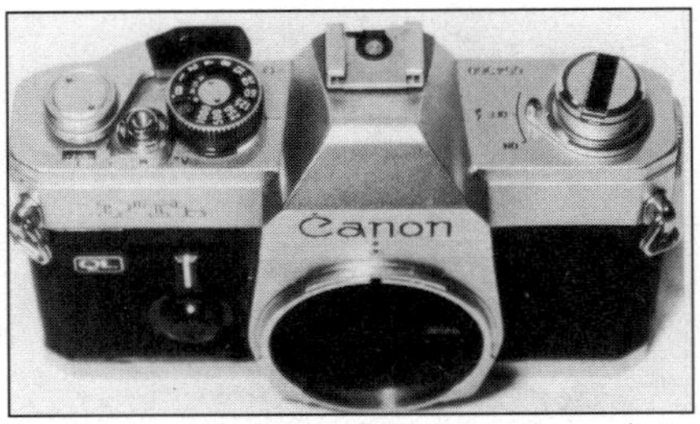

Canon FTbn with restyled film advance lever, shutter speed dial and self-timer shown

The main difference is the updated lens-to-body coupling, which allows full-aperture metering. Other differences include the mirror lock-up feature that, on the FTb, was combined with the self-timer/lens stop-down lever, resulting in an assembly that performs four separate functions. (See the accompanying section. explaining this ingenious four-in-one device.) The FTb has a hot shoe. The battery-check switch coaxial with the rewind crank was changed to a three-position meter on-off/ battery-check switch. The shutter speed dial was simplified. Because of its FD-mount lens design the FTb was the first Canon SLR to employ full-aperture, match-needle metering. Depth-of-field preview was retained, as was stop-down metering so FL lenses could still be used. Note: When mounting an FD lens to an FTb, the aperture ring must be moved off the "A" setting, or the lens will not mount.

In 1973, Canon introduced an updated version of the FTb. It was, and still is, referred to as the FTbn, but nowhere is this designation indicated on the camera. The differences are as follows: the all-metal film advance lever of the original model was redesigned for the FTbn and a black plastic tip was added; the shutter speed dial was changed slightly; shutter speeds are visible within the viewfinder of the FTbn. The FTb has a contoured stop-down/self-timer lever, whereas the FTbn's is a simpler-looking black affair with a white stripe in the center (identical in appearance to those on the EF and the original F-1).

Over twenty years after its introduction, the FTb still commands a large and loyal following. The FTb is an ideal, yet economical choice for photography students, Canon users with battery-dependent SLRs, or those who simply prefer to eschew automation.

Canon's QL Feature

QL (Quick Load), an ingenious film loading system Canon introduced in the mid-sixties, was the forerunner to almost all the various recent, quick-loading designs used on today's do-everything photographic techno-wonders. All Canon cameras with this feature display the QL symbol on the front of the camera. To use it is simplicity itself. You drop the film cassette into its well, draw the leader out to the red mark, close the camera back and advance the film to the first frame.

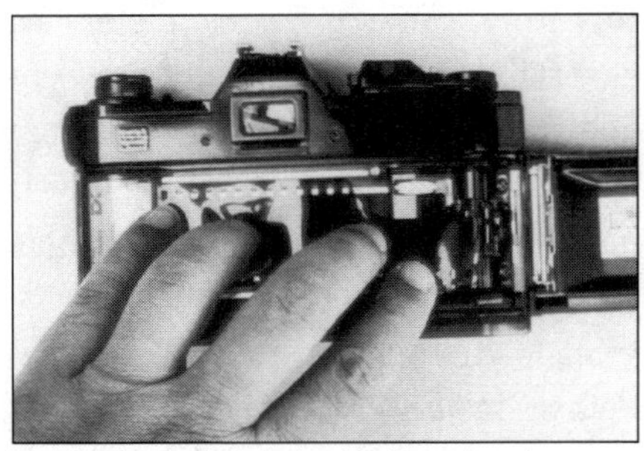

The film leader is pulled out to the red mark.

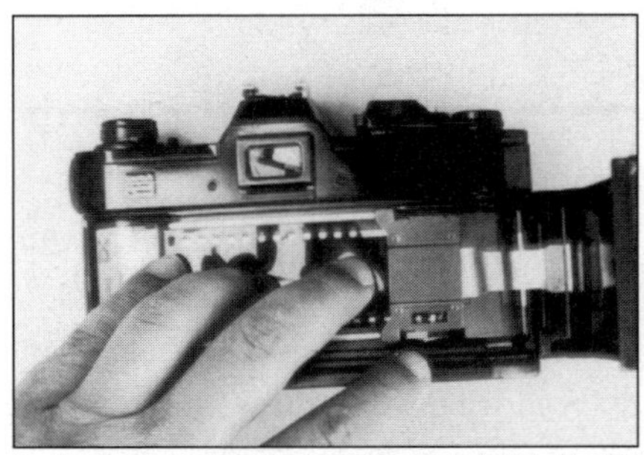

As the back is closed, a retainer plate holds the film in place.

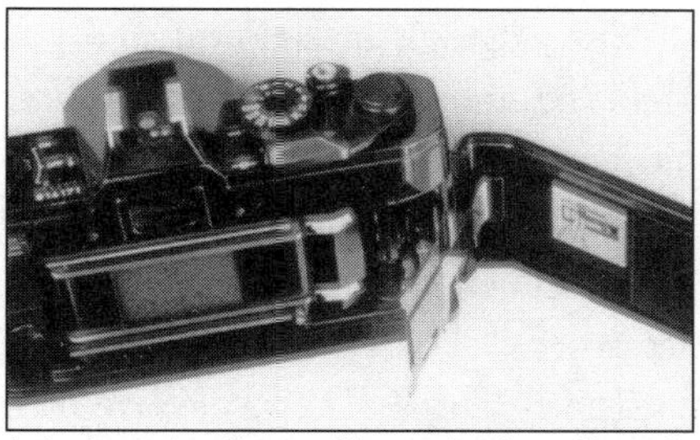

A look at the Canon QL mechanism. Note the illustration on the inside of the camera back.

Canon's 4-in-1 Stop-down/ Self-timer Mechanism

Unless you're mechanically inclined, it may take you a little while to puzzle out everything this arrangement can do. Let's examine the lever itself first. When facing the camera, rotating the lever fully counter-clockwise charges the self-timer. It's activated by depressing the shutter release. Pushing the lever clockwise stops the lens down momentarily for checking depth of field (this function operates only when the lens is off the "A" setting). By moving the small knob on the bottom of the assembly to the "L" position and pushing the lever clockwise, the lens is locked in its stopped-down position. This setting is used most often when FL or other non-FD lenses are mounted. After having done this, moving the small knob to the "M" position raises the mirror. To get everything back to the way it was before, just move the small knob on the bottom of the assembly back to its original position.

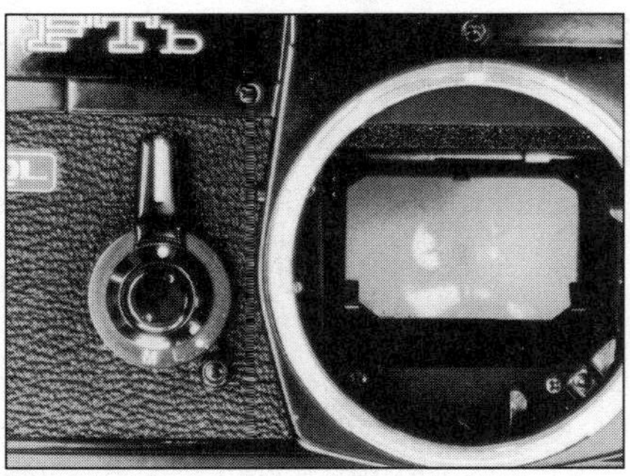

Canon's 4-in-1 self-timer/ mirror-lock/ stop-down mechanism. Shown in the normal position.

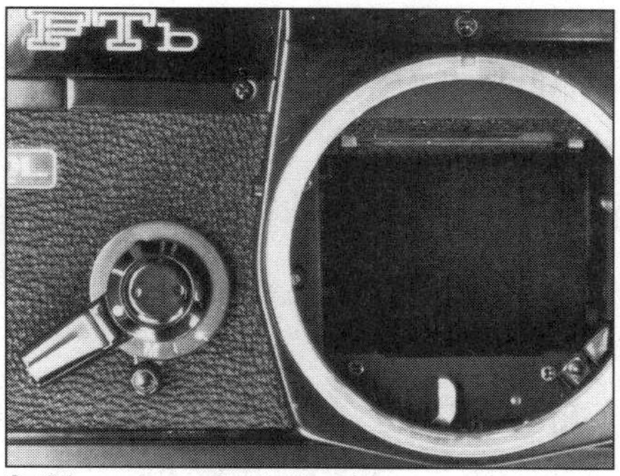

Self-timer charged with the mirror up.

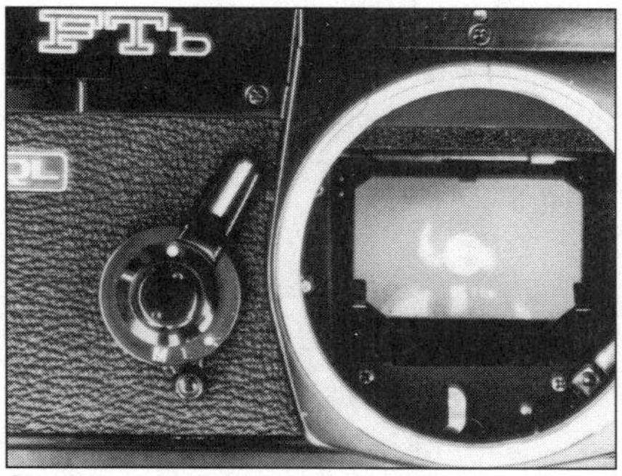

Stop-down metering position. The small knob is moved to 'L' (for Lock) and the stop-down/self-timer lever is moved to the right until it locks in place. Note that the aperture coupling lever at the bottom of the mirror box has moved to the left, exposing a red dot. The stop-down/self-timer lever can also be pushed to the left for checking depth of field without moving the knob to 'L'.

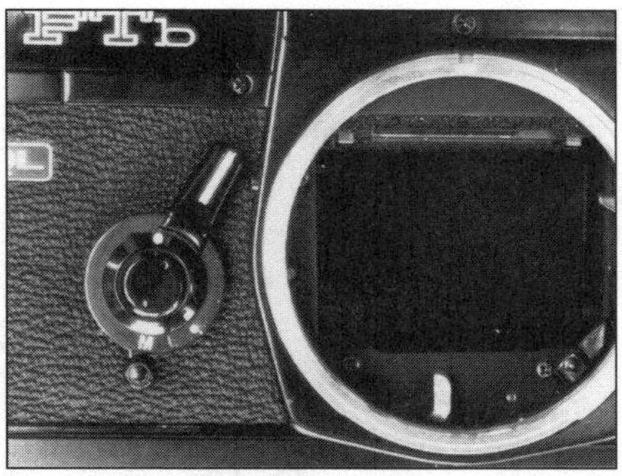

Mirror lock-up position. The small knob is moved to 'M' which raises the mirror.

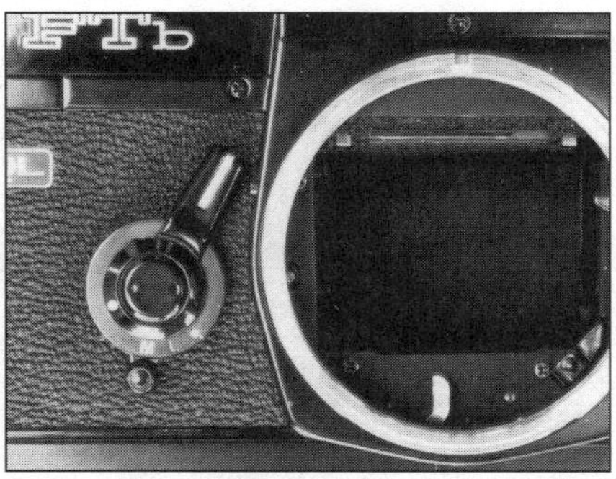

Same as before, but the lever has been moved back to its original position. Note the white dot above and to the left of the 'M'. This indicates the charged state of the self-timer.

Now, let's say you're out in your backyard and you want to take some close-up shots of your prize-winning snapdragons with your trusty F-1. You have everything set up: your camera and macro lens are mounted on a sturdy tripod, you've decided on your composition and the lighting's just right. You've loaded slow slide film and metered the scene at 1/4 second, so mirror lock-up will be essential — then your faithful dog Ralph eats your cable release. What to do? Use the self-timer, right? But wait! Remember how you had to push the lever clockwise to lock the aperture down, but that to use the self-timer, the lever has to be rotated counter-clockwise? What do you do now? Grab a stomach pump and chase after Ralph? Not to worry, Canon foresaw this problem when they designed this four-in-one unit. The lever itself does not lock in any position, only the mechanisms the lever actuates. It can still be rotated to charge the self timer and there is even a small white dot close to the hub to show when the self-timer has been charged.

Canon TLb & TX

The TLb, introduced a couple of years after the FTb, is a simplified, scaled down version of its big brother. It performs full-aperture, selective area metering with FD lenses, same as the FTb. The top shutter speed was trimmed to 1/500. It does not have the QL feature that the TL, its immediate predecessor, has. When introduced, it was a solid photographic workhorse and it remains so today.

The TX is a TLb with a hot shoe. Here's an aside for you: the Bell & Howell FD35 is virtually identical to the TX, the only differences being a few touches of cosmetics and the different name and logo. The FD35 was made by

Canon for Bell & Howell as a result of their marketing agreement in the U.S. When pricing an FD35, use the TX listing below.

Canon EF

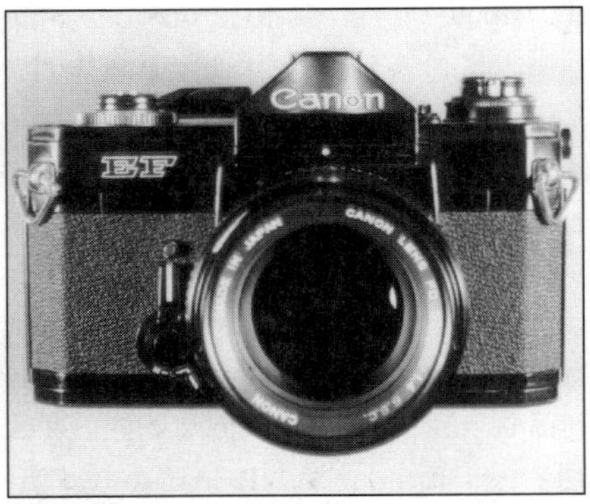

Canon EF

Fondly dubbed 'the Black Beauty,' the Canon EF was at the forefront of photo technology when it was introduced in 1973. It was expensive, selling for close to the same price as the professional model F-1. Sales of the EF were soft, and few were made. Clean examples are still highly prized and, even by today's standards, are capable, full-featured picture-takers.

The EF's exposure modes are shutter-priority AE and metered manual, using a centerweighted metering pattern. The extremely sensitive silicon photo cell meter has an ISO 100 EV range from -2 to 18 (-2 = 8 seconds at f/1.4). Shutter speeds range from 30 seconds to 1/1000, plus B, with X sync at 1/125. Speeds from 30 seconds to 1 second are electronically-controlled; the remainder are mechanical. Other features include an AE lock, multiple exposure capability, mirror lock-up, depth-of-field preview and a self-timer. Unique to the EF is a system that allows the user to advance a freshly-loaded roll of film to the first frame without having to trip the shutter. After inserting the film leader on to the take-up spool and closing the back, crank the film advance lever until it stops. The shutter is cocked and the film is set to the first frame.

Canon F-1 Systems: The Original Mechanical Marvel vs. The Modern Hybrid

Canon's F-1 cameras are regarded as some of the sturdiest and most accurate cameras ever built. Designed for the practicing professional, either system is fully modular, accepting interchangeable viewfinders, focusing screens, backs and both motor and winder options. Two principal versions have been produced since its introduction in 1971 and, since Canon elected to keep the same name for these two entirely different systems, keeping track of it all can be confusing.

Canon Original F-1 & F-1n

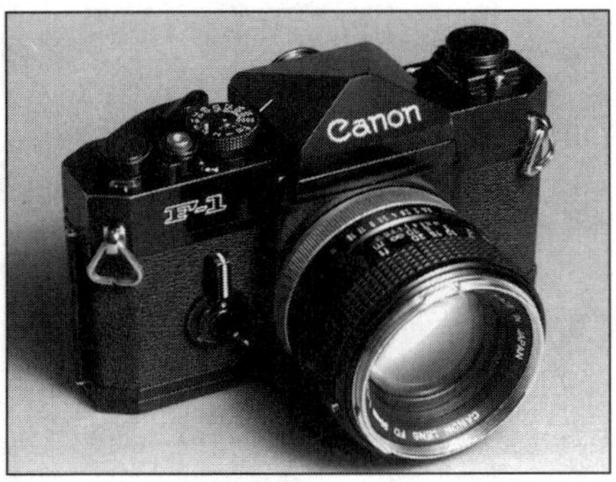

Canon F-1 original model

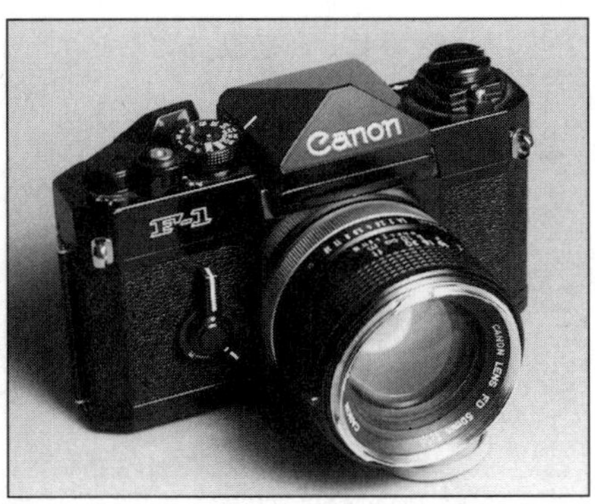

Canon F-1n. Note the plastic tip on the film advance lever.

The original, mechanical F-1 was produced in two versions. The later model, introduced in 1976, was essentially an update of the earlier one. Both accept Canon's full line of original F-1 accessories.

The F-1 uses a 12% selective area metering pattern, which is seen within the viewfinder as a slightly darker central rectangle. Match-needle manual metering is handled by an extremely accurate CdS meter. Shutter speeds range from 1 second to 1/2000, plus B, with X sync at 1/60. Other features include a self-timer, depth-of-field preview and mirror lock-up. The addition of the optional Servo-EE finder converts the F-1 into a shutter-priority AE camera. When the Booster-T finder is installed, the low-light metering sensitivity and slow shutter speeds are extended.

Now, for the obvious differences. The later model, commonly called the F-1n, differs from the original in a few noticeable areas. The most obvious are a redesigned film advance lever, now sporting a plastic tip, and the addition of a film memo holder to the back.

There are differences that aren't as apparent. The F-1n's meter switch is spring-loaded in the "C" (battery check) position, thereby preventing inadvertent drain. Multiple exposures are possible with the F-1n by depressing the film rewind button and cocking the advance lever (the film won't advance, but the counter will). The F-1n's film advance lever has a somewhat shorter stroke, and the shutter release collar was redesigned. Finally, the film ISO range was extended from 2000 to 3200.

Canon New F-1

The current F-1, called the New F-1 when it was introduced in 1981, is more commonly referred to in the trade as the F-1N (note the capital "N"). It's similar to the original F-1 in name only.

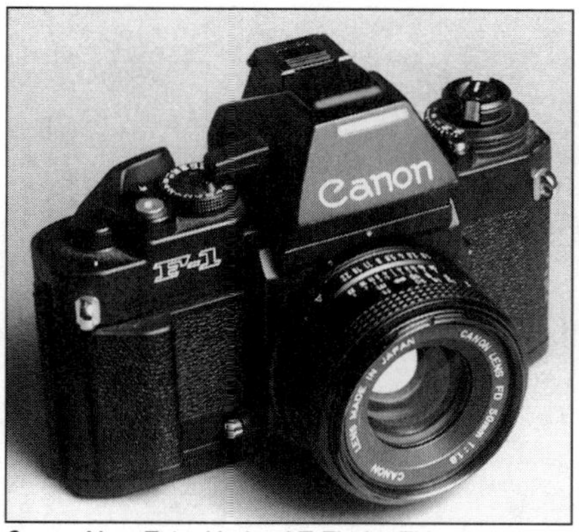

Canon New F-1 with the AE Finder FN

Exposure modes available depend on which viewfinder is attached and whether a film winding accessory is being used. With the Eye-Level Finder FN, match-needle manual is the only exposure mode. After attaching the AE Finder FN, the camera's available exposure modes expand to include both aperture-priority AE and metered manual. When either the Motor Drive FN or the Winder FN is attached, shutter-priority AE is available, independent of the finder being used.

Exposure metering is dependent upon the focusing screen installed. Three metering options are available through choice of the appropriate screens: centerweighted averaging, 12% selective area and 3% spot.

The New F-1 has a hybrid electro-mechanical shutter which provides electronically-controlled shutter speeds from 8 seconds to 1/60 and mechanical speeds from 1/90 to 1/2000, plus B. X sync occurs at 1/90. This dual-mode design provides the photographer with an adequate selection of shutter speeds in the event of battery failure.

Other features include: non-TTL flash AE, multiple-exposure capability, depth-of-field preview and a self-timer. Canon dropped the mirror lock-up feature from the new design.

Old & New F-1: Interchangeability

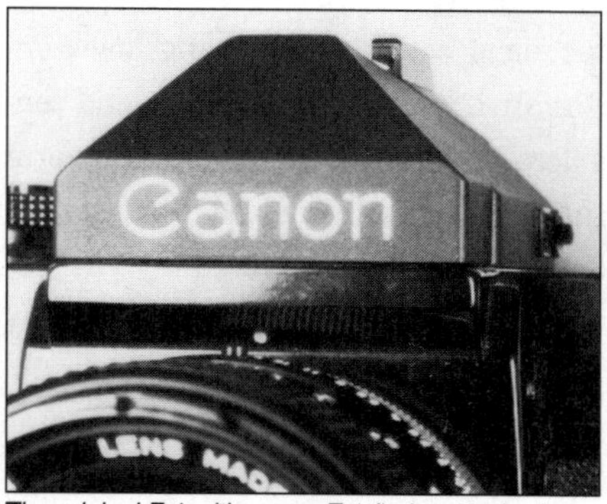

The original F-1 with a new F-1 finder attached.

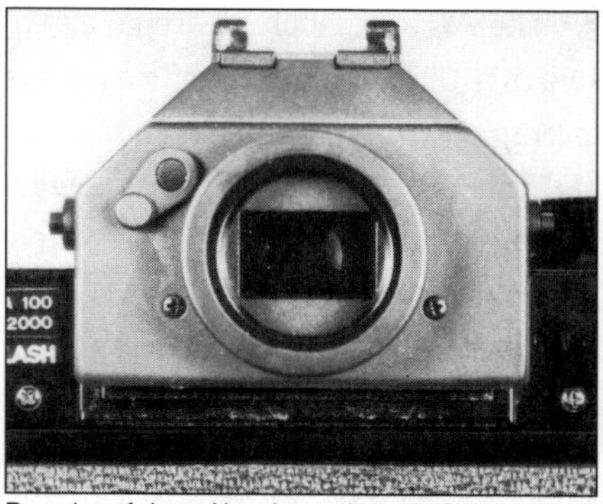

Rear view of above. Note the gap between finder and body.

While Canon claims that no interchangeability exists between the two F-1 systems (except for eyepiece rings, eyecups and diopters), there is more than they would have you believe. A New F-1 viewfinder will fit onto an original F-1 body, but not vice-versa. Though the finder will slide onto the body without being forced and will click into place, it is not a precise fit. There is a slight gap between the finder and the body in the front and a larger one in the rear. The eye relief seems to be somewhat mismatched between the two finders also, making focusing more difficult. So, if you try using late-model finders on your early-model F-1, expect to have a tougher time focusing and do so only in situations where there is no chance of dust or moisture entering the camera.

Canon A-Series Cameras

All A-series cameras are battery dependent and feature bottom-center-weighted metering, top shutter speeds of 1/1000 second and flash sync at 1/60. They also accept the standard A-series accessories, such as databacks and winders. The A-1 and AE-1 Program are the only two, however, which can use the Motor Drive MA. A brief explanation of each camera's features follow, listed in the order of their introduction to the market.

Canon AE-1

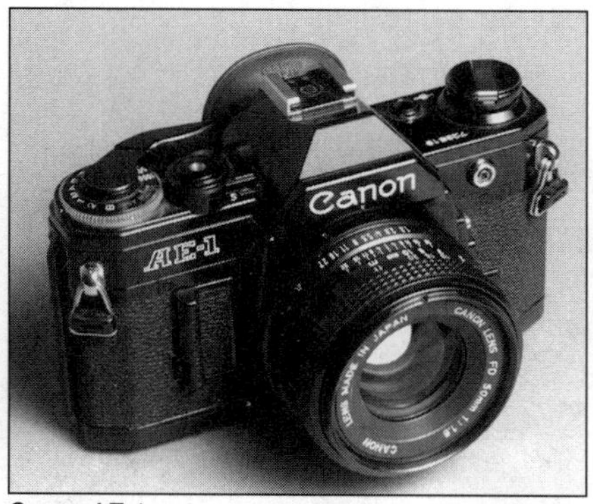

Canon AE-1

By today's standards the AE-1 is a simple, no-frills camera with limited auto options. When it was introduced in the mid-seventies, it was nothing less than revolutionary. Its lightweight design, incorporating state-of-the-art microcircuit technology, and its low price captured the interest of amateur photographers worldwide—leaving other manufacturers scrambling to catch up.

The AE-1 has two exposure modes: metered manual and shutter-priority AE. Non-TTL flash AE is also possible with dedicated flash units, as is stop-down metering for use with some of the older Canon FL and non-FD lenses. Shutter speeds range from 2 seconds to 1/1000, plus B. Other features include an AE lock, backlight control, multiple exposure capability, depth-of-field preview and a self timer.

Canon AT-1

Introduced shortly after the AE-1, the AT-1 is the only manual-exposure-only A-series model. It features match-needle metering, reminiscent of the FTb, and shutter speeds from B to 1/1000. It is also the only A-series Canon that has an exposure needle (or indicator) coupled to the lens aperture ring — a nice feature. While the AT-1 is a manual camera, it is not a mechanical one. The electronic shutter is the same as that in the AE-1 and requires a battery to operate. Other features include stop-down metering, multiple exposure, depth-of-field preview, a hot shoe and a self-timer.

Canon A-1

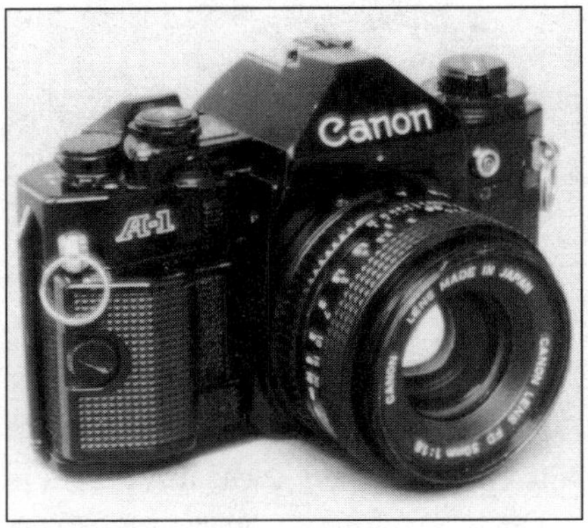

Canon A-1

Hexaphotocybernetic. Remember that mouthful? Just in case you weren't paying attention (or were a Nikon user or something), it was a word Canon's ad agency execs dreamed up to describe the feature-laden A-1 when it was introduced amidst much fanfare in 1978. Back then, its dazzling array of capabilities sent shock waves throughout the industry. A milestone in photography had been passed, portending what was to become commonplace in just a few short years. Photography would never be the same again.

Here's a little-known tidbit for you. As far back as 1976, Canon was testing working copies of the A-1, but it was called the New F-1. Apparently, Canon's management thought that professional photographers of the day would forsake their heavy, indestructible, mechanical cameras for the A-1's technical wizardry. Knowing how conservative working pros can be, and considering the departure from the norm the A-1 represented at the time, I would bet early responses were ... well, less than enthusiastic. But time has a way of proving worth, and such has been the case with the A-1. Ironically, many pros have come to depend on the features, lightness and reliability of the A-1.

The A-1's capabilities are so extensive that the following list of features is incomplete, but we'll take a stab at the high points. As the term Hexaphotocybernetic implies, the A-1 has six exposure modes: standard program, both shutter and aperture-priority AE, metered manual, non-TTL flash AE and stop-down AE. Shutter speeds range from 30 seconds to 1/1000, plus B. The A-1 has interchangeable focusing screens, but they must be interchanged by Canon or a qualified service center. Other features include exposure compensation, an ASA dial that ranges from 6 to 12,800, an AE lock, a back-light control, an eyepiece shutter, a multiple exposure switch, depth-of-field preview and a two-speed self timer (2 seconds and 10 seconds). The A-1 will accept all three film winding accessories Canon produced for the A-series cameras, the Winder A, the Winder A2 and the Motor Drive MA. With alkaline batteries, the Motor Drive MA will advance film at speeds up to 4.5 frames per second, slightly faster with the NiCad pack.

Canon AV-1

The AV-1, introduced in 1979, was targeted toward beginning photographers and those folks who preferred aperture-priority AE, but who didn't want to shell out the extra dollars for the host of other features one got with an A-1. The AV-1 is essentially an aperture-priority only auto exposure SLR,

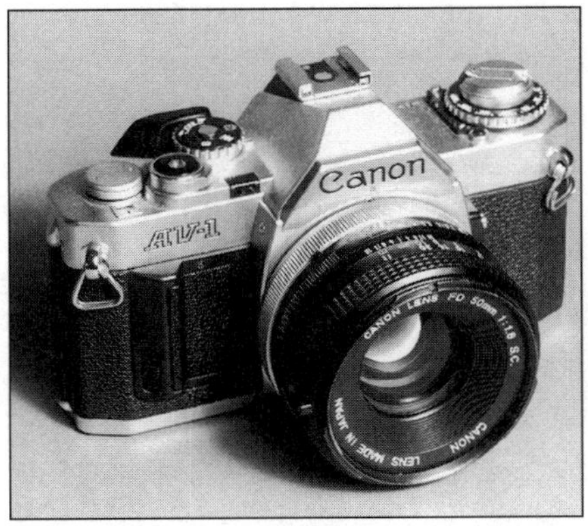

Canon AV-1

having just two user-selectable shutter speeds: 1/60 (flash sync) and B. The top dial, which on most cameras is a shutter speed dial, has those two selections, plus the "A" setting for aperture-priority AE, and the self-timer setting. Shutter speeds from 1/1000 to two seconds are available.

Canon AE-1 Program

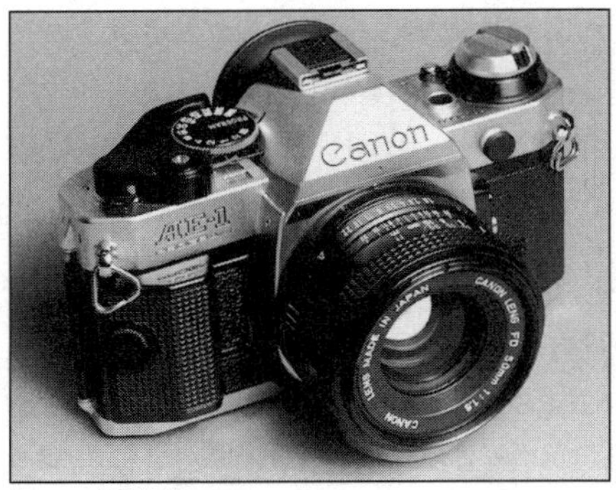

Canon AE-1 Program

The AE-1 Program, introduced in 1981, is not just an AE-1 with a program mode tacked on. It was totally redesigned, more closely resembling a scaled-down version of the A-1 than an evolution of the AE-1. As the name suggests, the AE-1 Program has a program mode in addition to shutter-priority AE and metered manual. It has the same range of shutter speeds as the AE-1. The meter needle was replaced with LEDs. One feature of the AE-1 Program that represents an improvement over even the A-1 is its user-interchangeable focusing screens. When coupled to the AE-1 Program, the Motor Drive MA provides film advance speeds up to about 4 frames per second, slightly less than it does when used with the A-1.

Canon AL-1

The AL-1 was the last variant of Canon's A-series cameras, introduced in 1983 or so. It is the only A-series camera with a focus-assist feature, identified by the "QF" badge (for Quick Focus) on the front of the body. This system, a predecessor to auto-focus technology, works reasonably well, even in subdued light or with somewhat slow lenses.

Basic features include two exposure modes, aperture-priority AE and metered manual, and a self-timer. Shutter speeds range from 2 seconds to 1/1000 (1/15 to 1/1000 in manual mode), plus B. The AL-1 is the only A-series Canon that is powered by penlight batteries (two required).

Of all the A-series Canons, the AL-1 is probably the most often overlooked. Many folks who switch to autofocus systems do so because their eyesight 'ain't what it used to be' and often find themselves overwhelmed, bewildered, even turned off by the computerized picture takers that today's autofocus cameras have become. Also, for people who use the Canon FD system, the switch to autofocus can be an expensive one, since there is no interchangeability between FD and EOS lens mounts. The AL-1 offers a serviceable alternative.

Canon T-Series Cameras

Canon's venture into the wonders of polycarbonate construction began with the introduction of the T-50 and the company hasn't looked back since. There is a lot to be said for using polycarbonate as a replacement for metal. When well-formulated and properly reinforced, it resists dings and dents because it can spring back to its original shape. Its tensile strength can even be greater than that of the metal it has replaced. But it isn't as hard as metal, so it scratches and abrades much easier.

Canon T-50

The T-50 is a simple-to-use beginner's camera, designed for the complete neophyte — or so you would think. I've known at least one professional who used a T-50 as a "grab-shot" camera. And I'll bet there are more out there who use T-50s, but who would rather be caught without film than be seen by their peers actually (gasp!) using one.

On the T-50, there is a shutter speed dial where one would expect to find it, but it only has three settings: Program, Self timer and Lock. It has a built-in motor drive with auto film advance and rewind only. Limited flash AE is available with dedicated flash units.

Canon T-60

Introduced in 1990, the T-60 represents a return to the basics, offering features most beginning photographers want and need. Its price should appeal to the budget-conscious photographer who may have wanted to buy a new camera, but who otherwise may have had to resort to buying a used one.

The T-60 has two exposure modes: aperture-priority AE and metered manual. Shutter speeds range from 8 seconds to 1/1000 (1 second to 1/1000 in manual), plus B, with X sync at 1/60. Film is advanced and rewound manually and there are no provisions for attaching a motor or winder accessory. It has a self-timer. There are no DX film contacts; film speeds must be set manually. The T-60 has a hot shoe, but no built-in flash automation.

Canon T-70

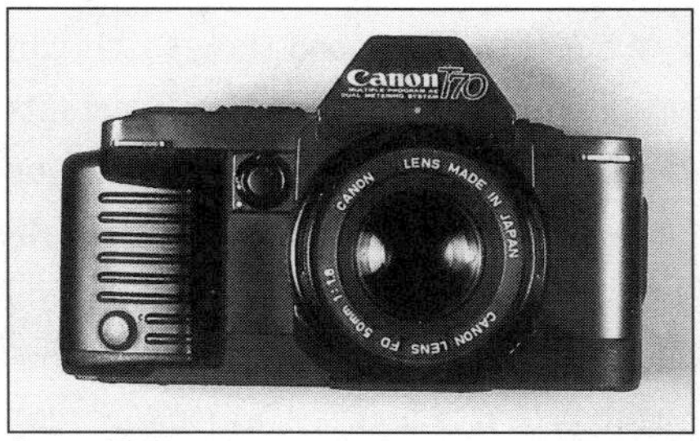

Canon T-70

Canon incorporated many of the best features of the A-1 into the T-70 and added a few more for good measure. Instead of having a single program mode it has three: a standard program, a telephoto program (high shutter speed bias) and a wide angle program (increased depth-of-field bias). Its other exposure modes are shutter-priority, metered manual, stop-down AE (for use with FL-mount and other non-FD lenses) and non-TTL programmed flash AE. The T-70 also features two metering patterns, either center-weighted averaging or partial, the latter of which is very tight and almost a spot pattern. This is a very nice feature for determining correct exposure in difficult lighting situations. Shutter speeds range from 2 seconds to 1/1000, plus B. X sync is at 1/90 with dedicated flash units, 1/60 with others.

Other features include multiple exposure capability, depth-of-field preview, a self-timer and integral winder.

Canon T-80

The T-80 was Canon's first attempt at an autofocus SLR and, because of bad timing or bad luck, became an Edsel almost overnight. The T-80 was introduced by Canon nearly the same time Minolta unveiled the Maxxum 7000. It wasn't a pretty sight, folks. The T-80 was blown away by the Maxxum's vastly superior autofocus technology and performance. But then, the Maxxum 7000 blew everyone away, and had virtually no competition for two years.

One of the few good things that can be said about the T-80 is that it accepts standard FD lenses and will provide focus confirmation with them. In addition to manual-focus override, the T-80 has two autofocus modes: single-shot (focus priority) and continuous (servo). The lenses meant to be used with the T-80 are designated "AC" for "Automatic Control." Only three focal lengths were made: the 50mm f/1.8, the 35-70 f/3.5-4.5 and the 75-200 f/4.5. AC lenses have their own drive motors, like the EF lenses, but can be easily told apart because of their humps. These lenses use the FD mounting style, so they can't be used on EOS cameras.

The T-80 has a built-in winder, which is good for 1.2 fps, and has powered film rewind. For exposure information, Canon used a pictograph system to illustrate the following exposure modes: standard program, deep focus (for maximum depth of field), stop action (high shutter speeds), shallow focus (for minimum depth of field) and "flowing" (low shutter speeds). Shutter speeds range from 2 seconds to 1/1000, plus B. X sync is at 1/90.

Canon T-90

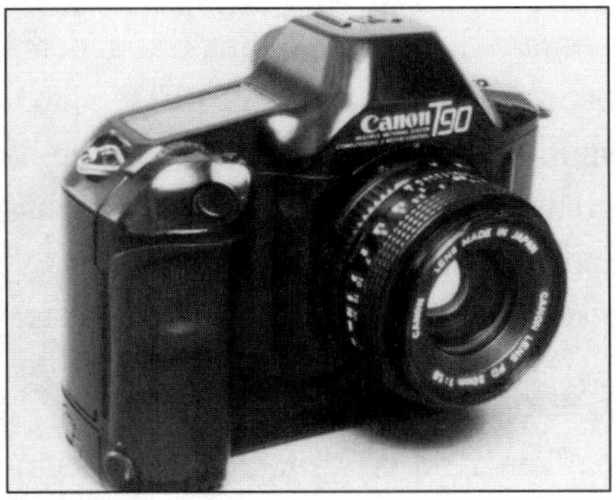

Canon T-90

It took a lot of courage for Canon to buck the trend in the mid-1980's toward auto-everything cameras and bring the T-90 to market, and many Canon users, professional and amateur alike, were glad they did. Sadly, Canon elected to discontinue the T-90 in 1991. Within days of Canon's announcement, warehouse stocks were sold out.

Originally targeted for the advanced amateur, the T-90 has found a loyal following among professionals, largely because until 1990 it stood alone as the most technically advanced manual-focus 35mm camera made. Now it shares that distinction with the Contax RTS III and ST.

The T-90's exposure modes include program with a seven-step shift adjustment and a safety shift, aperture and shutter-priority AE, and metered manual. Exposure options include TTL flash with the 300TL Speedlite or Macrolite ML 2, highlight/shadow compensation, exposure compensation and an AE lock. Available metering modes are centerweighted averaging, 13% central area, or 2.7% spot. Up to eight spot readings can be stored and averaged. The camera has DX contacts, but the DX coding can be overridden.

Shutter speeds range from 30 seconds to 1/4000, plus B. X sync occurs at 1/250. (Only two other Canons have this fast a flash sync and they're both EOS.) The built-in motor drive will advance film at speeds up to 4.5 fps. The camera features auto film load and auto rewind, as well as mid-roll rewind. Other features include interchangeable focusing screens, multiple exposure capability, a self timer, depth-of-field preview, stop-down metering and second-curtain flash sync with the 300TL.

Another handy feature is that everything is powered by only four AA alkaline batteries. While it is true the T-90 will not function at all without batteries, AAs are so common they can be obtained virtually anywhere in the world.

Canon FL and FD-Mount SLRs

Camera	Yrs Made	New	Mint	Excellent	User
A-1	1978-87		350 295	300 190	220 170
AE-1 chr	1976-85		180 150	150 115	120 90
AE-1 blk	1976-85			175 150	140 120
AE-1 Program chr	1981-87		220 175	200 130	150 125
AE-1 Program blk	1981-87			240 190	210 160
AL-1	1983-85			160 100	120 90
AT-1	1977-85		200 150	160 120	125 90
AV-1	1979-85			130 95	110 80
EF	1973-78		300 230	225 175	185 150
F-1	1971-76		400 325	310 245	260 210
F-1n	1976-81		525 370	400 300	290 245
F-1N, std. finder	1981-	1295 1170	850 650	575 450	480 360
F-1N, AE finder	1981-	1425 1250	900 750	680 550	575 470
FT QL	1966-72			125 80	95 80
FTb QL chr	1971-74		190 150	150 125	115 90
FTb QL blk	1971-74				180 130
FTbn QL chr	1973-78		225 185	180 125	125 100
FTbn QL blk	1973-78		285 250	230 180	180 130

Canon FL and FD-Mount SLRs

Camera	Yrs Made	New		Mint		Excellent		User	
FX	1964-69					120	90	90	65
TL QL	1968-72			125	100	100	85	90	75
TLb QL	1972-77					125	100	90	80
TX	1975-79			135	120	100	90	80	70
T-50	1983-89			130	115	110	90		
T-60	1990-	190	140						
T-70	1984-87			220	175	200	175	180	150
T-80 w/50/1.8AF	1985-86			250	200	185	150		
T-90	1985-91			800	625	600	450	440	380

Canon FL Lenses

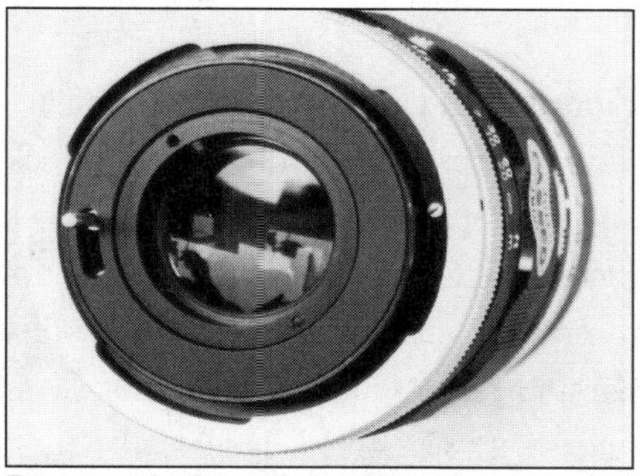

Rear view of a Canon FL lens. Note there is only one lens-to-body coupling lever.

FL lenses employ Canon's older meter coupling design that does not allow for full-aperture metering. A camera originally intended for use with FL lenses, such as the FT-QL or the TL-QL, meters the scene at the lens' taking aperture. For focusing ease, an FL lens has an additional ring next to the aperture ring or a button near the mount that can be used to momentarily open or close the diaphragm. FL lenses are interchangeable with FD lenses, but when using a camera designed to accept FD lenses, metering must be done in the camera's stop-down mode. If your camera was designed for use with FD lenses and does not have a stop-down function, it will not expose correctly with FL lenses. In addition, a few FL lenses will not work properly on some FD-mount cameras that do have a stop-down mode (for example, the 19mm f/3.5 FL will not work properly on the AE-1 or A-1 but works just fine on the FTb and mechanical F-1). The list of non-useable lenses varies from camera to camera. If in doubt check your owner's manual. One FL lens, though, should not be mounted on *any* camera except the Canon Pellix. This is the 38mm f/2.8 FLP.

FL lenses often go overlooked by users of FD cameras, mostly because they require a little more patience and thought to use. In my humble opinion, this is a big mistake. FL lenses are, with no doubt, the sturdiest of Canon's SLR lens styles. Regarding their optical quality, they still hold their own very well when compared to today's computer-designed optics, providing sharp images with great contrast and color.

Canon FL Lenses

Lens	Mint		Excellent		User	
19mm f/3.5	350	300	250	200	200	150
28mm f/3.5	75	50	50	35		
35mm f/2.5	75	60	70	50	60	40
35mm f/3.5	50	40	35	30		
38mm f/2.8 FLP (Pellix only)	125	100				
50mm f/1.4			60	50	50	40
50mm f/1.8	35	25	30	20		
50mm f/3.5 Macro (w/1:1)	175	150	160	125		
55mm f/1.2			150	90	90	70
58mm f/1.2			130	80	70	60
85mm f/1.8	250	200	175	150		
100mm f/3.5	150	120	140	100		
135mm f/2.5	75	60	50	40		
135mm f/3.5	50	40	40	35		
200mm f/3.5			125	90	90	60
200mm f/4.5	100	85	70	55		
300mm f/2.8 SSC Fluorite	1650	1200				
300mm f/5.6 SC Fluorite	500	400				
400mm f/5.6 (w/Focusing Unit)			700	500		
500mm f/5.6 SSC Fluorite	1350	1000				

Canon FL Lenses

Lens	Mint	Excellent	User
600mm f/5.6 (w/Focusing Unit)		900 700	
800mm f/8 (w/Focusing Unit)		1700 1500	
1200mm f/11 SSC (w/Focusing Unit)		2500 1800	

Canon FL Zoom Lenses

Lens	Mint	Excellent	User
55-135 f/3.5	150 120	100 60	
85-300 f/5	400 350	325 250	
100-200 f/5.6	120 95	100 60	

Canon FD Lenses

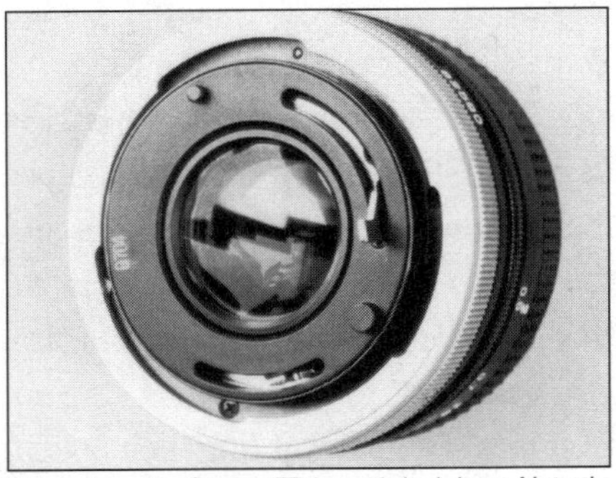

Rear view of a Canon FD breech-lock lens. Note the two coupling levers and two additional fixed posts.

Canon FD lenses exist in two main versions. The earlier version, commonly called the "breech-lock" style (abbreviated as "bl"), has a knurled chrome mounting ring that rotates an eighth to a quarter turn to lock the lens securely in place. The later version, which Canon calls "New FD," but everyone else calls "bayonet mount," is mounted by rotating the entire lens until it clicks into place. Both styles are interchangeable.

Many Canon aficionados prefer the older breech-lock style. They claim the lens mounts more securely and that the mount itself is less apt to wear out. Most breech-lock lenses are more massive in construction than their New FD counterparts, a feature that also fuels loyalty. But the disadvantage to the breech-lock style is that it takes practice and some dexterity to mount the lens with one hand while holding the camera with the other. Even when using both hands to mount the lens, the process is slower than when mounting a New FD lens one-handed. Nonetheless, the breech-lock lenses remain popular, so the price differential between equivalent examples of the old and new styles is small and, in some cases, somewhat more for the breech-lock style.

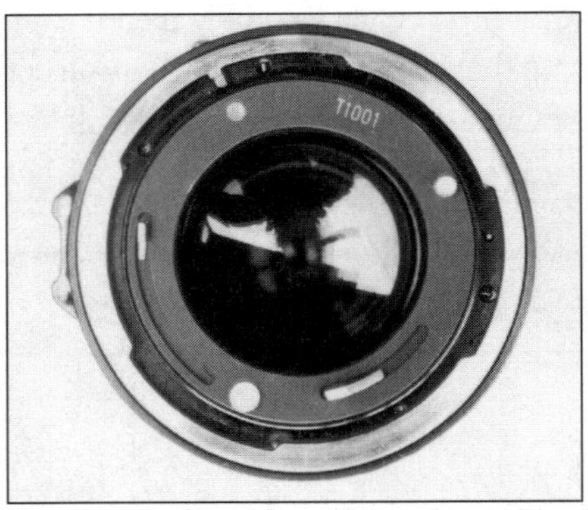

Rear view of a Canon New FD lens. The additional dot on the top is the mounting alignment mark. Note the lens release switch on the left side.

Lenses with an "L" suffix incorporate special low-dispersion glass elements and, in a few cases, internal fluorite elements for greatly reduced color aberration and increased sharpness at maximum apertures. Canon says the "L" stands for Luxury, and with the prices these lenses sell for, it's no wonder. Precursors to the L lenses were the breech-lock FL and FD Fluorite and FD Aspherical lenses, and three of the breech-lock super-telephotos. The Fluorite lenses include one or more fluorite elements to produce the same effect as low-dispersion glass, and are not to be confused with Canon FL lenses, although only one lens carrying the Fluorite label is an FD lens; the rest are FL lenses (got that?). "Al" in the listings below stands for Aspherical, a design using an aspherical surface to control a number of aberrations and to improve flare correction, much the same way current low-dispersion elements do. The 400mm f/4.5 SSC, 600mm f/4.5 SSC and 800mm f/5.6 SSC lenses all incorporate low-dispersion glass in their design, but this is not indicated anywhere on the lenses; you just have to know it. Canon made a distinction between the low-dispersion glass used in these three lenses and the glass used in the 500mm f/4.5 L when it was first introduced (the 500mm f/4.5 L was Canon's first L-series FD lens), referring to its glass at the time as "ultra-low dispersion" (UD). Confused yet?

Most breech-lock lenses are labeled SC or SSC. SC stands for Spectra Coating and SSC stands for Super Spectra Coating. Both are single-layer coatings that rivaled the quality of the best multi-layer coatings of their day (or so Canon claimed). Canon switched to multi-layer coatings with the bayonet mount lenses, however, and dropped the SC and SSC designations. (Canon still produces one breech-lock SSC lens, the TS35 f/2.8. The TS35 is designed to control perspective much as one would with a large format camera by allowing both tilt and shift movements of the front element.) The earliest model breech-lock FD lenses did not have either an SC or SSC designation. Price differences between early and later breech-locks are minor.

Most of Canon's later bayonet-mount long telephoto lenses include an internal focusing design, indicated by "IF" in the listings below. Focusing is achieved by moving inner elements, which keeps the overall length of the lens the same, hence no light loss when focusing from infinity to closest distance.

Canon FD Lenses

Lens	New		Mint		Excellent		User	
7.5mm f/5.6	1150	900	750	500	490	380	350	300
7.5mm f/5.6 bl			550	500	480	450	380	300
14mm f/2.8 L	2200	1850	1500	1350	1300	1000		
15mm f/2.8	1075	900	700	550	480	395	380	300
15mm f/2.8 SSC bl			480	425	400	325		
17mm f/4	525	450	375	325	300	250	250	190
17mm f/4 SSC bl			310	280	295	250		
20mm f/2.8	575	480	420	350	290	245	260	200
20mm f/2.8 SSC bl			340	290	325	250		
24mm f/1.4 L	1740	1450	1200	1000	900	700	650	600
24mm f/1.4 SSC Al bl			900	800	850	600	600	550
24mm f/2	695	600	540	480	400	300		
24mm f/2.8			215	150	200	140		
24mm f/2.8 SSC bl			230	175	190	145	150	125
28mm f/2	620	500	425	350	325	250		
28mm f/2 SSC bl			320	250	255	200	190	175
28mm f/2.8			85	60	75	55		
28mm f/2.8 SC b			100	75	80	50		
28mm f/3.5 bl			90	70	70	55		
35mm f/2	510	420	350	275	250	200	180	140
35mm f/2 SSC bl			200	160	185	150	160	125
35mm f/2.8			100	70	75	65	70	60
35mm f/2.8 TS SSC bl	1720	1350	950	750	700	575		
35mm f/3.5 SC b			95	85	85	65	60	50
50mm f/1.2 L	995	750	600	550	485	400		
50mm f/1.2	390	280	210	175	190	150		
50mm f/1.4	180	100	90	70	80	60		
50mm f/1.4 SSC bl			100	80	90	60	60	50
50mm f/1.8	95	70	50	40	40	25		
50mm f/1.8 SC b			45	30	45	25	25	20
50mm f/1.8 AC (T-80)			55	45				
50mm f/3.5 Macro (w/1:1)	480	350	300	250	200	165	150	135
50mm f/3.5 Macro SSC bl (w/1:1)			230	200	200	165		
55mm f/1.2 SSC Al bl			550	450	475	400		
55mm f/1.2 SSC bl			250	230	235	170	170	150
85mm f/1.2 L	1025	820	725	650	600	500		
85mm f/1.2 SSC Al bl			595	525				
85mm f/1.8			240	200	190	160		
85mm f/1.8 SSC bl			250	200	220	185		
85mm f/2.8 Soft Focus					450	380		
100mm f/2.0	565	450	375	320	290	225		
100mm f/2.8			160	140	145	120		
100mm f/2.8 SSC bl			180	140	150	110	120	100
100mm f/4 Macro (w/1:1)	785	600	415	350	350	275		
100mm f/4 Macro SC bl (w/1:1)			395	325	300	250		
135mm f/2.0	720	590	495	400	375	300	260	220
135mm f/2.5 SC bl			170	150	150	110		
135mm f/2.8			190	160	150	100	85	60
135mm f/3.5			75	50	60	45	50	40
135mm f/3.5 SC bl			80	55	65	50		

Canon FD Lenses

Lens	New	Mint	Excellent	User
200mm f/1.8 L IF	4500 3695			
200mm f/2.8 IF (latest)	750 600	525 470	450 350	
200mm f/2.8		400 370	375 300	
200mm f/2.8 SSC bl		400 350	330 270	
200mm f/4		150 125	140 105	110 95
200mm f/4 SSC bl		185 170	165 110	100 85
200mm f/4 Macro	970 750	675 595	550 400	
300mm f/2.8 L IF	4200 3500	2900 2600	2500 1750	
300mm f/2.8 SSC Fluorite		1850 1400	1500 1250	
300mm f/4 L IF	1500 1230	1000 850	800 650	
300mm f/4 IF	720 550	450 400	420 350	
300mm f/5.6 IF		250 180	200 170	
300mm f/5.6 SSC bl		250 190	200 160	
400mm f/2.8 L IF	6600 5600		4750 3500	
400mm f/4.5 IF	1700 1470	1100 950	875 650	
400mm f/4.5 SSC bl		975 900	950 700	665 500
500mm f/4.5 L IF	4650 4350	3750 3400	3200 2800	
500mm f/8 Mirror (New FD & bl)	695 570	450 400	350 280	
600mm f/4.5 IF	3200 2800		1995 1850	
600mm f/4.5 SSC bl		2050 1900	1950 1800	
800mm f/5.6 L IF	5100 4650	3895 3500	3200 2900	
800mm f/5.6 SSC bl		2750 2620	2500 2000	
Extender FD 1.4x-A	360 300	225 200	180 150	
Extender FD 2x-A	300 230	195 150	160 120	
Extender FD 2x-B	360 300	225 200	180 150	

Canon FD Zoom Lenses

Lens	New	Mint	Excellent	User
20-35 f/3.5 L	1350 1100	895 750	680 500	
24-35 f/3.5 L		590 500		
24-35 f/3.5 SSC Al bl		620 500	550 430	370 350
28-50 f/3.5		375 325	300 200	
28-50 f/3.5 SSC bl		400 325		
28-55 f/3.5-4.5		160 145	150 125	
28-85 f/4		350 300	290 225	
35-70 f/2.8-3.5		490 400	350 280	
35-70 f/2.8-3.5 SSC bl		470 375	350 250	
35-70 f/3.5-4.5	170 130	100 80	90 75	
35-70 f/4		125 100	120 80	
35-70 f/4 AF		200 125		
The 35-70 f/4 AF will autofocus on any Canon camera that accepts FD lenses.				
35-70 f/3.5-4.5 AC (T-80)		165 120		
35-105 f/3.5		275 200	225 180	
35-105 f/3.5-4.5		235 180	160 135	
50-135 f/3.5		220 175	200 165	
50-300 f/4.5 L		1700 1450	1300 1100	
70-150 f/4.5		155 120	130 80	
70-210 f/4		225 170	180 150	140 100
75-200 f/4.5		160 130	140 120	100 80
75-200 f/4.5 AC (T-80)		180 160		
80-200 f/4 (2 ring)		320 250	250 190	200 145
80-200 f/4 SSC bl (2 ring)			270 225	195 150
80-200 f/4 L	795 600	480 420	460 380	
85-300 f/4.5		900 750	800 650	
85-300 f/4.5 SSC bl		950 750	795 625	650 480
100-200 f/5.6		125 100	115 90	
100-200 f/5.6 SC bl		110 80	85 50	
100-300 f/5.6 L		400 355	375 325	
100-300 f/5.6 (latest)		225 190	200 150	
100-300 f/5.6 (early)		280 190	220 185	
150-600 f/5.6 L			9000 6000	

Original F-1 System Accessories

Lens	New		Mint		Excellent		User	
Std. Eye Level Finder			100	75	50	40		
Speed Finder			250	200	210	180		
Waist Level Finder			100	70	60	50		
Booster T Finder			250	175	200	150		
Servo EE Finder			250	165	150	125		
w/case, EE Coupler, battery magazine and cord, or connecting cord MF								
Motor Drive Unit			300	250	280	225		
w/cord, Battery Magazine 15V or Battery Case D								
Motor Drive MF			400	375	350	280	275	220
Connecting Cord MF			40	30				
Winder F			250	200	225	180		
Data Back F			150	100	100	50		
Film Chamber 250 (w/magazines)			250	200	220	150		
Film Loader 250 or 250-II	225	170	140	120	120	100		
NPC or Forscher Polaroid Back	700	630			450	385		
Flash Coupler D			30	25				
Flash Coupler F	45	30			35	30		
Flash Coupler L	60	45			50	40	40	35
Finder Illuminator F					35	25	25	20

New F-1 System Accessories

Item	New		Mint		Excellent		User	
AE Finder FN	280	230	150	120	130	100		
Eye Level Finder FN	160	120	100	80	70	50		
Speed Finder FN	310	240	240	185	190	145		
Waist Level Finder FN	150	120	95	70				
Waist Level Finder FN-6X	340	260	170	150				
AE Motor Drive FN Set	590	500	400	325	350	275		
AE Motor Drive FN (w/Nicad Pack)	600	535	395	350				
AE Motor Drive FN (w/Hi-Pwr Nicad Pack)	630	570	450	400				
Nicad Pack FN	175	135	75	65				
Hi-Power Nicad Pack FN	260	170			150	125		
Nicad Charger MA/FN	150	110						
AE Power Winder FN			250	200	210	160		
AC/DC Converter Set AD-1	410	300						
Data Back FN			120	100	90	75		
Film Chamber FN-100 (w/magazines)	580	500			350	300		
Film Loader 250 or 250-II	230	170	150	130	120	100		
NPC or Forscher Polaroid Back	700	630			400	385		
Remote Switch 3 (MD & Winder FN)	15	15						
Remote Switch 60 (MD & Winder FN)	10	10						
Extension Cord E1000 (MD & Winder FN)	30	25						

A-Series Accessories

Item	New		Mint		Excellent		User	
Data Back A			90	75	75	50		
Motor Drive MA set			300	240	250	195	200	175
Motor Drive MA (w/Nicad Pack MA & Chgr)			400	325	350	285		
The Motor Drive MA fits A-1 and AE-1 Program only								
Nicad Charger MA/FN	150	110						
Power Winder A			95	75	75	50		
Power Winder A-2	160	135	120	100	100	85		
Generic Winder (Not Canon)	30	45	35	25	30	20		
Remote Switch 3 (MD MA, Winder A2)	15	15						
Remote Switch 60 (MD MA, Winder A2)	10	10						
Extension Cord E1000 (MD MA, Winder A2)	30	25						

T-Series Accessories

Item	New	Mint	Excellent	User
T-70 Command Back 70		75 65	60 50	
T-80 Command Back 80		75 65		
T-90 Command Back 90		140 100	100 80	
T-90 Data Memory Back		200 150	120 95	
Forscher Pro Back (T-90)	700 630			
NPC Pro Back II (T-90)	750 675	600 550		
Remote Switch 60 T3 (T-50/70/80/90)	35 25	25 20	20 15	
Remote Switch Adapter T3 (T-50/70/80/90)	25 20			
Cable Release Adapter T3 (T-50/70/80/90)	30 25			
Extension Cord 1000 T3 (T-50/70/80/90)	35 30			

Close-up Accessories

Item	New	Mint	Excellent	User
20mm f/3.5 Macrophoto lens	195 140	125 95		
35mm f/2.8 Macrophoto lens	225 170	150 120		
The 20/3.5 Macrophoto and 35/2.8 Macrophoto are special high-magnification lenses that must be used in conjunction with bellows.				
Angle Finder A-2		40 30		
Angle Finder B (w/adapter S)	110 75	55 35	50 35	
Auto Bellows (w/double cable release)	245 195	150 140	130 120	
Slide Duplicator 35-52R	120 95	65 50		
w/roll film stage and adapter ring — for use with Auto Bellows only				
Bellows FL		125 100	90 80	
Slide Duplicator FL (w/adapter ring)			80 50	
Bellows M		60 50		
Extension Tube FD 15	85 65			
Extension Tube FD 25	80 60		35 25	
Extension Tube FD 50	90 70			
Extension Tube FL 25		25 20		
Extension Tube M set (manual diaphragm)	70 55			
FD Auto Extension Tube set (not Canon)		75 50		
Variable Extension Tube set M15-25	85 65			
Variable Extension Tube set M30-55	100 70			
Focusing Rail	120 100	75 60		
Macro Auto Ring	60 45			
Macrophoto Coupler FL (55mm or 58mm)		25 20	20 15	
Macro Stage	90 70	60 50	45 40	
Magnifier R or S	50 35	30 20		
Copy Stand 4		125 100		
Copy Stand 5	620 480	350 300		
Macrophoto Adapter	30			
Macrophoto Coupler	50			
Photo Micro Unit F	45			

Other Canon Accessories

Item	New	Mint	Excellent	User
Canon Booster Meter (Pellix, FT, FTb, FTbn)		45 40	40 30	
LC-1 Wireless Controller Set	160 140	135 115	95 85	
LC-2 Wireless Controller Set	140 100	80 70		
TM-1 Quartz Interval Timer	160 110			

The Wireless Controller LC-1 set is compatible with the AE Motor Drive FN, Power Winder FN, Motor Drive MA and Winder A2. When combined with the Remote Switch Adapter T3, it can also be used with T3-compatible T-series and EOS cameras. The Wireless Controller LC-2 is for use with T3-compatible T-series and EOS cameras only. The Quartz Interval Timer TM-1 has the same compatibility requirements as the LC-1.

Canon Flashes

Item	New		Mint		Excellent		User	
011A			40	30	20	15		
133A					30	20		
133D "CAT" w/ring					50	40		
155A			50	35	45	30		
166A			55	45	45	30		
177A					50	35		
188A			55	45	55	40		
199A			100	80	85	65		
244T (T-50)			50	40	40	30		
277T			60	50	45	35		
299T			120	100	110	90		
300TL (TTL flash w/T-90)			250	200	180	120	115	90
533G Set			200	175	170	140		
577G Set			290	250	265	200		
Transistor Pack G set (533G/577G)			100	75				
Transistor Pack G set (NiCads: 533G/577G)			200	150				
ML-1 Macro Light			350	275	250	180		
ML-2 Macro Light (TTL w/T-90)			210	170	175	140		
ML-3 Macro Light (TTL w/T-90)	290	200	180	150	160	125		
TTL Distributor (T-90)	60	40						
TTL Hot Shoe Adapter 2 (T-90)	60	45						
Connecting Cord 60 (T-90)	45	30	20	15				
Connecting Cord 300 (T-90)	50	35	25	20				
Off Camera Shoe Adapter (T-90)	30	25						
Off Camera Shoe Cord (T-90)	60	45						
60F (T-60)	15							

Canon EOS

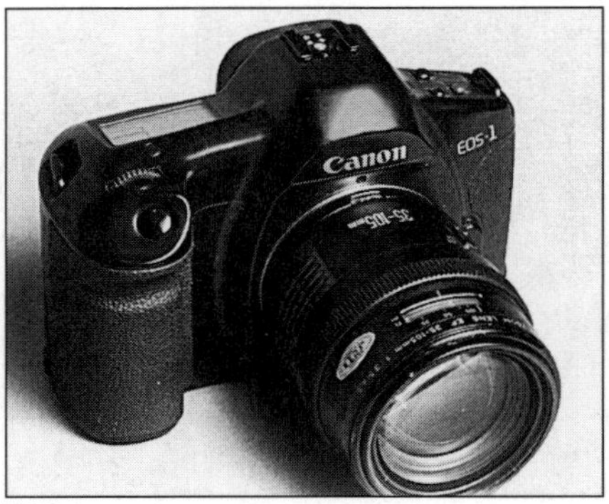

EOS-1

Canon's line of EOS autofocus cameras and lenses continues to grow in popularity among amateurs and professionals alike. EOS cameras have arguably the most advanced lens mount in the industry, which can be coupled with some of the best performing lenses ever made.

Currently (and presumably for the foreseeable future) competition is extremely intense between major autofocus SLR manufacturers. The result is an almost uninterrupted stream of new models being introduced, superceding older ones as technology evolves. In these days of computer-controlled manufacturing processes, look for such trends to continue.

Because there have been so many EOS models introduced since the original EOS 650, the following camera descriptions are listed alphanumerically rather than chronologically.

EOS A2 & A2E

In the ultra-competitive autofocus SLR market, either a camera maker constantly pushes the limits of the envelope, or it quickly becomes an also-ran. Canon is obviously determined not to let this happen with its EOS line, and the new A2E convincingly reinforces this point.

Imagine being able to look at a subject within the viewfinder and having the camera focus on it *automatically*. The A2E comes very close to making the dream become reality. Instead of having one, two, or even three autofocus sensors, the A2E has five, any of which can be triggered just by *looking* at it. Using a system called Eye Controlled Focus, Canon has applied its experience in the design of optometric instruments to the world of autofocus camera technology. Putting it simply, the camera analyzes a ghost image reflected from the eye's cornea via four infrared diodes located around the viewfinder and a CCD (charge coupled device) located next to the pentaprism. This system also tracks the eyeball as it moves, which is what enables it to determine which sensor the eye is looking at. In order for the Eye Controlled Focus System to work at all, however, the camera must be calibrated to each user's eye (a total of five calibrations can be stored). Fortunately, the calibration process is easy to do and takes only seconds to complete. This can be very handy if more than one person uses the camera, or if one wears glasses and/or contacts.

Canon feels that the A2E will appeal primarily to advanced amateurs, but that professionals will prefer the A2, with its more straightforward approach and lack of the Eye Controlled Focus System. Based on what I've observed, though, I'd say don't count on it. A professional will use every tool at his or her disposal to get that one unique, timeless shot that will separate them from the rest of the pack. I predict there will be a strong demand for the A2E, with its unique eye-point autofocus capability, among professional EOS users.

Canon didn't limit this eye-point concept in the A2E just to the autofocus sensors, however. Another, smaller rectangle is visible in the top left corner of the viewfinder. By glancing there, the lens will stop down to taking aperture to allow a momentary preview of depth of field. This is a dazzling concept, and strikes one as being not so much a depth-of-field preview only, but a preview of things to come. One can only speculate as to what sort of tantalizing offshoots will be incorporated into later cameras based on this technology — control of autoexposure modes, exposure compensation, or metering patterns, for example.

Other new features are incorporated into the A2 and A2E, as well. Both cameras use the aforementioned 5-segment autofocus sensor array (the A2 works like an updated 10s in this respect), but coupled with this expanded capability is a new 16-segment evaluative metering pattern. Both cameras also have a high-speed integral motor drive, capable of burning through a roll of film at the rate of five frames per second. The motor drive uses a belt transport similar to the Elan's, but has a quiet rewind mode claimed by Canon to be 2 and ½ times quieter. It also has a higher speed rewind mode which is slightly louder, but which is twice as fast (9 seconds for a 36-exposure roll versus 18 seconds).

With the exception of the new features outlined previously, the A2 and A2E's autofocus systems closely resemble those of other contemporary EOS cameras, which include autoswitching from single-shot AF to AI Servo when subject movement is detected, and predictive autofocus. The central autofocus sensor is cross-based, which will enable the camera to focus easily on both horizontal and vertical lines.

Exposure modes include what has become a standard array of selections on EOS cameras: program, full-auto, portrait, landscape, close-up, sports, aperture- and shutter-priority, depth-of-field, and metered manual. Both the A2 and A2E have the thumbwheel found on the EOS-1 and Elan, located on the camera back. The wheel can be used to alter either aperture or shutter speed selections, depending on the user's preference. Other available exposure modes include autobracketing, ±2 EV exposure compensation, multi-exposures, TTL-flash with the built-in flash (GN 43 @ 28mm) and accessory units such as the 430 EZ, second-curtain flash sync, and red-eye reduction with the built-in flash.

Shutter speeds range from 30 seconds to 1/8000 second, plus B, with X sync occurring at 1/200. Some of the many other features include 16 user-set custom functions, a 3% spot metering pattern which can be shifted between five different areas (set by one of the user-set functions), interchangeable focusing screens, a threaded manual flash PC socket, a T3 remote switch socket, a two-position self-timer, mirror lock-up (set by one of the user-set functions), a built-in focus aid light, and with the A2, built-in eyepiece dioptric correction. Add the optional accessory grip VG10 to either camera and you have the main input dial, shutter release, manual-focusing point-selection button and AE lock button located conveniently for vertical operation — a worthwhile addition any serious photographer will consider indispensible.

EOS EF-M

If you've ever felt the need for a camera that accepts autofocus lenses, but doesn't autofocus, then the EF-M (EF lenses-Manual focus) may be the one for you. Canon designed the EF-M with the photography student in mind, since often students are not allowed to use autofocus cameras in their course work.

The EF-M's exposure modes consist of program, shutter and aperture-priority AE, and metered manual. The metering modes include 3-zone evaluative (for program), centerweighted (for shutter-priority AE, aperture-priority AE and manual), and partial metering. The latter can be selected by the user at any time. Other exposure features include exposure compensation and AE lock.

Shutter speeds range from 2 seconds to 1/1000 second, plus B, with X sync at 1/90. The hot shoe has dedicated flash contacts for the Speedlite 200M, but does not offer TTL flash metering. Other features include DX film coding with override and a self-timer.

The EF-M has a built-in single-shot winder that prewinds to the end of the roll. Auto film rewind and mid-roll rewind are available.

EOS Elan

Intended to replace the now-discontinued 630, the Elan has many of the features found on higher-priced EOS cameras, yet is priced to fit snugly between the 10s and the Rebel XS. It is the first EOS to feature a unique film winding system called Whisper Drive. Instead of using the traditional gear train to advance the film, the Elan uses a belt drive, which goes a long way toward reducing winder noise.

Autofocus modes are single shot (focus priority) and AI Servo (predictive continuous autofocus). Manual focus is also available.

Exposure modes include program with shift, shutter-priority and aperture-priority AE, depth-of-field AE, and metered manual. The Elan also has the same four PIC (Program Image Control) modes found on the Rebel models and has the Bar Code program similar to that found on the 10s, but which can store up to five programs at a time (the 10s can store only one at a time). TTL flash AE is available with the built-in flash or dedicated accessory units. The built-in flash will zoom to adjust its coverage from 28mm to 80mm, and has a pre-flash red-eye-reduction system.

Metering modes include a six-zone evaluative mode, centerweighted averaging, and partial (the central 6.5% of the viewfinder). Shutter speeds range from 30 seconds to 1/4000, plus B, with flash sync at 1/125.

Other features include the Quick Control dial found on the EOS-1, seven built-in Custom Functions (including depth-of-field preview, second-curtain flash sync and mirror lock-up), a self timer, DX film coding with override, automatic film rewind and mid-roll rewind.

EOS Rebel: S, II & S II

The EOS Rebel was sold both as a camera body only or as part of a kit, which included the EF 35-80 f/4-5.6 lens and the 200E flash. Canon took polycarbonate construction to new heights with this puppy. Gone are the metal film guide rails and metal lens mounting flange of an older, bygone era. The result is a compact and almost unbelievably light camera that is so feature-packed and fun to use, it's almost habit-forming.

The autofocus control system used in the Rebel is the same as that in the 630, although the way it works for the user has been simplified in the Rebel. Depending upon the shooting mode the user selects, it will use either single shot, continuous (called "Predictive AI Servo"), or a combination of the two. The shutter will not fire until focus is correct. Manual focus override exists, also.

Exposure modes include a user-shift program, shutter and aperture-priority, metered manual, depth-of-field AE and the same four PIC modes used on the 10s. The metering options available (depending on the mode selected) are three-segment evaluative, centerweighted and partial (9.5%). Other exposure options include: exposure compensation, exposure preview, an exposure/focus lock, multi-exposures and TTL flash with dedicated Canon Speedlites.

Shutter speeds range from 30 seconds to 1/1000, with flash sync occurring at 1/90. Other features include: auto film prewinding as used with the 700, 750 and 850, auto rewind, mid-roll rewind, DX film coding with override and a self timer.

The Rebel S has all the above features plus a built-in flash. It was available as a camera body alone, or in two kit packages: with the 35-80 f/4-5.6 lens, or with the 35-105 f/3.5-4.5 lens.

The Rebel II and Rebel S II, now replaced by the X and XS, are minor updates of the original Rebels. The most significant differences are: a musical self-timer with four different selections: beep, Bach, Beethoven and Vivaldi (the Rap models never made it); a 1/2000 second top shutter speed; a quieter film transport; and a Soft Focus mode, which takes a double exposure on a single frame, defocusing the lens slightly between exposures. The amount of soft focus can be controlled somewhat —the mode has two settings: weak and strong (like something one might find on a coffee maker.). Both the Rebel II and Rebel S II are available with the same kits as the original Rebel models.

EOS Rebel X & XS

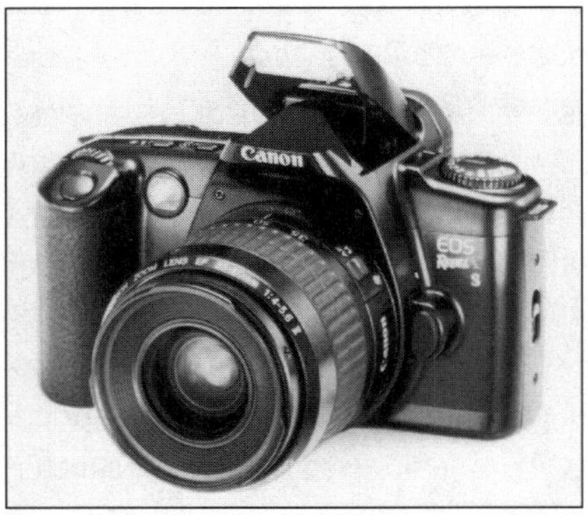

Canon EOS Rebel XS w/EF 35-80mm 1:4-5.6II (with flash up)

I'll bet you didn't think an interchangeable-lens SLR could get any lighter than the EOS Rebel, did you? Well, you're right — and wrong. This new camera by Canon is still labeled the EOS Rebel, however, while it shares some style points with the older Rebels, it has nevertheless undergone a major update.

When compared to the EOS Rebel and Rebel II, the Rebel X is noticeably smaller and lighter. Canon accomplished the weight loss feat by — you guessed it — using even more plastic on the Rebel X than on its predecessors and by doing away with the traditional one-piece glass pentaprism and replacing it with a hollow, plastic and glass, roof-type prism. Now, it's well known among optics buffs that this arrangement is not as bright as a pentaprism, but Canon was able to make up for the light loss somewhat by reducing viewfinder magnification slightly (from 77 to 72 percent). To the user's eye, light loss is negligible.

As part of the update, the Rebel X is fitted with a new three-sensor, wide-area autofocus system. The central sensor is of the cross-type BASIS variety, which is sensitive to both horizontal- and vertical-lined subjects, while the two outer sensors are vertical CCD arrays, which are sensitive to horizontal-lined subjects.

The Command Dial for controlling built-in AE settings is still located in its old place, but it has been reduced in size to match the rest of the camera's pint-sized proportions. Its settings include four PIC modes (Sports, Close-up, Scenic and Portrait), plus Full Auto (displayed as a green square — this is a no-brainer snapshot mode that works surprisingly well), Intelligent Program AE, shutter- and aperture-priority AE, Manual, a simplified depth-of-field mode which requires only a single push of the shutter release, a beeper and ISO override. Gone is the soft focus feature found on the Rebel II, but added is a mid-roll rewind feature — a welcome change from the old method of dismounting the lens, setting the Command Dial to ISO and pushing both of those two small buttons on the right side of the back of the camera. Now, you just set the Command Dial to the rewind setting and push one of two new buttons on the top of the camera. All other exposure controls from previous Rebels have been retained.

The Rebel X's meter now uses a six-zone evaluative system tied in directly to the AF system. This is a highly effective method of determining exposure, since the meter will bias exposure toward the AF sensor in use. The meter also will handle exposure compensation with backlit subjects automatically, but will not dial in enough compensation in very strongly backlit situations. Not to worry, the Rebel X has a ±2 stop exposure compensation capability when you need it. Another effective tool for unusually lit scenes found on the Rebel X is partial metering — first implemented by Canon on the FT and later employed with great success in the FTb and F-1 cameras. The Rebel X's partial metering pattern uses the central AF sensor, the central metering zone and AE lock to achieve critical exposure. The pattern is so tight, however, that it's really more effective to think of it as a spot meter, even though it's a bit broader than the spot metering patterns found on other EOS models.

The Rebel XS has a new, three-zone, four-segment TTL flashmeter, which uses the active AF sensor to determine flash exposure — a surprisingly advanced feature for a camera of this type. This camera is so advanced, in fact, the new EOS-1n uses virtually the same system. The XS's built-in pop-up flash's range (GN 39 @ ISO 100 in feet) has been expanded from 35mm to 28mm — a welcome addition for those tight group shots come holiday time. It also has a combined low-light focus assist beam and red-eye reduction light, located next to the lens, where one would normally expect to find the infrared focus-assist beam on most autofocus SLRs. By locating the red-eye reduction feature in this way, Canon was able to shrink the XS's pop-up flash. Apparently, though, this little halogen lamp throws out a good imitation of a high-beam headlight, and can catch potential subjects off guard in low-light situations, causing them to squint from the bright light. If you've been trying to catch subjects who will provide you with that elusive deer-in-the-headlights expression, this bright little guy may be just what you're looking for.

Shutter speeds range from 30 seconds to 1/2000 second, plus B, with flash sync occurring at 1/90. Although all Rebels have a "B" setting, the Rebel X and XS are the first ones where it can be put to practical use. Located on the side of the camera is a jack that will accept an electronic remote release. The built-in winder has single-frame and continuous modes. Set to the latter, the camera will burn through a roll of film at the blazing speed of 1 fps. Other features include a self-timer and a camera-shake alert.

Finally, a word about an accessory available for the X and XS that most owners will want to think about purchasing: the GR-80TP accessory grip extender. If you have large hands, this accessory will make the camera easier to hold, but that's incidental. Built into the bottom of the grip is a handy little table-top tripod that's a snap to set up — perfect for those situations when you need a stable platform, but didn't want to lug around a tripod.

EOS RT

RT (Real Time) is the feature that separates the RT from all other EOS cameras (and most others, regardless of make). The RT contains a fixed, pellicle mirror, the same arrangement used with the Canon Pellix and the high-speed F-1 cameras, in which about 30% of the light entering the camera is reflected upward by the semi-transparent mirror and then through the viewfinder, while the remaining light travels directly to the film plane. The primary advantage to this arrangement is that the photographer can "capture the moment" much more decisively with a RT than with conventional SLRs, which, by their very nature, do not allow the photographer to see the subject at the moment of exposure. Other advantages are reductions in shooting-time lag, vibration and noise. Light fall-off due to the fixed mirror is minimal.

The EOS RT has all the features of the 630, except "Programmed Image Control". It also has Canon's "Custom Function Control" feature, which provides eight additional user-set custom functions.

EOS-1

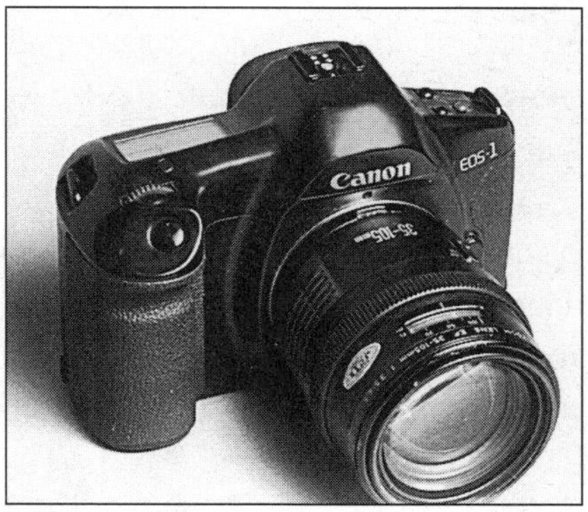

EOS-1

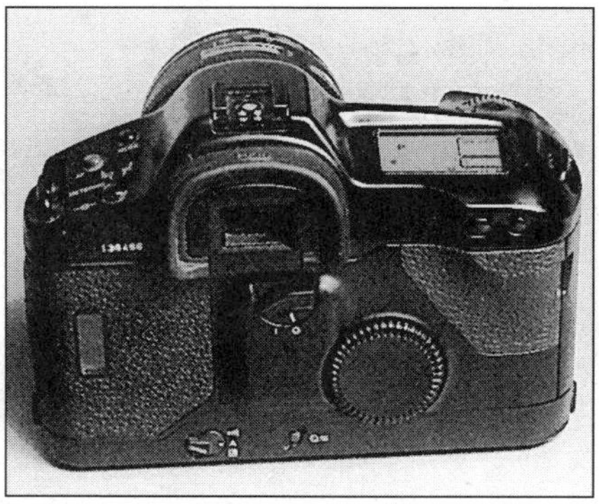

Rear view of the EOS-1 showing thumbwheel

Canon's most recent flagship, the EOS-1 (now the EOS-1n), was obviously designed to go toe-to-toe with the only other autofocus heavyweight on the block at the time of its introduction, Nikon's F4. While the F-4 is still the more popular of the two cameras among working professionals, many have deserted the Nikon ranks and switched to the EOS-1. Such a pivotal (and costly) move is justified by those who have made the switch for a couple of reasons. Perhaps the most significant reason is that the EOS-1 outperforms the F-4 in terms of sheer autofocusing speed. In the super-competitive world of photojournalism, even the slightest edge in performance can be the difference between an award-winning photograph and an honorable mention. Secondly, as sophisticated as the EOS-1 is, ultimately it is only as good as its lenses. Canon's high-performance, ultra- expensive L-series EF lenses have been consistently rated as top performers, and are establishing a reputation among photo professionals as some of the finest 35mm SLR lenses ever made.

The EOS-1's autofocus modes include one-shot (focus priority) or continuous (servo) with "Focus Prediction" at speeds up to 4.5 fps with the optional power drive booster (up to 2.5 fps with the standard built-in drive). The EOS-1's "cross-type" AF sensors detect both horizontally-lined or (with f/2.8 and faster lenses) vertically-lined subjects.

Shutter speeds range from 30 seconds to 1/8000, plus B (which includes an elapsed time indicator). Flash sync occurs at 1/250. DX film coding is there, but so is the option to override it. Metering options include six-zone evaluative, centerweighted, partial (5.8%), or spot (2.3%). Exposure modes include program (w/shift), aperture and shutter priority, depth-of-field program and, of course, metered manual. Other exposure features are exposure compensation, AE lock and auto-bracketing. With the Canon 430 EZ (or the discontinued 420 EZ), TTL flash, auto fill-flash, adjustable fill ratios, second-curtain sync, multi-strobe effects and variable power levels are all at your fingertips. The most innovative feature of the EOS-1 is the Quick-Control Dial (aka thumbwheel) on the back, which the user can choose to select either shutter speeds or apertures. In addition, the EOS-1 has eight user-set custom functions for AF control, AE control, meter patterns, film advance and DX coding. And a first for Canon SLRs: the EOS-1 has a viewfinder that displays 100% of the actual image (almost all other SLRs offer a viewfinder image that covers from 90% to 97% of the actual image area), a basic requirement for critical copy work or exact framing.

Some other features are built-in diopter correction, multi-exposure, a self timer, and auto film loading and rewind with mid-roll rewind. The optional Power Drive Booster advances film at speeds up to 5.5 fps.

EOS-1n

The EOS-1n was announced just before this book was sent to the publisher, so the following description will only address the high points. Regarding price, it appears that the EOS-1n will retail for about the same price as its predecessor.

If you feel the temptation to believe the "n" in the EOS-1n's name stands for "minor update," you'd be dead wrong. This is an entirely new camera that just happens to share some of the same subcomponents as the original.

The EOS-1n's AF system has been tweaked to render even faster performance, especially with moving subjects. It also benefits from the same 5-sensor AF technology that is found in the A2, although the central sensor is more similar to the original EOS-1's than the one used in the A2. The EOS-1, like the A2, does not have the Eye Controlled Focus System found on the A2E. Why not? The explanation being given is that the folks at Canon are still working on an ECF system that will work reliably when the camera is held either horizontally or vertically. It would appear that, as far back as the A2's introduction, Canon was already preparing a cushion for the letdown many users would feel when the EOS-1n would be released without ECF, by referring to the A2 as the camera designed with the professional in mind. (Translation: get used to the A2 and you won't be as angry at us when the EOS-1n is released with no ECF.) Despite this omission, however, this update is impressive, and still worth a look.

The EOS-1n's metering system now has five different patterns from which to choose: 16-zone evaluative (similar to that found on the A2 and A2E), a 3.5% spot pattern that is coupled to the active AF sensor, 9% spot, 2.3% spot, and centerweighted. Flash exposure is measured by employing a 3-zone selective system linked to the active AF sensor for improved flash and fill flash performance.

The EOS-1n's range of user-selectable custom functions has increased from six to fourteen. Included in the list of options are such choice selections as mirror lock-up, AF sensor selection with the quick-control dial, adjustment of shutter speed and aperture increment sizes, various auto bracketing adjustments, and more. The camera has a redesigned film rewind system that manages to be whisper quiet without forsaking the ruggedness of a gear drive. When using the new Power Drive

Booster (interchangeable with the old one), the maximum film advance speed was edged up to a full 6 fps.

EOS 10s

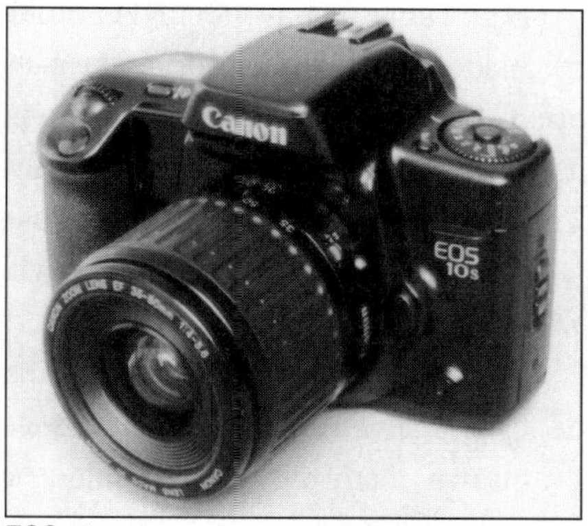

EOS 10s

Introduced with EOS 10s were several advances that have found their way into subsequent EOS SLRs. The focusing control system in the 10s has been enhanced considerably with the addition of Canon's new "Multi-Basis" system's three focusing sensors, which provide the user greater flexibility for subject positioning and also improve tracking of moving subjects.

The 10s autofocus modes include the "One-shot AF Mode" (focus-priority) and the "AI Focus AF Mode" (predictive, continuous autofocus). One program selection switches the AI Focus mode between one-shot and continuous, depending on whether or not the subject is moving.

Exposure is determined either by an eight-zone evaluative metering system, due to the three active AF points, or by the partial-metering method, which places heavy emphasis on the center of the viewfinder. Exposure modes include program (same as in the 650), shutter and aperture priority AE, depth-of-field AE, metered manual, Canon's "Programmed Image Control" (PIC), which, on the 10s, includes four different preset exposure modes, and, a first for Canon, a bar code system. Using the optional bar code reader and bar code book, the user can program the 10s for special shooting situations.

Other exposure features include: TTL flash with the built-in flash or accessory Canon speedlites, auto exposure bracketing, exposure compensation, multi-exposures and an interval timer.

Shutter speeds range from 30 seconds to 1/4000, plus B, with flash sync occurring at 1/125. Other features include: DX film coding with override, a self timer, film transport speeds up to 5 fps with the built-in motor drive (up to 3.3 fps in AI Servo Mode), and auto film loading and rewind. The 10s has fourteen custom function controls that let the user tailor functions such as film rewind, DX coding, shutter-speed lock, depth-of-field check and, something that has been missing from Canon's lineup for way too long, a mirror lock-up feature.

EOS 620

The EOS 620 has been out of production for a while now, but remains popular on the used market because of its top flash sync speed: 1/250 second. The only other EOS cameras with this fast a flash sync are the EOS-1 and the EOS-in.

Available autofocus modes are one-shot (focus priority) or continuous (servo). Metering patterns include a six-zone evaluative pattern or partial area (6.5%). Exposure modes include a program mode with manual shift override, aperture and shutter-priority AE and metered manual. Additional exposure controls include auto-bracketing, multi-exposure capability and a depth-of-field check button. Shutter speeds range from 30 seconds to 1/4000, plus B, with the above-mentioned X sync of 1/250 second.

Other features include interchangeable focusing screens, exposure compensation, DX coding with manual override, a self timer, TTL flash, auto fill-flash, second-curtain flash sync and multi-strobe effects. The integral motor drive advances film at speeds up to 3 fps with auto film loading and rewind, and mid-roll film rewind.

EOS 630

The EOS 630 replaced the 620, although it lacks a couple of features its predecessor has, most notably the top shutter speed and flash sync. Both speeds got bumped down a notch with the 630 to 1/2000 and 1/125, respectively.

The 630 makes up for this with a host of improvements. For starters, Canon claimed the 630 focuses twice as fast as previous models (the 620 and 650). It still has two AF modes, one-shot (focus-priority) and continuous (servo), but the latter was improved with an added "Focus Prediction" feature for sharper results when shooting high-speed action photos. To complement this faster autofocus capability, the motor drive's speed was boosted to 5 fps (slower when tracking moving subjects in the continuous AF mode).

The 630 combines the best exposure modes of the 650 and 620, plus a lot more. In addition to program with shift, aperture and shutter-priority AE, and metered manual modes, are both depth-of-field AE and auto-bracketing. It also has Canon's "Programmed Image Control" (PIC) system, a set of seven preset program modes, and "Custom Function Control," a set of seven user-set custom functions for film advance, DX coding, AF control, AE control and metering patterns. Other features include multi-exposure capability and a depth-of-field check button.

TTL Flash AE options are the same for the 630 as with the 620.

EOS 650

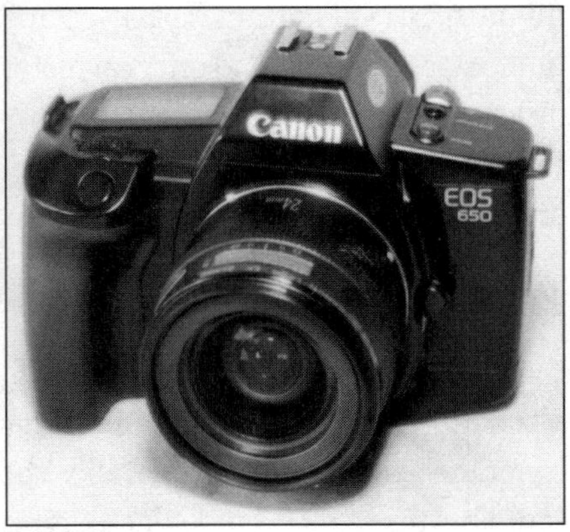

EOS 650

Available autofocus modes are one-shot (focus priority) or continuous (servo). Metering patterns include a six-zone evaluative pattern or partial area (6.5%). Exposure modes include a program mode that shifts automatically depending on the lens mounted, aperture and shutter-priority AE, metered manual and depth-of-field AE. Other features include interchangeable focusing screens, exposure compensation, DX coding with manual override, a self timer, TTL flash, auto fill-flash, second-curtain flash sync and multi-strobe effects.

Shutter speeds range from 30 seconds to 1/2000, plus B, with X sync at 1/125. The integral motor drive advances film at speeds up to 3 fps with auto film loading and rewind, and mid-roll film rewind.

EOS 700

The EOS 700 was released after the EOS 750. The two cameras look similar, but shouldn't be confused. The EOS 700 is an entirely different camera with a broader array of features.

The autofocus system used in the 700 is similar to that used in the 630, ensuring rapid autofocus. Two modes are possible: one-shot (focus-priority) or "One-Shot/AI Servo Automatic Changeover." The latter selection will switch automatically from single shot to continuous predictive autofocus based on subject movement.

Exposure options, using the six-zone evaluative metering pattern, include the same program mode as the 650's, depth-of-field AE, and Canon's "Programmed Image Control" with 8 settings, Shutter-priority and TTL programmed flash with the built-in flash or other EOS speedlites. Shutter speeds range from 2 seconds to 1/2000 (¼-1/2000 in shutter-priority), with flash sync at 1/125.

The 700 uses the same film prewind system as in the 750/850 and, like them, has DX film speed settings only with no manual override. The built-in motor winds the film at speeds up to 1.2 fps.

EOS 750 & 850

Both cameras have a single autofocus mode, one-shot (focus priority) operation. The 750 has a built-in flash and a hot shoe, the 850 has a hot shoe only. The E-160E flash was designed for use with the 850, but other EZ units will work as well.

Exposure modes are program and depth-of-field AE using the six-zone evaluative metering pattern, ala the 650. Shutter speeds range from 2 seconds to 1/2000. Film ISO is set automatically by DX film coding. There is no manual DX override. The built-in motor provides film wind speeds to 1.5 fps. Mid-roll rewind is not possible. When film is inserted, the film is prewound to the end of the roll, then drawn back into the film cassette with each exposure, thereby protecting exposed frames if the camera back is accidentally opened. The frame counter shows the number of frames remaining on the roll.

TTL flash and fill-flash are possible with either the built-in flash (750 only, GN of 39 at ISO 100), or add-on EZ speedlites.

EOS Autofocus SLRs

Camera	Yrs Made	New	Mint	Excellent	User
EOS A2	1992-	685 600			
EOS A2E	1992-	805 700			
EOS EF-M w/50 f/1.8	1991-	300 220			
EOS EF-M w/35-80	1991-	350 260			
EOS Elan	1991-	450 370	340 295		
EOS Elan kit w/28-80 USM	1991-	650 590			
EOS Rebel	1990-91		150 130		
EOS Rebel kit	1990-91		275 225		
EOS Rebel II	1991-94		220 170		
EOS Rebel II kit	1991-94		310 230		
EOS Rebel S	1990-91		200 175		
EOS Rebel S w/35-80	1990-91		325 280		
EOS Rebel S w/35-105	1990-91		360 330		
EOS Rebel S II	1991-94		200 180		
EOS Rebel S II w/35-80	1991-94		300 260		

EOS Autofocus SLRs

Camera	Yrs Made	New	Mint	Excellent	User
EOS Rebel S w/35-105	1990-91		360 .. 330		
EOS Rebel S II	1991-94		200 .. 180		
EOS Rebel S II w/35-80	1991-94		300 .. 260		
EOS Rebel S II w/35-105	1991-94		420 .. 330		
EOS Rebel X	1994-	225 .. 180			
EOS Rebel X w/35-80 II	1994-	320 .. 275			
EOS Rebel XS	1994-	270 .. 230			
EOS Rebel XS w/35-80 II	1994-	365 .. 325			
EOS RT	1989-		300 .. 250		
EOS 1	1989-	1525 .. 1150		925 .. 825	
EOS 1 w/pwr drv	1989-	1850 .. 1325		1100 .. 950	
EOS 1n	1994-	2095 .. 1550			
EOS 10s	1990-		325 .. 280		
EOS 620	1986-89		300 .. 270	280 .. 200	
EOS 630	1989-91		265 .. 225		
EOS 650	1986-89		250 .. 185	200 .. 160	
EOS 700 w/35-80	1990-90		260 .. 240		
EOS 750	1988-90		175 .. 150		
EOS 850	1988-90		170 .. 150	150 .. 100	

EOS (EF) Autofocus Lenses

EOS optics have established a reputation for optical quality, especially the ultra-expensive L-series and the various almost-silent Ultrasonic models. More and more members of the photographic press and others whose work requires the finest lenses available seem to agree that Canon's L-series EF lenses are superior to all other 35mm SLR lenses currently being produced. But that shouldn't be too surprising, considering the prices tags these optics carry.

When Canon decided to switch from the tried-and-proven, backward-compatible FD mount with its millions of users to an altogether new mount with no backward-compatibility, you can bet that the company had some pretty good reasons for doing so. For starters, Canon was getting clobbered by Minolta. Clearly, Canon engineers saw the necessity of coming up with a design which would not only meet the competition's capabilities, but which would give Canon a decided edge. So, instead of another attempt at an autofocus design based on the FD mount (they had already been burned pretty good trying that before — remember the T-80?), Canon elected to start with a clean slate.

Once again, in a departure from the industry norm, Canon decided to locate autofocus motors in its lenses instead of camera bodies. Even though this idea didn't work so well with the T-80, Canon was on the right track, largely due to its own advances in motor design. By foregoing a mechanical autofocus power coupling between the camera and lens, and instead providing each lens with its own motor, the number of moving parts was reduced, which translates directly into a focusing system that is not only inherently faster, but, with the new Ultrasonic lenses, the quietest in the industry — although your dog may not agree.

If you're an experienced photographer, but new to EOS, something else you're sure to notice right away is perhaps the second most significant aspect of an EOS lens. There is no aperture ring. Lens apertures are controlled by setting the aperture value on the camera instead of the lens. To many photographers from an earlier, bygone era, this may seem to be unnecessary gimmickry — more retraining for the end user disguised as convenience. Maybe not, though. For example, the new TS (Tilt-Shift) lenses for EOS have automatic diaphragms, whereas the FD-mount TS 35 does not. Because EOS lenses communicate aperture information electronically, an automatic diaphragm on a TS lens is no longer the stumbling block it once used to be with the FD lens' mechanical design. Look for other new products that will take advantage of the EOS electrical-contact coupling. Like what? How about an EOS auto bellows that doesn't need a double cable release? Makes sense, doesn't it.

Another improvement over the FD mount is the larger diameter of the EOS mount. It has been reported that Canon felt the larger mount size was necessary to prevent vignetting in the viewfinder when using super telephoto lenses with focal lengths of 800 millimeters and greater. This is an interesting tidbit, since the longest focal length EOS telephoto currently available is the 600mm f/4. Can this mean that Canon has even longer focal lengths planned for the EOS system?

One other peculiarity found with many of the L-series lenses should be mentioned: the 50mm f/1.0 L, 85mm f/1.2 L, 200mm f/1.8 L, 300mm f/2.8 L, 400mm f/2.8 L and 600mm f/4 L all have power-assisted manual focus. The traditional helical or rack-and-pinion methods of mechanical focusing have been abandoned in favor of an electronic coupling between the focusing ring and the movable elements, allowing manual focus to be performed by the internal drive motor. Because of this the camera must be switched on to focus one of these lenses manually.

In the lens listings below, the following abbreviations are used: L = Low dispersion glass (See the FD lens section for an explanation), USM = UltraSonic Motor, TS = Tilt-Shift, and A = Autofocus only.

EOS Autofocus Lenses

Lens	New	Mint	Excellent	User
14mm f/2.8 L USM	2450 2120			
15mm f/2.8	795 670			
20mm f/2.8 USM	575 470	400 300		
24mm f/2.8	405 320	250 200		
24mm f/3.5 L TS	1470 1300	1100 950		
28mm f/2.8	230 190	125 95	100 85	
35mm f/2	335 220			
45mm f/2.8 L TS	1470 1300			
50mm f/1.0 L USM	2995 2500			
50mm f/1.8	95 75	55 45	50 40	
50mm f/1.4	400 370			
50mm f/2.5 Macro	420 300	220 190	200 160	
Life Size Converter EF	250 190	150 120	120 90	
85mm f/1.2 L USM	1975 1500			
85mm f/1.8 USM	430 360			
90mm f/2.8 L TS	1470 1300			
100mm f/2 USM	490 420			
100mm f/2.8 Macro	610 550			
135mm f/2.8 Soft Focus	440 370		190 170	
200mm f/1.8 L USM	4695 4190			
200mm f/2.8 L USM	950 690			
300mm f/2.8 L USM	4900 4400			
300mm f/4 L USM	1200 1000			
400mm f/2.8 L USM	7000 6300			
400mm f/5.6 L	1750 1420			
500mm f/4.5 L USM	5750 5300			
600mm f/4 L USM	9100 8400			
1.4X APO	475 390			
2X APO	380 310			

EOS Autofocus Zoom Lenses

Lens	New	Mint	Excellent	User
20-35 f/2.8 L	1800 1470	1200 1000		
20-35 f/3.5-4.5 USM	600 450			
28-70 f/3.5-4.5		225 175		
28-70 II f/3.5-4.5		170 160		
28-70 f/2.8 L USM	1650 1370			
28-80 f/2.8-4 L USM		1200 950		
28-80 f/3.5-5.6 USM	325 260			
28-80 f/3.5-5.6 II USM	275 200			
28-105 f/3.5-4.5 USM	405 335			
35-70 f/3.5-4.5		150 125	125 100	
35-70 f/3.5-4.5 A	140 110			
35-80 f/4-5.6		100 80		
35-80 f/4-5.6 USM	170 150			
35-80 f/4-5.6 II	150 105			
35-105 f/3.5-4.5		175 150		
35-105 f/4.5-5.6	200 160			
35-105 f/4.5-5.6 USM	275 200			

EOS Autofocus Zoom Lenses

Lens	New	Mint	Excellent	User
35-135 f/3.5-4.5		350 275		
35-135 f/4-5.6 USM	375 310	225 200		
35-350 f/3.5-5.6 L USM	2450 2000			
50-200 f/3.5-4.5		215 180	195 170	
50-200 f/3.5-4.5 L		580 400		
70-210 f/3.5-4.5 USM	395 290			
70-210 f/4		180 170	160 150	
75-300 f/4-5.6 USM	325 250			
80-200 f/2.8 L	1425 1200		750 650	
80-200 f/4.5-5.6	225 160			
100-200 f/4.5 A		100 80		
100-300 f/4.5-5.6 USM	375 310			
100-300 f/5.6		260 200		
100-300 f/5.6 L	680 575	450 400		

EOS Accessories

Item	New	Mint	Excellent	User
Command Back E-1 (EOS-1)	250 175			
NPC Polaroid Back (EOS-1)	750 630	570 500		
Quartz Data Back E (620/630/650/RT)	80 65	70 50		
Technical Back E w/kbrd (620/630/650)	690 550			
Interface Unit TB	150 120			
Connects Technical Back E to IBM PC or compatible computers				

EOS Motor & Remote Accessories

Item	New	Mint	Excellent	User
Power Drive Booster (EOS-1)	330 290			
Handstrap E-1 (for Power Drive Booster)	30 25			
Nicad Pack E-1 w/charger	315 285			
BP-E1 Battery Pack (EOS-1)	200 130			
BP-5 Battery Back (A2/A2E)	80 55			
RC-1 Remote Controller (10s/Elan)	20 20			
Remote Switch 60 T3*	45 30	25 20		
Remote Switch Adapter T3	25 20			
Cable Release Adapter T3*	30 25			
Extension Cord 1000 T3*	35 30			
LC-2 Wireless Controller Set*	125 100	80 70		
TM-1 Quartz Interval Timer*	160 110			

**The Remote Switch 60 T3, Cable Release Adapter T3, Extension Cord 1000 T3 and LC-2 Wireless Controller Set are for use with T3-compatible EOS cameras. The TM-1 Quartz Interval Timer requires the Remote Switch Adapter T3 to be used with T3-compatible EOS cameras.*

EOS Grips

Item	New	Mint	Excellent	User
GR-10 Grip (620/630/650/RT)	45 35	20 15		
GR-20 Grip (620/630/650/RT: w/T3 socket)	45 35	20 15		
GR-50 Grip (700/750/850)	35 25			
GR-60 Grip (10s)	45 35			
GR-70 Grip (Rebel/Rebel S)	35 25			
GR-80TP (Rebel X/XS)	45 35			
VG-10 Grip (A2/A2E)	130 80			

EOS Close-up Accessories

Item	New	Mint	Excellent	User
Angle Finder B (w/adapter S)	110 ... 75	55 ... 35	50 ... 35	
Magnifier S	50 ... 35	30 ... 20		
EF-12 Extension Tube*	100 ... 70			
EF-25 Extension Tube*	125 ... 95			
FD to EOS Adapter (not Canon)*	60 ... 40			
Macro Lens Mount Converter FD-EOS	85 ... 65			

**The EF-12 and EF-25 Extension Tubes provide fully coupled extensions (12mm and 25mm respectively) between body and lens, and can be used with all EOS cameras. The Macro Lens Mount Converter FD-EOS is designed to couple EOS cameras to FD close-up accessories, such as the Auto Bellows, for high-magnification photography. Although an FD lens can be mounted directly to an EOS camera using this accessory, infinity focus will be lost.*

Miscellaneous EOS Accessories

Item	New	Mint	Excellent	User
Bar Code Reader E (10s & Elan)	65 ... 45			
Bar Code Book	20 ... 15			

EOS Flashes

Item	New	Mint	Excellent	User
160E (EOS 850)			35 ... 25	
200E (EOS Rebel)	80 ... 60			
200M (EOS EF-M)	75 ... 55			
300EZ	155 ... 140	90 ... 80	75 ... 60	
420EZ		175 ... 140	150 ... 125	
430EZ	350 ... 275	215 ... 190		
480EG Set	580 ... 500			
540EZ	400 ... 315			
Compact Battery Pack E	120 ... 80			
Transistor Pack E set	165 ... 120	90 ... 75	75 ... 60	
Trans Pack E set w/NiCads, chgr	300 ... 230	200 ... 150		
The Compact Battery Pack E and the Transistor Pack E set are for use with the 430EZ and 480EG only.				
ML-3 Macro Light	290 ... 200	180 ... 150	160 ... 125	
TTL Distributor	60 ... 40			
TTL Hot Shoe Adapter	80 ... 60			
Connecting Cord 60	45 ... 30	20 ... 15		
Connecting Cord 300	50 ... 35	25 ... 20		
Off Camera Shoe Adapter	30 ... 25			
Off Camera Shoe Cord (except 630, RT) 60	45			

Contax / Yashica

Contax SLRs

Modern Contax 35mm cameras (as opposed to the Contax rangefinders and SLRs of the 1930's-50's) are the result of a 1973 cooperative agreement between Carl Zeiss of Germany and Yashica of Japan.

The Contax mystique was reborn when the RTS was introduced in 1976. Sporting a sleek exterior created by Porsche's design studios, Contax cameras have always been a sensual experience to hold and, well, just to look at. The modern Contax is not just a beautifully-designed machine, it is a well-engineered and constructed photographic tool that accepts some of the finest optics ever made, the Zeiss T* lenses.

Contax G-1

The Contax G-1 was announced just before this book was sent to the publisher, thus the following description is not comprehensive.

The Contax G-1 is the first genuinely new design in interchangeable-lens rangefinder cameras since the introduction of the Leica CL. Comparisons with the only other currently produced high-end rangefinder camera, the Leica M6, are inevitable. However, other than the fact that they're both interchangeable-lens rangefinder cameras, the G-1 and the M6 have virtually nothing in common.

It remains to be seen if the G-1 truly is Leica's wake-up call, as many are suggesting. Two big items the G-1 has in its favor are price and features. Its street price will be approximately half that of the Leica M6 and less than half that of the M6 Titanium. Regarding its features, if one were to poll Leica rangefinder users and tabulate a list of features they'd like to see, the result would likely resemble the G-1. So, what did Contax come up with?

Right off the bat, the engineers at Contax decided to house the G-1 in titanium — a smart move. Press-corps duty can be brutal and housing a camera in titanium is the most effective means of prolonging its life. Underneath the titanium skin is an all-metal frame made from copper-silumin alloy, a material that Contax is using in all its latest SLRs now.

The G-1's most significant feature is also a big departure from the Contax philosophy of "user control": autofocus. At this date, I have no details on the precise method by which the autofocus mechanism operates, but it is reported to be an advanced passive AF system with an extended base length to enhance autofocus accuracy.

The TTL meter is of the center-weighted averaging variety. The exposure modes provided are aperture-priority AE, manual, and TTL auto flash. Shutter speeds range from 16 seconds to 1/2000 (1 second to 1/2000 in manual), plus B, with X sync occurring at 1/100 second. The G-1 has an integral motor that provides what has become the standard array of features: auto first-frame film wind and auto rewind, plus single and continuous frame advance modes. Other features include an AE lock, eyepiece dioptric adjustment, and an adapter that will allow the user to fit Contax SLR lenses on the G-1.

Initial lens offerings for the G-1 include a 16mm f/8 Biogon (which will use an external meter and viewfinder), a 28mm f/2.8 Biogon, a 45mm f/2 Planar, and a 90mm f/2.8 Sonnar.

Contax RTS

The RTS' exposure features include aperture-priority AE and metered manual modes using a bottom-center-weighted metering pattern, exposure compensation and multi-exposure capability. Shutter speeds range from 4 seconds to 1/2000, plus B, with X sync at 1/60. Other features include user-interchangeable focusing screens, a self-timer and depth-of-field preview. The RTS Winder can be attached for motor-driven speeds up to 2 fps. There was also a motor drive made for the original RTS, called the Professional Motor Drive. The W-6 Professional Motor Drive (not to be confused with the aforementioned one), while designed for the RTS II, will function on the RTS, as well.

Contax RTS II

The RTS II features the same exposure options and metering pattern as the RTS. The shutter speed range was extended on the low end to 16 seconds (4 seconds in manual mode), plus B, with X sync at 1/60 (apparently, even though it's labeled as being 1/60, the actual mechanical shutter speed is 1/50 second). Only B and X sync operate without batteries. Other features include TTL flash automation with dedicated flash units, exposure compensation, an AE lock, interchangeable focusing screens, a self-timer and depth-of-field preview. Either the accessory 3 fps W-3 Winder or the 5 fps W-6 Motor Drive can be attached.

Contax RTS III

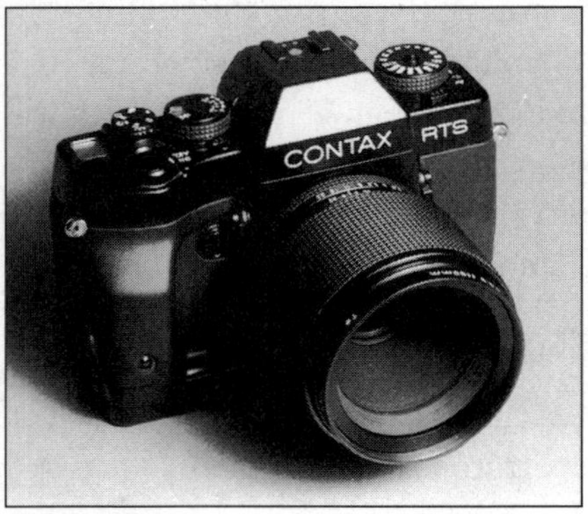

Contax RTS III

The RTS III is the new leader in the dubious "Most Expensive Japanese 35mm SLR" category. Being that it's more expensive than the Nikon F4 and the Canon EOS-1n by several hundred dollars, you'd probably expect it to be crammed with features, offering the latest state-of-the-are technology and, of course, exhibiting the very best of craftsmanship The response to such expectations is an unqualified "Sort of." For example, your 2,000 plus semolians doesn't buy you autofocus, nor do you get even a single program mode, and you can forget about the latest smart technology in multi-segmented metering patterns. But what you do get is impressive.

The RTS III has a unique vacuum mechanism coupled with a ceramic pressure plate that sucks the film flat at the film plane, insuring maximum sharpness. Another unique feature is its TTL pre-flash spot metering system, which allows the user to check exposure with any flash, from wink lights to studio strobes, not just dedicated units. The RTS III joins the Nikon F family and the EOS-1 as one of a handful of 35mm SLRs that offer a 100% field of view through the viewfinder (most other 35mm SLRs have a field of view ranging from 90% to 97%).

Exposure modes include shutter or aperture-priority AE and metered manual using centerweighted or spot metering. Other exposure features include TTL flash metering with dedicated flash units (second-curtain sync with the TLA280 flash), autobracketing, an AE lock and exposure compensation. Shutter speeds range from 32 seconds to 1/8000 (4 seconds to 1/8000 in manual), plus B, with X sync at 1/250.

Other features include a built-in databack that records information between the frames, mirror lock-up, interchangeable focusing screens, diopter correction, an eyepiece shutter, depth-of-field preview, multiple exposure capability, DX film coding with override, a die-cast aluminum body with a magnesium top plate and a titanium bottom plate, and an integral motor drive that provides continuous speeds up to 5 fps.

Contax RX

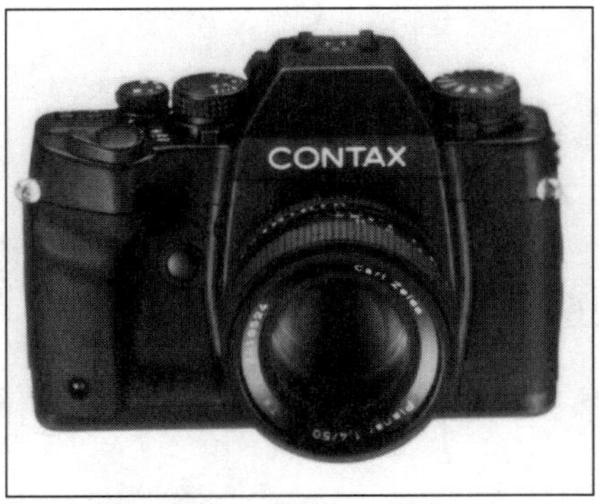

Contax RX with Planar T* 50mm F1.4mm Lens

One must be familiar with Contax's tenacious adherence to manual focus technology to appreciate the milestone the Contax RX represents. The engineers at Contax have finally conceded that a focus-assist feature, called the Digital Focus Indicator on the RX, could be of some value. Contax still draws the line at autofocus, though, claiming that the Zeiss T* lenses cannot be enhanced by adding autofocus capability, mostly due to weight and focus accuracy. The RX nevertheless represents a fundamentally new direction for Contax, so let's take a look at what they've come up with.

The RX bears a strong resemblance to the ST. Its body components are made from the same materials, the same type of precision drive motor system is used; the same metering components and oversized pentaprism are found in the RX as in the ST. But the differences between the two cameras are considerable.

The RX's Digital Focus Indicator (DFI) function is a unique focus-assist system that uses the principle of the Circle of Confusion to determine best focus. Put simply, the circle of confusion is the minimum size of a light source when projected onto the film plane. Have you ever noticed how, when you defocus a lens in either direction, the image not only blurs but grows in size?

That's the principle at work here. The RX is able to determine the minimum size of the subject at the point of focus, and as a result is able to indicate when critical sharpness has been reached. The RX also has two Focus Indicator Scale modes. Not only will the DFI render the subject in absolute focus, but it can also provide the user with a depth of field scale, showing an acceptable focus range and where within that range the point of focus lies. For the photographer who prefers focus accuracy over focus speed, the RX, with its DFI system, could be just the ticket.

The RX has six exposure modes: aperture preferred AE, shutter preferred AE, program AE, manual, TTL auto flash AE and manual flash. Also found on the RX is Automatic Bracketing Control, which will bracket three shots either in single or continuous frame advance in ½ EV increments. AE lock, ±2 EV exposure compensation and second-curtain flash sync with dedicated TLA flashes are also available.

The user can select between two metering systems: centerweighted averaging and spot. Shutter speeds range from 16 seconds to 1/4000 second (4 seconds to 1/4000 in manual and shutter preferred AE), with X sync occurring at 1/125, plus B. The RX can be personalized, as well, with a selection of nine user-defined Custom Functions to choose from.

Other features include a self-timer, DX-film coding with override, dioptric adjustment, interchangeable focusing screens, auto film loading and rewind with mid-roll rewind available, single or continuous frame advance (speeds up to 3 fps), a PC connector, a built-in data back that prints data between frames and a depth-of-field preview button.

Contax S2 & S2B

If you're like many photographers who cut their teeth on mechanical, manual-focus, manual-exposure SLRs, and if you find yourself longing for the good old days, then news of the release of the Contax S2 may come as sweet comfort to your soul. Imagine a rugged, titanium-housed Nikon FM2, and you'll have a pretty good picture of the Contax S2 (even the shutter speed dial is located where a non-Contax user would expect to find it). One unusual feature of the S2 is its metering pattern: indicated by the focusing screen's microprism circle, the pattern is a 5mm spot, which works out to about 2% of the image area — an unusual choice for a single metering pattern. Contax sees the prospective S2 user as a meticulous photographer, either a dedicated amateur or professional who needs the tight discrimination a spot meter provides. The S2B, however, employs the more conventional centerweighted metering pattern, which is, as far as I've been able to determine, the only feature that distinguishes the S2B from the S2.

The S2's mechanical, vertical-travelling, metal-bladed shutter provides speeds from 1 second to 1/4000, plus B, with X sync occurring at 1/250. Other features include interchangeable focusing screens, a mechanical self-timer, depth-of-field preview, a multiple-exposure lever, a semi-dedicated hot shoe (with dedicated Contax strobes, a ready light will illuminate in the viewfinder), a PC connector, and a manual ISO film-speed setting dial (No DX coding here, folks.).

Contax ST

The Contax ST represents a superb balance of form and function. Its form can only be described as elegant. Its function, however, is very traditional by today's auto everything standards. Nevertheless, the elements of the ST combine to provide the serious photographer with a perfect extension of his view. Designed to accompany the professional or ardent amateur into most any environment — be it friendly or hostile — the ST is as rugged as it is sleek. The camera is housed entirely in metal: the body is composed of copper-silumin alloy, while the top and bottom cover are brass. Contax engineers opted for brass covers over higher-tech substances because of brass's inherent shock-absorbing properties. And, given the fact that the ST is designed to accept the Carl Zeiss T* lenses, one has the capability to produce images of unrivaled quality.

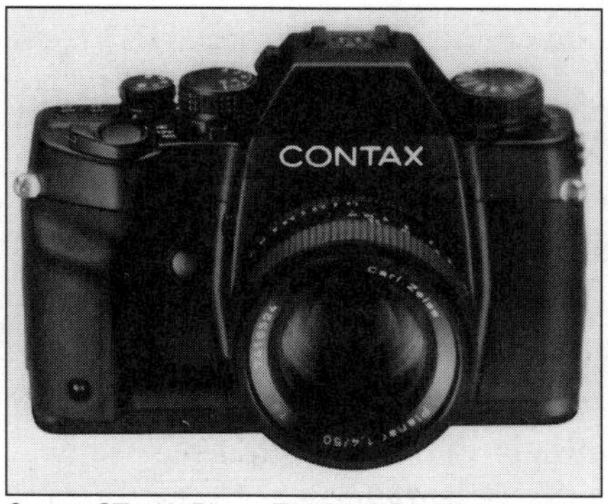

Contax ST with Planar T 50mm F1.4 lens*

The ST is billed as having seven exposure modes. These are aperture-priority AE, shutter-priority AE, programmed auto, manual, TTL auto flash, manual TTL auto flash and manual flash. Exposure compensation is available (±2EV in third-stop increments) as is AE lock. An auto-bracketing mode can be selected as well, which will provide a 3 frame continuous exposure control by switch-over from ±0.5EV to ±1.0EV. Available metering patterns are centerweighted averaging and spot. The spot pattern is indicated by the 5mm diameter microprism ring in the viewfinder. Another nice feature that makes viewing and composition all the more easier is an oversized high-eyepoint pentaprism.

Shutter speeds range from 16 seconds to 1/6000 second (1 second to 1/4000 second in manual and shutter-priority AE), plus B with an elapsed time indicator. X sync occurs at 1/200. Second curtain flash sync is available with Contax flashes (such as the TLA 280) that support the feature.

Other features include auto film loading and rewind with the built-in winder, single or continuous film advance with speeds up to 3 fps, mid-roll film rewind, user-interchangeable focusing screens, a cable release socket and a PC connector (two features overlooked all too often by other manufacturers), a self-timer, dioptric adjustment from -3 to +1 diopters and DX film coding with override.

Contax 137 MD Quartz

The 137 Quartz, introduced in 1979, offers aperture-priority AE as its single exposure mode. Shutter speeds range from 11 seconds to 1/1000, plus B, and X sync at 1/100. Other features include TTL flash with dedicated flash units, a self-timer, and an integral winder, which provides film advance speeds up to 2 fps. It has no manual film advance lever, but it does have a rewind crank, lacking auto-film rewind.

Contax 137 MA Quartz

The 137MA superseded the 137 MD Quartz, and came with the following improvements: A manual exposure mode was added. The shutter speeds remain the same in the aperture-priority AE mode, but are 1 second to 1/1000 in the manual mode. Frame numbers are visible inside the full-information viewfinder. Exposure compensation was added, as was an AE lock. The integral winder's speed was boosted to 3 fps.

Contax 139 Quartz

The Contax 139, released in 1979, is in some areas a scaled down version of the RTS and in other areas has a few features the RTS lacks. Like the RTS, the 139's exposure modes are aperture-priority AE and metered manual, with exposure compensation. Added to the 139 is an auto-exposure lock and TTL flash with dedicated flash units.

Shutter speeds range from 11 seconds to 1/1000 (manual mode speeds are 1 second to 1/1000), plus B, with X sync at 1/100. Other features include a self-timer and a multiple exposure lever located on top of the camera.

Contax 159MM

The Contax 159MM was the first Contax to utilize the new-style Zeiss MM lenses. To engage any of its three program modes, an MM lens must be used, although any bayonet Zeiss or Yashica lens may be used for its other exposure modes.

The 159MM's program modes are: HP, a high-speed program for shallow depth of field and/or stop-action photography; P, the standard program; and LP, a low-speed program for maximum depth of field. In addition, aperture-priority AE and metered manual are available, as well as an AE lock and exposure compensation. Centerweighted metering is handled by silicon photo cells.

Shutter speeds range from 60 seconds to 1/4000 (1 second to 1/4000 in manual mode), plus B, with X sync occurring at 1/250 (1/100 in AE modes). TTL-OTF flash metering is available with dedicated flash units. Other exposure options include an AE lock and exposure compensation.

Other features include a self timer, depth-of-field preview, multiple exposure capability, interchangeable focusing screens (although not by the user) and power film winding with the optional W-7 Winder.

Contax 167MT

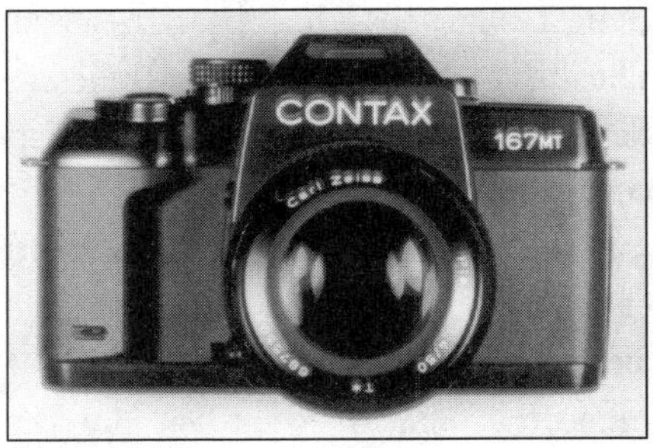

Contax 167MT

The Contax 167MT was the second Contax SLR designed to accept Contax MM lenses and was the sole remaining current production model until the introduction of the RTS III. As was mentioned with the 159MM, the Contax MM lenses must be used to engage either the 167MT's program or shutter-priority mode. Exposure modes include program with a three-stop shift feature, aperture and shutter-priority AE, and metered manual. Other exposure features include a safety shift, three-shot autobracketing, an AE lock and exposure compensation. Metering choices are centerweighted averaging and spot.

Shutter speeds range from 16 seconds to 1/4000, plus B, with X sync at 1/125. Other features include DX film coding with override, user-interchangeable focusing screens, depth-of-field preview, a self timer, TTL flash with dedicated units and a PC socket. Film is advanced via an integral motor drive at speeds up to 3 fps. The film handling features also include auto film loading and motorized rewind.

Yashica SLRs

Ever since the reintroduction of the Contax marque, Yashica SLRs have languished in the shadows of their more upscale cousins. It isn't that they aren't good cameras. In fact, they're quite well made, as one would expect when considering that Yashica also manufactures the Contax. Nevertheless, they haven't enjoyed near the popularity or attention. All this tends to depress a Yashica's value on both the new and used market, which means that one can obtain a nice camera for a minimum investment. Yashicas are often purchased by Contax owners to be used as back-up or second cameras when they don't wish to make another heavy investment, but when they need another camera body that will accept their Zeiss lenses.

The Yashica SLRs listed below are the later generation, bayonet-mount cameras. They will accept both Zeiss T* and Yashica ML lenses. Those employing the Universal Screw lens mount are not listed. These older cameras are capable, but nowadays are even more rare than their bayonet-mount successors. Nowadays, a screw-mount Yashica in clean used condition can be picked up for as little as $50 to $75 with a normal lens.

Yashica FX-1

The Yashica FX-1 was the first SLR bearing the Yashica name to use the Contax/Yashica bayonet mount. Exposure options include metered manual and aperture-priority AE. Shutter speeds range from 2 seconds to 1/1000 (1 second to 1/1000 in manual), plus B, with X sync at 1/60. Other features include a hot shoe, a self timer and depth-of-field preview.

Yashica FX-2

Back to the basics was the theme of the FX-2 when it was introduced. This is a manual-mode, center-the-needle SLR with the standard array of features. Shutter speeds range from 1 second to 1/1000, plus B, with X sync at 1/60. The camera has a hot shoe, a self-timer and depth-of-field preview.

Yashica FR, FR-I & FR-II

The FR uses the same shutter and mirror assembly found in the RTS. Its features are the same as those of the FX-2. It accepts the Winder FR for film advance up to 2 fps. The FR-I has all the features of the FR, plus the addition of an aperture-priority mode and exposure compensation. The FR-II is essentially an FR-I without a manual exposure mode. The Contax W-3 and RTS winders can be used with these three cameras.

Yashica FX-3, FX-3 Super 2000 & FX-7

The FX-3 is essentially the same as the FX-2 with a couple of improvements: The flash sync speed was increased to 1/125 and the meter needle was replaced by an LED array.

As its name implies, the FX-3 Super 2000 has a 1/2000 second top shutter speed. All other features of the FX-3 were retained. The FX-7 is identical to the FX-3, except it sports a chrome body (the FX-3 is all black).

Yashica FX-D

The FX-D offers two exposure modes: aperture-priority AE and match-diode metered manual using a centerweighted metering pattern. Shutter speeds range from 11 seconds to 1/1000 (1 second to 1/1000 in manual mode), plus B. Other features include non-TTL flash automation with dedicated units, an AE lock and exposure compensation.

Yashica FX-70

The FX-70 has a single exposure mode: aperture-priority AE using a centerweighted metering pattern. Shutter speeds range from 11 seconds to 1/1000, plus B, with X sync at 1/100. Other features are exposure compensation, an AE lock and a self-timer.

Yashica FX-103 Program

The FX-103 Program offers two program modes (normal and high speed) in addition to aperture-priority AE and metered manual. Also, TTL flash capability was added with dedicated flash units. Auto mode shutter speeds range from 16 seconds to 1/1000 (1 second to 1/1000 in manual mode), plus B, with X sync at 1/100. Other features are exposure compensation, an AE lock and a self-timer.

Yashica 107 Multi Program & 108 Multi Program

The 107 Multi Program has three program modes, normal, high speed and low speed, plus non-metered manual. Shutter speeds range from 16 seconds to 1/2000, plus B, with X sync at 1/90. Other features include exposure compensation, DX film coding and a built-in winder with auto loading. Film must be rewound manually.

The 108 Multi Program updates the 107, with changes in exposure modes: There's no low-speed program mode, aperture-priority AE was added and the manual mode is metered.

Yashica 200 & 230-AF

Yashica autofocus SLRs accept Yashica autofocus and Contax/Yashica bayonet mount lenses. Manual focus lenses can only be used on these cameras with the AF 1.6X teleconverter. Both cameras have three standard autofocus modes: one-shot (focus-priority), continuous (servo), and trap-focus. Both have AF-lock buttons and manual focus override.

Several exposure modes include: program (with program shift on the 230-AF), aperture-priority AE, shutter-priority AE, and metered manual. In the shutter or aperture-priority modes, the system will shift to the closest appropriate setting if the user-selected value will result in incorrect exposure. Metering patterns are centerweighted averaging and, on the 230-AF, 3% spot. The 230-AF also has exposure compensation, AE lock and auto-backlight compensation, a system that switches automatically to spot metering if the frame edges are lighter than the center.

Shutter speeds differ between the two models. On the 230-AF, speeds range from 16 seconds to 1/2000. On the 200-AF, they extend from 8 seconds to 1/2000. Both cameras have a B setting with an elapsed time indicator, flash sync at 1/90 and DX film coding. Manual override of DX coding is possible on the 230-AF. Each has a self timer, built-in motor drive with speeds up to 1.8 fps, auto-film loading and mid-roll rewind, if so desired.

TTL flash is possible with the 230-AF's built-in flash (GN 19 @ ISO 100), or with a dedicated flash. The 200-AF has auto-flash capability, called "CPU-matic," but it isn't TTL.

Yashica 230-AF Super & Kyocera 270-AF

The Yashica 230-AF Super and the Kyocera 270-AF are the same camera. Kyocera, Yashica's parent company, markets Yashica cameras under the Kyocera brand name outside of the U.S. A small number of 270 AF cameras were sold in the U.S. to fulfill contractual obligations. Except for the few improvements listed below, the 230-AF Super more closely resembles the now-discontinued 200-AF in features, price and performance.

The 230-AF Super shares many features of its predecessor, the 230-AF, but is a totally new camera. Instead of listing all the similarities, let's look at the differences and improvements. The 230-AF Super has an integral, near-infrared AF light, which projects a beam onto dimly lit subjects as a low-light autofocus aid — pretty standard fare for modern autofocus cameras, but something its predecessor lacked. It has red-eye reduction preflash with the built-in flash. Yashica has included what it calls "Advanced Autofocus Function," otherwise known as predictive autofocus. Unique to the 230-AF Super is a built-in autofocus zone selector, which allows the user to choose between two focus ranges (up to three meters, and three meters to infinity). This can greatly reduce focusing time. The ergonomically redesigned body cloaks a few other differences, which include a simplified viewfinder readout, a dual-exposure program determined by lens focal length, a shutter speed range that has been trimmed to 8 seconds on the low end, no spot meter, and non-TTL flash.

Yashica 300 Auto Focus

Kyocera's latest entry into the super-competitive amateur autofocus SLR market is the Yashica 300 Auto Focus (for the balance of this description, we'll refer to it as the 300 AF). It is a sleek-looking camera, just what you might expect from the same company that produces the Contax, and it is a capable camera, with a sufficient array of features to satisfy most any amateur's needs.

The 300 AF has a 3-speed power zooming feature with the new AF Power Zoom lenses. The zoom rate is controlled by how firmly one twists the zoom ring: a light pressure will cause it to zoom at the slowest rate, a moderate pressure will bump the rate up a notch, and rotating it to its stop will engage the high speed zoom mode. There is also a manual zoom override.

The autofocus system employs a single CCD sensor and provides the user with three AF modes: standard, continuous predictive autofocus and trap focus. In addition, the camera has a 3-step AF zone selector, which allows you to select a range in which the AF system will operate. Also included is a near-infrared focus assist beam for reliable autofocus in low-light.

Exposure modes include program AE with a 3-selection shift, aperture- and shutter-priority modes, a metered manual mode and automatic backlight compensation. Exposure compensation is also available: ±2 EV in half-stop increments. The metering system employs centerweighted averaging.

The 300 AF has a built-in pop-up flash (GN 39 @ ISO 100 in feet) with an angle of coverage down to 35mm, and will also accept optional dedicated TTL units, such as the CS-240 or CS-250. Flash exposure modes include auto fill-flash and slow shutter flash in addition to the standard TTL mode. A pre-flash function for red-eye reduction is also available.

Other features include AE Lock, a self-timer, a built-in winder that provides single frame and continuous advance at speeds up to 2 fps, auto film loading and rewind, mid-roll rewind, DX film coding with no override, capability to attach the optional DA-5 data back, and a panoramic adapter which stores in the camera back.

Contax G-1 System

Camera	Yrs Made	New	Mint	Excellent	User
G-1	1994-	1395			
16mm f/8 Biogon w/meter and finder	1994-	2295			
28mm f/2.8 Biogon	1994-	495			
45mm f/2 Planar	1994-	320			
90mm f/2.8 Sonnar	1994-	495			
TLA 140 Flash	1994-	170			
GA-1Contax SLR Lens Adapter	1994-	190			
GD-1 Databack	1994-	160			
GP-1 Power Pack Adapter	1994-	60			

Contax SLRs

Camera	Yrs Made	New	Mint	Excellent	User
RTS	1976-80		425 320	325 225	
RTS II Quartz	1980-88		695 575	500 425	
RTS III	1990-	2600 2300	1800 1595	1600 1395	
RX	1994-	1345 1200			
S2	1992-	1225 1100	920 750		
S2b	1993-	1225 1100			
ST	1993-	1500 1400	1195 950		
137 MA Quartz	1983-87		295 225	225 200	
137 MD Quartz	1978-83		295 220	250 175	165 150
139 Quartz	1978-87		210 150	170 125	
159 MM Quartz	1985-89		300 250	260 200	
167 MT Quartz	1987-	540	400 375	350 275	

Yashica SLRs

Camera	Yrs. Made	New	Mint	Excellent	User
FR	1976-80			130 80	
FR-I	1978-81			150 100	
FR-II	1978-81			140 100	
FX-1	1975-78			95 65	
FX-2	1976-80			100 75	
FX-3, FX-7	1979-?		125 100	90 65	
FX-3 Super 2000	1987-	195 150	120 90		
FX-D Quartz	1980-?		125 100		
FX-70			120 100	110 80	
FX-103 Program			170 125		
107 Multi Program	1988-90			150 130	
108 Multi Program	1988-	225 165			
200AF	1987-91		190 165		
230AF	1987-91		200 175		
230AF Super	1991-93		225 190		
300 Auto Focus	1993-	295 220			

Contax T* Lenses

Contax MM lenses are backward compatible to all bayonet-mount Contax and Yashica SLRs. They must be used with the Contax 159MM, 167MT, RX and ST to access the shutter-priority and program modes. AE lenses are the predecessors of the MM lens, but are still the current design with some focal lengths. The easiest way to differentiate between MM and AE lenses is by looking at the smallest aperture (i.e., highest aperture number). It will be green on an MM lens. Pricing information on new lenses is a bit sketchy; any question marks in the following listings reflect this. Yashica AF lenses are not compatible with Contax or Yashica manual focus SLRs.

Lens	New		Mint		Excellent		User	
15mm f/3.5 Distagon AE		6200						
16mm f/2.8 Distagon AE		4200						
18mm f/4 Distagon AE			750	600				
18mm f/4 MM Distagon		1300	900	800				
21mm f/2.8 MM Distagon		1650	1400	1200				
25mm f/2.8 Distagon AE			650	525	470	395		
25mm f/2.8 MM Distagon		850	750	645	620	550		
28mm f/2 Distagon AE			690	650				
28mm f/2 MM Distagon			890	770				
28mm f/2.8 Distagon AE					250	200		
28mm f/2.8 MM Distagon	425	365	350	295				
35mm f/1.4 Distagon AE					800	675		
35mm f/1.4 MM Distagon		1200	1000	825				
35mm f/2.8 Distagon AE			225	180	170	145		
35mm f/2.8 MM Distagon		320	275	220	205	150		
35m f/2.8 PC Distagon AE		3350	2470	1895				
45mm f/2.8 Tessar AE	380	350	200	180				
45mm f/2.8 MM Tessar		350	275	240				
50mm f/1.4 Planar AE			190	135	140	100		
50mm f/1.4 MM Planar		300	220	160	150	120		
50mm f/1.7 Planar AE			100	75	80	65		
50mm f/1.7 MM Planar	225	190	135	120	95	70		
60mm f/2.8 S-Planar (Macro) AE			890	775	775	700.	670	550
60mm f/2.8 MM Macro Planar C	1150	900						
85mm f/1.2 MM Planar	3300	2995						
85mm f/1.4 Planar AE			790	670	650	590		
85mm f/1.4 MM Planar		950	845	695	700	650		
85mm f/2.8 Sonnar AE			430	350	320	250		
85mm f/2.8 MM Sonnar			480	420	400	320		
100mm f/2 Planar AE			1200	850	825	750		
100mm f/2 MM Planar		1600	1275	1150	1095	950		
100mm f/2.8 Makro Planar AE		1750	1535	1370				
100mm f/3.5 Sonnar AE			300	250				
100mm f/3.5 MM Sonnar			450	325				
135mm f/2 Planar AE			990	775				
135mm f/2 MM Planar			1490	1270				
135mm f/2.8 Planar AE			275	225				
135mm f/2.8 MM Sonnar		440	365	250	325	200		
180mm f/2.8 Sonnar AE					950	700		
180mm f/2.8 MM Sonnar		1380	1150	950	850			
200mm f/2 APO Sonnar MM		7700						
200mm f/3.5 Tele-Tessar AE			520	420	440	385		
200mm f/4 Tele-Tessar AE			475	400	400	350		
200mm f/4 MM Tele-Tessar			550	475				
300mm f/2.8 Tele-Apotessar AE	19200	17000						
300mm f/4 Tele-Tessar AE			650	550	550	500		
300mm f/4 MM Tele-Tessar		1600	1080	950	850	760		
500mm f/4.5 Mirotar *(special order only)*								
1000mm f/5.6 Mirotar *(special order only)*								
100 DX Medical Macro-flash			1200	900				
Mutar I		720	550	400				
Mutar II		700	540	400				

Contax T* Zoom Lenses

Lens	New	Mint	Excellent	User
28-85 f/3.3-4 Vario-Sonnar MM	1450 1140			
35-70 f/3.4 Vario-Sonnar MM	1200 950	850 695	595 495	
35-105 f/3.3-4.5 Vario-Sonnar MM	2350 2000	1700 1450		
40-80 f/3.5 Vario-Sonnar AE		600 550	550 500	
70-210 f/3.5 Vario-Sonnar AE			1250 1000	
80-200 f/4 Vario-Sonnar MM	1170 900	775 650		
100-300 f/4.5-5.6 Vario Sonnar MM	2250 1800			

Yashica ML Lenses

Lens	New	Mint	Excellent	User
15mm f/2.8	390 350	350 250		
24mm f/2.8		175 125		
28mm f/2.8	100 90	75 60		
35mm f/2.8		80 60		
50mm f/1.4	190 140	85 65		
50mm f/1.7		60 45	50 40	
50mm f/1.9	60 30	45 40	35 30	
55mm f/2.8 Macro		150 135		
100mm f/3.5 Macro		175 150		
135mm f/2.8		95 75		
200mm f/4		120 80		
300mm f/5.6		175 150		
500mm f/8 Reflex		250 200		
1000mm f/11		700 650		

Yashica ML Zoom Lenses

Lens	New	Mint	Excellent	User
28-50 f/3.5	150 100			
28-85 f/3.5-4.5	220 160			
35-70 f/3.5-4.5	125 85			
38-90 f/3.5		100 80		
42-75 f/3.5-4.5		100 70	75 50	
70-210 f/4.5		150 125		
70-210 f/4.5-5.6	160 135			
75-150 f/4		95 70		
75-200 f/4.5	150 100			
80-200 f/4.5		120 100		

Yashica AF Lenses

Lens	New	Mint	Excellent	User
24mm f/2.8	280 240	220 195		
28mm f/2.8	120 105	80 70		
50mm f/1.8	75 70		50 40	
60mm f/2.8 Macro	390 330	280 250		
28-70 f/3.5-4.5	160 125			
28-70 f/3.5-4.5 PZ	190 140			
28-85 f/3.5-4.5	250 220			
35-70 f/3.3-4.5	140 125	100 80		
35-105 f/3.5-4.5	240 210			
70-210 f/4-5.6	210 165	150 125		
70-210 f/4-5.6 PZ	245 185			
75-300 f/4.5-5.6	360 320			
80-200 f/4-4.8		150 100		
1.6 AF Teleconverter	130 115			

CONTAX/YASHICA

Contax/Yashica Accessories

Item	New		Mint		Excellent		User	
RTS Winder (Contax RTS/RTS II)					110	85	70	65
139 Winder 2 (Contax 139/Yashica FX-D)	100	90	80	70	70	60		
W-3 Winder (Contax RTS/RTS II)			110	85	90	75		
W-6 Motor Drive (w/PMD Pack)			400	325	300	250		
W-7 Winder (Contax 159MM)			100	80	80	65		
Winder FR (Yashica FR)	115	85	60	35				
Winder FX (Yashica FX)	85	65	50	35				
Data Back D-4 (RTS II)	130	100						
Data Back D-5 (137MA/MD)	130	110	90	80				
Data Back D-6 (139/159MM)	130	80	100	75				
Data Back D-7 (167MT)	250	230						
Data Back DA-1 (Yashica 200/230 AF)	80	60						
FR Data Back (Yashica FR)			75	50				
FX Data Back (Yashica FX)			85	65				
Contax 250 Exp Back	700	650						
Yashica Dental Eye			600	550				
Yashica Dental Eye II	1030	900						
2x Lens for Dental Eye	85	70						
Quartz Data Back for Dental Eye	180	150						
AC Adapter for Dental Eye II	85	50						
Contax Auto Bellows PC	260	210						
Yashica (FX) Auto Bellows	150	120						
Auto Ext Tube Set (Y or C)	160	100						
Focusing Rail (Y or C)	80	50						
Slide Copier (Y or C)	150	80						
Macro Stand (Y or C)	90	40						
Right Angle Finder (Y or C)	110	95						
Contax/Hasselblad Adapter	185	150						
Mounts Hasselblad lenses on Contax cameras								
AC Control Box	660	550						
IR Remote Control Set S	120	100	80	70				
Interval Timer			100	70				
TLA-20 Flash	70	60	60	45	40	30		
TLA-30 Flash			120	80	75	65		
TLA-140 Flash (G-1)	225	170						
TLA-280 Flash	395	310	225	180				
TLA-360 Flash		475						
TLA-480 Flash		850						
TLA-480 Battery Pack		225						
RTF 540 Flash w/bracket	360	300	250					
RTF 540 Power Pack	100	80						
RTF 540 510v Battery Pack	90	75						
CS-14 Flash	25	15						
CS-140 Flash	35	25						
CS-220 Auto Flash	45	30						
CS-240 Auto Flash	60	40						
CS-250 AF Flash	110	90						

Leica & Canon Screw-Mount Rangefinder Cameras

In spite of the age of many models, screw-mount Leicas and Canons still see regular use by an active, hard-core group of anachronists. Certainly one endearing feature of these cameras is their small size. With a collapsible lens, a screw-mount Leica or Canon is the same size as a point-and-shoot camera and fits easily into a jacket pocket — a true, take-anywhere camera. It may not have autofocus, a built-in flash or a meter, or any of the other bells and whistles of modern P&S cameras, but the features these cameras lack are more than made up for by their craftsmanship, durability and the optical quality of most lenses available in Leica thread.

Leica Screw-Mount Cameras

This section is not intended to replace, or compete with, Leica collector's guides or collector's guides that have comprehensive Leica listings. Because this is a book intended for the practicing photographer, only the most common Leica screw-mount cameras are listed. Still, any screw-mount Leica is collectible — even models from huge production runs, like the IIIa and IIIc (in mint condition).

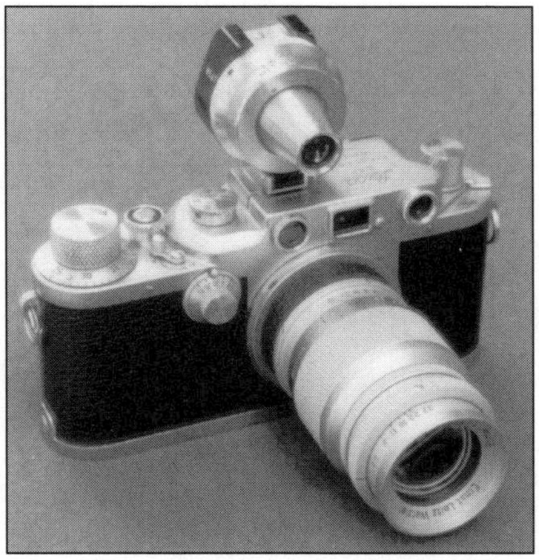

Leica IIIC with 90mm f/4 Elmar and Imarect finder

If you're buying a Leica with collecting in mind, or if you would just like to know more about the various models, I strongly recommend that you pick up one or more of the several publications currently available that cover the subject of Leica from a collectible standpoint. Why? Because minor differences in these cameras and lenses can translate into major differences in price. Probably the handiest publication is a three-volume, pocket-size set from Hove Photo Books: *Leica Pocket Book, Leica Accessory Guide,* and *Leica International Price Guide.*

You should keep in mind a couple of other caveats. *Any* alterations made to a camera affect its collectible value. Many early Leica models were converted by Leitz to later models. Many have been refinished (especially black ones), some by Leitz, some by others. Such modifications, even when done by Leitz, have a negative impact on a camera's collectible value. Also, because some models command exceedingly high prices due to their rarity, counterfeits exist. As always, it pays to be informed.

The cameras below are listed in chronological order. The following listings are for German-made (Wetzlar) Leicas. Canadian-made screw-mount Leicas are rarer and are not listed. Those listings followed by a letter in parentheses are known by that designation also. For example, a Leica III is also known as a Leica model F, not a IIIf; a Leica IIIa is also known as a Leica model G, not a IIIg.

While the following prices are for cameras bodies only, frequently they're offered for sale only with normal lenses. Depending on the lens, the difference in price can be from minimal to substantial.

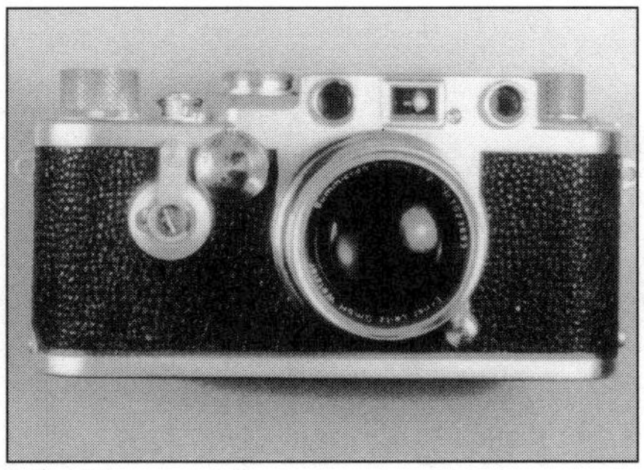

Leica IIIf

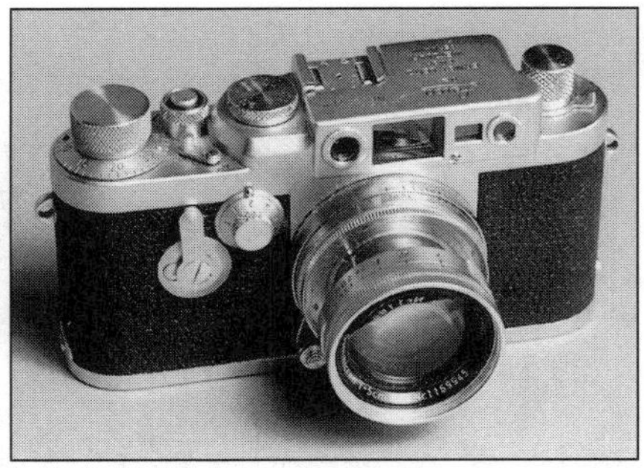

Leica IIIg

Leica Screw-Mount Cameras

Camera	Yrs. Made	Mint	Excellent	User
II (D) chr	1933-48		350 225	250 180
II (D) blk	1932-39		550 300	270 200
III (F) chr	1933-39		250 150	150 125
III (F) blk	1933-39		400 300	250 170
IIIa (G) chr	1935-48		250 150	170 120
IIIb chr	1938-46		300 250	250 200
IIIc (SN<400,000)	1940-45		450 375	300 250
IIIc (SN>400,000)	1946-51		250 200	200 130
IIc	1948-51		320 200	
Ic	1949-52		450 350	
IIIf black dial	1950-52		350 280	250 175
IIIf red dial	1952-53		450 350	320 250
IIIf red dial/ST	1954-57		475 370	350 280
IIf black dial	1951-52		350 260	250 200
IIf red dial	1952-56		350 225	
If red dial	1952-58		700 425	
IIIg	1957-60	1200 850	1025 650	550 390

Leitz Screw-Mount Lenses

With many of the lenses listed, variations exist that often greatly affect price. Only the most common Leitz screw-mount lenses are listed.

Lens	Mint	Excellent	User
28mm f/5.6 Summaron		600 500	
28mm f/6.3 Hektor		450 350	
35mm f/2.8 Summaron		450 300	
35mm f/3.5 Elmar		250 195	
35mm f/3.5 Summaron	300 250	275 225	
50mm f/1.5 Summarit		200 125	
50mm f/2 Summar collapsible		80 50	
50mm f/2 Summicron collapsible		395 250	
50mm f/2 Summitar		170 120	
50mm f/2.8 Elmar collapsible		200 150	
50mm f/3.5 Elmar chr collapsible		150 85	
65mm f/3.5 Elmar chr		450 350	
90mm f/4 Elmar blk or chr (A36 filter)		175 100	
90mm f/4 Elmar chr (E39 filter)	225 175	180 125	
135mm f/4.5 Elmar		295 180	
135mm f/4.5 Hektor	150 125	130 100	90 70

Canon Screw-Mount Cameras

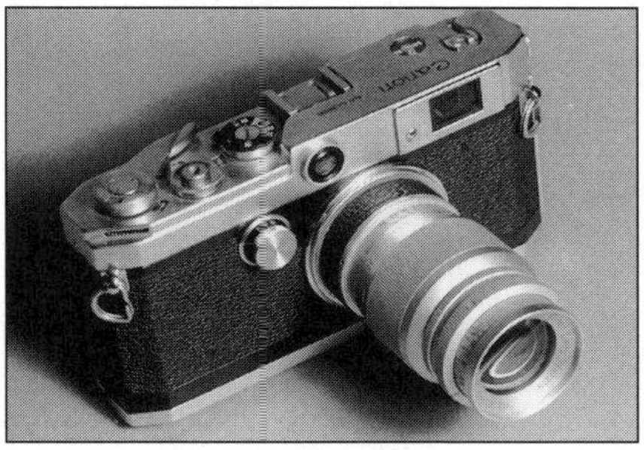

Leitz 90mm Elmar lens on a Canon L-1

During the heyday of screw-mount Leicas, a host of copycat manufacturers sprang up in Japan and elsewhere. Most of the cameras produced were direct copies of the most popular Leica models. Of all the copies, however, the Canon screw-mount cameras are the most common. In fact, Canon produced more screw-mount cameras than all the other Leica copy-cats put together. Canon rangefinders are also not direct Leica copies, either, which lends them their own personality.

Canon screw-mount cameras as a class are slowly increasing in collectible value. A few of the earliest Canon rangefinders, such as the legendary Hansa and the S, are extremely rare and highly sought after.

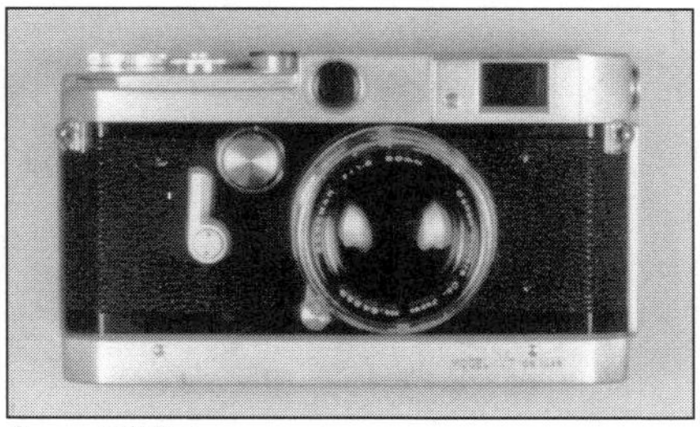

Canon VT Deluxe

Some late model Canon rangefinders were produced in both chrome and black enamel finishes. The black ones were made in small numbers and are rare. Black examples of the VT-Deluxe (all versions), VI-L, VI-T, 7, L1 and P exist, but are not included in the listings. They are highly collectable and are often five to ten times the price of chrome models in the same condition. If you're buying a camera to use, get a chrome one. You'll save a lot of money and the chrome is more durable. As with the Leicas, only Canons you are most likely to find are listed.

For more detailed information about Canon screw-mount cameras, several good source books are available. The most notable is Peter Dechert's *Canon Rangefinder Cameras — 1933-1968,* which is the most exhaustive study of Canon rangefinders undertaken to date. It does not list prices, however.

While the following prices are for cameras bodies only, frequently they're offered for sale only with normal lenses. Usually, price differences are minimal.

Canon Screw-Mount Cameras

Camera	Yrs. Made	Mint	Excellent	User
IIB	1949-52		300 175	
IID	1952-55		250 175	
IID1	1952-54		350 200	
IID2	1955-56		250 175	
IIF	1953-55		200 150	125 100
IIF2	1955-56		400 250	
IIS	1954-55		350 250	
IIS2	1955-56		250 150	
III	1951-52		200 125	
IIIA	1951-53		225 125	
IV	1951-52		350 225	
IVF	1951-52		250 175	
IVS	1952-53		200 150	
IVSB (IVS2)	1952-55		250 180	
IVSB2	1954-56		200 150	
VT	1956-57		275 175	200 150
VT-Deluxe	1957-57		325 225	220 180
VT-Deluxe-M	1958-58		350 225	
VT-Deluxe-Z	1957-58		325 225	
VL	1957-58		325 225	
VL2	1958-58		325 225	
VI-T	1958-60		300 200	
VI-L	1958-61		275 200	
7	1961-64		350 225	220 170
7S	1965-67		350 275	
7Sz	1967-68		400 300	
L1	1957-57		250 175	
L2	1956-57		275 200	
L3	1957-58		250 175	
P	1958-61		325 220	200 150

Canon Screw-Mount Lenses

Canon lens prices do not include accessory viewfinders. For the more common lenses, prices with finders are only moderately higher. For others, especially a few of the wide angles, expect to pay significantly more.

Lens	Mint	Excellent	User
25mm f/3.5		500 300	
28mm f/2.8	425 425	400 275	
28mm f/3.5 Serenar		250 200	
35mm f/1.5	400 350	340 280	
35mm f/1.8		250 150	100 50
35mm f/2		200 125	
35mm f/2.8 Serenar		225 150	
35mm f/3.2 Serenar		150 100	
35mm f/3.5 Serenar		120 80	
50mm f/0.95 (7/7S/7Sz only)	750 700	600 500	
50mm f/1.2	295 270	250 200	
50mm f/1.4		300 200	
50mm f/1.5	165 140	130 90	
50mm f/1.8 Serenar	100 70	70 50	
50mm f/1.8 chr	100 70	80 60	50 40
50mm f/1.8 blk	125 100	90 60	
50mm f/1.9 Serenar		90 50	
50mm f/2.8	225 160	175 125	
85mm f/1.8	300 250		
85mm f/1.9 Serenar	200 180	175 100	
85mm f/2 Serenar	150 130	100 65	
100mm f/2 blk	575 500	500 350	
100mm f/3.5 Serenar		150 120	
100mm f/4 Serenar		125 90	
135mm f/3.5 chr or blk	150 100	130 75	80 50
135mm f/4 Serenar		80 50	

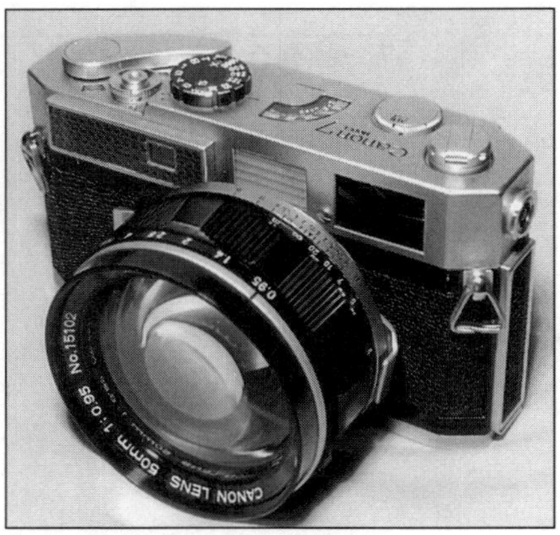

Canon 7 with 50mm f/0.95 lens

Aftermarket Screw-Mount Lenses

Until 1948, the lenses Canon offered with their rangefinder cameras were mostly Nikkors. Back then, Canon was a camera maker, and Nippon Kogaku Tokyo (later known as Nikon) was primarily a lens maker. Some of the more pedestrian varieties of screw-mount Nikkors are listed below. Others, deemed rare or desirable by collectors, are not listed because of their scarcity and extremely high prices. Still others, which are quite collectible but which remain popular as user lenses because of their focal lengths, are listed.

Unless indicated otherwise, the prices are for lenses without accessory viewfinders. Expect to pay slightly more for lenses with viewfinders in the more common focal lengths, and substantially more for lenses in less common ones — especially the wide angles.

Aftermarket Screw-Mount Lenses

Lens	Mint	Excellent	User
20mm f/5.6 Russian (Jupiter?) w/finder		425 350	
25mm f/4 Nikkor (w/finder)		650 550	
28mm f/3.3 SOM Berthiot		250 175	
28mm f/2.8 Soligor		120 75	
28mm f/3.5 Nikkor		300 225	
35mm f/1.8 Nikkor		450 350	
35mm f/2.5 Nikkor		225 175	
35mm f/2.8 Jupiter		180 145	
35mm f/2.8 Schneider Xenogon		150 95	
35mm f/2.8 Tanar		100 80	

Aftermarket Screw-Mount Lenses

Lens	Mint	Excellent	User
35mm f/2.8 Topcor		125 80	
35mm f/3.5 Alcall		90 75	
35mm f/3.5 Komura		100 75	
35mm f/3.5 Nikkor		125 95	
35mm f/3.5 Soligor		100 75	
35mm f/3.5 Staeble Linogon		100 75	
35mm f/3.5 Travegon		95 75	
35mm f/4.5 Steinheil Orthostigmat		140 80	
45mm f/2.8 Steinheil		80 60	
47mm f/2 Kodak Ektar		100 90	
50mm f/1.4 Nikkor		200 100	
50mm f/1.5 Zeiss Sonnar		100 80	
50mm f/1.8 Yashinon		100 70	
50mm f/2 Cooke Amatal		125 100	
50mm f/2 Nikkor		175 125	
50mm f/2 Tanar		100 75	
50mm f/2.8 Steinheil Collapsible		100 70	
80mm f/1.8 Komura		100 70	
85mm f/2 Nikkor		200 120	
85mm f/2 Zeiss Sonnar		125 95	
90mm f/4.5 Wollensak		100 80	
105mm f/2.5 Nikkor	350 350	300 200	175 140
105mm f/3.5 Komura		100 75	
105mm f/3.5 Schneider Xenar		150 100	
105mm f/3.5 Super Acall		75 50	
127mm f/4.5 Wollensak		125 95	
135mm f/2.8 Komura		90 75	
135mm f/3.5 Komura		75 50	
135mm f/3.5 Nikkor		125 90	80 70
135mm f/3.5 Steinheil		80 50	
135mm f/3.5 Super Acall		75 50	
135mm f/3.5 Topcor		150 100	
135mm f/4 Tele Rokkor		150 100	
135mm f/4.5 Steinheil		60 40	40 20
200mm f/4.5 Komura w/finder		150 120	

Leica M-Series Rangefinders

The Leica M-series rangefinder camera is an enduring classic, much sought after by professionals and collectors alike. Because anything with the name Leica on it is collectible to some degree, minor differences among cameras of the same model can translate into major differences in price. The fine points of Leica collecting are beyond the scope of this book, so only a few differences that affect price will be addressed below. If you're buying or selling Leica with collecting in mind, several fine publications are available. Probably the handiest is a three volume pocket-size set from Hove Photo Books: Leica Pocket Book, Leica Accessory Guide, and Leica International Price Guide. Since this book is intended primarily for the practicing photographer and not the collector, I have omitted the special edition Leicas (such as the Everest, Jubilee and Safari editions), those cameras that were made in very small quantities (such as the MP and M4 MOT) and the cameras intended primarily for scientific use (such as the MD, MDa and MD2). These Leicas are prized by collectors and are bought and sold almost exclusively with collecting in mind, hence it serves no purpose to include them in a price guide for the practicing photographer.

Leica M3, M2 & M1

For the Leica M3, the following abbreviations are used: DS = Double Stroke advance lever, SS = Single Stroke advance lever. Some other abbreviations you may run across (not shown here) are: ST (Self Timer) and PV (Preview lever, which shows frames in the viewfinder for different focal lengths). Some M2s and DS M3s have no self timer and no preview lever. Some have a self timer, but no preview lever. I haven't listed the variants because the price differences are small. Many double-stroke M3s were converted by Leica to single stroke. These cameras, while not listed, sell for about the same as single-stroke M3s with serial numbers below 1 million. Because many sellers price their single-stroke M3s according to the serial number, I've listed separate prices for single-stroke M3s with serial numbers above and below 1 million.

The M3 was Leica's first bayonet-mount rangefinder camera and, while the design dates back to 1954, it is still considered one of the finest cameras ever made. The M3 has a bright viewfinder, incorporating a parallax-corrected rangefinder and brightline frames for 50mm, 90mm and 135mm lenses. Shutter speeds range from 1 second to 1/1000, plus B, with M and X sync. M3s with serial numbers greater than 915,000 have single-stroke film advance levers.

The M2 was originally intended as a less-costly alternative to the M3 and is very similar to its immediate predecessor. The main differences include an external film-counter that must be manually reset and viewfinder frames for 35mm, 50mm and 90mm lenses. Early models have a button release for rewinding the film, later ones have a lever, like the M3. Some collectors make a distinction in price between these two models, but I haven't here since the price variance is small.

Less than 10,000 M1s were made, although they are not particularly hard to find on the used market at this time. I suspect this is because they are not very practical for photographic use. Essentially a simplified M2, the M1 lacks a coupled rangefinder and has brightline frames for the 35mm and 50mm lenses only.

Leica M4, M4-2 & M4-P

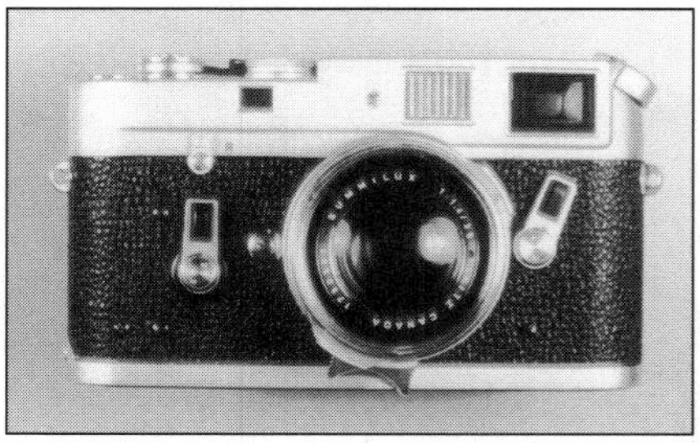

Leica M4

The Leica M4 was made in chrome and black. About 2,500 of them were made in Canada in both chrome and black. Altogether, less than 9,000 black M4s were made. Black M4s, whether Canadian, black enamel or black anodized, fetch quite a premium because of their relative scarcity and popularity among collectors, and aren't listed. Neither are chrome Canadian M4s (for the same reason). None of the above cameras should be confused with the M4-2 and M4-P.

The M4's physical appearance is similar to that of the M3, the most notable differences being the slanted film rewind knob with a built-in crank and a plastic-tipped film advance lever. Other differences are brightline frames for 35mm, 50mm, 90mm and 135mm lenses and a three-pronged drop-in film loading system that speeds film loading considerably.

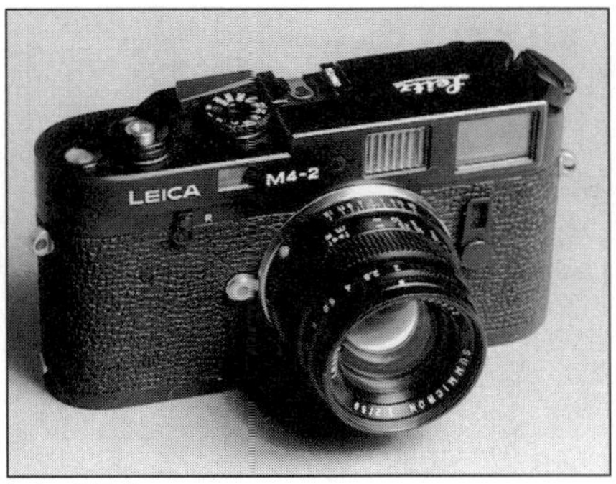

Leica M4-2

The M4-2 is an M4 with the following differences: it has a hot shoe, it does not have a self-timer and, most significantly, it was the first regular production M-series Leica to which a separate electric winder could be attached.

The M4-P is similar to the M4-2, with one notable difference: 28mm and 75mm viewfinder frames were added, necessitating that all frames be shown in pairs. They are paired as follows: 28mm and 90mm, 50mm and 75mm, 35mm and 135mm. Like the M4-2, a separate winder can be attached.

Leica M5

The Leica M5 represented a departure from Leitz's traditional rangefinder design in a couple of ways. It was the first Leica rangefinder with a meter and it also was much larger than its predecessors. Its popularity never really caught on, although it is a fine picture taker. The semaphore-style behind-the-lens metering system hasn't been without its problems over the years and, because of this arrangement, a few lenses cannot be used on this camera; namely the 21mm Super Angulons and 28mm lenses with serial numbers below 2,315,000.

Leica M6

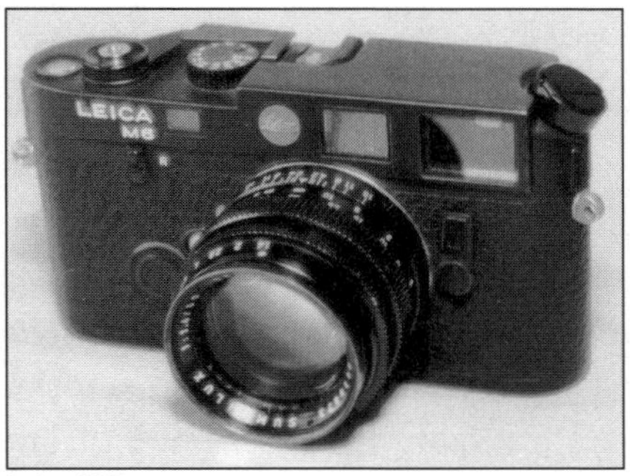

Leica M6

The Leica M6 is similar to the M4-P and differs primarily from its predecessor in that it has an integral TTL light meter. Unlike the M5, the M6's meter employs a backward-facing silicon diode that reads a white spot on the shutter curtain to determine exposure. This provides the user with match-diode metering of the central 13% of the framed viewfinder area. The electronics for the meter are located where the self-timer is on the M4. As with the M4-2 and M4-P, a winder can be attached.

Leica CL, Leitz-Minolta CL & Minolta CLE

The Leica CL was designed by Leitz, but manufactured by Minolta under license from Leitz. It has a built-in semaphore-style TTL light meter (similar to the M5's) and is considerably more compact and lighter than M-series Leicas. Leitz built a 40mm Summicron and a 90mm Elmar C especially for the CL. At almost the same time as the advent of the CL, Minolta began producing the Leitz-Minolta CL. It was the same camera, available with a 40mm M-Rokkor and a Leitz made 90mm M-Rokkor. Later, Leitz marketed the Leitz-Minolta in the US after supplies of the original Leitz CL ran out. As with the M5, most all M-style bayonet mount lenses will work on these cameras, but there are a couple that won't. These are the 21mm Super Angulon and 28mm lenses with serial numbers below 2,315,000. It is my understanding that these lenses will bayonet onto the camera, but should not be used because of the risk of damaging the semaphore mechanism.

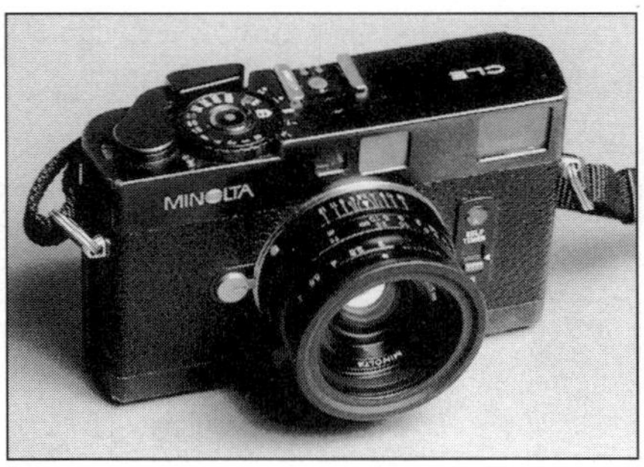

Minolta CLE

After the CL was discontinued around 1981, Minolta introduced the CLE. It resembles the CL in outward appearances only. Just a few of its features include off-the-film-plane metering (instead of the troublesome semaphore in the CL), TTL flash metering, exposure compensation, and aperture-priority AE. Minolta also introduced a 28mm M-Rokkor, made especially for this camera. Until the release of the Contax G-1 in 1994, the CLE had been the most advanced mass produced interchangeable-lens 35mm rangefinder ever. Largely because of this, the CLE is highly sought after. It is also quite collectible. As a result, prices for clean examples remain high.

Leica M-Series Rangefinder Cameras

Camera	Yrs. Made	New	Mint	Excellent	User
Leica CL	1972-81			600 450	350 300
Leica CL w/40 Summicron	1972-81		800 680	700 500	
Leitz-Minolta CL	1972-81			500 375	350 300
Leitz-Minolta CL w/40 Rokkor	1972-81		700 625	650 500	
Minolta CLE	1981-84		1000 850	900 725	
Minolta CLE w/40 Rokkor	1981-84			1000 725	
M1	1959-64			730 500	
M2 chr	1957-67			600 400	
M3 DS	1954-58			695 550	485 420
M3 SS (SN<<1,000,000)	1958-60			750 500	500 415
M3 SS (SN>>1,000,000)	1960-66			995 750	
M4 chr (Wetzlar)	1967-70		1500 1300	1200 825	800 650
M4-2	1978-80		1080 850	900 780	800 750
M4-P	1981-87		1200 950	1100 800	825 750
M5 chr (2 lug)	1971-?			1050 800	
M5 blk (2 lug)	1971-?		1050 980	950 750	750 680
M5 chr (3 lug)	?-75		1400 1100	1050 700	
M5 blk (3 lug)	?-75		1400 1000	1100 800	
M6 chr	1984-	2600 2495	2050 1700		
M6 blk	1984-	2600 2495	2050 1600	1700 1400	
M6 Titanium	1993-	3200 2995			

Leitz M-Series Lenses

The many permutations that exist among Leitz lenses can make decisions about which one should buy difficult at the very least. One focal length may have more than a half-dozen varieties, each difference having a substantial affect on the value of the lens. Some were made in very small quantities and are quite rare. Lenses with low production numbers are not listed below. For the more pedestrian varieties, there are separate listings when significant price differences warrant it, but I would caution the buyer or seller to be well-informed before the sale is made.

Leitz M-Series Lenses

Lens	New	Mint	Excellent	User
21mm f/2.8 Elmarit	2300 2095	1500 1200	1300 1000	
21mm f/3.4 Super Angulon		995 950	795 550	
21mm f/4 Super Angulon		690 500	550 480	
28mm f/2.8 Elmarit (early)		750 700	600 500	
28mm f/2.8 Elmarit (late)	2100 1795	1400 1200	1100 800	
28mm f/2.8 M Rokkor (CLE)		750 595	550 495	
35mm f/1.4 Summilux Aspherical	2900 2695			
35mm f/1.4 Summilux chr or blk	2150 1895	1295 1000	995 750	
35mm f/1.4 Summilux (M3 Windows)		1095 850		
35mm f/1.4 Summilux Titanium	2350 2095			
35mm f/2 Summicron blk (late)	1600 1395	1000 895	725 650	
35mm f/2 Summicron blk		895 695	665 550	500 450
35mm f/2 Summicron chr (late)	1700 1495	1095 995	950 700	
35mm f/2 Summicron chr		750 600	650 425	395 280
35mm f/2 Summicron (M3 Windows)		600 550	595 450	
35mm f/2.8 Summaron		395 275		
35mm f/2.8 Summaron (M3 Windows)			395 250	
35mm f/3.5 Summaron		295 250	250 150	
35mm f/3.5 Summaron (M3 Windows)		260 225	235 190	
40mm f/2 M Rokkor (CL,CLE)		200 175	190 145	
40mm f/2 Summicron (CL,CLE)		425 320	310 250	
50mm f/1.0 Noctilux	3100 2895	2100 1750	1500 1200	

Leitz M-Series Lenses

Lens	New	Mint	Excellent	User
50mm f/1.4 Summilux blk (late)	2100 1845	1400 1200	1100 825	
50mm f/1.4 Summilux blk		1000 900	835 525	
50mm f/1.4 Summilux chr		750 700	695 500	
50mm f/1.5 Summarit Wetzlar		320 280	250 200	195 100
50mm f/2 Summicron blk (late)	1200 945	795 695	550 450	
50mm f/2 Summicron blk		595 500	450 365	335 295
50mm f/2 Summicron chr		595 485	495 395	280 200
50mm f/2 Summicron chr (late)	1300 1095	900 795		
50mm f/2 Summicron Collapsible chr		475 395	395 250	200 190
50mm f/2 Summicron Rigid chr		400 350	325 280	
50mm f/2 Summicron DR (w/finder)		750 495	450 325	
50mm f/2.8 Elmar			495 350	300 250
50mm f/3.5 Elmar			395 325	
75mm f/1.4 Summilux	2900 2695	2100 1695	1595 1300	
90mm f/2 Summicron chr	2050 1795			
90mm f/2 Summicron blk (late: E49 filter)	1750 1595	1200 1000	900 650	
90mm f/2 Summicron (early: E48 filter)		750 625	650 450	400 295
90mm f/2.8 Elmarit blk (late)	1400 1150	995 750		
90mm f/2.8 Elmarit chr			795 450	445 350
90mm f/2.8 Tele-Elmarit		695 550	595 400	420 350
90mm f/4 Elmar		250 175	200 130	
90mm f/4 Elmar C (CL, CLE)		400 370	350 250	
90mm f/4 Elmar Collapsible		695 400	395 325	
90mm f/4 Leitz-Rokkor (CL, CLE)		400 350	275 250	
90mm f/4 M Rokkor (CL, CLE)		375 300	325 270	
135mm f/2.8 Elmarit (S7 filter)		600 550	495 395	
135mm f/2.8 Elmarit (E55 filter)	2150 1895	1400 1200	1000 750	
135mm f/4 Elmar			395 200	200 150
135mm f/4 Tele-Elmar	1950 1695	1100 900	800 550	450 375
135mm f/4.5 Hektor		210 145	150 100	90 70

Leitz Viso Lenses

Lens	New	Mint	Excellent	User
65mm f/3.5 Elmar		450 350	380 300	
125mm f/2.5 Hektor			1000 800	
200mm f/4 Telyt		350 300	375 200	
200mm f/4.5 Telyt		450 295	250 150	
280mm f/4.8 Telyt			575 450	
400mm f/5 Telyt (late: built-in hood)			700 600	
400mm f/5.6 Telyt			700 600	
400mm f/6.8 Telyt		500 390	450 350	
560mm f/6.8 Telyt		1000 850		

Leica M-Series Accessories

Item	New	Mint	Excellent	User
M Rapid Winder (not Leica)	550 425			
M Winder (#14214: M4-2 only)		200 140	155 120	
M Winder (#14400: M4-2/M4-P/M6)		250 225	230 175	
M Winder (#14401: M4-P, M6)		250 200		
M Winder (#14402)		450 300		
M Winder (#14403: M6)	800 700	550 460		
Note: All the above winders will work with the M6 except #14214				
MC Meter chr			50 30	
MC Meter blk			45 40	
MR Meter chr/blk			180 125	110 90

Leica M-Series Accessories

Item	New		Mint		Excellent		User	
MR-4 Meter chr			230	170	170	140		
MR-4 Meter blk chr			255	240	230	150		
Dual Range Finder					100	60		
For 50mm f/2 Dual Range Summicron								
Imarect Finder					90	50		
21mm BL Finder	400	350	295	270	265	200	175	150
28mm BL Finder	375	335	270	250	250	200	175	150
35mm BL Finder			250	200	225	150		
90mm BL Finder					125	95		
135mm BL Finder					125	90		
A variety of accessory universal viewfinders, commonly called "Imarect" finders (for Erect Image), was produced by Leitz for use with screw-mount Leicas. The most common ones offer parallax correction and viewfinder frames for 35mm, 50mm, 73mm, 90mm and 135mm lenses. For the single-focal-length finders above, "BL" stands for the Bright Line frame visible when looking through the viewfinder. Those made in Canada are more rare, hence more $. Finders originally designed for screw-mount cameras will work with the M-series as well.								
R to M adapter (#22228)			190	150				
Screw-mount to M adapter			95	60				
M Grip (fits most M cameras)	100	80						
Bellows I			220	190	175	90		
Bellows II			200	180	200	140		
Visoflex I					100	85		
Visoflex II					140	90		
Visoflex III			350	300	295	200		

Leica SLRs

Included below are price listings for the original Leicaflex, SL and R-series Leicas with explanatory notes. Since this book is intended primarily for the practicing photographer and not the collector, I have omitted from the following list such commemorative models as the R3 Gold, R3 Safari, the Anniversary models, and models with low production runs such as the SL MOT and SL2 MOT. These Leicas are highly prized by collectors and are bought and sold almost exclusively with collecting in mind, hence it serves no purpose to include them in a price guide designed for the user.

Leicaflex, Leicaflex SL & SL2

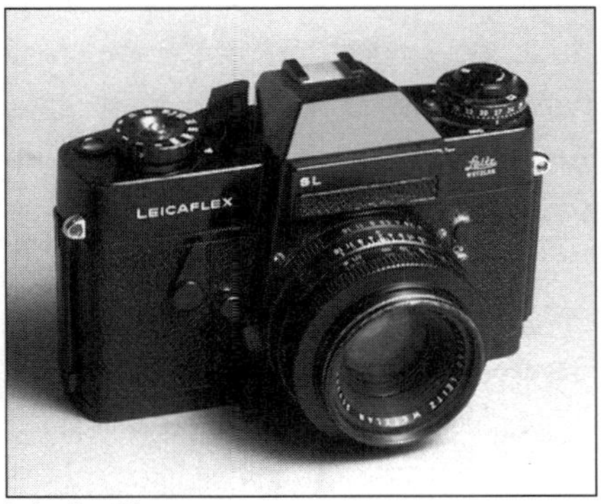

Leicaflex SL

Introduced in 1964, the Leicaflex is the original Leica SLR. It incorporates a non-TTL, match-needle meter, visible as a small window on the face of the pentaprism housing. Shutter speeds range from 1 second to 1/2000, plus B, with flash sync at 1/100. Other features include mirror-lock-up, a self-timer and PC sockets for x and m sync. The original Leicaflex takes the 1-cam R-mount lenses.

The SL is similar in appearance to the Leicaflex, the most notable exterior difference being the lack of a meter window. A TTL light meter was incorporated into the SL design, providing the user with a selective area metering pattern (confined to the microprism area of the focusing screen). A depth-of-field preview button was also added, but the mirror-lock-up feature was dropped. Shutter speeds and flash options remained the same as with the previous model. A new series of 2-cam lenses was designed to be used with the SL because of its TTL meter. 1-cam lenses can be used, but the meter will not operate.

The SL2 incorporated several improvements over its predecessor, the SL. The SL2's light meter sensitivity was increased by a factor of four, full exposure information is visible in the viewfinder, the mirror was redesigned to allow the use of the new-at-the-time 16mm and 19mm wide angle lenses, and a hot shoe was added. Shutter speeds remain the same as on the two previous models.

Leica R3

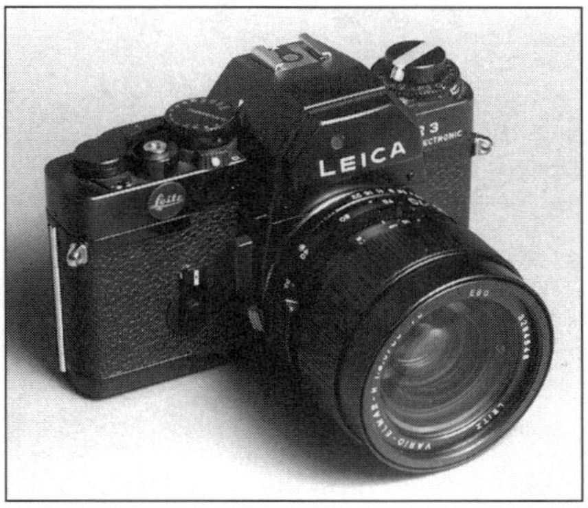

Leica R3

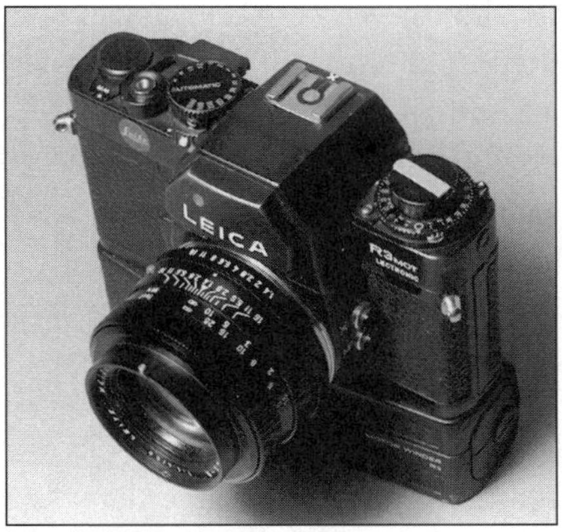

Leica R3 MOT with motor drive attached

Introduced in 1974, the R3 was the first Leica SLR to emerge from the cooperative agreement between Leitz and Minolta and was a radical departure from its manual, mechanical predecessors. A new series of 3-cam lenses was also introduced with this camera, which remains the current lens-to-body coupling style. The R3's two exposure modes are aperture-priority AE and metered manual. The electronic shutter provides speeds from 4 seconds to 1/1000, plus B, with X sync at 1/90. In the event of battery failure, only B and 1/90 will operate. Metering patterns are centerweighted and spot. Other features include a memory lock, self-timer, depth-of-field preview and a hot shoe. The R3 MOT was designed to accept a compact motor winder, which would provide continuous speeds up to 2 fps.

Leica R4, R4-S & R4S-P

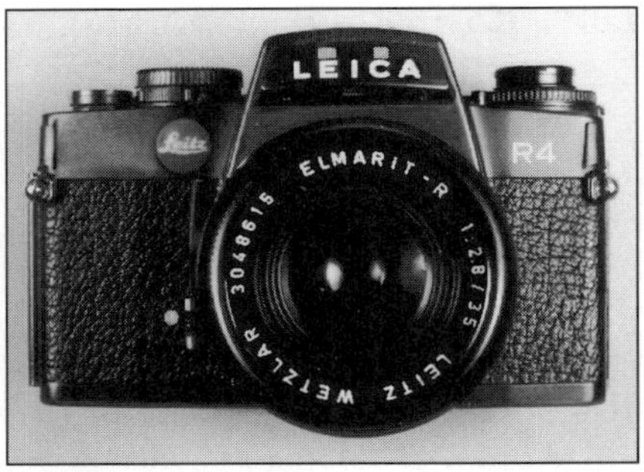

Leica R4

The R4 was updated three times following its debut. Apparently it took Leica four tries to get it right, because the first three were plagued with electronics problems. So, if you're considering the purchase of an R4 (or R4-S), avoid those with serial numbers below 1,600,000 unless the seller provides you with some sort of warrantee. As always, caveat emptor, forewarned is forearmed and all that.

The R4 comes with five exposure modes: program, aperture priority, shutter priority, metered manual and limited flash AE. Two metering patterns are available: centerweighted and spot. Shutter speeds range from 1 second to 1/1000, plus B, with X sync at 1/100. Other features include a motor drive option, interchangeable focusing screens, depth-of-field preview, exposure compensation, AE lock, a hot shoe and a self-timer. Earlier models of the R4 were labeled R4 MOT ELECTRONIC. Prices for these cameras have been included in the R4 listings.

The R4-S is a simplified R4, having aperture-priority and metered manual exposure modes only. All other R4 features were retained.

The R4-S MOD P (or MOD 2) is an update of the R4-S. The Model P designation was used for those cameras imported to the United States. In Europe, it's known as the Model 2. The most significant differences are: the Model P displays shutter speeds in the viewfinder and switching from spot to centerweighted metering is accomplished by pushing the program selector. A few other minor improvements were made, such as an enlarged film rewind crank, a sliding switch instead of a button for the exposure compensation feature, and a redesigned eyepiece that will accept eyecups, etc.

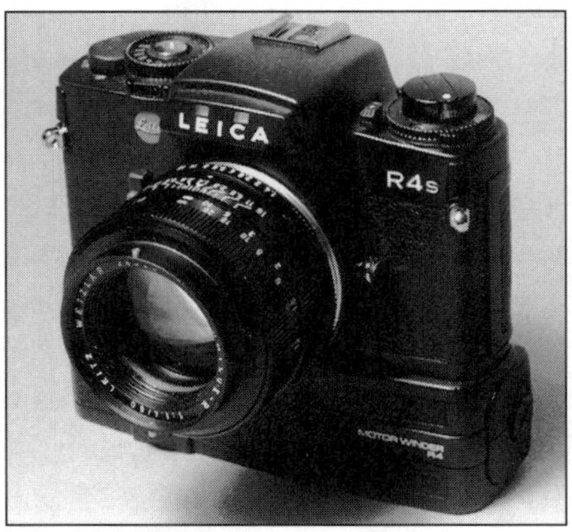

Leica R4-S MOD P with winder attached

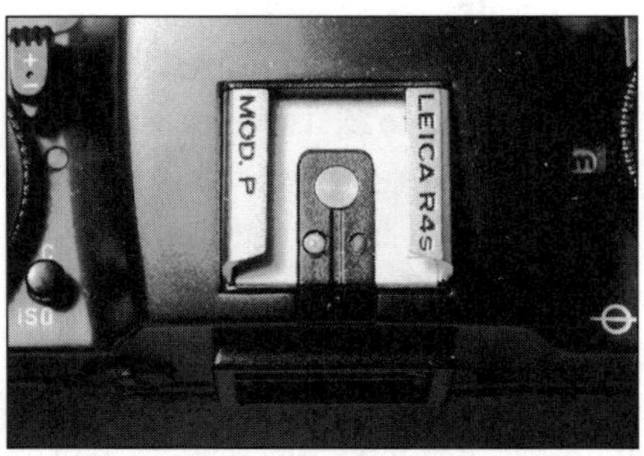

Leica R4-S MOD P — the easiest way to tell the R4-S and the R4-S MOD P apart.

Leica R5 & RE

The Leica R5 is best looked at as an improved and updated R4. It has the same exposure modes, except the program mode has an 11-step shift capability. TTL flash exposure with SCA-series flash units was added as was an eyepiece with built-in diopter adjustments. The viewfinder was also redesigned for greater eye-relief. The shutter speed range was increased: 15 seconds to 1/2000. All other features of the R4 were retained on the R5. The RE is basically an R5 without a program mode.

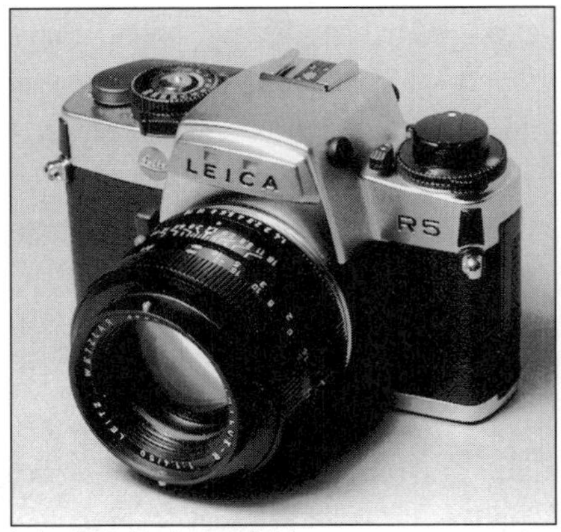

Leica R5 with chrome finish

Leica R6 & R6.2

The R6 was the first mechanical, manual-exposure-only SLR produced by Leica since the SL2 was discontinued. Metering modes are center-weighted averaging or a central 7mm spot. Metering is done via a match-diode display in the viewfinder. Shutter speeds range from 1 second to 1/1000, plus B, with X sync occurring at 1/100. Other features include a motor drive option, mirror-lock-up (the first Leica since the original Leicaflex to have one), interchangeable focusing screens, TTL flash metering with SCA-compatible flash units, depth-of-field preview, a self-timer and viewfinder diopter adjustments.

The R6.2 is an update of the R6. The two most significant changes are a higher top shutter speed (1/2000 second) and an improved TTL flash mode that will meter flash exposure at any shutter speed from 1/100 to B.

Leica R7

If you're a long-time Leica purist, you probably know already that Leica prefers the steady, evolutionary approach to product development over the totally new and sensational gee-whiz kind of gimcrackery. The R7 once again reinforces the Wetzlar philosophy. It's best, perhaps, to think of the R7 as being an R5 to which several features found on the more up-to-date R6 (now R6.2) have been added.

The R7 has a more full-featured TTL flash mode. Using SCA-compatible flash units, fill flash is now available with shutter-priority AE, and the system will switch automatically between fill flash and full flash in Program mode. Exposure compensation has been increased from ±2 EV (in ⅓ stop increments) to ±3 EV (in ½ stop increments). The R7 also takes four 1.5 volt batteries instead of the R5's two, extending service life between battery changes. Finally, the frame counter was repositioned for easier viewing. All other features of the R5 were retained.

Leica SLRs

Camera	Yrs. Made	New	Mint	Excellent	User
Leicaflex chr	1964-68			350 250	
Leicaflex blk	1964-68			800 650	
Leicaflex SL chr	1968-74		495 420	395 300	300 230
Leicaflex SL blk	1968-74		695 495	450 300	
Leicaflex SL2 chr	1974-76		1295 1200	1100 800	
Leicaflex SL2 blk	1974-76			1250 1150	
R3 blk or chr	1976-79		495 450	395 300	300 210
R3 MOT w/winder	1978-79		550 450	450 380	
R4	1980-86		500 380	450 300	
R4-S	1983-85		550 400	420 350	
R4-S MOD P (MOD 2)	1985-88		800 700	700 550	
R5	1987-92		1500 1250	1200 900	
R6	1988-92		1600 1300	1450 1000	
R6.2	1992-	2785 2595			
R7	1992-	2500 2395			
RE	1990-	1700 1300	1100 1000		

Leica SLR Lenses

All lenses are 3-cam unless noted. 2-cam lenses that have been converted to 3-cam are not listed. Such converted lenses sell for more than 2-cam lenses, but less than factory original 3-cam.

Lens	New	Mint	Excellent	User
15mm f/3.5 Super Elmar	6100 5595	4400 3120	3300 3000	
16mm f/2.8 Elmarit	2650 2245	1500 1370	1220 950	
19mm f/2.8 Elmarit (latest)	3000 2645			
19mm f/2.8 Elmarit		1500 1200	1150 1000	
21mm f/3.4 Super Angulon			800 650	
The 3.4 Super Angulon is for Leica SLRs with Mirror Lock Up.				
21mm f/4 Super Angulon	2250 1995	1395 1000	995 830	
21mm f/4 Super Angulon (2-cam)		800 750	700 620	
24mm f/2.8 Elmarit	2250 1995	1350 895	1000 650	
28mm f/2.8 Elmarit	1850 1645	1050 800	825 600	
28mm f/2.8 Elmarit (2-cam)			500 350	
28mm f/2.8 PC Super Angulon	3100 2745			
35mm f/1.4 Summilux	3000 2645	1995 1750	1695 1300	
35mm f/2 Summicron	1850 1645	1200 1000	995 750	
35mm f/2 Summicron (2-cam)		650 500	450 300	
35mm f/2.8 Elmarit	1150 995	820 750	600 525	
35mm f/2.8 Elmarit (2-cam)			325 250	
35mm f/2.8 Elmarit (1-cam)		250 200	195 170	
35mm f/4 PA Curtagon	2400 2195	1595 1400	1395 950	
50mm f/1.4 Summilux	2195 1895	1295 1050	995 750	

Leica SLR Lenses

Lens	New		Mint		Excellent		User
50mm f/1.4 Summilux (2-cam)			600	550	580	500	
50mm f/2 Summicron	850	695	495	395	450	300	
50mm f/2 Summicron (2-cam)			350	250	250	195	
50mm f/2 Summicron (1-cam)			150	100	90	80	
60mm f/2.8 Macro Elmarit	1900	1695	1195	1000	950	700	
1:1 Tube (14256) for above	240	200	150	100	90	75	
60mm f/2.8 Macro Elmarit (2-cam)					600	500	
1:1 Tube (14198) for above					100	75	
80mm f/1.4 Summilux	3000	2645	1895	1750	1695	1300	
90mm f/2 Summicron	2195	1895	1295	1050	950	800	
90mm f/2 Summicron (2-cam)			600	450	500	350	
90mm f/2.8 Elmarit	1350	1195	695	600	640	375	
90mm f/2.8 Elmarit (2-cam)			495	350	400	300	
90mm f/2.8 Elmarit (1-cam)					350	225	
100mm f/2.8 APO Macro	2700	2495	1895	1495			
1:1 Elpro (16545) for above	600	495					
100mm f/4 Macro Elmar (Bellows)			425	300	280	200	
100mm f/4 Macro Elmar	2000	1745	995	800	760	550	
1:1 Tube (14262) for above	240	200	150	100	95	70	
135mm f/2.8 Elmarit	1600	1445	950	750	690	400	
135mm f/2.8 Elmarit (2-cam)			375	270	290	200	
135mm f/2.8 Elmarit (1-cam)					250	150	
180mm f/2.8 Elmarit (E67 filter)	2700	2495	1795	1550	1495	895	
180mm f/2.8 Elmarit (S8 filter)			800	695	650	450	
180mm f/2.8 Elmarit (2-cam)			550	500	475	400	
180mm f/3.4 APO-Telyt	3150	2895	1895	1395	1400	795	
180mm f/3.4 APO-Telyt (2-cam)					950	600	
180mm f/4 Elmar	1950	1695	1095	800	750	600	
250mm f/4 Telyt (latest)	3300	2995	2000	1400	1300	1100	
250mm f/4 Telyt (S8 filter)			750	595	570	480	
250mm f/4 Telyt (2-cam)			600	550			
280mm f/2.8 APO-Telyt	7700	6995	5500	4000	5000	3400	
350mm f/4.8 Telyt	4200	3795	2400	1920			
400mm f/2.8 APO-Telyt	16000	13000					
400mm f/5.6 (w/stock)					1400	1100	
400mm f/6.8 (w/stock)			1100	1000	900	725	
400mm f/6.8 (lens only)					800	600	
400mm f/6.8 (w/stock, 2-cam)			995	895	640	530	
400/560 Tube	595	500					
500mm f/8 MR-Telyt Mirror	2700	2495	1750	1495			
560mm f/5.6 (w/stock)			1600	1450			
560mm f/6.8 (w/stock)			1400	1240	1200	1095	
560mm f/6.8 (lens only)			1400	1300	1250	1095	
800mm f/6.3 R Telyt	25000	18995	20500	17500			
800mm f/8 Minolta Reflex					1000	800	
The 800mm f/8 Minolta was produced in both Minolta and Leica R lens mounts.							
1.4X APO Extender R	1450	1295	985	775			
2X (for SL, SL2)			650	500			
2X Tele-Extender R			795	695	550	460	
2X APO Extender R	1550	1395	1000	800			

All lenses are 3-cam unless noted. 2-cam lenses that have been converted to 3-cam are not listed. Such converted lenses sell for more than 2-cam lenses, but less than factory original 3-cam.

Leica SLR Zoom Lenses

Lens	New	Mint	Excellent	User
28-70 f/3.5 Vario Elmar	1150 995	795 695		
35-70 f/2.5-3.3 Angenieux	1050 850	800 695	750 500	
35-70 f/3.5 Vario-Elmar (Germany)	2250 1795	1500 1300	1100 850	
35-70 f/3.5 Vario-Elmar (Japan)		950 750	795 695	
45-90 f/2.8 Angenieux		900 800	750 600	
70-210 f/3.5 Angenieux	1400 1200	850 740	700 600	
70-210 f/4 Vario-Elmar	2350 2195	1400 1200	1200 900	
75-200 f/4.5 Vario-Elmar		1000 850	900 600	
80-200 f/4.5 Vario-Elmar		750 675	595 475	

Leica SLR Accessories

Item	New	Mint	Excellent	User
Motor Winder R3 (14270: R3 MOT)		100 75	80 60	
Motor Winder R4 (14282)		170 120	110 75	
Motor Winder R (14208: R4/5/6/E)	400 330	280 200	200 150	
Motor Drive R4 (14292)		260 200	240 160	150 120
Motor Drive R (14309: R4/5/6/E)		300 225	250 200	
Motor Drive R (14310: R4/5/6/E)	700 590	450 350	375 275	
Handgrip R3 (14271)		30 20		
Handgrip R4 (14283)		40 30		
Handgrip R (14308)	80 75	60 55	55 40	
Handgrip R7 (14317)	65			
Universal Handgrip (14188)			150 100	
Universal Handgrip R (14239)	380 335		220 175	
Remote Control R (14277)	150 130	95 80		
Electric Release MD-R/MW-R (14237)	90 80			
Electric Release R (14238)	65 55			
Tripod Holder R3 (14276)		30 25		
Tripod Holder R (14284: R4/5/6/E)	100 80			
APO Macro Tripod Holder (14636)	85			
Data Back DB (14297: R4)			150 100	
Data Back DB2 (14230: R4)	590 495	350 290	250 140	
Data Back DB2 (14216: R5/R6/RE)	590 495	400 320	295 200	
Minolta Data Back D (fits R4/5/6)		100 90		
Right Angle Fndr (14186/286: SL/SL2)		125 100		
Right Angle Fndr (14287/288: R3)		125 100		
Right Angle Fndr (14326: R4)		125 100		
Right Angle Fndr 1X/2X (14329: R3)		150 130		
Right Angle Fndr 1X/2X (14328: R4)		140 120		
Right Angle Fndr 1X/2X (14300: R5/6/7/E)	500 420			
Bellows R (3-cam: 16860)	1100 925	650 500	400 300	
Bellows R (2-cam)			275 200	
Bellows R (1-cam)		200 180		
Macro Adapter R (14256)	500 420	300 250		
Elpro 1 or 2	125			
Elpro 3 or 4	160			
Leitz-Braun 340M SCA Flash		110 95	90 80	
Leitz-Braun 340 SCA Flash		100 90		
Leitz-Braun 400M Logic Flash	140	120 100		
Leitz-Braun 400M Flash Cord	30			
Leitz-Braun SCA 351 Module	80 60		35 30	
Braun Macro Flash		70 65		

Numbers shown in parentheses are Leica catalog numbers.

Minolta

Minolta's history as a camera manufacturer dates from 1928. Early on, the company established a reputation for innovation, a Minolta tradition that has continued for over six decades. To name just a few firsts for which Minolta was responsible, it was the first Japanese camera company to manufacture every component of its cameras, it marketed the first 35mm SLR with a coupled meter (SR-7), as well as the first 35mm SLR with an integral motor drive (SR-M). Minolta was the first to introduce a multi-exposure mode 35mm camera (XD-11) and, of course, it marketed the first successful autofocus interchangeable-lens 35mm SLR (Maxxum 7000).

Minolta SRs

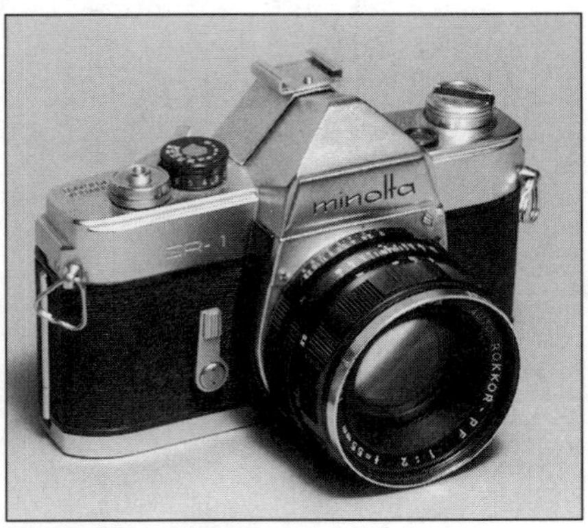

Minolta SR-1 with accessory 'cold' shoe

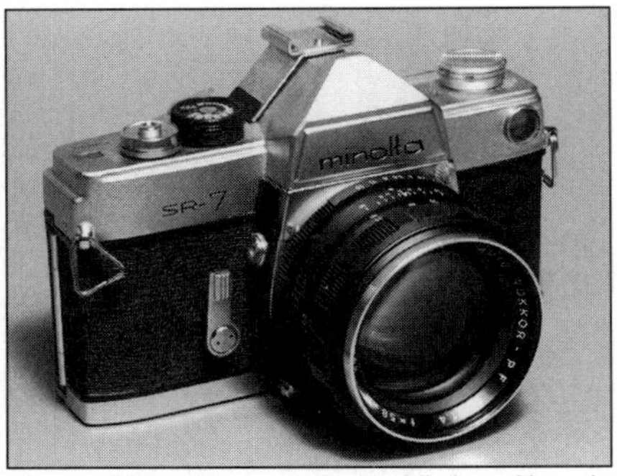

Minolta SR-7 with accessory 'cold' shoe. Note the meter window just below the film rewind crank.

Minolta's first series of SLRs consists of the various SR models. With the possible exception of the SR-M, all bear close resemblance to each other with only minor differences in features. Following is a brief overview.

The SR-1 has shutter speeds which range from 1 second to 1/500, plus B, with X sync at 1/60. Early SR-1's have no depth-of-field preview button. Late SR-1's have mirror lock-up and an attachment point for a non-TTL CdS exposure meter. The SR-1s appears to be identical to the late SR-1 (also known as the SR-1 Model V), and was produced concurrently with the SR-T 101. The SR-2 (Minolta's first SLR) has a full range of shutter speeds, from 1 second to 1/1000, plus B, with X sync at 1/60. It was replaced by the SR-3, which featured a detachable selenium non-TTL exposure meter.

The SR-3 was superseded by the SR-7, which has a built-in non-TTL exposure meter coupled to the camera's shutter speeds, and was the first Minolta SLR (as far as I've been able to tell) with mirror lock-up. The SR-M was Minolta's first motorized camera and was introduced four years after the SR-T 101. It has a built-in motor drive with a large, detachable hand grip and features both motorized film advance and rewind. It also has mirror lock-up. The SR-M has no meter, nor does it have a provision for attaching one of the above accessory meters. All the above SR-series cameras have self-timers except the SR-M.

Minolta SR-Ts

The success of the workhorse SR-T-series was largely responsible for positioning Minolta as a major player in the 35mm camera market. There are six basic models, most which underwent slight modifications during their production lives. Just to make matters confusing, though, the model numbers varied according to the countries in which they were sold. Following is a more-or-less chronological listing of SR-T cameras, with brief descriptions of features.

Minolta SR-T 101

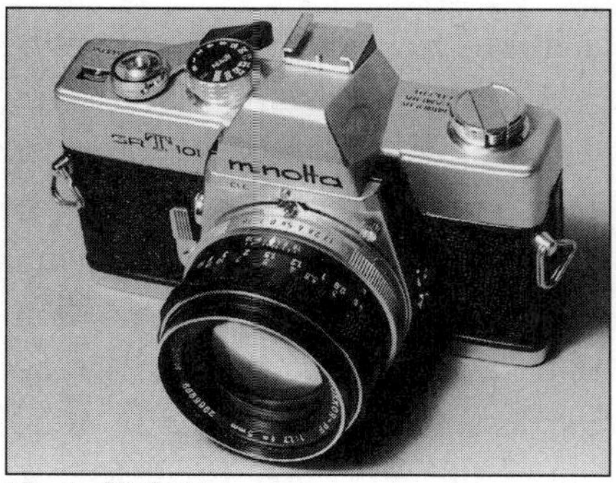

Minolta SR-T 101

The SR-T 101 debuted in 1966. It is a full-size, full-featured, manual, mechanical SLR. The TTL CdS meter provides centerweighted average metering. Exposure is determined by the match-needle method. Shutter speeds range from 1 second to 1/1000, plus B, with X sync at 1/60. The camera has a "cold shoe" (an accessory shoe without flash contacts) and PC sockets for X sync and FP bulbs. Other niceties include a depth-of-field preview lever and a self-timer. Most SRT-101s have mirror lock up, although those made at the very end of the production run do not.

Minolta SR-T 100

Introduced in 1971, the SR-T 100 is a scaled-down version of the 101. The top shutter speed is 1/500. It doesn't have a self-timer, depth-of-field preview, or mirror lock-up.

Minolta SR-T 102, SR-T 303 & SR-T Super

The SR-T 102, introduced in 1973, is basically a 101 with improvements. It has a hot shoe, multiple exposure capability and lens apertures are visible in the viewfinder. Examples can be found with or without mirror lock-up. The SR-T 303 and SR-T Super are identical to the 102, marketed in Europe and Japan, respectively.

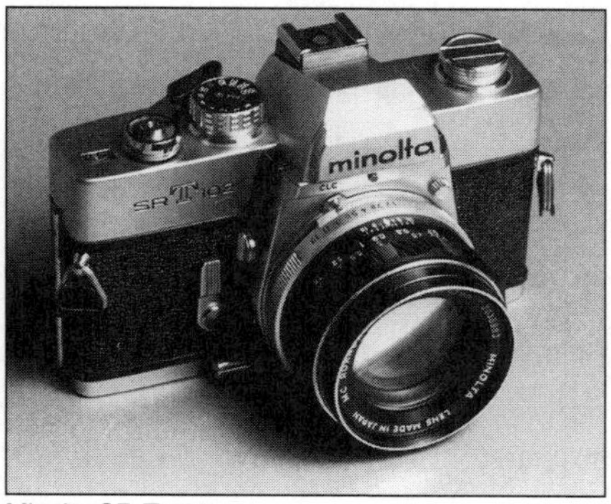

Minolta SR-T 102

Minolta SR-T 201, SR-101 & SR-T 101B

Things get a little confusing at this point. Introduced in 1975, the SR-T 201 is a 101 with a hot shoe. Most examples do not have mirror lock up. It almost seems as if Minolta still had a few 101s lying around that got new top covers. The SR-101 and SRT-101B are identical to the SR-T 201, marketed in Japan and Europe, respectively.

Minolta SR-T 202, SR-T 303B & SR-505

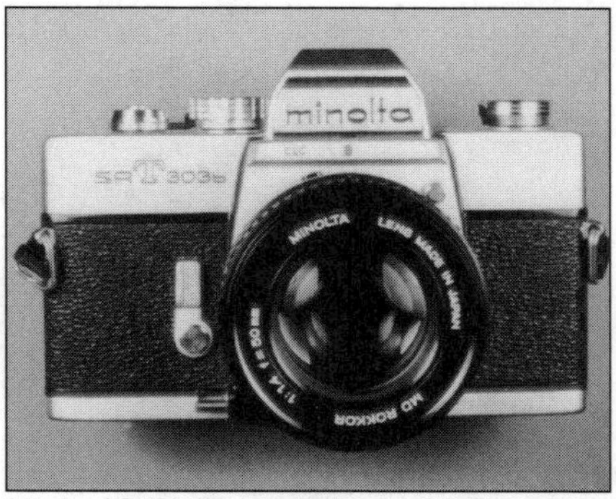

Minolta SR-T 303b. Identical to the SR-T 202.

The SR-T 202 was introduced in 1975 and is almost identical to a late SR-T 102. Most 202s do not have mirror lock-up. Two features added to this camera are a window under the film advance lever that has an indicator for correct film transport and a memo holder. The SR-T 303B and SR-505 are identical and were marketed in Europe and Japan, respectively.

Minolta SR-T 200

Also introduced in 1975, the SR-T 200 replaced the 100. It has a full range of shutter speeds, however.

Minolta SR-T MC, SR-T MCII, SR-T SC & SR-T SCII

These cameras were marketed through major national department stores, such as K-Mart and others. As far as I could determine, the SR-T MC is the same as the SR-T 101, the SR-T MCII is an SR-T 202, the SR-T SC is an SR-T 100 and the SR-T SCII is an SR-T 200. Don't hold me to this, though. If you have specific details on these models, I'd be interested in finding out how close I am.

Minolta XD-11, XD-7, XD-5 & XD

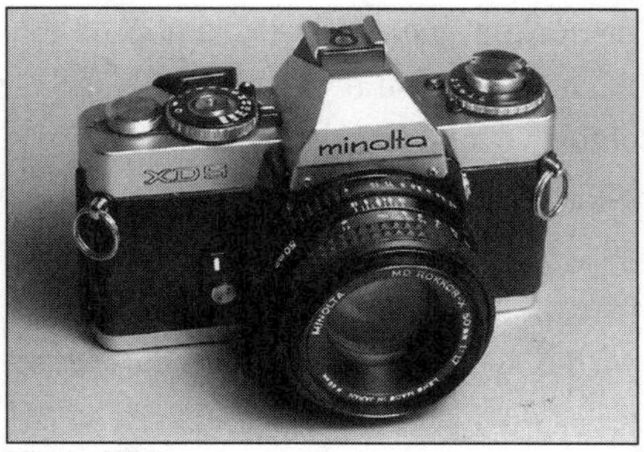

Minolta XD-5

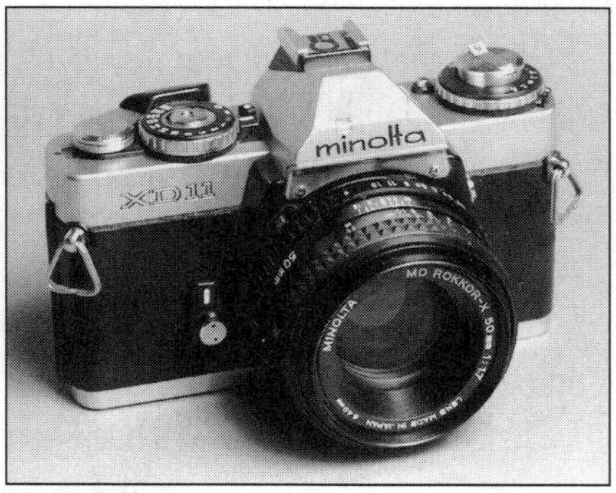

Minolta XD-11

The XD-11, when introduced back in 1977, was billed as the first SLR with more than one auto-exposure mode and caused the photo industry to take notice. It's an elegantly-designed camera; controls are uncluttered and easily understood. If you happen to run across an XD or an XD-7, these are XD-11's originally marketed in Japan and Europe, respectively.

The XD-11's exposure modes include both aperture and shutter-priority AE, and metered manual. Minolta MD lenses must be used to engage the XD-11's shutter priority mode (see illustration in lens section). In shutter-priority AE, if the user has selected a setting that will result in improper exposure, the camera will automatically adjust things so that a well-exposed photo will result. Though it was never billed as such by Minolta, what this override function amounts to is a program mode, because the camera is selecting both shutter speeds and apertures. Thus, it could be argued that the XD-11 was the first SLR featuring multi-exposure modes that included program. Non-TTL flash AE is also available (auto-setting of flash sync) with dedicated flash units. Silicon photo diodes provide center-weighted metering. Shutter speeds range from 1 second to 1/1000, plus B, with X sync at 1/100. Should the battery fail, two mechanical speeds are available: B and "O". The latter will sync with a flash at about 1/100 second.

Other features include multiple-exposure capability, a viewfinder window for direct aperture readout, a viewfinder shutter, depth-of-field preview, a variable self-timer and a 2 fps winder option with the Minolta Auto Winder D.

The XD-5, as far as I have been able to ascertain, is identical to the XD-11, except it lacks the direct aperture readout window.

XE-7, XE-5, XE-1 & XE

The XE-7 was available in black finish only and bears more than a passing resemblance to the Leica R3 for a very good reason. This camera was Minolta's first payoff from the shared technology agreement between the two companies. The XE-1 and XE are identical to the XE-7, marketed in Japan and Europe, respectively.

Exposure modes include aperture-priority AE, metered manual and stop-down metering for non-MC or preset lenses. Shutter speeds range from 4 seconds to 1/1000, plus B, with X sync at 1/90. Without batteries, only B and 1/90 are available. Other features include exposure compensation, an eyepiece shutter, a direct aperture readout window in the viewfinder, a film transport indicator, a hot shoe and a PC socket, multi-exposure capability, depth-of-field preview and a variable self-timer.

The XE-5 is much the same camera, except for the following differences: It was available only in chrome finish with a black finder. It lacks depth-of-field preview, the direct aperture readout window, the eyepiece shutter and multiple exposure capability.

XG-1, XG-7, XG-9, XG-A, XG-M & XG-SE

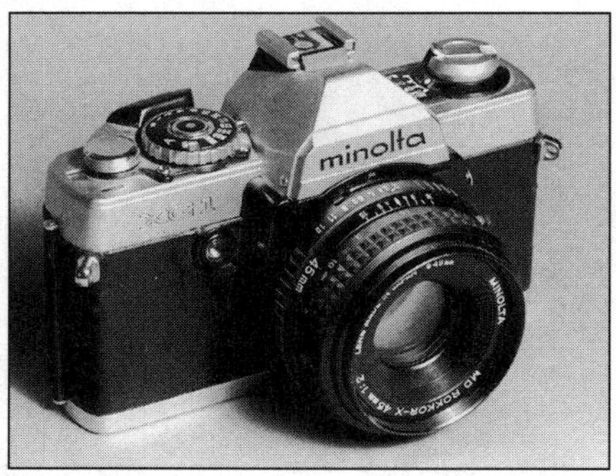

Minolta XG-1

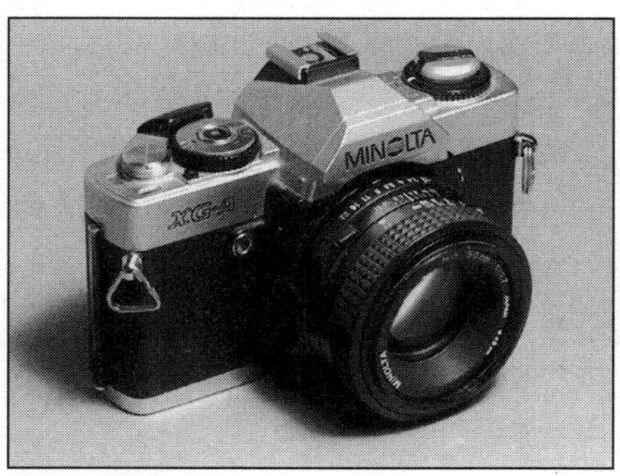

Minolta XG-A

These five cameras are almost identical in features and most are almost identical in appearance. Exposure modes are aperture-priority AE, employing a centerweighted averaging meter, non-metered manual (except the XG-A) and limited flash AE (shutter speed is set automatically with dedicated flash units). Shutter speeds range from 1 second to 1/1000, plus B, with X sync occurring at 1/60. Other features include exposure compensation and a self-timer. All models accept the Winder G for film advance speeds up to 2 fps.

Now, for the differences:

The XG-1 was made in two models, known within the trade as the XG-1 and XG-1n. At least these two are easy to tell apart. The XG-1 has the older-style body, while the XG-1n has an updated body, similar to that of the X-370 and X-570. It also has the current Minolta logo on its nameplate. The XG-1 will not take the Databack G, whereas the XG-1n will. The XG-7 is an XG-1 with a film memo holder and the capability to accept the Data Back G. The XG-9 is an XG-7 with a window in the viewfinder for direct aperture readout and a depth-of-field preview lever. The XG-A is an XG-7 without a manual exposure mode. The XG-M is an XG-9 with AE lock and a body similar to the XG-1n's. The XG-SE is a black XG-7 with an Acute Matte focusing screen (much brighter). There was also an XG-7A, which is apparently a black XG-M.

There. I hope that's been settled.

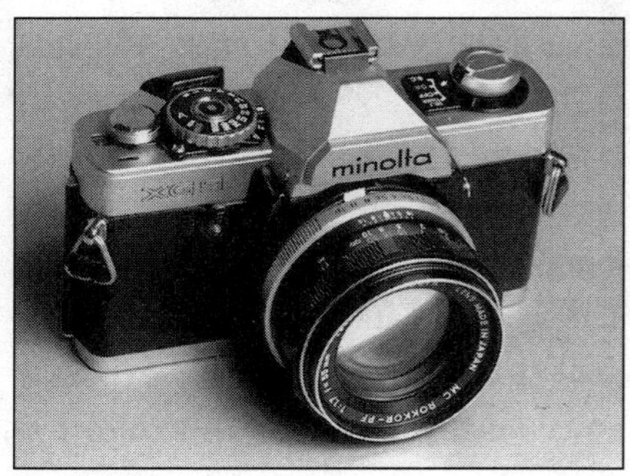

Minolta XG-9

Minolta XK & XK Motor, XM, & X-1

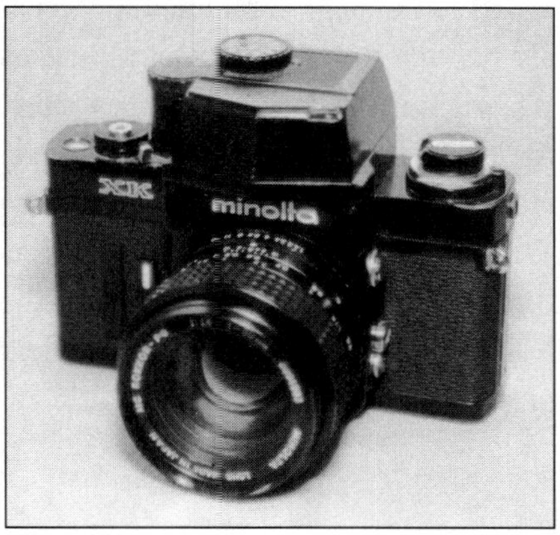

Minolta XK

The XK was the first Minolta that used the X prefix in its model designation. Introduced in 1973, it was an attempt by Minolta to go up against the Nikon F and F2, and the Canon F-1. Built in that tradition, it is a solid, heavy camera, obviously designed to withstand years of hard use. Minolta may have been more successful with the original XK if it had had motor drive capability when introduced. Instead, the company waited until 1976 before finally introducing the XK Motor. Another difference that may have contributed to its lack of acceptance is the fact that it is an electronic, battery-dependent camera. If one looks at the XK's features, though, it was years ahead of its time.

The XK has two basic exposure modes: aperture-priority AE and metered manual. Shutter speeds range from 16 seconds to 1/2000 (1 second to 1/2000 in manual), plus B, with X sync at 1/100. B and X sync are the only mechanical speeds. A variety of interchangeable viewfinders were offered, although the camera is usually found with the AE finder. Other features include interchangeable focusing screens, depth-of-field preview, mirror lock up and a self-timer.

The XK Motor is an XK adapted for the XK motor drive, and came with the improved AE-S finder when new. An interesting addition to the XK Motor is a microswitch that allows the motor drive to operate only when film is in the camera. The motor drive is built every bit as ruggedly as is the camera, yet its grip is sculpted to fit one's hand comfortably. When new, the XK Motor was usually sold with the motor drive. The set was expensive, as well. Discount new prices for the outfit in the mid-to-late 1970's were over $1,000. The XK Motor is a beautiful combination for the diehard Minoltaphile, but clean examples still fetch a high premium on the used market.

The XM and X-1 cameras are identical to the XK and were marketed in Europe and Japan, respectively.

Minolta X-700

This lightweight camera just feels good resting in the palm of your hand. Years before radical streamlining became chic, Minolta came up with the subtle ergonomics responsible for the way it feels. In addition to looking good, it functions well and remains a very popular camera on both new and used markets.

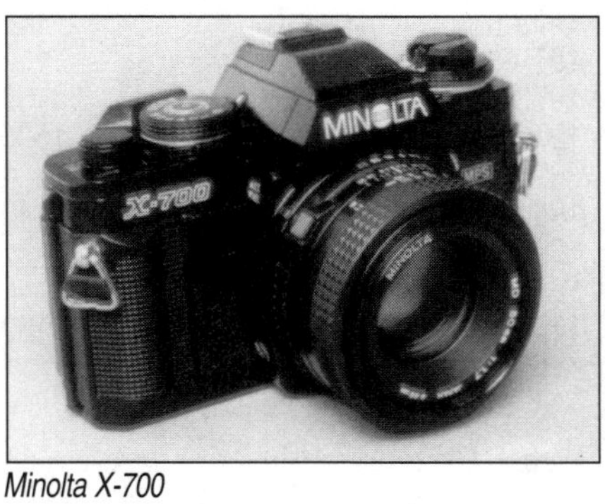

Minolta X-700

The X-700 has four exposure modes: program, aperture-priority, metered manual, and TTL flash with dedicated flash units. Other exposure features include AE lock and exposure compensation. The metering pattern employed is the tried-and-true centerweighted method. Shutter speeds range from 4 seconds to 1/1000 (1 second to 1/1000 in manual mode), plus B, with X sync at 1/60. Other features include interchangeable Acute Matte focusing screens, a direct aperture readout window, a PC socket, depth-of-field preview and a self-timer. The X-700 will accept either the winder G for film advance speeds up to 2 fps, or the Motor Drive 1, for continuous speeds up to 3.5 fps. MD lenses must be employed to engage the X-700's program mode (see illustrations in lens section).

Minolta X-570

At first glance, this camera appears to be a scaled-down version of the X-700 and it is — sort of. It lacks the X-700's program mode, as well as the X-700's exposure compensation, depth-of-field preview and PC socket. Like the X-700, the X-570 accepts both the Winder G and the Motor Drive 1.

The big difference between the two cameras, and one reason why many people prefer the X-570 to the X-700 has to do with the LED readout. In manual mode, the LED readout in the X-570 viewfinder is coupled to both the lens aperture ring and the shutter speed dial, allowing one to do match-diode metering without having to remove one's eye from the viewfinder. With the X-700, the selected apertures are shown in the viewfinder, but the shutter speed shown is that which the camera recommends for correct exposure. It does not change as the shutter speed dial is adjusted. This forces the user to look away from the viewfinder, glance at the shutter speed dial to see what's been set, then recompose and shoot. As a result, the X-570 is a much more convenient camera to use for manual work.

Minolta X-370 & X-7A

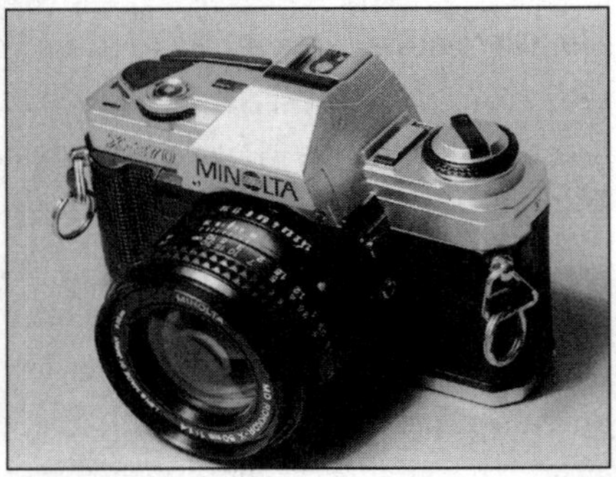

Minolta X-370

The only differences between the X-370 and the X-570 is that the X-370 does not have TTL flash automation and it will not accept the X-series data backs. beside this, they're the same camera. The X-7A is a domestic Japanese X-370, available in black only. Although never officially imported into the U.S., it is common on the used market.

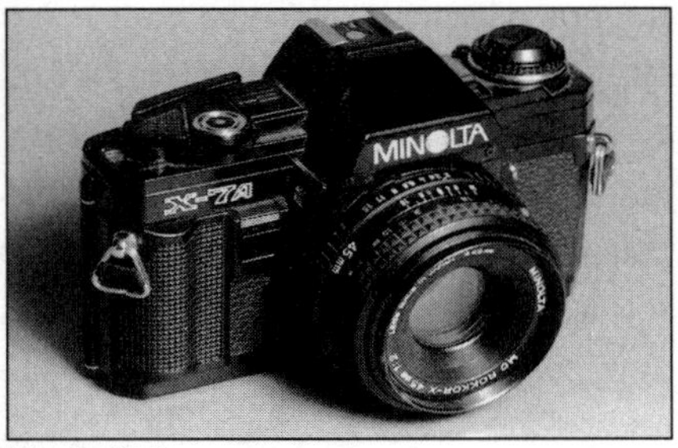

Minolta X-7A

Minolta X-370n & X-9

The X-370n is a redesigned X-370, styled to be more ergonomic. It probably has the same amount of plastic as the original, but looks as if it has more. As far as I can tell, the only improvement over the original X-370 is that the X-370n has a window for direct aperture readout. The X-9 is identical to the X-370n, except it has a depth-of-field preview lever.

Minolta Manual Focus SLRs

Camera	Yrs. Made	New	Mint	Excellent	User
SR-M w/grip	1970-75			550 400	
SR-1 or SR-1s	1959-70			100 60	
SR-2	1958-61			95 50	
SR-3 w/meter	1961-62			100 80	
SR-7	1962-66			110 90	
SR-T 100	1971-75			100 80	75 50
SR-T 101	1966-75		150 120	130 100	90 55
SR-T 102	1973-75		175 150	150 110	
SR-T 200	1975-81			120 75	
SR-T 201	1975-81		180 160	150 95	
SR-T 202	1975-78		190 175	160 125	
XD-5	1979-83		170 140	150 120	
XD-11 chr	1977-82		225 185	180 150	140 120
XD-11 blk	1977-82		300 265	250 175	
XE-5	1975-78		170 150	160 115	
XE-7	1975-78		225 180	170 150	
XG-A	c1981-85		100 90	80 70	
XG-M	1981-84		125 100	100 90	
XG-1	1979-84		125 110	115 80	
XG-7, XG-SE	1978-81		140 110	125 90	
XG-9	1979-84		150 125	130 100	
XK w/AE finder	1973-77		450 400	370 300	275 195
XK Motor W/AES fndr & mtr drv	1976-87		1500 1200	1150. 950	850 780
X-9	1990-	190 160		120 110	
X-370, X7A	1984-89		140 110	125 100	
X-370n	1990-	190 160			
X-570	1984-87			150 125	
X-700	1983-	270 220	190 150	160 125	

Minolta Lenses

Minolta Auto, MC and MD lenses will fit all manual focus Minolta cameras, allowing varying degrees of automation depending on the camera.

The first generation of lenses produced for Minolta SLRs were the Auto Rokkor-PF lenses. Most of these lenses have auto diaphragms, but none have meter couplings. Many of these early lenses can be used on later cameras that support stop-down metering. Chances are pretty good, though, that if your Minolta has a meter, you'll probably want to use lenses that will couple to it.

MC or MD — what's the difference, and which style do you need for your camera? MC lenses have a tab on the aperture ring of the lens that engages the meter coupling pin on the camera. MD lenses have an additional tab, which, when the lens is set to its smallest aperture (highest number), engages another pin on the camera (see illustration). Only three Minolta cameras support the MD feature: the XD-11, the XD-5 and the X-700. With the X-700, for example, the engagement of this pin lets the camera know everything is ready to go when the shutter speed dial is set to program. Thus, if your camera has shutter-priority exposure automation (XD-11 or XD-5) or a program feature (X-700), and if you wish to use these functions, you will need MD lenses. If your camera does not have a program mode or shutter-priority AE, or if you don't use these features, then you can get by just fine with MC lenses and your camera will never know the difference.

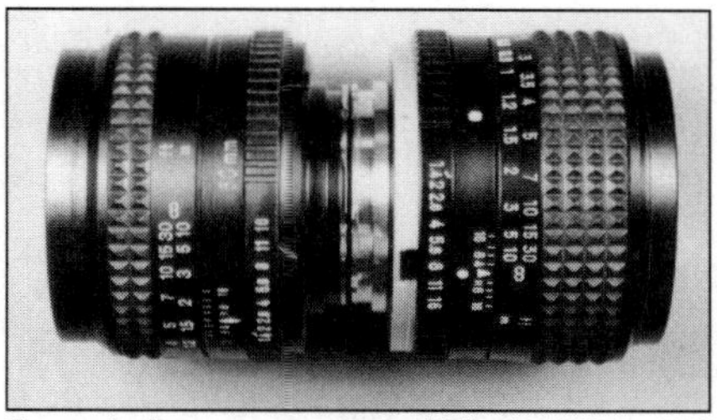

Flange to flange comparison of Minolta MD and MC lenses. Note the additional tab on the aperture ring of the MD lens (left).

MC lenses were made in three styles: the early Rokkors, most of which have metal focusing rings; the Rokkor-X lenses, which have rubberized inserts on the focusing rings; and the MC Celtic lenses. The Celtics were priced and marketed as economy models and are fine lenses optically, although not as sturdy as their Rokkor and Rokkor-X counterparts.

MD lenses exist in two basic styles. The earlier style, labeled MD Rokkor-X (sometimes MD Rokkor), resemble late MC lenses in appearance and are generally larger than the later MD style (labeled Minolta MD). Price differences between MD Rokkor-X and Minolta MD lenses are usually negligible, although it is not unusual to see Rokkor-X lenses commanding higher prices than their latest-generation plastic counterparts. Another difference is that Minolta MD lenses have a sliding switch that locks the lens aperture ring in the AE setting (see illustration). The earlier style does not have this switch, so it is easier for the aperture ring to be moved inadvertently from the AE position. Minolta also produced MD Celtic lenses.

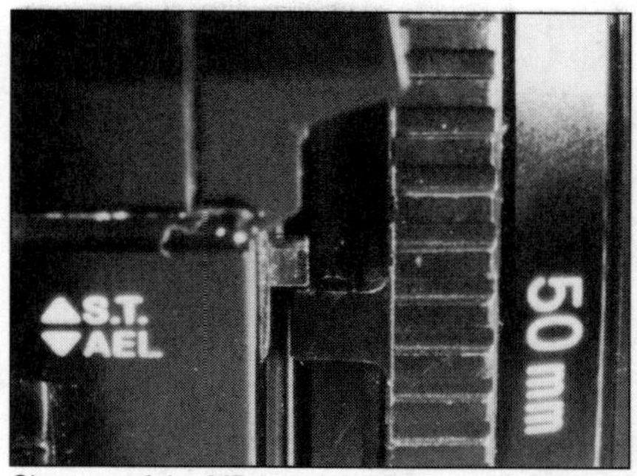

Close-up of the MD len's program coupling tab and the body switch it engages. Minolta X-700 shown.

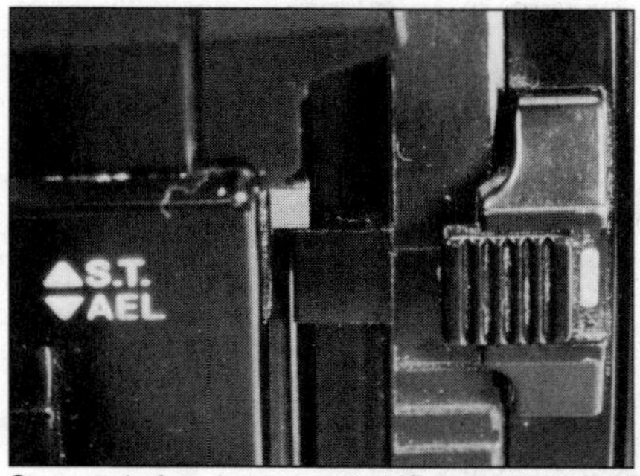

Same as before, but new style MD lens with lens AE lock engaged. A green mark is uncovered when the lens is unlocked.

There are also a variety of Minolta lenses concurrent with the MC and MD lenses, which lack meter-coupling tabs. Those listed here are the mirror and bellows lenses. Both groups are listed separately following the MD lens listings.

Minolta Auto Rokkor-PF Lenses

Lens	Mint	Excellent	Use
18mm f/9.5 Fish-eye		250 .. 100	
21mm f/4 w/finder		150 .. 125	
The 21mm f/4 is for Minolta SLRs with mirror lock-up			
35mm f/2.8		50 ... 35	
55mm f/1.8		30 ... 20	
55mm f/2		25 ... 15	
58mm f/1.4		50 ... 30	

Minolta MC Lenses

Lens	New	Mint	Excellent	User
7.5mm f/4 Fish-eye			350 .. 300	
16mm f/2.8 Fish-eye		375 .. 350	300 .. 275	250 .. 180
17mm f/4			350 .. 250	
21mm f/2.8		260 .. 200	225 .. 180	
24mm f/2.8			125 .. 100	
24mm f/2.8 VFC		350 .. 300		
28mm f/2			200 .. 150	
28mm f/2.5		100 ... 80	70 ... 60	

Minolta MC Lenses

Lens	New	Mint	Excellent	User
28mm f/2.8		95 75	60 50	
28mm f/2.8 Celtic			40 30	
28mm f/3.5			50 40	
35mm f/1.8			175 125	
35mm f/2.8			60 40	
35mm f/2.8 Celtic			50 35	
50mm f/1.4		65 50	55 50	
50mm f/1.7			50 25	
50mm f/2		30 25	25 20	
50mm f/3.5 Macro (w/1:1)		165 145	160 120	
50mm f/3.5 Celtic Macro			100 85	
55mm f/1.7			40 25	
55mm f/1.9			35 25	
58mm f/1.2			150 125	
58mm f/1.4		75 50	60 40	
85mm f/1.7			175 125	
85mm f/2.8 Varisoft	700 600	500 425	400 345	
100mm f/2.5			125 80	100 75
100mm f/3.5 Macro w/1:1			250 200	
135mm f/2.8			70 45	
135mm f/2.8 Celtic			55 40	
135mm f/3.5			60 30	
135mm f/3.5 Celtic			40 30	
200mm f/3.5			100 75	
200mm f/4.5 Celtic			60 50	
200mm f/4.5			75 60	
300mm f/4.5		300 280	290 225	
400mm f/5.6 APO			850 600	
600mm f/5.6		1000 800		
MC 2X APO Teleconverter			240 200	
MC 2X 200L Teleconverter		125 100		
SR 2X M/A Teleconverter		120 100		

Minolta MC Zoom Lenses

Lens	New	Mint	Excellent	User
40-80 f/2.8			160 125	
80-160 f/3.5			125 100	
80-200 f/4.5		200 190		
100-200 f/5.6 Celtic			60 40	
100-500 f/8			500 400	

Minolta MD Lenses

Some of the following MD lenses for which new prices are listed may be limited to existing stock. Minolta is trimming down its manual focus line and, as stocks of some of these lenses become depleted, they may not be replenished.

Lens	New	Mint	Excellent	User
7.5mm f/4	800 500		400 300	
16mm f/2.8	550 450	375 300	275 225	
17mm f/4	600 490	425 350		
20mm f/2.8	550 450	375 300	290 225	
24mm f/2.8	260 220	200 160	160 130	

Minolta MD Lenses

Lens	New	Mint	Excellent	User
24mm f/2.8 VFC	540 375		290 225	
28mm f/2	450 320	250 175	200 150	
28mm f/2.8	150 120	100 80	80 65	
28mm f/2.8 Celtic			60 40	
35mm f/1.8	400 300		180 135	
35mm f/2.8		100 80	70 40	
35mm f/2.8 Shift			600 400	
45mm f/2		40 30	30 20	
50mm f/1.2		200 170		
50mm f/1.4		90 75	70 60	
50mm f/1.7	80 60	50 40	40 20	
50mm f/2		35 30	30 25	
50mm f/2.8		40 25		
50mm f/3.5 Macro (w/1:1)		200 180	190 150	
85mm f/1.7		220 180	175 150	
85mm f/2	460 350	250 190		
100mm f/2.5	240 200	175 140	150 125	
100mm f/3.5 Macro (w/1:1)		350 270		
100mm f/4 Macro (w/1:1)	560 450	380 320	300 240	
135mm f/2		350 300	285 250	
135mm f/2.8	140 120		80 65	
135mm f/3.5 (MD or Celtic)		50 35	35 30	
200mm f/2.8	595 480	400 350	325 250	
200mm f/4			75 50	
300mm f/4.5	595 480	400 350	325 250	
300mm f/5.6			180 90	
400mm f/5.6 APO	1695 1350	1100 1000	950 800	
600mm f/6.3 APO	2495 2000			
MD-2X 300S	250 190		160 120	
MD-2X 300L	170 130		100 80	

Minolta MD Zoom Lenses

Lens	New	Mint	Excellent	User
24-35 f/3.5	290 225			
24-50 f/4	430 355	330 260	270 150	
28-70 f/3.5-4.5	160 110			
28-85 f/3.5-4.5	240 240	225 170	175 140	
35-70 f/3.5			150 100	
35-105 f/3.5-4.5		250 200	190 150	
35-135 f/3.5-4.5		280 250	225 150	
50-135 f/3.5		200 180	170 140	
70-210 f/4		175 150	160 120	
70-210 f/4.5-?	195 150			
70-300 f/4.5-?	325 240			
75-150 f/4		140 115	110 85	
75-200 f/4.5			150 120	
100-200 f/5.6			110 85	
100-300 f/5.6			265 200	
100-500 f/8 APO		1200 950	900 750	

Minolta Mirror Lenses

Lens	New	Mint	Excellent	User
250mm f/5.6		160 120	125 90	
500mm f/8	430 345	300 275	285 190	
800mm f/8	1395 1100	850 690	700 500	
1000mm f/6.3			1800 1250	
1600mm f/11	2995 2500		2000 1600	

Minolta Bellows Lenses

Lens	New	Mint	Excellent	User
12.5mm f/2 Micro (Bellows)	230 . . 145			
25mm f/2.5 Micro (Bellows)	230 . . 145			
50mm f/3.5 Macro (Bellows)	220 . . 180		125 . . 100	
100mm f/4 Macro (Bellows)	250 . . 155			

Minolta Accessories

Item	New	Mint	Excellent	User
Data Back D (XD-series)			140 . . 100	
Data Back G (XG-series)			85 . . 65	
Multi Function Back (X700/570)	170 . . 140			
Quartz Data Back 1 (X700/570)	195 . . 155			
Motor Drive 1 (X700/570/370)	250 . . 190	180 . . 140	160 . . 135	125 . . 120
Auto Winder D (XD-11/XD-5)		100 . . 80	100 . . 80	
Auto Winder G (XG's/X700/X570/X370)	140 . . 120	100 . . 85	80 . . 50	
Remote Control Cord L (X700/X570)	45 . . 30			
Remote Control Cord S (X700/X570)	50 . . 35			
Auto Bellows I		75 . . 50		
Auto Bellows II		100 . . 75		
Auto Bellows III	240 . . 165	135 . . 125		
Bellows I		50 . . 45		
Bellows II		75 . . 60		
Bellows III	140 . . 100		85 . . 75	
Bellows IV	140 . . 100		95 . . 75	
Compact Bellows	100 . . 80			
Slide Copier		50 . . 40		
Slide Copier II		60 . . 50		
Slide Copier III	110 . . 80			
Focusing Rail III	130 . . 90			
Macro Stand III	70 . . 50			
MC Auto Extension Tube Set	100 . . 80	50 . . 40		
Copy Stand I		60 . . 50		
Copy Stand II	150 . . 100			
Copy Stand III	210 . . 160			
Transmitter IR-1 Set	200 . . 150		130 . . 100	
Eyepiece Magnifier V or Vn	50 . . 30	25 . . 20		
Angle Finder V or Vn	110 . . 85	70 . . 55		
SR Right Angle Finder			40 . . 25	
XK AE Finder		140 . . 130	125 . . 100	
XK AE-S Finder		170 . . 155	150 . . 120	
XK Prism P		100 . . 75		
XK Waist level Finder		60 . . 40		
XK Magnifier Eyepiece		75 . . 65		

Minolta Flashes

tem	New	Mint	Excellent	User
45FPX			60 . . 45	
80PX Macro Ring Flash	325 . . 250	220 . . 170	180 . . 125	
118X			25 . . 15	
128			40 . . 30	
132PX	110 . . 75	30 . . 20		
132X		45 . . 40	35 . . 25	
200X		45 . . 35	35 . . 25	
220X	55 . . 30			
280PX	130 . . 90	75 . . 50	60 . . 40	
320X			70 . . 50	
360PX		170 . . 140	150 . . 125	
Power Grip I Set		150 . . 125		
Power Grip II Set	210 . . 140	140 . . 125	115 . . 85	

Minolta Maxxum

Maxxum cameras accept only Maxxum bayonet-mount lenses (or aftermarket equivalents). There is no direct interchangeability between the Maxxum mount and the earlier Minolta MC/MD-style bayonet mount. Minolta does offer a teleconverter that will allow the use of these lenses on Maxxum cameras, but they won't autofocus. The following cameras are listed in the order of their introduction.

Maxxum 7000

Minolta's introduction of the Maxxum 7000 shook the 35mm photo industry to its very foundations. This single camera is responsible for the subsequent explosion in autofocus technology that has continued unabated since its 1985 release. But a good thing can't last forever; the Maxxum 7000 now suffers at the hands of the very revolution it began. By today's standards, the 7000's autofocus mechanism moves lenses into focus in a positively leisurely fashion. This isn't to say its autofocus mechanism is slow, it's just that the latest generation of autofocus cameras, such as the current Maxxum xi-series, now focus at seemingly instantaneous speeds.

The 7000 has two autofocus modes: one-shot (focus priority) and continuous (servo), with AF lock. Exposure modes are program with shift, aperture and shutter priority AE, metered manual and TTL-OTF (Off The Film plane) flash metering with dedicated flash units. Metering is performed by silicon photo cells in a centerweighted pattern. Shutter speeds range from 30 seconds to 1/2000, plus B, with X sync at 1/125.

Other features include interchangeable focusing screens, a built-in film winder with continuous speeds up to 2 fps, a self-timer, DX film coding with override, auto film loading and rewind.

Maxxum 5000

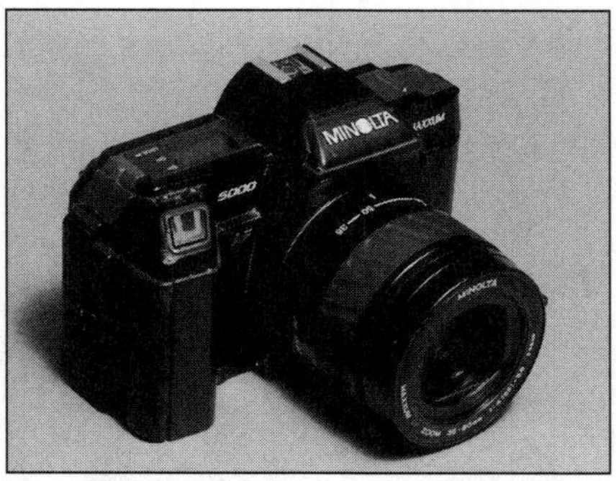

Maxxum 5000

The Maxxum 5000 is a simplified, less-costly version of the 7000 that retains its most often used features. A single autofocus mode, single-shot (focus priority), is available. Exposure modes are program and metered manual. Shutter speeds range from 4 seconds to 1/2000, plus B, with X sync at 1/100. Other features include DX film coding, backlight compensation, a self-timer and a built-in 1.5 fps motor drive that provides auto film loading and rewind.

Maxxum 9000

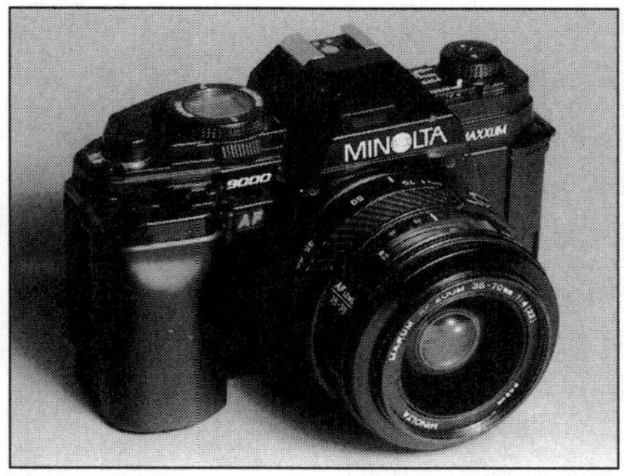

Maxxum 9000

The Maxxum 9000 garnered rave reviews when it was released in 1986 — and for good reason. It was the first member of a very select group, currently occupied by only three other cameras: professional-quality autofocus SLRs. Its robust construction, numerous built-in features and wide array of accessories still make it a very useful, full-featured SLR. But, because it uses Minolta's first generation of autofocus technology, it won't focus with the speed of its two competitors, the Canon EOS-1 and the Nikon F-4, and is miles behind the new Maxxum 9xi. Until the 9xi's introduction, the Maxxum 9000 had been the only Minolta SLR with a top flash sync speed of 1/250 second.

The 9000's standard autofocus mode is continuous (servo) operation with an AF lock located in the shutter release. When the motor drive or winder is attached, single-shot (focus-priority) is also available. Metering modes are centerweighted averaging and a tight 0.7% spot. Exposure modes include program with shift, aperture and shutter priority AE, metered manual and TTL flash with dedicated flash units. The metering can be biased for shooting in highlighted situations or shadows. Shutter speeds range from 30 seconds to 1/4000, plus B with an elapsed time indicator. Flash sync occurs at 1/250.

Other features include exposure compensation, a PC socket, built-in diopter correction, an eyepiece shutter, interchangeable focusing screens, multiple exposure capability, the retention of manual film advance and rewind capability, and a self-timer. A host of accessories has been made for the 9000, from either a winder or motor option (continuous advance speeds to 5 fps with the motor) to a still video back with a video recorder.

Maxxum 7000i

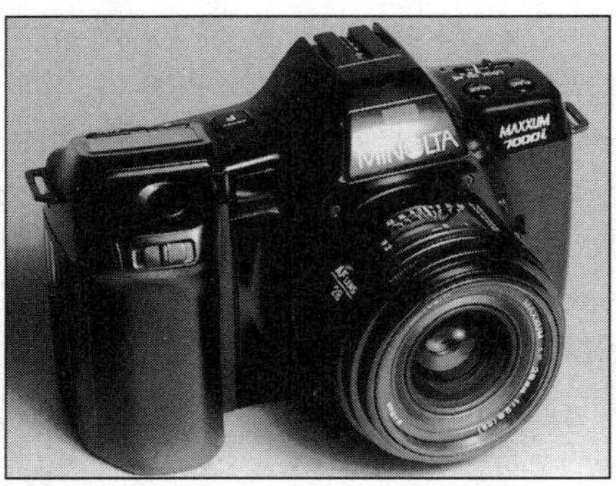

Maxxum 7000i

The 7000i's autofocus features: the system switches automatically between continuous and one-shot, depending upon subject movement. Predictive focus was added, which allows the camera to track a moving subject, anticipating its location at the time of exposure. It has a wide-area, three-element array of focus sensors, sensitive to both horizontal and vertical subjects.

Exposure modes are program with shift, aperture and shutter priority AE, metered manual and TTL flash with auto fill flash, variable fill ratios and multi-strobe effects when using i-series flash units. The i-series Minoltas' hot shoes will accept only i-series flashes, although Minolta does make an adapter that will allow use of standard ISO flashes. Metering modes are six-zone multi-pattern and 2.3% spot, with standard centerweighted metering in the manual exposure mode. Shutter speeds range from 30 seconds to 1/4000, plus B, with X sync at 1/125.

Other features include exposure compensation, a standard PC socket, multi-exposure capability, DX film coding with manual override, a built-in motor drive with film advance speeds up to 3 fps, and auto film loading and rewind.

A feature introduced with the 7000i is Minolta's Creative Expansion Card library. The Creative Expansion Cards are plug-in modules that will customize the camera for fine-tuned control over such exposure situations as autobracketing, program shift, fantasy effects, data memory, highlight/shadow biasing and more.

Maxxum 5000i

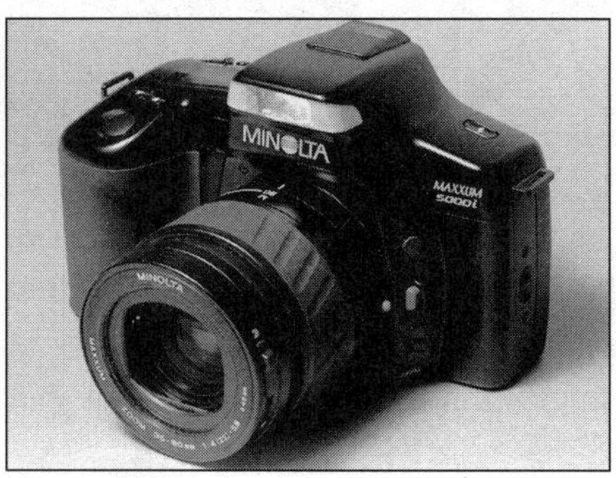

Maxxum 5000i

The 5000i is a scaled-down little brother to the 7000i with many of the same features. Its wide area array of focus sensors provide one standard autofocus mode: one-shot (focus priority). Continuous AF is possible with the "Sports Action" Creative Expansion Card. Its exposure modes include program and metered manual. Shutter and aperture priority AE modes are available with optional Creative Expansion Cards. Metering choices are two-zone evaluative in the program mode or centerweighted averaging in the manual mode. Shutter speeds range from 4 seconds to 1/2000, plus B with an elapsed-time indicator.

The 5000i has a built-in flash (GN 50 @ ISO 100) that fires only in low-light and backlit situations when in program and shutter-priority AE. It fires with every shutter release in aperture-priority AE and manual exposure modes (sounds like a bug in the software, doesn't it?). The camera has an i-series hot shoe that accepts only i-series units. As with the 7000i, it will take an adapter that will allow the user to mount standard ISO flash units. Flash sync occurs at 1/90.

Other features include the line of Creative Expansion Cards as mentioned with the 7000i above, AE lock, a self-timer and an integral motor drive with single frame advance, auto film loading and rewind. Film is DX coded with no override capability.

Maxxum 3000i

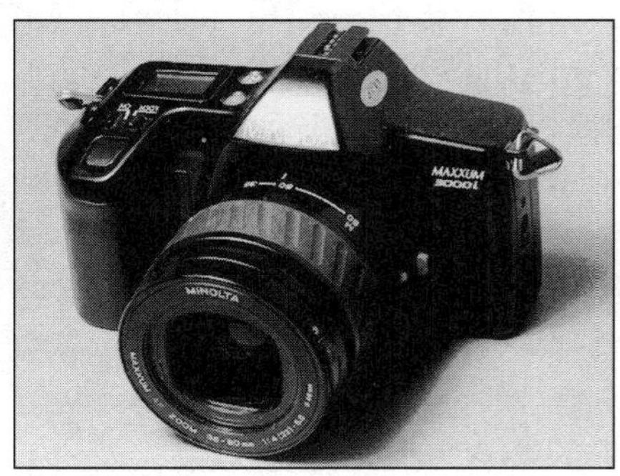

Maxxum 3000i

An even further simplified i-series camera, the 3000i is designed for the snapshot shooter who may wish to change lenses from time to time. Its wide-area AF sensor array provides one autofocus mode: one-shot (focus priority) with a limited predictive focusing capability. Metering modes are the same as those in the 5000i. It has two program modes: normal and high-speed program, but no manual exposure control. As with other i-series cameras, its hot shoe accepts only i-series flashes, but standard ISO units can be mounted with an optional adapter. Shutter speeds range from 4 seconds to 1/1000, with X sync at 1/60. Other features include a self-timer, integral motor drive with single frame advance, auto film loading and rewind.

Maxxum 8000i

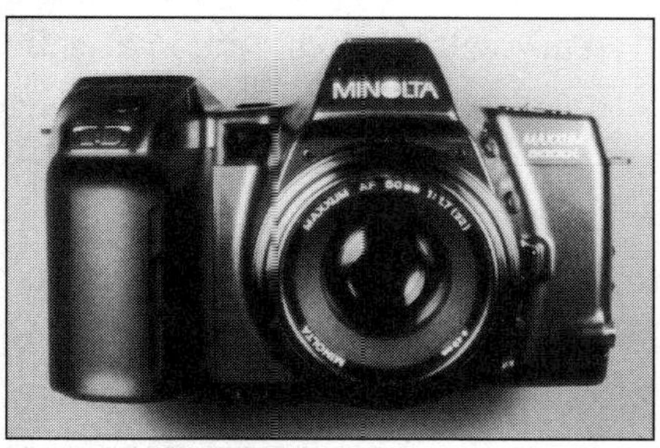

Minolta Maxxum 8000i

As if the 7000i didn't have enough souped up capabilities, Minolta introduced the 8000i to leave little room for doubt that they could still go head to head with Nikon and Canon. Targeted at the Nikon N8008, the Maxxum 8000i is similar to the 7000i with the following additional features:

The top shutter speed was boosted to 1/8000, with X sync at 1/200 (1/180 with non-Maxxum flash units). A new, on-demand centerweighted metering pattern was added, as was an AF lock button. The 8000i has a high-eyepoint finder, a handy feature for eyeglass wearers. User-redefined ISO settings can be entered for any given DX code. Thus, if you expose your Kodachrome 64 at EI 80, for example, you can change the DX setting on the camera so that you don't have to override the DX code manually every time you load a new roll — a nice feature.

Maxxum xi-series SLRs

The Maxxum 7000 was considered a pretty smart camera when it was released in 1985. Then along came the i-series Maxxums, where the "i" stood for "intelligence," and which were a whole lot smarter. The xi-series features what Minolta calls "expert intelligence," hence "xi." It makes one wonder what the next generation will bring. Omniscience, perhaps?

The following xi cameras are listed in numerical, rather than chronological order.

Maxxum 2xi

The littlest brother in the xi line to date, the Maxxum 2xi has enough features to keep most occasional photographers perfectly content. It is compact, lightweight and easy to use, yet contains the same fuzzy logic Expert Program routines that its more full-featured siblings have.

The 2xi's autofocus system uses a single wide-area CCD sensor to handle the focusing chores. The AF system will detect movement and switch automatically to the continuous focus mode, with predictive focus control.

Exposure modes include the following: Program AE, aperture and shutter-priority AE, and manual mode. The 2xi has two metering patterns: a seven-segment honeycomb pattern plus the background, and a spot meter, which uses the central honeycomb segment only. Shutter speeds range from 30 seconds to 1/2000 second. TTL flash exposure is also provided when a dedicated accessory flash is attached. An interesting flash option available with the 2xi is the slow shutter sync option. By depressing and holding the spot-metering button while taking the picture, a slower shutter speed will be used, thereby increasing exposure of the background — handy for night scenes when one wants background detail brought out.

Other features include auto film advance and rewind, mid-roll rewind, single-frame film advance, DX film coding with no override, and a cancelable self-timer.

Maxxum 3xi & SPxi

Although these two baby brothers to the 7xi have fewer features, the features they have still set them apart from almost all other current-technology AF SLRs. Both cameras are almost identical, except for the differences shown below.

The autofocus system uses a single, wide CCD (charge-coupled device) sensor, activated by the Eye Start feature (see the 7xi section for a description of Eye Start). Depending on subject movement, the system will select either single-shot (focus-priority) or Predictive Focus Control, and will switch automatically between the two modes should the subject move or stop.

An 8-segment honeycomb metering pattern (seven central segments plus the background) determines correct exposure and is the only metering mode in the 3xi. The SPxi has this, plus it also uses the center segment for a spot meter. Exposure modes available include Expert Intelligence program, aperture and shutter-priority AE, metered manual, and TTL flash using either the built-in flash on the 3xi (GN 39 @ ISO 100) or dedicated accessory units. The SPxi has no built-in flash. Shutter speeds range from 30 seconds to 1/2000 second, plus B, with x-sync at 1/90. Another feature supported by the

3xi and SPxi is Auto Stand-by Zoom (ASZ) (see the 7xi section for a description of ASZ).

Other features include DX coding with no override, a built-in winder that provides single-frame advance, auto film loading and rewind, and mid-roll rewind.

Maxxum 5xi

Just as the 7xi and 3xi replaced their respective i-series models, so does the 5xi replace the now-discontinued 5000i. And, like the 5000i, the 5xi fits squarely between the other two xi models in terms of price and features. The 5xi is housed in the same shell as the 3xi's, but has many more of the 7xi's features, and only weighs two ounces more than the 3xi.

The autofocus and exposure systems used in the 5xi are virtually identical to those found in the SPxi — single-shot, predictive autofocus, two metering modes (eight-segment evaluative and spot). Exposure modes available and shutter speed selections on the 5xi are the same as those found on the 3xi and SPxi.

As with other xi cameras, the 5xi supports the Eye-Start and Auto-Standby Zoom features when using xi lenses. The built-in winder can be set for either single-shot or continuous operation, and provides auto film loading and rewind, plus mid-roll rewind. DX coding is automatic, with no override. Many Creative Expansion cards can be used with the 5xi, some with only part of their features implemented. Some, like the function-change card, can't be used at all.

Now, for the new stuff: The 5xi is the first Maxxum camera with a built-in flash that pops up and fires automatically when needed and retracts when not needed. This flash also has a zooming feature, which covers lens focal lengths from 28mm to 85mm and greater. Further, the flash works as an AF illuminator in low light. The 3500xi flash can be used with the 5xi and can be triggered off-camera, without the use of a PC cord (maximum flash-sync shutter speed when doing this is 1/45 second).

Maxxum 7xi

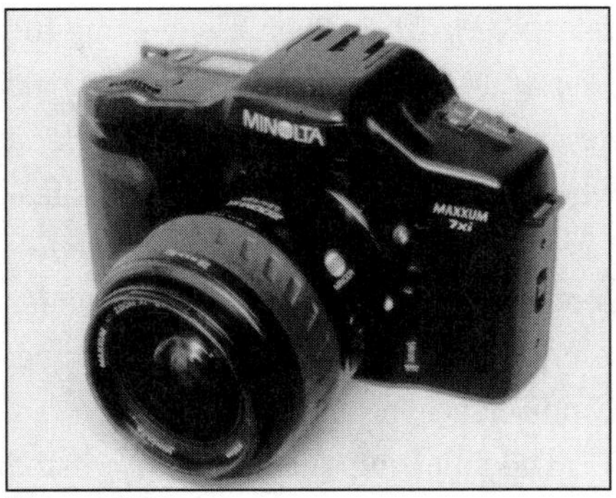

Maxxum 7xi

Minolta inserted a new term into the still photographer's lexicon when the Maxxum 7xi was released -- fuzzy logic. Already a familiar concept to many computer experts and camcorder users, fuzzy logic is a computer algorithm that differs from digital logic by allowing for gradations between the absolute states of on or off. Put in terms more amenable to the photographer, if we let "on" represent white and "off" represent black, then fuzzy logic can interpret the gray scale in between these two absolute values, whereas digital logic cannot (at least, not without lots of added subroutines and more memory requirements). Thus, by incorporating fuzzy logic into the 7xi, Minolta has come up with a memory-management scheme that makes much more efficient use of the camera's computer memory than would be possible using conventional digital logic alone. But, in order to make the most effective use of fuzzy logic with the camera's various "Expert" features, the Minds at Minolta knew a more powerful on-board computer would be needed. In 'computerese', the heavier requirements led to the adoption of a 16-bit CPU running at a clock speed of 20 MHz, with 64 kilobytes of ROM and 2 kilobytes of RAM. It wasn't that long ago when specs like these would have been impressive for a full-sized desktop computer. The 7000i, by comparison, sports an 8-bit 10.5 Mhz CPU, with only 20 kilobytes of ROM and 640 bytes of RAM. In plain English, the Maxxum 7xi has roughly four times the computing speed and three times the memory capacity of earlier i-series models.

According to Minolta, the Maxxum 7xi focuses twice as fast as its i-series predecessors. Partially responsible for this feat is its ultra wide angle phase-detection system, which has four high-density CCD sensors.

The 7xi's wide-area autofocusing system will switch automatically between sensors depending on subject location or movement. It will also switch sensors automatically to accommodate horizontal or vertical subjects. And, if the user desires, he or she may select any of the four sensors at any time. Autofocus modes are single shot (focus priority) and continuous predictive autofocus. Manual focus is assisted with a focus confirmation indicator in the viewfinder.

Like most other advanced AF SLRs, the 7xi will detect subject movement and switch automatically to continuous predictive autofocus. A system called Omnidirectional Predictive Focus Control will track a subject moving at variable rates of speed in three-dimensional space as fast as 187 miles an hour (that's 300 kilometers an hour for you metric-minded folks). What this means is that not only will the camera track fast-moving subjects, but it will track them as they accelerate, decelerate, change direction, or all of the above. Assuming *you* can track a subject with these kind of moves, you can get off more than one shot. The built-in motor drive will burn through a roll of film at the respectable rate of four frames a second.

Whether tracking a fast-moving subject or framing a carefully composed still life, the way an auto-exposure camera's meter responds to light is crucial. Thus, to accommodate most any exposure situation, the 7xi's meter employs a 14-zone honeycomb pattern (13 hexagonal segments plus the background). The 7xi's computer, using the fuzzy logic algorithm, determines the precise metering pattern and the weighting each of the 14 segments is given. The metering pattern and spot metering (the center hexagonal segment only) are available in all exposure modes, including manual.

To complement the 7xi's advanced metering capabilities, a variety of exposure modes are available. Perhaps the most significant of these is the Expert Program Selection mode. Exposure in this mode is determined based on a number of variables, including lens focal length, subject type, size, movement and distance from the camera. Expert program can be overridden to an "expert" aperture- or shutter-priority mode, which is really just a program shift feature but which allows the photographer to fine tune either shutter speeds or apertures without having to leave the program mode. Standard shutter and aperture-priority AE modes are also available, as is full-metered manual. Other exposure features include exposure compensation, an AE lock, and additional custom exposure control through the use of Minolta's Creative Expansion Cards.

Another feature introduced with the 7xi and unique to xi-series cameras, is the Eye-Start System, a feature which switches on the camera when you pick it up and activates several things at once when you bring it to your eye. Specifically, a pressure switch in the camera's grip detects when its been gripped, which triggers an infrared sensor at the eyepiece. When this sensor detects an object (your face, for example), the camera comes to life and, if you have an xi-series zoom attached, three things happen: the meter evaluates the scene, the AF system decides what your likely subject is and focuses on it, and the ASZ system (more on that in just a second) automatically zooms the lens to a starting focal length. If you're not prepared for all this the first time you pick up one of these cameras, having it suddenly spring to life in your hands can be a bit startling.

With an xi-series Autozoom lens attached to the 7xi, the user has four Expert Autozoom functions at his or her disposal: ASZ, APZ, Image Size Lock, and 150% Wide View Mode. ASZ (Auto-Standby Zoom), is automatically activated by the Eye-Start System, which selects a focal length based on subject distance. APZ (Auto Program Zoom), continuously sets focal length based on changing subject position (currently available only with the "Child" Creative Expansion Card). Image Size Lock is a continuous focal-length adjustment which maintains image size while a subject is moving. Wide-View Modeis a focal-length reset which allows viewing of 50% more of the picture area until the shutter release is pressed partway down.

Shutter speeds range from 30 seconds to 1/8000 second, plus B, and can be selected in half-stop increments. Flash sync tops out at 1/200 using either the built-in TTL flash (GN 40 @ ISO 100) or dedicated accessory units. Other features include DX film coding with override, a self-timer, a remote-control socket, auto film loading and rewind with mid-roll rewind. The built-in motor has single-frame, 2 fps and 4 fps settings.

Maxxum 9xi

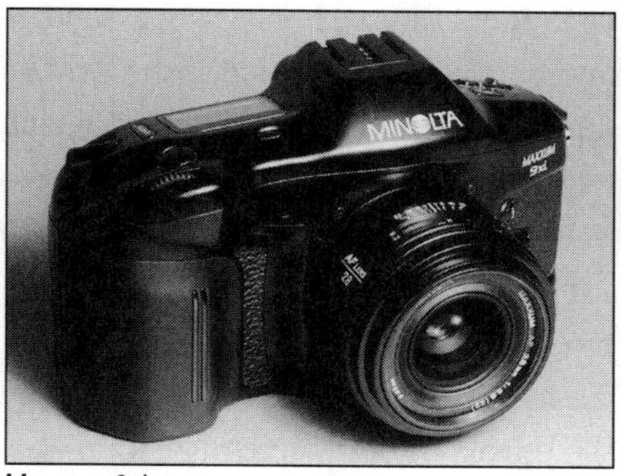

Maxxum 9xi

In the high-stakes game of hi-tech camera one-upsmanship, Minolta has put together another winning combination with the 9xi. While the rest of us waited for a 9000i replacement to the robust, but dated, Maxxum 9000, Minolta had other plans. Was the wait worth it? You be the judge. Instead of repeating all the details about Minolta's xi technology that have already been explained under the 7xi's heading, we'll take a look at what sets the 9xi apart from the other xi cameras — and other professional level SLRs.

First of all, almost all the features found on the 7xi exist on the 9xi. Only a few amateur oriented ones, such as the built-in pop-up flash and autozooming composition mode, have been dropped. While the body's styling is very close to that of the 7xi, there are both major and minor differences. Minor differences, such as the addition of leatherette coverings to the front, are a nice touch. Major differences are much more than cosmetic. The 9xi's body is made up of several durable sub-components. The mirror box is made from stainless steel and zinc, and is coupled to a cast zinc baseplate. Where polycarbonate is used, it is of the fiber-reinforced variety. The controls are well-sealed against moisture and dust intrusion.

The 9xi supplanted the 7xi as the fastest-focusing SLR in the industry (when it was introduced, but it has been edged out by the 700si). Although both the 9xi and 7xi share the same fuzzy logic autofocus technology, AF sensors and autofocus mechanisms, the 9xi has an improved mirror-return mechanism, which allows the 9xi to begin autofocusing between exposures sooner than the 7xi. As a direct result of this, the integral motor will burn through a roll of film at 4.5 frames per second when shooting in the predictive omnidirectional autofocus mode (the 7xi is good for "only" 4 fps when in this mode).

Because the 9xi performs autofocus with such speed, the default AF mode is focus priority; that is, the camera will not fire until the subject is in focus. This default can be overridden, however, by shutting off the camera, then depressing the self-timer button while turning the camera back on.

The 9xi is on the top of the technological heap in another category. Its highest shutter speed is 1/12,000 second and its highest flash sync speed is 1/300 second when using the 3500xi, the 5400xi, or the 5400HSS flash (1/250 second for non-dedicated flash units, including studio strobes). Its slowest shutter speed is 30 seconds.

Other features include a threaded PC sync terminal, a genuine depth-of-field preview lever, built-in eyepiece diopter correction, a variety of TTL flash options (including off-the-camera, cordless flash), and a "quick-adjust" button, which allows the user to customize override settings for the various controls.

Remember the EV locks found on older manual-exposure cameras and others like the Hasselblad? This same function is available at the touch of a button with the 9xi. You can change the shutter speed or aperture and its counterpart will follow along, providing you stay within available aperture or shutter-speed ranges.

The built-in motor drive has a high-speed rewind mode that will suck the leader back into a 36-exposure roll's cassette in under six seconds. A much quieter and only slightly slower rewind mode is also available for times when the high-speed mode's noise may be intrusive.

Five new Creative Expansion Cards were introduced with the 9xi: the Bracketing Card 2, the Auto Shift Card 2, the Sports Action Card 2, the Fantasy Effect Card 2 and the Memory Card 2. The Bracketing Card 2 allows for auto-bracketing of exposures with both ambient and flash, providing ⅓, ½ or full-stop exposure increments, and frame counts of 3, 5, or 7. The Auto Shift Card 2 is an automated "program shift" feature, allowing the user to fire off three frames at varying shutter-speed/aperture combinations, while retaining the same overall exposure. The Fantasy Effect Card 2 defocuses the lens during exposure, thereby providing a soft-focus effect. The Sports Action Card 2 biases the program toward higher, action-stopping shutter speeds. The Data Memory Card 2 will memorize up to four rolls of film's worth of exposure data, and will then play it back to the user via the LCD display.

Maxxum 700si

The 700si may still fall short of being omniscient, but Minolta is obviously working hard toward that ultimate goal. It is Minolta's fourth generation AF technology release. Instead of looking at the 700si as an entirely new camera, view it as a 7xi with a major facelift. It shrank a bit and even shed a little weight (four ounces, to be exact). Controls were rearranged for more logical placement; some being discarded altogether. Other controls were added, correcting a few minor but annoying oversights with the 7xi. Improvements in the image processing routines were made, as well, leading to even faster AF times than those of the 7xi and 9xi. However, the 700si lists for $100 more than the 7xi, with a street price of about $50 less than the 9xi as I write this, so it's my hunch that the 7xi will remain in production for a while yet. For the most part, it will be the differences between the 700si and 7xi that will be addressed in the following paragraphs.

Beginning with the Eye-Start system that was first introduced on the 7xi, the 700si now has an on-off switch for this feature. A good move, in my view, since I still find it unsettling to have a camera spring to life in my hands when I pick it up. Admittedly, though, this is only plainly noticeable when an xi-series zoom lens is attached to the camera.

The 700si's autofocus sensor array is the same as that used in the 7xi: Minolta's TTL phase-detection system with four CCD sensors. To let the user know which AF sensor is in use, or to toggle between the four, there is a new AF button located within easy reach of the right thumb on the camera back. Pushing the button will highlight the sensor in use. Holding it down while rotating the front control dial allows the user to select which sensor he or she would like to use. The built-in AF illuminator will automatically switch on in low-light or low-contrast situations to improve AF response times. Either focus-priority or release-priority is now available in all AF modes.

The 14-segment honeycomb metering pattern used in the 700si is identical to the 14-segment pattern used by the 7xi, except it would seem the background segment is now included as part of the metering area. Apparently that wasn't the case with the 7xi. The spot meter button has been relocated for greater ease of use to the right rear of the top deck, just above the AF button — an ideal placement when the shooter must take quick spot readings with a minimum of fuss. And, if you prefer to do things your own way, the 700si has an enhanced manual metering scale that shows the difference in exposure values between spot and centerweighted metering.

The built-in flash found atop the 700si (GN 39 in feet at ISO 100) has been improved to allow the use of 24mm wide-angle lenses (the widest coverage of any built-in flash). It does not pop up automatically as is the case with the 7xi, however. A flash button still exists, but instead of the flash head popping up, it forces the camera into fill-flash mode. Below the flash button is the button used for exposure bracketing. Normally this button will allow the user to fire off a three-shot bracket. But when it and the above button are pressed simultaneously, the camera will render a three-shot fill-flash bracket.

On the bottom right of the lens mount is another new and long-overdue feature: an electronically operated depth-of-field preview button. And yet another push-button control was added for the 700si's new "memory" feature: now you can store and retrieve a particular camera setting you might wish to save. Unfortunately, the 700si has only one level of memory storage. Among many other features available are ±3EV autoexposure bracketing in f-stop increments, multiple exposures, variable fill-flash, your choice of fast or quiet rewind modes, mid-roll rewind, and a frame counter in the viewfinder that counts down the last 9 frames.

Anyone who is considering buying a 700si should seriously consider purchasing the new 5400HS flash, as well. Actually, the 5400HS is such a versatile — and powerful — flash, that I wouldn't be surprised if many serious shooters will purchase a 700si just so they can use this flash. Why would I think this? Well, probably its most remarkable feature is its ability to provide flash sync at all shutter speeds, from 30 seconds to 1/8000 second (available only with the 700si). From 30 seconds to 1/200 second, flash sync is handled normally, but above 1/200 second, the HSS mode is used. While flash output is reduced in the HSS mode, for most work where it'll be used, the output should be sufficient. And speaking of output, the 5400HS is one of the most powerful shoe-mount flashes ever made. It has a very impressive guide number of 177 (in feet at ISO 100), which should be ample for most situations. It also has a built-in modeling light with two settings: one and four seconds. Another very handy feature is its wireless capability. With any si or xi camera, the 5400HS can be fired off-camera without having to worry about connecting cables. Other features include a multi-burst function to provide a strobe effect on a single exposure, two-way head pivoting, and bounce and zoom coverage from 24mm to 105mm.

Another accessory well worth considering is the VC700 vertical control grip. This handy add-on reorients the 700si's most important controls vertically so that they can be accessed easily when doing portraits and other vertical work. Relocated for easy vertical use are the shutter release, the front and rear control dials, and the AF and spot buttons. Added to the control grip is a PC terminal, just in case the photographer wishes to employ even more powerful flash units than the 5400HS. And should the situation ever arise where the VC700's controls become an intrusion, they can be activated or deactivated via an on/off switch. When the grip is attached, its battery supply is used to power the camera. Either a lithium battery or 4 AA-size alkalines or NiCads can be used. This feature alone will probably cause many folks to consider buying the grip, not so much because of the difference in price between AA's and lithium batteries (which can be substantial, by the way), but because of the much wider availability of AA's.

Maxxum 400si

The 400si is similar to the 700si in name only. These are two very different cameras that just happen to share a few common features. Obviously intended for the tyro on a budget, the 400si is still a very capable, full-featured camera, but it would be a mistake for one to think of it as a less-costly alternative to the 700si.

The 400si uses a single wide area CCD sensor and employs an AF system that switches between single-shot or continuous predictive AF automatically, depending upon subject movement. Manual focus is also available.

The 400si uses an eight-segment honeycomb metering pattern. Exposure modes include program AE, shutter- and aperture-priority AE, five preconfigured program modes (portrait, landscape, close-up, sports-action and night-portrait), and metered manual. Shutter speeds range from 30 seconds to 1/2000 second, plus B, with on-camera flash sync of 1/90 second (1/45 second using a wireless remote flash, such as the 5400HS).

The 400si's flash system includes a built-in pop-up flash (GN 39 @ ISO 100) that provides coverage down to 28mm and has a red-eye-reduction mode. The flash does not pop up and down automatically, however. There is also a hot shoe, if you prefer a more powerful external unit.

Following a trend that's becoming increasingly popular, the 400si does not use a traditional pentaprism, but a "penta-mirror" arrangement. The advantage is it saves weight. There is a slight amount of light loss when compared to the traditional pentaprism, but with today's bright focusing screens the amount is negligible.

Other features include a 10-second self-timer, DX film coding with no override, a built-in winder with auto film loading and rewind that provides single or continuous advance (up to 1 fps), mid-roll rewind and a non-interchangeable Acute-matte focusing screen.

Maxxum SLRs

Camera	Yrs. Made	New	Mint	Excellent	User
Maxxum SPxi	1991-	295 220			
Maxxum SPxi w/28-80, 2000xi flash.	1991-	485 370			
Maxxum SPxi w/35-80, 2000xi flash.	1991-	370 295			
Maxxum 2xi	1993-	225 165			
Maxxum 3xi	1991-	280 225	200 175		
Maxxum 5xi	1992-	425 350			
Maxxum 7xi	1991-	595 470	380. 340		
Maxxum 9xi	1992-	795 700			
Maxxum 400si	1994-	350 265			
Maxxum 700si	1994-	725 600			
Maxxum 3000i	1987-91		125 100		
Maxxum 5000	1986-88		160 145	135 115	
Maxxum 5000i	1989-91		210 190		
Maxxum 7000 crossed x's	1985-86		400 325	290 250	
Maxxum 7000	1986-88		185 160	150 125	
Maxxum 7000i	1987-91		270 250	250 220	
Maxxum 8000i	1990-91		450 400	370 340	
Maxxum 9000	1986-90		390 300	320 250	

Maxxum Autofocus Lenses

Lens	New	Mint	Excellent	User
16mm f/2.8	900 730	500 395		
20mm f/2.8	550 425	420 385	350 340	
20mm f/2.8 N	625 540			
24mm f/2.8	420 340	220 180	200 180	
28mm f/2.0	520 350		310 280	
28mm f/2.8	240 175	110 95	95 80	
35mm f/1.4	995 800	625 550	575 470	
35mm f/2	320 225	200 180		
50mm f/1.4	295 220	125 100	115 90	
50mm f/1.7	120 80	55 45	45 35	
50mm f/2.8 Macro (early)		250 225	220 185	
50mm f/2.8 Macro (late)				
50mm f/3.5 Macro	280 210			
85mm f/1.4		450 410	400 340	
85mm f/1.4 N	780 360			
100mm f/2	520 400	290 250	240 180	
100mm f/2.8 Macro w/1:1		430 420		
100mm f/2.8 Macro w/1:1 (late)	625 560			
135mm f/2.8	170 120	125 85	90 70	
200mm f/2.8 APO			600 420	
200mm f/2.8 APO (late)	1100 830			
300mm f/2.8 APO		2500 2400	2350 2200	
300mm f/2.8 APO (late)	4200 3700	2650 2500		
500mm f/8 Reflex	595 485			
600mm f/4 APO		3800 3500		
600mm f/4 APO (late)	7550 7100			
1.4X APO		250 200		
1.4X APO-II	470 340			
2X APO		270 225		
2X APO-II	490 350			
MA-S or -L 2X (MD to Maxxum)	160 120	100 80		
3X-1X Macro Zoom	2100 1700			

Maxxum Autofocus Zoom Lenses

Lens	New	Mint	Excellent	User
24-50 f/4	425 300	260 200		
28-85 f/3.5-4.5		200 175	160 140	
28-105 f/3.5-4.5	320			
28-135 f/4-4.5		315 245	250 215	
35-70 f/3.5-4.5	130			
35-70 f/4		125 110	100 85	
35-105 f/3.5-4.5		200 180	170 140	
70-210 f/4		150 120	125 90	
70-210 f/4.5-5.6	185 130			
75-300 f/4.5-5.6	500 280	300 240	250 180	
80-200 f/2.8 APO		880 750	700 600	
80-200 f/2.8 Super H.S. APO	1495 1200			
100-200 f/4.5		100 80		
100-300 f/4.5-5.6 APO	580 460			

Maxxum i-Series Autofocus Lenses

Lens	New	Mint	Excellent	User
24-85 f/3.5-4.5	550 420			
28-70 f/2.8	1250 980			
28-80 f/4-5.6	260 200			
28-85 f/3.5-4.5	420 300			
35-80 f/4-5.6	160 115	120 80		
35-105 f/3.5-4.5	300 195	180 140		
70-210 f/3.5-4.5	320 230			
70-210 f/4.5-5.6	200 130			
80-200 f/4.5-5.6	220 170	150 125		
100-300 f/4.5-5.6	380 275	245 200	210 180	

Maxxum xi-Series Autofocus Lenses

Lens	New	Mint	Excellent	User
28-80 f/4-5.6	230 170			
28-105 f/3.5-4.5	400 310			
35-80 f/4	140 110			
35-200 f/4.5-5.6	620 540			
80-200 f/4.5-5.6	240 175			
100-300 f/4.5-5.6	400 310			

Maxxum Accessories

Item	New	Mint	Excellent	User
MD-90 Motor Drive only	250 220	200 160	150 125	
MD-90 w/BP-90M	370 310	270 250	250 220	
MD-90 w/NP-90M	440 380	330 275	290 250	
AW-90 Autowinder	180 155	140 115	120 85	
External Battery Pack Ep-70	60 40			
Battery Pack B (9xi)	95			
Holding Strap 9xi	70			
Holding Strap 7xi	40			
Holding Strap 7000i/8000i	30			
Data Back DB-3/DB-5/DB-7 (i-series)	80 75			
Data Back 70 (5000/7000)		50 40		
Data Back QD-7	80			
Data Back QD9xi	80			
Program Back PB-7 (7000i/8000i)	180 150			
Program Back 70 (5000/7000)		140 120	100 70	
Program Back Super 70 (7000)		255 225	225 185	

MINOLTA

Maxxum Accessories

Item	New		Mint		Excellent		User	
Program Back 90	215	150	150	125	120	90		
Program Back Super 90	340	295	255	180	185	160		
EB-90 100-frame Back (9000)	930	840						
Film Magazine Set for EB-90	300	225						
FL-90 Film Loader for EB-90	220	160						
NPC or Forscher Polaroid Back	750	650	500	400				
Creative Expansion Cards	35	25						
AF Extension Tube 25		70						
Macro Stand 1000	265	190						
Slide Copy Unit 1000	275	220						
IR-1n Set	265	190						
RC1000L	55	35						
RC1000S	55	35						
Panorama Set	55	35						

Maxxum Flashes

Item	New		Mint		Excellent		User	
D314i	55	35						
D316i	80	55	45	35				
1200AF Macro			250	210				
1200AF-N Macro (i/xi-series)	395	320						
1800AF	85	65	55	45	45	35		
2000i	95	70						
2000xi	105	65						
2800AF	120	90	85	65	70	50		
3200i	130	105						
3500xi	220	150						
4000AF			170	150	140	110		
5200i			200	160				
5400xi	295	265						
5400 HS	420	320						
EP-1 Set External Battery Pack	190	130						
TC-1000 Triple Connector	55	35						
Off-Camera Cable OC-1100	50	30						
Off-Camera Shoe OS-1100	50	30						
FS-1100 Shoe	45	25						
FS1200 Shoe	45	25						
Wireless Remote Flash Controller	145	100						
Control Grip CG-1000 Set (2800AF/4000AF)	220	175	155	135	145	120		
VC-700 Grip	200	140						

Nikon

Explanatory notes for Nikon cameras are grouped by series. F-series cameras (F, F2, F3 and F4) are grouped at the beginning, followed by the Nikkormats (including the Nikon EL2), compact Nikons (FE/FE2, FG/FG-20/EM, FM/FM2/FM2n), and finally, the N-series (N2000/2020, N4004/4004s, N5005, N6000/6006, N8008/N8008s and N90).

Nikon F-Series Cameras

All Nikon F-Series Cameras, from the original, meterless, mechanical F of 1959 to the high-tech marvel F4 of 1989, have a few things in common. All are system cameras, meaning each model has interchangeable viewfinders, focusing screens, backs, and motor drive capabilities. All have a mirror lock-up feature. They provide 100% image visibility within the viewfinder. And, of course, all accept the F-type bayonet mount lenses.

The Nikon F

The original Nikon F was introduced in 1959. In its various derivations, the F was in production for fifteen years with over a million units produced. Nikon had already assembled a loyal following of professionals with their fine line of rangefinder cameras by the time the F was introduced. But it was the F, with its system concept and robust construction — along with a healthy dose of shrewd marketing — that was largely responsible for earning Nikon its world-wide reputation as a builder of rugged, professional quality equipment — a reputation that has endured for over thirty-five years.

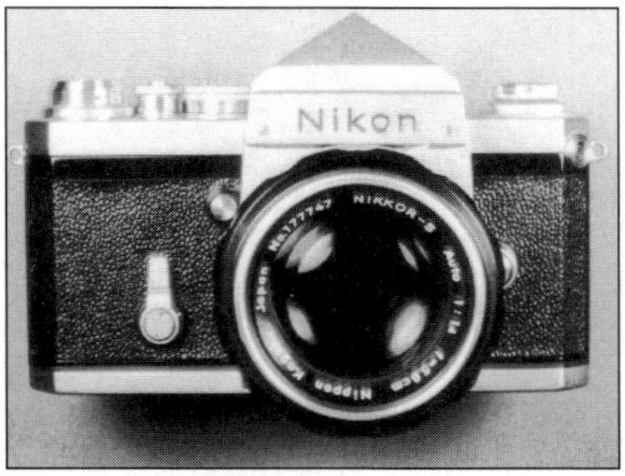

Nikon F with standard prism

There have been many misconceptions about the serial numbering system Nikon instituted with the F and continued with the F2. This misconception often leads to misunderstandings and warrants clarification, so that which follows is a brief explanation: Serial numbering for the Nikon F began at 6400001. During the mid-to-late 1960's, as a matter of coincidence, the first two digits of the serial numbers began to approximate the years of manufacture. Some people say that when this took place, Nikon adopted it into their numbering process and from then on the first two digits of a camera's serial number reflected its year of manufacture. Others claim that the serial number on a later camera could differ by as much as a couple of years from the actual date of manufacture. Either way, there is no disputing the fact that the numbers remained close, and it does seem probable that once the coincidence occurred there was some intentional design on Nikon's part to keep the numbers close to the year of manufacture.

One thing to be aware of is that many used camera dealers price their Nikon Fs (and F2s) according to these first two digits, due to the assumption that later models will have experienced less use and also because very early Fs are becoming collectible. So, all else being equal, expect to pay a little more for later model Fs (especially those that came from the factory with F2-style film advance and self-timer levers) and expect to pay a lot more for Fs with very low serial numbers.

Exposure metering with the Nikon F is handled by the viewfinder, so it's common to see early model bodies with late model finders. The derivations of the Nikon F are determined by its viewfinder. For those of you who may not know the differences between them, they are:

NIKON

The **meterless F** has the standard, traditional-looking, pentaprism-shaped viewfinder with a large "F" inscribed on the front.

The **F Photomic**, introduced in 1962, has a large, non-TTL finder with a round meter window in front of the shutter speed dial. An angle of acceptance restrictor and an incident light attachment came with the finder when new. Either one or both can be threaded into the meter window for use. When not in use, they are threaded into the finder's side, one on top the other. It is not unusual to find Fs with early Photomic meters that are missing these accessories.

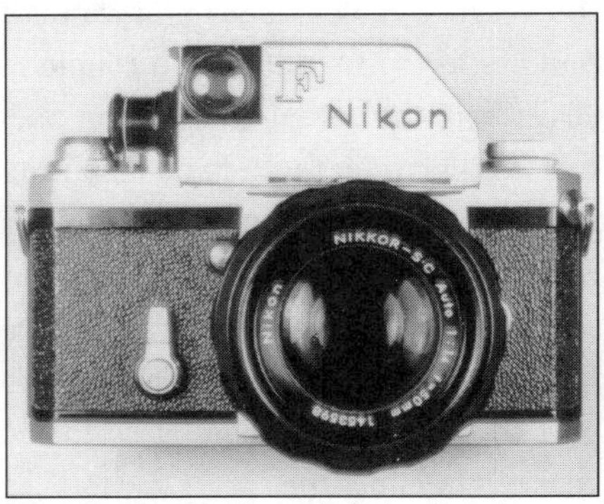

Nikon F with early Photomic finder. Note the round meter window. Also note the angle of acceptance restrictor mounted to the side of the finder.

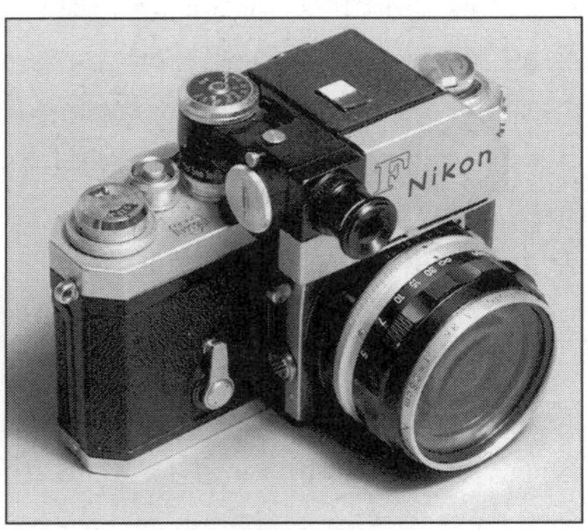

Nikon F with early Photomic finder showing the angle-of-acceptance restrictor positioned for use.

The **F Photomic T**, introduced in 1965, has a finder with a TTL meter (Nikon's first) that is a little smaller than the early Photomic finder and lacks the round window.

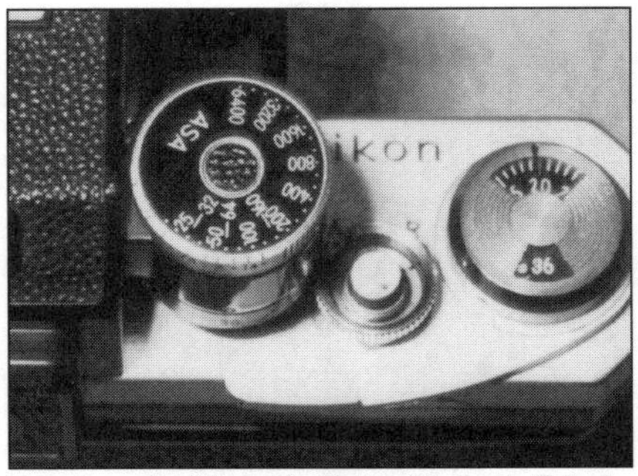

Top view of a Nikon F with the Photomic T finder. Note the aperture numbers on the side of the ASA setting dial.

The **F Photomic Tn,** introduced in 1967, looks like the F Photomic T, but performs centerweighted metering and has an "N" on the top of the finder just below the meter on-off button.

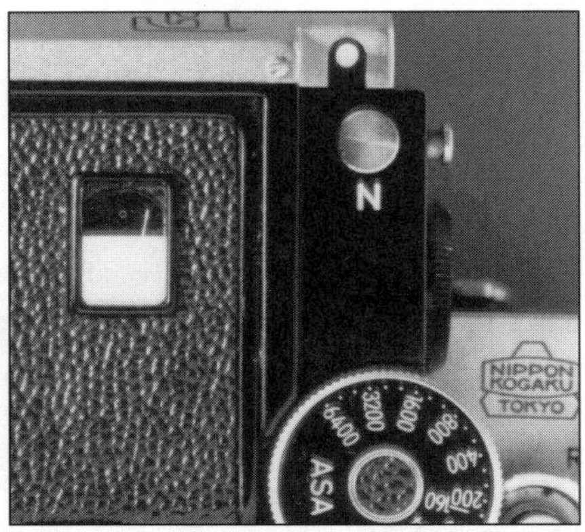

Top view of a Nikon F with the Photomic Tn finder. Note the 'N' just below the meter on/off button.

Lastly, the **F Photomic FTn**, introduced in 1968, provides semi-automatic maximum aperture indexing, done by rocking the aperture ring back and forth. It can be identified easily by the short aperture index slot located on the front face of the viewfinder with the numbers 5.6 — 2.8 — 1.2 above it. This is also the only F finder that displays shutter speeds in the viewfinder. Of all the metered finders for the F, the FTn finder is, by far, the most popular and the most useful. With earlier finders, the photographer had to readjust the ASA dial each time he or she changed lenses of a different maximum aperture so they would index correctly with the meter.

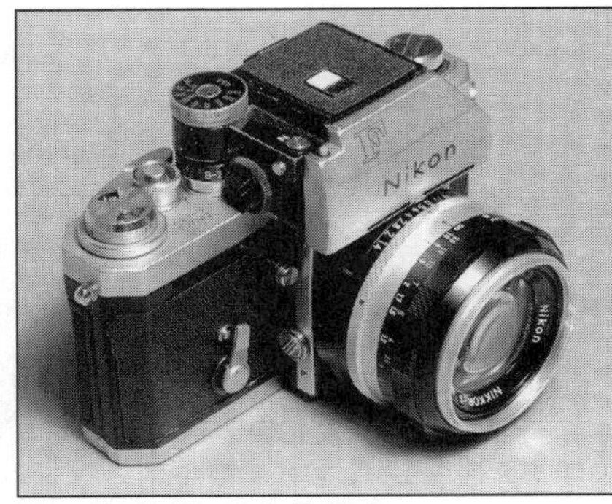

Nikon F with Photomic Tn finder

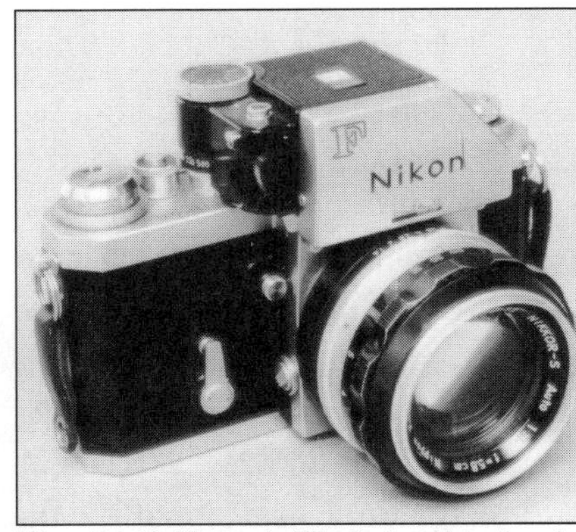

Nikon F with Photomic FTn finder. Note the short aperture slot with numbers 5.6—2.8—1.2 above.

The metered F finders have proven themselves to be generally accurate and reliable, but they do wear out after lots of use. When trying out an F's meter, rotate the aperture ring or shutter speed dial while keeping the viewfinder centered on a well-lighted subject. Observe the needle. It should track smoothly from one end of its range to the other. If it quivers or jumps, chances are the variable resistor inside the finder is either dirty or scratched. If it's scratched the problem will deteriorate. If it's dirty and not cleaned promptly, the dirt could scratch the resistor and...well, you get my drift. This procedure for checking the meter applies not only to the F, but to the various F2 metered finders and to mechanical Nikkormats, as well. Nowadays, there are lots of dead F Photomic meters out there and parts for them are from scarce to impossible to come by. So test before you buy and buy with caution.

A couple of other aspects of Nikon Fs bear mentioning. The first has to do, once again, with finders. If you have an early F and wish to mount a later style finder on the camera, a slight modification will be required if it hasn't already been done. It involves a little bit of grinding that any qualified repair technician can do in a few minutes for a nominal charge. The second has to do with adapting a motor drive, such as the F-36, to the camera. Two small holes must be drilled into the inside baseplate of the camera. Only a small number of Fs came from Nikon predrilled, so if your camera has never had a motor drive attached, chances are the necessary holes aren't there. Most any qualified repair technician can do this in minutes for a nominal charge.

In addition to the metering options discussed above, the Nikon F's basic features include: shutter speeds ranging from 1 second to 1/1000, plus B and T, with X sync at 1/60; depth-of-field preview; mirror lock-up; a self-timer; interchangeable focusing screens, viewfinders and backs; and a motor drive option.

The Nikon F2

The Nikon F2, billed by Nikon as an improved version of the original F during its 1971 debut, was in reality a totally new design. Many regard the F2 as the finest mechanical 35mm SLR ever built. It was Nikon's last hand-built camera. Clean examples are highly prized and much sought after. This may explain why some later models of the F2 now command higher prices on the used market than the F3 in equivalent condition.

The serial numbering system that evolved with the F continued with the F2, which allows one to arrive at its approximate date of manufacture by looking at the first two digits. It should be reemphasized that this method only approximates years of manufacture. The most convincing argument in favor of this view is based on Nikon's later habit of coordinating serial numbers with trim. F2s displaying serial numbers beginning with 74, 76, 78 and 80 have chrome trim, whereas F2s having serial numbers beginning with 75, 77 and 79 have black trim. It seems highly unlikely that Nikon would have devoted an entire year's production to only one type of finish. Earlier F2s having serial numbers beginning with 71, 72 and 73 can be either black or chrome. It seems likely that these cameras' serial numbers more closely approximate their actual years of manufacture than later ones do.

The F2, like the F, depends on the viewfinder that is attached for its exposure metering options, and it is the meter that determines the model (e.g., an F2 with a DP-1 finder is an F2 Photomic). Also, as with the F, it is not uncommon to see earlier F2s with late model finders, especially the DP-11 (F2A) and DP-12 (F2AS) finders.

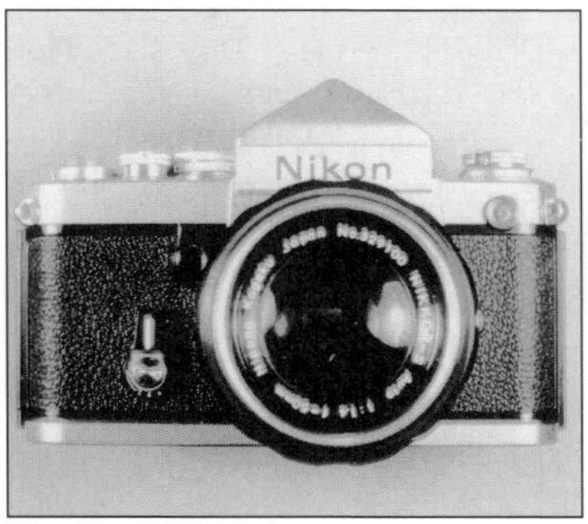

Nikon F2 with DE-1 finder

When first introduced, the F2 was available in two models: the **standard F2** (meterless DE-1 eye-level finder), and the **F2 Photomic** (DP-1 finder). The latter provides TTL full-aperture 60/40 center-weighted metering with the shutter speeds, aperture and meter needle shown in the viewfinder.

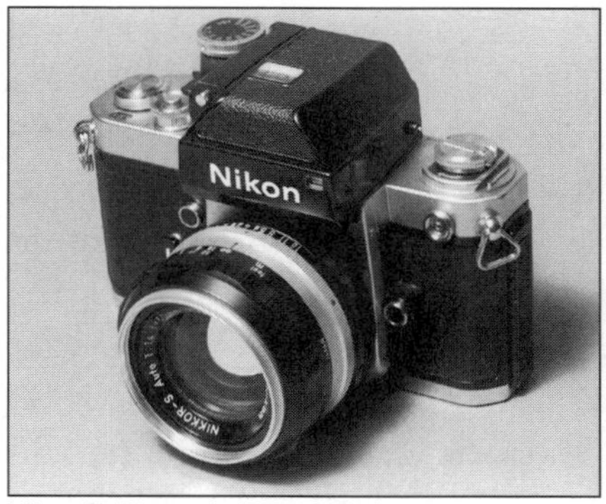

Nikon F2 Photomic (DP-1 finder)

The **F2 Photomic S** (DP-2 finder) was introduced in 1973. The three principal differences between the F2S and the F2 Photomic were: 1. The addition of a slow-speed ring above the shutter speed ring, which, when engaged, allows the DP-2 to meter down to 10 seconds. 2. Nikon had caught LED fever by then and substituted the meter needle for two LEDs. When both are lit, exposure is correct. 3. The addition of a coupler for the EE Aperture Control Attachment DS-1 or DS-2, which allowed the camera to be used in shutter-priority AE. The DP-2 finder also developed a strange hump on top to house the LEDs.

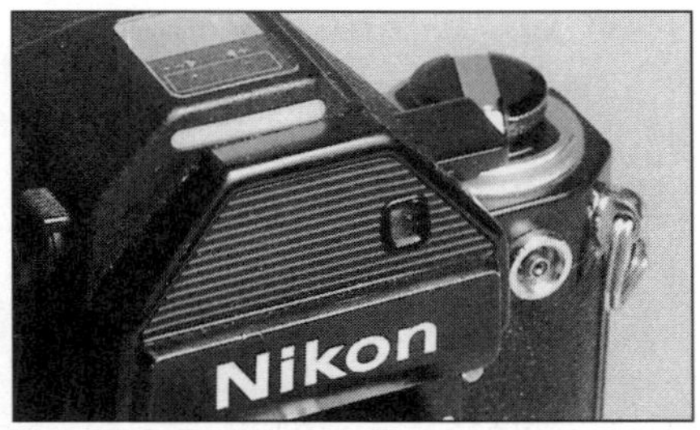

Nikon F2S (DP-2 finder). Note the aperture index window above the small 'n', the coupling attachment for the DS-1 or DS-2 (right side), and the hump.

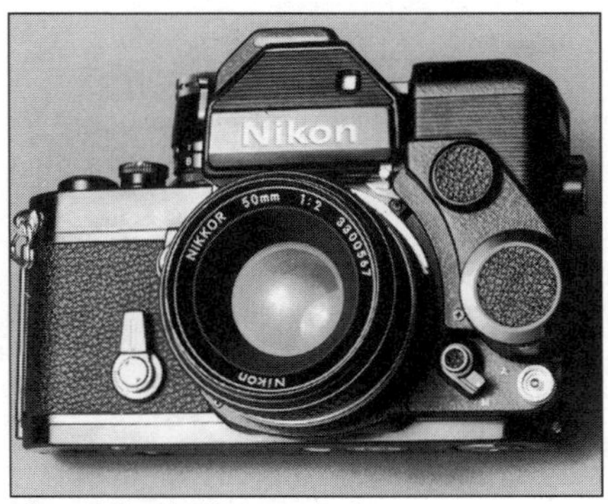

Nikon F2S with DS-2 attached

In 1976, Nikon refined the F2S and called it the **F2 Photomic SB** (DP-3 finder). The F2SB differs from the F2S in several areas, the most useful being an easier-to-use 3-LED readout in the viewfinder in the shapes of a minus sign, a zero and a plus sign. Obviously, the minus sign indicates underexposure, the plus sign indicates overexposure and the zero indicates correct exposure. Silicon photodiode metering cells were incorporated into the DP-3 for faster metering response, as was an eyepiece shutter. Nikon also got rid of the hump. The slow speed metering ring and provision for the DS-1 or DS-2 were retained.

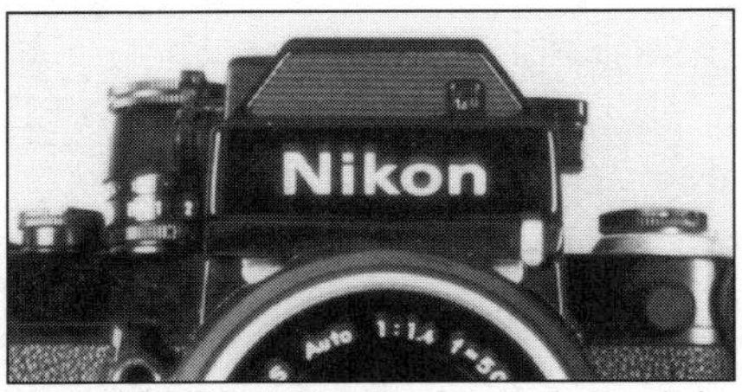

Nikon F2SB (DP-3). Note the aperture index window above the second 'n' and the coupling attachment for the DS-1 or DS-2 (right side).

The **F2 Photomic A** (DP-11 finder), introduced in 1977, was the first Nikon to allow automatic indexing (AI) of the lens' maximum aperture. The F2A's appearance is very close to that of the original F2 Photomic, but can be told apart easily by the small white "A" at the lower right front of the viewfinder just above the AI coupling lever. The F2 Photomic A has no provisions for attaching the DS-1 or DS-2.

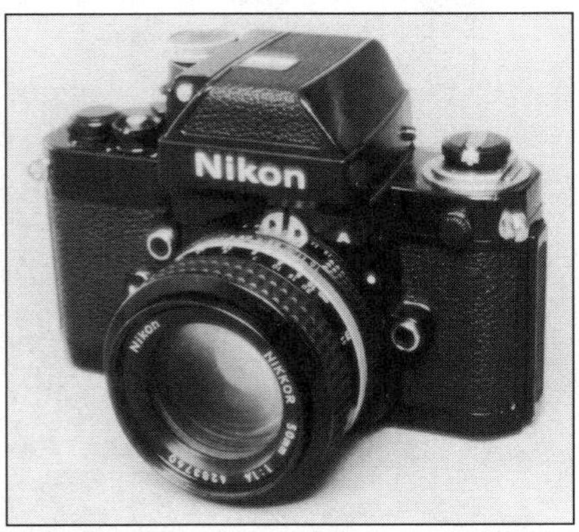

Nikon F2A (DP-11 finder). Note the 'A' at the bottom right hand corner of the finder.

Nikon's last variant of the F2, the **F2 Photomic AS** (DP-12 finder), also introduced in 1977, is the AI version of the F2SB. Like the F2A, the F2AS can be identified by the white "AS" located above the AI coupling lever. Shutter-priority AE is possible with the F2AS when using the Aperture Control Attachment DS-12.

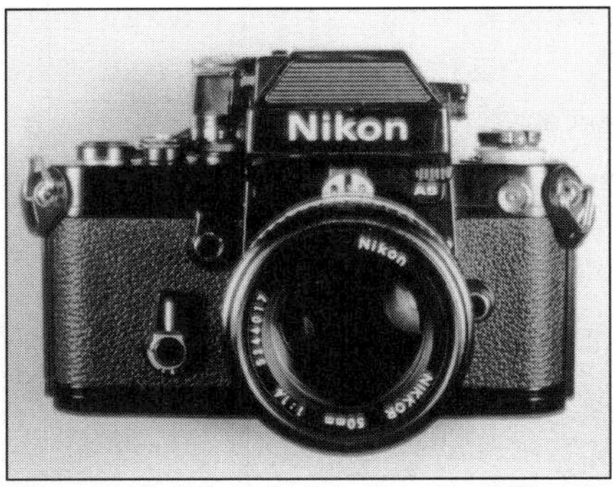

Nikon F2AS (DP-12 finder). Note the 'AS' at the bottom right hand corner of the finder and the attachment for the DS-12 (right side).

Nikon also built a few **F2Ts**. The T stands for titanium. The F2T came with a standard eye level prism, which was made from titanium as were the top plates and base plate. The F2T was produced in two models, the more common of the two apparently intended for use by the Japanese press corps. It seems some excess F2Ts were shipped to the U.S. and Canada. The other model, known as the F2 Titan, is much more rare. I've only seen one of these beauties. It had a textured matte black finish and the word Titan was engraved in script on the front left (facing the camera). The Titan was a special model built in small numbers for NASA. A few have made their way out into the public sector and, when they appear on the used market, command prices as astronomical as their originally intended destination.

The F2T is built like a tank and is the ultimate photographic workhorse. Even the pedestrian variety is somewhat rare and expensive. I haven't listed prices for the F2 Titan because of its rarity, and because prices for rare pieces like the Titan are usually determined entirely by one party's eagerness to buy and the other party's lack of eagerness to sell.

In addition to the various finders discussed above, other features of the Nikon F2 include: shutter speeds ranging from 1 second to 1/2000, plus B, with X sync at about 1/90 (it's an intermediate setting between 1/60 and 1/125); interchangeable finders, focusing screens (interchangeable with those used in the F) and backs; depth-of-field preview; mirror lock-up; a variable self-timer that's good for more than just delaying the shutter; and an optional choice of three different motor drives.

Here's something I'll bet many of you who have F2s and have used them for years may not know, especially if your camera does not have a finder with low light metering capability (DP-2, DP-3 or DP-12). The Nikon F2 is possibly the only mechanical 35mm SLR with slow shutter speeds that will go all the way down to 10 seconds. "Wait a minute!" you say. "The shutter speed dial's slowest setting is 1 second!" You'd think so, wouldn't you? But with the Nikon F2, the slowest shutter speed on your dial is accessed from the B setting. And, no, I'm not talking about tripping the shutter with a cable release and counting "one thousand one, one thousand two…"

Lets say, just for the sake of this discussion, you have absolutely no rhythm (either that or you can't count to eight), but you want to take an eight second exposure of a dimly-lit scene. Set your shutter speed dial to B and the collar surrounding the shutter release to T (*See* Illustration 1). Advance the self timer to the 8 second mark (*See* illustration 2). Then, trip the shutter using a cable release. (Do not push the button above the self-timer; as this will cause the self-timer to work in its usual fashion.) The shutter opens and the self-timer activates, timing out eight seconds. When the self-timer finishes, the shutter closes. Presto! A mechanical, eight-second exposure.

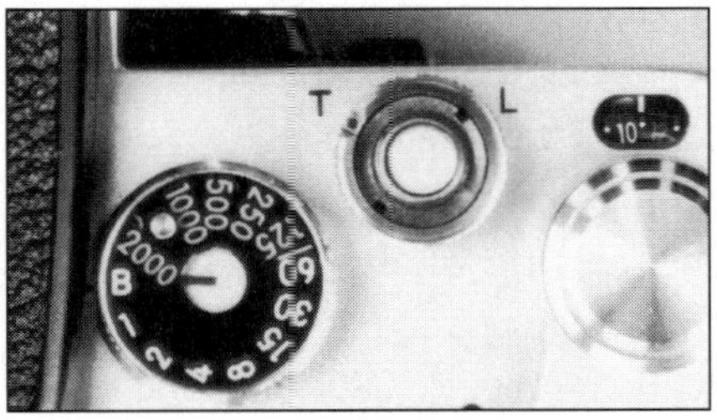

Illustration 1

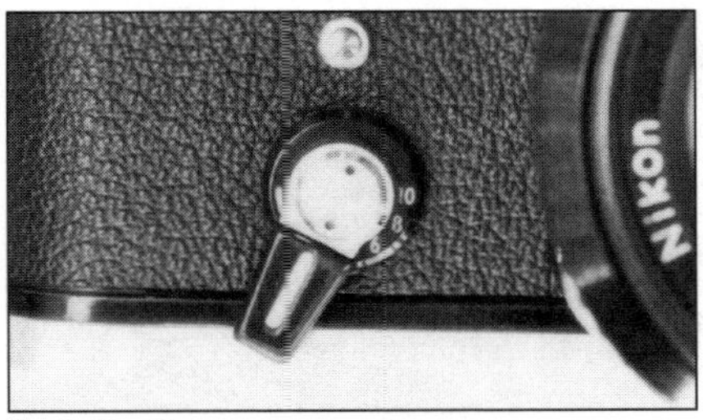

Illustration 2

For those of you who do have one of the finders with low-light metering ability, you may be nodding your head right about now and thinking, "So that's what that slow speed ring is for."

The Nikon F3

Although the F3 designation may lead the uninformed to believe that this camera was a continuation of the traditions set by its mechanical predecessors, one who is better informed might at best reply, "Well, maybe…" This is not meant to belittle the F3. An excellent camera it is, but, when introduced, it did represent a departure in Nikon's approach toward professional cameras. Many pros took a dim view initially to the battery-dependent F3 (okay, so you still have B and 1/80 without the battery, but that's not much of a selection) and took to hoarding F2s. Many still do. In the ensuing years, however, the F3 has proven its ability to take the hard use a professional camera is often subjected to, such that most pros have come to rely on it, although they'd sooner be caught with an expired passport than be without spare batteries.

The F3 offers several niceties that earlier F-series cameras did not, such as TTL flash automation, both aperture priority AE and metered manual exposure modes, an AE lock, exposure compensation, a six frame per second motor drive option, which will power the camera in the event of battery failure, and an exposure meter built into the body instead of the viewfinder. The **F3HP,** released in 1982, offers greater ease of use for eyeglass wearers by allowing one inch of eye-relief from the viewfinder while still providing total visibility of the viewing area and viewfinder exposure information.

Besides the standard F3 and the F3HP, Nikon makes or has made other models: the **F3AF**, the **F3P**, and the **F3T**.

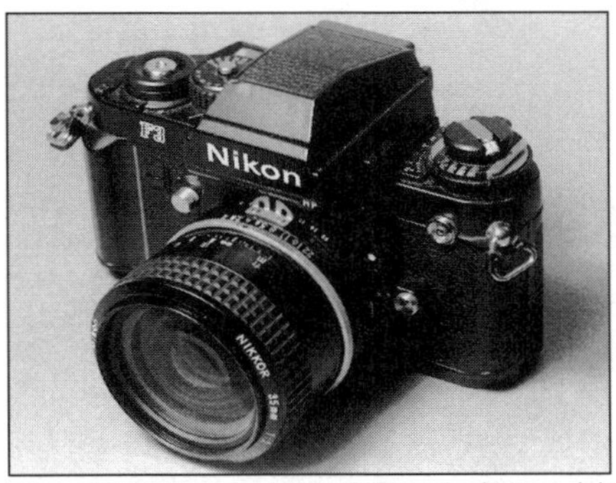

Nikon F3HP. Note the letters 'HP' on the bottom right of the finder.

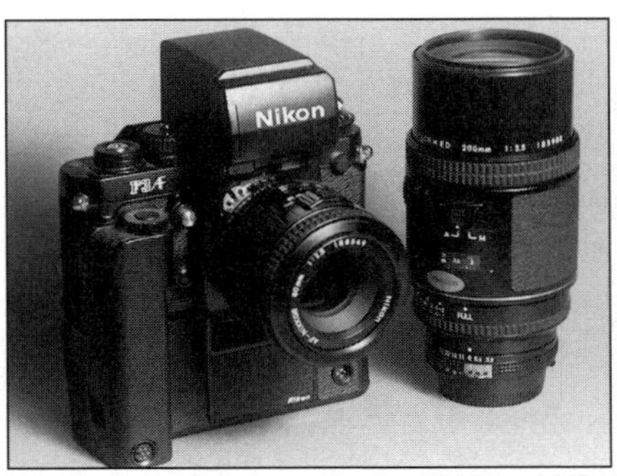

Nikon's first autofocus outfit: the F3AF and MD-4 motor drive with the 80mm f/2.8 AF and 200mm f/3.5 ED AF lenses.

The **F3AF** debuted in 1983 and was an early attempt at autofocus. Its autofocus system provides continuous focusing only, and is housed entirely in the removable finder, which results in a very large finder and a top-heavy-looking camera. Unlike other autofocus Nikon SLRs, the F3AF does not autofocus by using a mechanical drive coupling between camera and lens. Instead, focus information is communicated by a series of electrical contacts in the base of the finder through a set of pin contacts in the camera body to electrical contacts on the two autofocus lenses made for this camera. These lenses, the AF 80mm f/2.8 and the AF 200mm f/3.5, contain their own drive motors and will autofocus on the F3AF only (power for the motors is supplied by two AAA batteries housed in the finder). The F3AF accepts manual focus lenses and provides focus confirmation with lenses of f/3.5 and faster maximum apertures. Standard F3 finders can be used on the F3AF and the F3AF finder (DX-1) can be used on a standard F3. It will provide focus confirmation, but not autofocus.

The **F3P** is the "professional" model F3HP. Many people find this designation confusing since the F3 is supposedly a professional camera. It turns out the F3 often becomes temperamental in the damp and just flat refuses to work in very cold weather. It has to be "winterized" to work properly. Nikon's answer to this problem was the F3P, conceived plainly with the idea of inclement weather in mind.

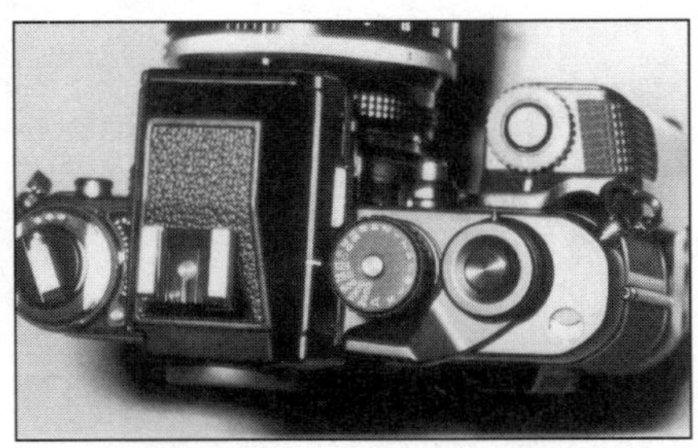

Nikon F3P with MD-4 motor drive attached. Note: non-TTL hot shoe on finder, no self timer switch, no cable release socket on shutter release, redesigned on/off switch, restyled frame counter, and no multiple exposure lever.

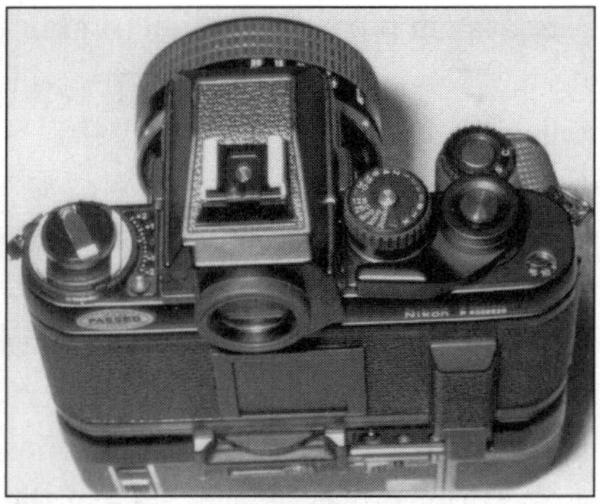

Nikon F3P rear view. Note the serial number and the MF-6B back (standard).

It is thoroughly gasketed against moisture intrusion. The shutter speed dial is oversized and the main on-off switch was redesigned, both changes made for ease of operation with gloved hands. The cable release socket was eliminated, as was the self-timer and the multiple-exposure lever. One nice addition is a hot shoe atop the removable finder (although it's non-TTL). The camera comes standard with the MF-6B back, which leaves the film leader protruding from the film cassette after power-rewinding the film with the MD-4 motor drive. Many pros grouse that this camera is the F3 Nikon should have built from the beginning. Did Nikon take this well-meaning criticism to heart? Apparently not. The camera was discontinued in 1989.

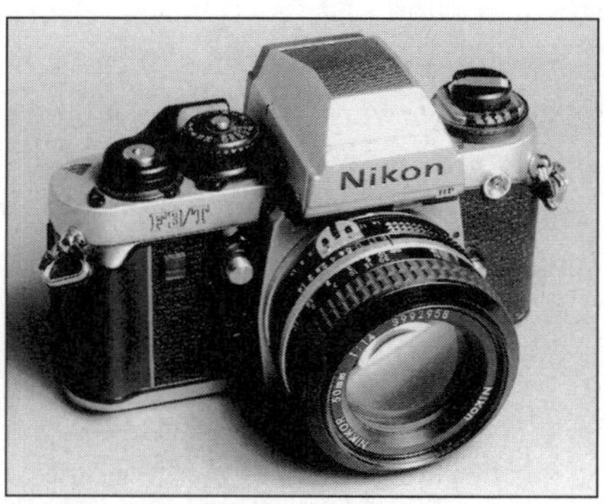

A pre-war Nikon F3T Champagne

The **F3T** is an F3HP housed in Titanium. It has been produced in two color schemes: standard black and champagne. The champagne model's top plate, bottom plate and finder are a muted pink chrome color. That's right, pink. If you've never seen one, trust me, the camera looks much better than it sounds. In fact, the champagne F3 is the more durable of the two cameras, because there is no paint to chip or wear off. I once came across a few champagne F3Ts that were veterans of several years of heavy press corps duty. It was obvious they had been used heavily because of the deep wear they exhibited. But, amazingly enough, not one had a dent or ding anywhere! When Nikon says in the brochure, "Bump it. Bang it," they aren't kidding.

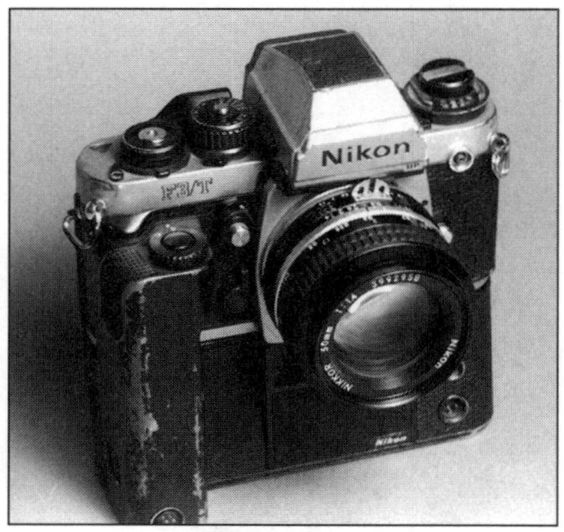

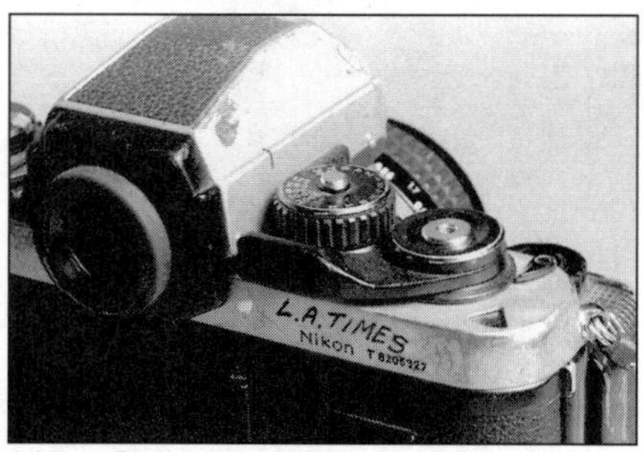

A Nikon Champagne F3T veteran of the press corps wars, complete with an equally battle-scarred MD-4 motor drive. Note the engraving.

Now that the F4 has been out for a while and working professionals have begun to rely on its impressive capabilities, many are dumping their F3s. And even though a new F4 commands a price fifty percent more than a new F3, for every pro who sells or trades in his or her F3, there is probably a dozen amateurs doing the same thing. This activity has resulted in a deluge of F3s on the used market. Despite the fact that the F3 is still available new at record high prices, it is so plentiful on the used market that used prices have dropped substantially for the more common models (F3 and F3HP). Nikon says it will continue to produce the F3 for as long as there is a demand for the camera, but if current trends continue its days are numbered.

Other basic features not listed above, yet common to all F3s include: a strongly centerweighted (80/20) metering pattern; shutter speeds ranging from 8 seconds to 1/2000, plus B and T, with X sync at 1/80; interchangeable focusing screens, finders and backs; depth-of-field preview; and mirror lock-up.

The Nikon F4

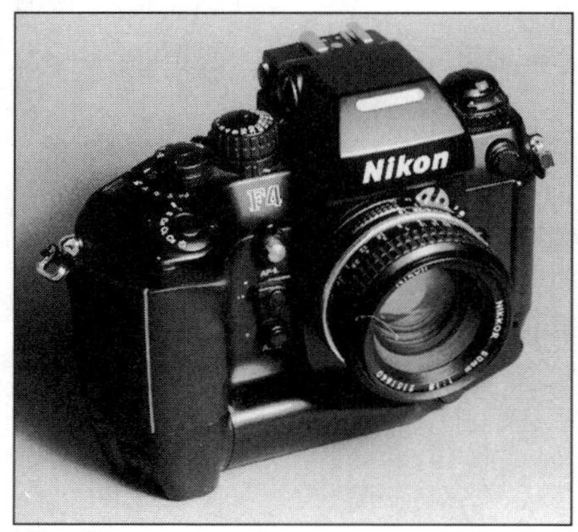

Nikon F4s

The F4 is marketed in two versions: the F4 and the F4s, the difference being the battery pack included with the camera. The F4s is the standard U.S. model. It has the larger battery pack/grip (the MB-21) that accommodates six AAs and powers the motor drive to a conservatively-rated 5.7 fps. The smaller MB-20 battery pack, which takes four AAs, is the standard battery pack in Japan and Europe, and is available as an option in the States. The F4 with the MB-20 is good for a top speed of "only" 4 fps, but the package is considerably lighter and more compact. A lot of folks opt for the MB-20 option to reduce weight. Another optional battery pack, the MB-23 is gaining in popularity. It allows the use of NiCads and offers increased performance over the MB-21, or so Nikon claims, but the motor's maximum continuous rate is still supposed to be the same as that when using the MB-21. The MB-23 also adds another 5 ounces of weight to an already heavy system.

The F4's autofocus modes are one-shot (focus priority) and continuous (servo), with predictive autofocus. "Freeze focus" (trap focus) is available with the MF-21 Multi-Control Back. The camera has an AF lock button. Exposure modes include program, high-speed program, shutter and aperture priority AE, and metered manual. Metering options include Nikon's acclaimed five-zone matrix metering system, 60/40 centerweighted averaging and a 5mm central spot selection. The matrix metering option switches automatically between two sensitivity patterns depending on whether the camera is held horizontally or vertically and will choose between four different metering programs: centerweighted, highlight-bias, shadow-bias, or a five-segment averaging method.

Shutter speeds range from 30 seconds to 1/8000 (4 seconds to 1/8000 in manual mode), plus B and T, with X sync at 1/250. The integral motor has three continuous advance modes: hi-speed (5.7 fps), low speed (3.4 fps) and "silent" (1 fps), although "stealth" seems a more appropriate label for the latter. The motor makes this strange, subdued chugging sound as it sneaks the film to the next frame. Single frame advance is also available.

Flash photography with the SB-24 or SB-25 speedlight provides the user with a variety of TTL exposure options, including auto fill flash with variable fill ratios, multistrobe effects, second-curtain sync and variable power levels. And, yes, Nikon did think to include a PC socket.

Other features include interchangeable viewfinders and screens, interchangeable backs, DX film setting with override, multiple exposure capability, AE lock, exposure compensation, built-in diopter correction, an eyepiece shutter, mirror lock-up, a manual rewind option, depth of field preview, a rubberized body, moisture resistant seals and a whole lot more.

The F4 accepts all F-mount Nikkor lenses. Focus confirmation is provided for with non-AF lenses. Matrix metering is possible with AI or AIs (non-AF) lenses, but when using non-AI lenses centerweighted metering is the only mode available.

The Venerable Nikkormat

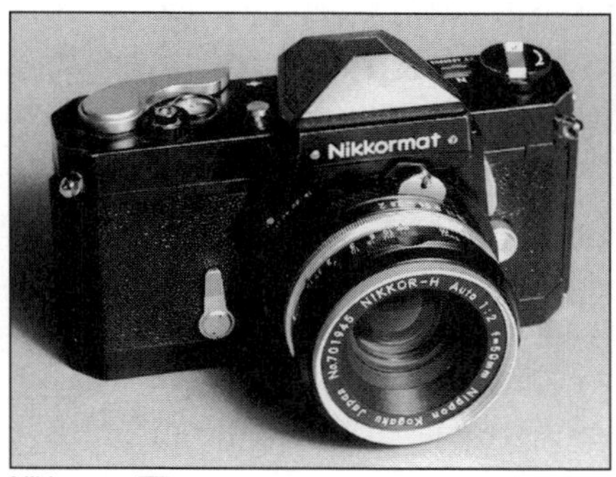

Nikkormat FT

Nikon introduced the Nikkormat **FT** and **FS** in 1965 as lower cost alternatives to the F. These were the first models in the series of mechanical Nikkormats. The FT features a TTL exposure meter, mirror lock-up and shutter speeds from 1-1/1000 plus B, with X sync at 1/125. The FS is a simplified FT with no exposure meter and no mirror lock-up.

In 1967, the Nikkormat **FTN** was introduced. It differs from the FT in one primary area: the meter was given a centerweighted pattern. An update of the FTN was released in the early 1970's. The new camera had a film advance lever with a plastic tip and an improved mechanism for setting film ASA speeds.

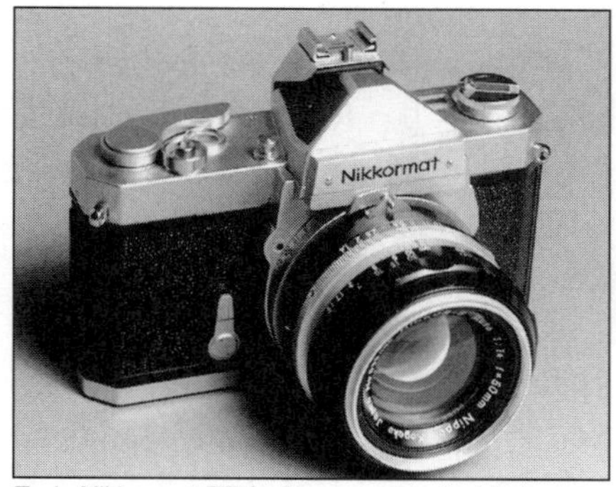

Early Nikkormat FTN with accessory 'cold' shoe

The next mechanical Nikkormat, the **FT2**, was introduced in 1975. The FT2 is essentially a late FTN with a hot shoe.

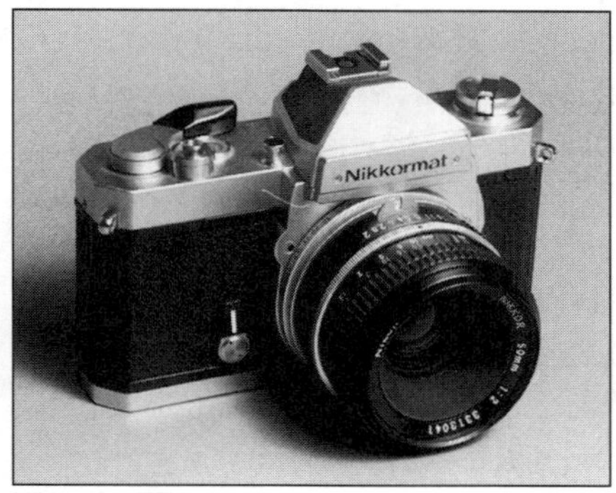

Nikkormat FT3

In 1977 the final version of the mechanical Nikkormat, the **FT3**, was introduced. The FT3 is an FT2 that takes AI lenses.

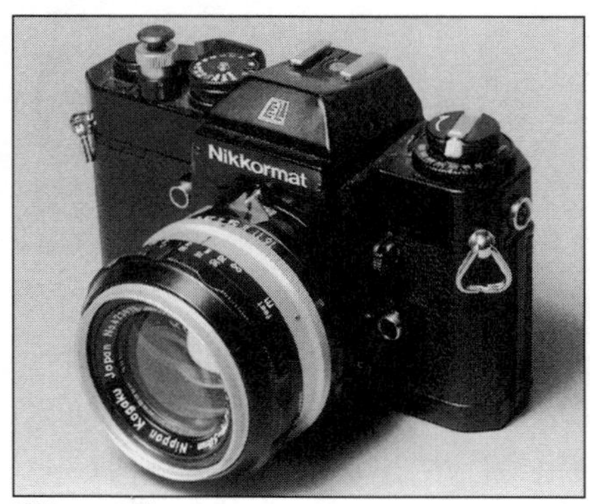

Nikkormat EL

The first of the electronic Nikkormats appeared in 1972. Dubbed the **EL**, it was Nikon's first auto-exposure SLR. It features aperture-priority AE, electronically-controlled shutter speeds from 8 seconds to 1/1000, plus B,

1/125 second flash sync (the speed available without a battery), match- needle manual metering and mirror lock-up.

An "improved" version of the EL, the ELW, was introduced in 1976. It is identical to the EL, except it can use the single-shot-only AW-1 winder.

The final electronic Nikkormat received a name change. The *Nikon* EL2 is an ELW with SPD (silicon photo diode) metering cells and an AI lens mount. The EL2 is the immediate predecessor to the FE and shares several characteristics with the FE. The similarities are: shutter speeds from 8 seconds to 1/1000, 1/125 flash sync, match-needle manual metering and battery dependence. The major differences are: non-interchangeable focusing screens on the EL2 (interchangeable screens on FE), mirror lock-up (the FE comes close) and the EL2 takes the sluggish, single-frame AW-1 winder only (the FE takes the MD-11 or MD-12 motor drive). The EL2 is also heavier than the FE and is a much sturdier camera.

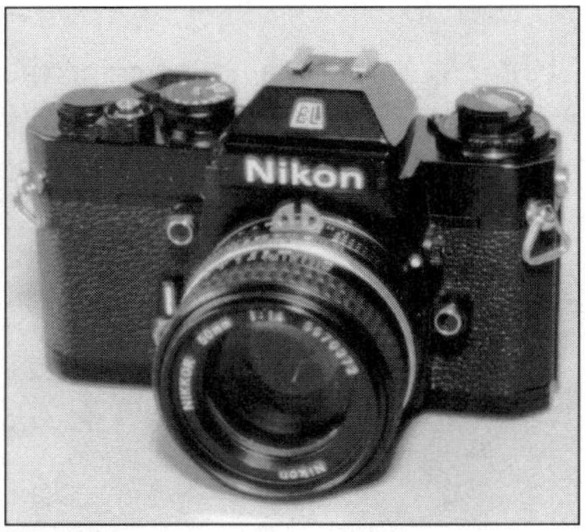

Nikon EL2

Of all the Nikkormats, the most highly prized (and most expensive) are the AI-mount FT3 and EL2. If you can live without the AI mount, it's not difficult to find clean examples of older FTNs, FT2s, and ELs for more reasonable prices. Regardless of the mounting style or features, all Nikkormats have two things in common: they are extremely rugged and very reliable cameras that often go overlooked because the name plate says Nikkormat instead of Nikon.

Incidentally, some of these cameras have name plates that say Nikomat. A Nikomat is a domestic (Japanese) market Nikkormat. The reason for the name difference? Well, Nikomat is easier for a Japanese person to pronounce than Nikkormat, that much is fact. Apparently though, Zeiss objected to Nikon's use of a name so similar to their own trademark, Ikomat, and brought legal pressure to bear, to which Nikon relented and changed the name plates on the export cameras to Nikkormat.

The Compact Nikons

The following grouping of cameras consists of the FA, and the FE, FG and FM families. When introduced, these cameras were considered to be amateur-oriented SLRs, but they have proven their value as reliable photographic tools over the ensuing years. Several models now enjoy a loyal professional and advanced amateur following.

One handy feature most of the following cameras have in common is a pseudo-mirror-lock-up capability, done by using the self-timer. The mirror rises when the self-timer is activated, providing about ten seconds for vibration to settle down before the photo is taken, which is usually plenty of time.

A word of caution: of the cameras listed in this grouping, only the FE and FM will allow the use of Non-AI lenses. Damage can result to any of the other camera if one attempts to mount a Non-AI lens. Non-AI lenses that have been "AI'd," that is, converted to the AI-style meter coupling design, will mount properly and can be used without problems.

Nikon FA

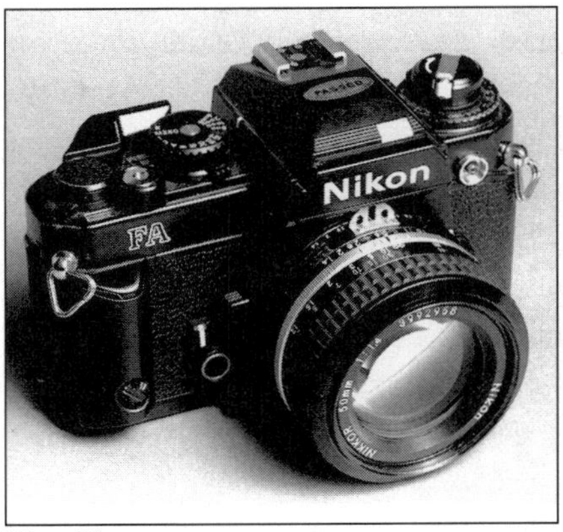

Nikon FA

The Nikon FA, as a discontinued camera, is more popular now than when it was available new. Nikon's Automatic Multi-Pattern Metering (AMP) system, originally introduced with the FA, is the same basic metering pattern still employed in the latest Nikons, such as the N8008s and F4. The FA was also the first Nikon to support the AIs feature.

The FA features a 1/4000 second top shutter speed with flash sync at 1/250 and five exposure modes: metered manual, aperture and shutter-priority AE, and two program modes: standard and high-speed (with AIs lenses, the camera will bias shutter speeds automatically according to the focal length mounted), plus cybernetic override just in case the user makes a mistake with one of his or her choices.

Other features include exposure compensation, interchangeable focusing screens, TTL flash metering with dedicated flash units, multiple exposure capability, depth-of-field preview, a self-timer and a motor drive option using either the MD-11, MD-12 or MD-15. While the MD-11 and MD-12 motor drives offer slightly higher top speeds (3.5 fps vs. 3.2 fps), the MD-15 will supply power to the FA in the event of on-board battery failure.

Nikon FE & FE2

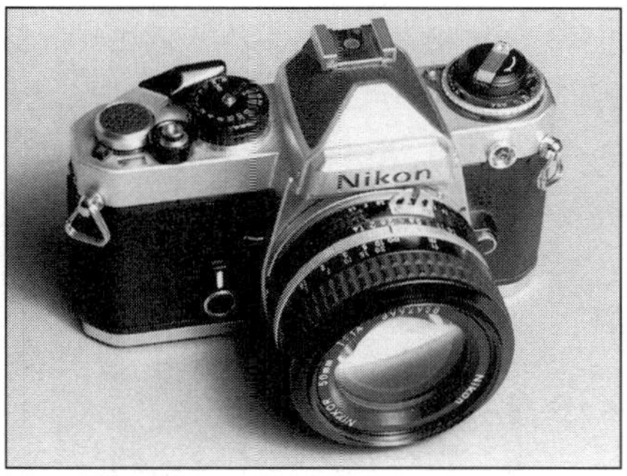

Nikon FE

The Nikon FE was the immediate successor to the Nikon EL2 and shares many of its features. It has two exposure modes: aperture priority AE and match-needle-metered manual. The metering pattern is Nikon's tried-and-true 60/40 averaging method, that is, 60% of the metering is concentrated within a moderately large circle seen within the viewfinder, while the other 40% of the weighting is given to the remainder of the image. Shutter speeds range from 8 seconds to 1/1000, plus B, with X sync at 1/125. Other features include exposure compensation, interchangeable focusing screens, non-TTL flash automation, multiple exposure capability, depth-of-field preview, a self-timer and a 3.5 fps motor drive option using either the MD-11 or MD-12.

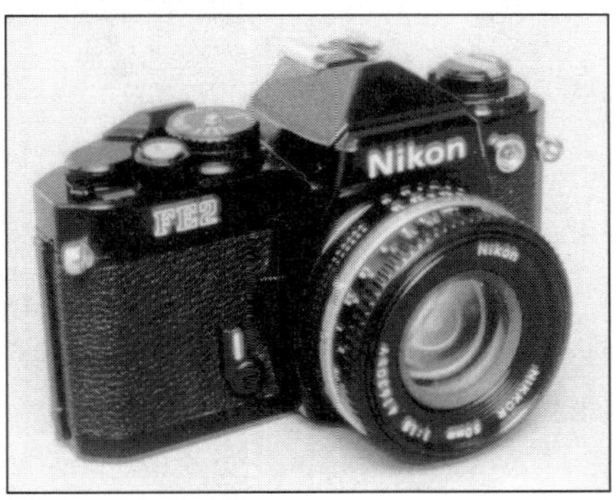

Nikon FE2

The FE2 differs from the FE in a few important areas. The FE2 was given a high-speed shutter. Slow speeds stayed the same, but the top speed was increased to 1/4000, and X sync was increased to 1/250. Brighter focusing screens were also introduced with the FE2, as was TTL flash metering.

When offered new, the FE2 was a popular camera. Since its discontinuation, it has become something of a modern classic. The demand for the camera is so heavy, in fact, that it frequently commands higher prices than its more full-featured cousin, the FA. In the case of the FE2, less does indeed seem to be more.

Nikon FG, FG-20 & EM

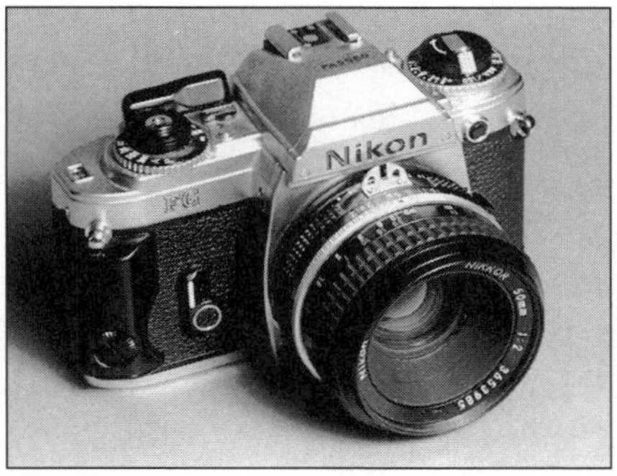

Nikon FG

The Nikon FG was the first Nikon to offer a program mode. Often thought of as a camera for the tyro, it is frequently the butt of much derision voiced by elitists who think more (i.e., more money, more features, more weight) is better. I say this in a self-deprecating fashion because I was one of those souls until I had the occasion to play around with an FG for a few weeks. I came to appreciate, of all things, its performance in manual mode, and the amazing accuracy of its quartz-controlled shutter.

The FG employs Nikon's 60/40 centerweighted metering (see FE for explanation) for its three exposure modes: program, aperture-priority AE and metered manual. Shutter speeds range from 1 second to 1/1000 in manual (longer in program or aperture-priority AE), plus B, with a mechanical X sync at 1/90. TTL flash automation is available with dedicated flash units. Other features include exposure compensation, a backlight control, a self-timer and a motor drive option with the MD-14 or MD-E.

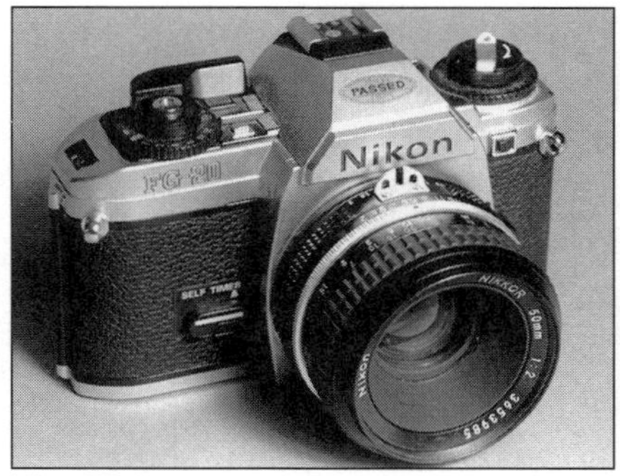

Nikon FG-20

The FG-20 is a scaled-down version of the FG. Gone are the program mode and TTL flash automation. All other features are the same as the FG.

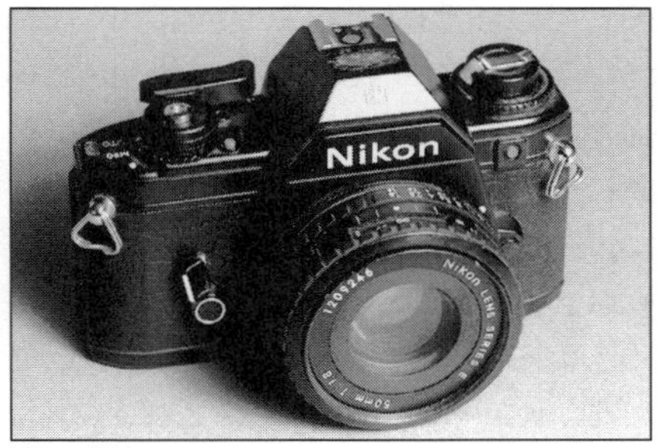

Nikon EM

The EM is the simplest 35mm SLR Nikon has produced. Designed for the neophyte, the EM features aperture-priority AE as the only exposure mode. Shutter speeds range from 1 second to 1/1000. The only manual shutter speed settings, though, are 1/90 and B. The 1/90 setting is flash sync. Both these speeds are the only ones that will operate if the battery fails. The EM has a self-timer and will accept the same motor drive options as the FG and FG-20.

Nikon FM, FM2 & FM2n

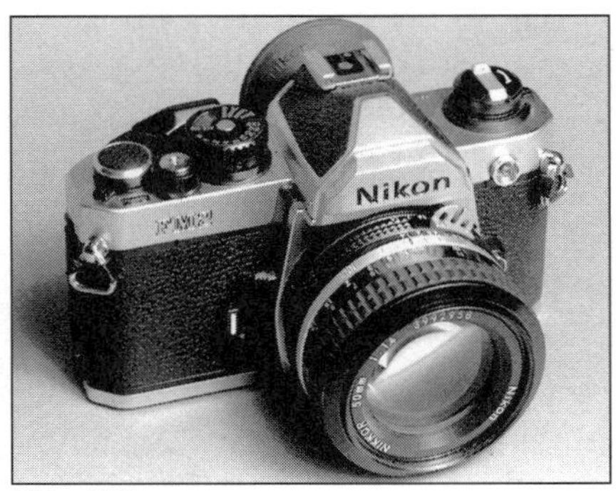

Nikon FM2n

The Nikon FM is a perfect camera for the student on a budget, or for a professional who has no need for bells and whistles, but who is looking for a low-priced, reliable camera that won't cause him or her to wince in sympathetic agony every time it picks up a new ding. It is lightweight, yet full-featured enough for most any photographic occasion.

The FM is a manual exposure only camera, using Nikon's 60/40 centerweighted metering system. It employs an array of three, cross-coupled LEDs (i.e., coupled to both apertures and shutter speeds) that light up next to either a plus, a minus or a zero sign on the edge of the viewfinder. Zero is correct exposure. Its all mechanical shutter provides speeds ranging from 1 second to 1/1000, plus B, with X sync at 1/125. Other features include multiple exposure capability, depth-of-field preview, a hot shoe and PC socket, a self-timer and a 3.5 fps motor drive option with the MD-11 or MD-12.

Because the demand for FM2s is so strong, FMs can often be purchased for very reasonable prices. Thus, if you don't need the FM2's features, you can save a sizable chunk of change.

The FM2 differs from the FM in almost the same way as the FE2 differs from the FE. The FM2 has the high-speed shutter with a top speed of 1/4000 and flash sync at a non-metered 1/200. It takes the bright, interchangeable FE2 focusing screens (the FM's screen is non-removable). Also, the meter information in the viewfinder was improved. Instead of having LEDs next to plus, minus and zero signs, the signs have become LEDs. This greatly aids metering in low light situations.

The FM2n has one big improvement over the FM2. The 1/250 setting on the shutter-speed dial became the flash sync setting also. There are two ways to tell the FM2n apart from the FM2. One is to look at the shutter speed dial. The FM2n has a red 1/250 setting. Another way is to check the serial number. If the number is preceded by an N, then it's an FM2n.

Nikon N-Series SLRs

The N-series Nikons, from the original, manual-focus N2000 to the high-tech N90, have a few things in common—integral motor drives and polycarbonate construction are the most obvious. Additionally, as is true with some of the above-mentioned models, N-series cameras will not accept Non-AI lenses. Damage to these cameras may result if you attempt to mount Non-AI lenses. So don't.

Nikon N2000 & N2020

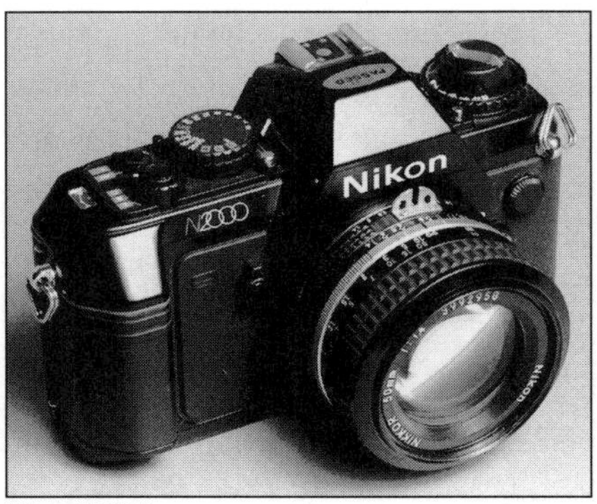

Nikon N2000

The **N2000** was Nikon's first 35mm SLR with a built-in motor drive and the second Nikon to support the "s" feature of AIs lenses. Its centerweighted metering pattern is used for all four exposure modes: standard program, high-speed program (AIs lenses are necessary to engage this function), aperture-priority AE and metered manual. Other exposure features include TTL flash metering with dedicated flash units, an AE lock and exposure compensation. Shutter speeds range from 1 second to 1/1000, plus B, with X sync at 1/125. Other features include DX film coding with override, a self-timer and, as was mentioned above, an integral motor drive that has continuous speeds up to 2.5 fps. The motor features auto film loading, but film must be rewound manually.

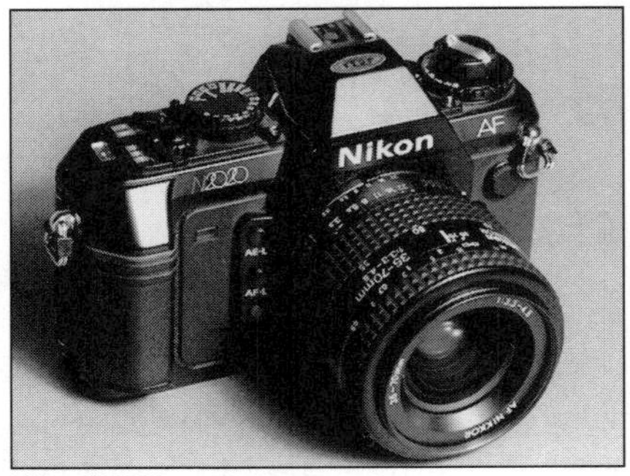

Nikon N2020

Nikon's second autofocus SLR, the **N2020**, is an N2000 with the addition of two autofocus modes: single shot (focus priority) and continuous (servo). All AF-Nikkors will autofocus on the N2020 (except those for the F3AF and some of the D-type AF Nikkors). Focus confirmation is provided for with AI'd, AI, or AIs lenses.

Nikon N4004/N4004s & N5005

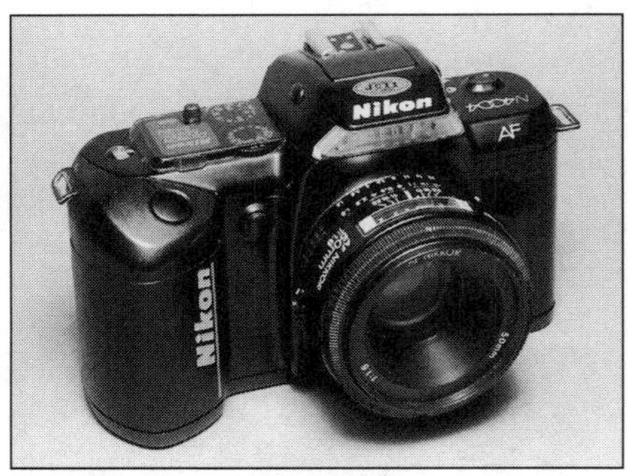

Nikon N4004s

Nikon's bid for the entry-level autofocus consumer's dollar back in 1987 was the **N4004**. Its autofocusing system provided rather ho-hum performance and offered only one autofocus mode: single shot (focus priority). The shutter will not release unless the subject is in focus. For what it's worth, this fail-safe feature can be circumvented with the self-timer. Manual focus with focus confirmation is provided for when using lenses that have maximum apertures of f/5.6 or faster.

Exposure modes available are two program modes (normal and high-speed), aperture- and shutter-priority modes, and manual. A three-zone matrix metering system evaluates exposure in the camera's AE modes. The camera switches over to Nikon's 60/40 centerweighted metering for manual exposure or when the AE lock is used. In any of the above auto-exposure modes, the shutter will lock when lighting conditions are unfavorable. Shutter speeds range from 1 second to 1/2000, plus B, with X sync at 1/100.

The N4004 has a built-in, dedicated flash (GN 39 @ ISO 100), which provides TTL flash automation and auto fill flash. TTL and autofocus TTL flash are also possible with dedicated accessory flash units. Other features include DX film coding with no override, an integral winder with single-frame advance only and a self timer.

While most lenses employing Nikon's AI meter-coupling style will mount onto the N4004 and the camera will provide focus confirmation, the metering systems will operate only when autofocus lenses are mounted. In other words, with Non-AF lenses, the N4004 becomes a non-metered, manual-focus camera. Please read the cautionary notes regarding the use of some lenses with this camera, following the description on the N5005.

The **N4004s** superceded the N4004 in 1989 and is basically the same camera. Most significantly, it inherited the N8008's autofocus system, which drastically improved focusing performance. The other improvement was the addition of a locking pin on the top deck to prevent the dials from being bumped off their settings. All other features of the N4004 were retained.

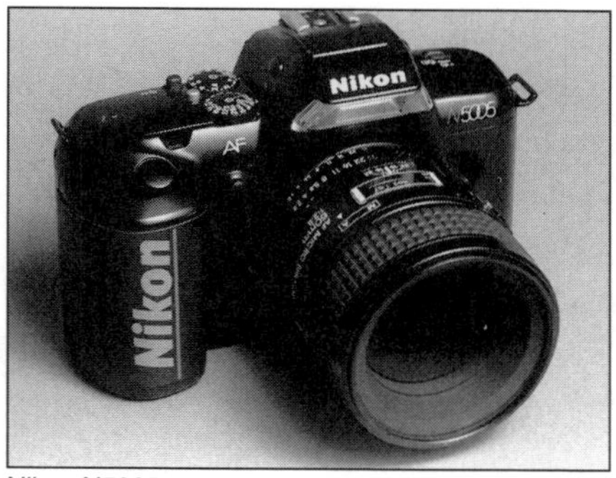

Nikon N5005

The **N5005** is Nikon's latest entry-level autofocus SLR. It closely resembles the N4004s, the model it superceded, and boasts several nice improvements. For starters, the autofocus system was given a boost with the addition of predictive-focus capability. The shutter speed range was extended also: 30 seconds to 1/2000 second (1 second to 1/2000 in shutter-priority and manual modes); and the flash sync speed was increased to 1/125. The built-in flash has the same rated guide number, but its angle of coverage was increased to include 28mm lenses (35mm lenses on the N4004/N4004s). Additionally, matrix balanced fill-flash is available using either the built-in flash or dedicated accessory units. The N5005 also has a T setting, an unusual feature for this class of camera. All other features of the N4004s are on the N5005.

Caution: *Do not attempt to mount Non-AI lenses or lenses that have been "AI'd" (by having notches machined in their aperture rings) on the above three cameras. These cautionary notes apply only to the N4004, N4004s and N5005. Read on to find out why.*

Beginning with the N4004 and continuing through to the N5005, Nikon did away with the AI meter-coupling tab that communicates lens aperture settings to the camera's meter. Instead, the electrical contacts shared by the camera and AF lenses are used for this. (This is why these cameras' meters operate only with autofocus lenses) To access the program or shutter-priority AE modes, however, Nikon borrowed another idea from from the Mind of Minolta and incorporated a minimum-aperture sensing switch to tell the camera when the lens was set to its minimum aperture, which doubles as the AE setting. When facing the camera, this switch is located at about the 8 o'clock position and engages a seldom-used and often-ignored additional tab found on the aperture rings of AI and later lenses. (See the photo of the AI lens in the Nikon lens section. On the far right of the lens, you'll notice this tab protruding from the back of the aperture ring.)

This minimum-aperture sensing switch can present a potentially costly problem to the unsuspecting user. If a photographer owns a non-AI lens they had "AI'd" by someone other than Nikon, they may think that it will work just fine. Unfortunately, if they mount such a lens, they run the risk of crushing this switch, just as if the lens had never been AI'd to begin with. Why? Because a lens AI'd by someone other than Nikon has a single, long notch cut in the aperture ring for the AI meter tab. No notch is cut for the sensing switch. Nikon circumvented this problem by replacing the entire aperture ring when it updated lenses to the AI meter-coupling style.

Nikon N6006 & N6000

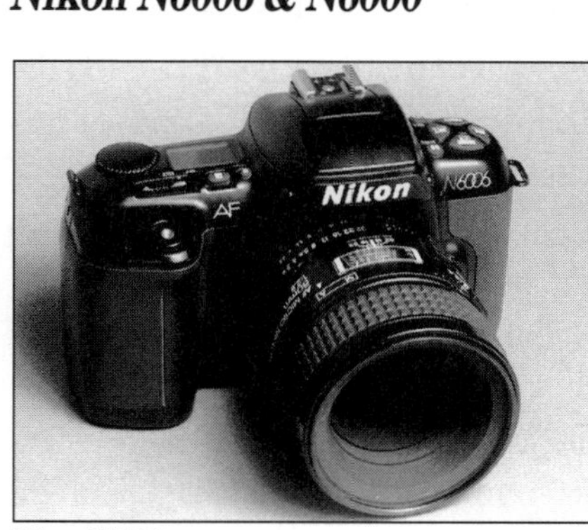

Nikon N6006

Released simultaneously, both cameras filled gaping holes in Nikon's two SLR camera lines that had existed prior to their introduction. Ever since the N2020 was discontinued, there was a rather large gap in both capabilities and price between the N4004s (now the N5005) and the N8008s. The N6006 fits snugly between the two cameras, although a little closer to the N8008s in both price and performance. Prior to the introduction of the N6000, if one wished to buy a new manual-focus Nikon, the choice had been reduced to two cameras: the FM2n and the F3. Both are very fine cameras, but that isn't much of a selection.

The N6006 offers a somewhat simplified autofocus selection when compared to the N8008s. Its autofocus modes, both single and continuous, operate in focus-priority only. There is no continuous servo. And, with a maximum film winding speed of 2 fps, there doesn't seem to be the slightest need for it either.

Exposure options include two program modes with shift, shutter and aperture-priority AE, and metered manual. Metering patterns include Nikon's Matrix metering, 75/25 centerweighted averaging and spot. Other exposure features are an AE lock, exposure compensation and autobracketing. Shutter speeds range from 30 seconds to 1/2000, plus B, with X sync at 1/125.

The N6006 has a built in flash (GN 43 @ ISO 100) that provides TTL exposure automation, fill flash and second- curtain sync. The N6006 also has a hot shoe, which will provide the above features with more powerful dedicated units.

Other features include DX film coding with override, a self-timer and the integral motor drive. The motor offers two continuous speeds (2 fps and 1.2 fps), single-frame advance, and auto film loading and rewind.

Manual focus Nikkors with the AI meter-coupling style can be used on the N6006 without losing a host of features. Focus confirmation is provided. Exposure modes still available are aperture priority and metered manual. In aperture priority, the Matrix metering pattern is employed; in manual, either centerweighted metering or spot is available.

The N6000 shares most of the features of the N6006. Those that were not included on the N6000 are the spot meter, the autobracketing function, the built-in flash (although TTL flash is still available with dedicated units) and, of course, autofocus. Interestingly, the N6000 was designed to be used with AF Nikkors — all the electrical contacts are there. When using AIs, AI or AI'd Nikkors, available exposure modes are aperture-priority AE and metered manual using centerweighted metering only. Matrix metering is not available except with AF Nikkors.

Nikon N8008 & N8008s

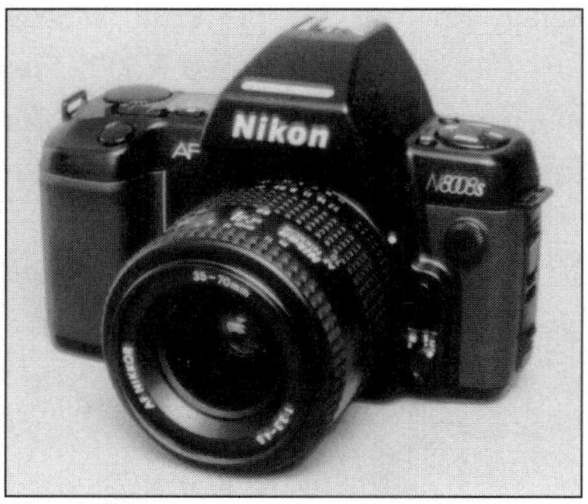

Nikon N8008s

The N8008 was the first 35mm SLR in the world to offer a top shutter speed of 1/8000 second. At the time of its introduction, this single feature caused quite a stir among photographers and competitors alike. Such a speed could freeze action in a way that had not been possible previously unless one used high speed strobes. In addition to this, the N8008 was packed full of other innovations, which made it the autofocus hit of 1988. Now the N8008s, this camera continues to be a runaway best seller for Nikon.

Autofocus modes available with the N8008 are: single shot (focus priority) or continuous (servo) operation. It has an AF lock button. "Freeze focus" (trap focus) is available with the optional MF-21 Multi-Control Back. Exposure modes include program with shift, high speed program, "dual" program, aperture or shutter priority AE, and metered manual. The "dual" mode switches automatically between normal and high-speed programs depending on the lens focal length. Other exposure features include exposure compensation and an AE lock. Metering patterns available on the N8008 are Nikon's five-zone segmented Matrix pattern, 75/25 centerweighted averaging and, with the N8008s, spot metering.

Shutter speeds range from 30 seconds to 1/8000, plus B, with X sync at 1/250. TTL flash automation is available with dedicated units. When using the SB-24 or SB-25, auto fill flash, variable fill ratios, multistrobe effects, second curtain sync and variable power levels are all at the user's fingertips.

Other features include DX film coding with override, interchangeable focusing screens, interchangeable backs, depth-of-field preview, a variable self-timer with up to 30 seconds of delay and a one or two shot option, multiple exposure capability and a built-in motor drive that provides continuous film advance speeds up to 3.3 fps.

If one wishes to use manual focus lenses on the N8008, it will accept AIs, AI and AI'd lenses, with varying degrees of flexibility. Focus confirmation is possible with all the above lenses. Matrix metering is retained with AIs lenses only. The camera defaults to centerweighted metering with all others.

Nikon N90

The N90, Nikon's latest entry to its stable of autofocus thoroughbreds, falls between the N8008s and the F4 as far as price is concerned, but as one would expect with a latest-generation AF SLR, the N90 contains several state-of-the-art features not found on any of its cousins. Its styling, switch and button placement are very similar to that found on the N8008s, but housed beneath the familiar exterior is a broadly updated tool.

The most significant new feature found on the N90 is its 3D Matrix Metering exposure system. Sounds impressive, but what does it mean, you may ask? Well, most anyone who has advanced beyond the snapshot level of photography knows that a proper composition often requires that the principal subject be located off center. True, having the camera stay focused on a stationary off-center subject is easy enough with most AF cameras, but what about exposure? In deference to the snapshot crowd, most camera makers design their autoexposure systems to bias exposure toward the center of the image. But this exposure method will not always expose correctly for an off-center subject, especially if the lighting conditions are unusual. With the N90, this is no longer a problem.

To enable this feature, one of the new AF D lenses must be used. An AF D lens will communicate distance information to the 3D Matrix Metering exposure system, which will then adjust exposure for the subject at that distance. This same system is available for TTL flash exposure when using the new SB-25 strode unit.

Other new features include a user-selectable P multiprogram mode, which biases autoexposure based on the lens focal length, Vari-Programs (close-up, high speed, hyperfocal depth, landscape, sihouette and sports, plus provisions for adding user-customized ones), and a new set of AF sensors: one broad-based horizontal sensor with a vertical cross sensor, which can be switched to a tight, high-density cross spot sensor. One other new feature worth noting is the provision for linking the N90 to selected Sharp Electronic Organizers via Nikon's Data Link IC Card AC-1E. Using a Sharp Electronic Organizer (like the Wizard 8000) the photographer can customize exposure modes, lengthen exposures, store up to five rolls worth of exposure data and more.

The exposure system also includes aperture and shutter-priority AE, plus metered manual. Metering patterns include the eight-segmented 3D Matrix Metering pattern, 75% centerweighted metering, and a 1% spot meter. Other exposure features include an AE lock and ±5 EV exposure compensation in ⅓ steps. Shutter speeds range from 30 seconds to 1/8000, plus B. X sync is available up to 1/250 second.

Some of the N90's many other features include: a built-in motor drive with single frame and continuous advance (to 3.8 fps), autoloading and power rewind, interchangeable focusing screens, and a self-timer.

Nikon SLRs

Camera	Yrs. Made	New	Mint	Excellent	User
EM	1979-84		140 120	125 90	
F no prism chr	1959-74		120 105	110 75	
F no prism blk	1959-74		200 140	140 100	90 70
F std prism chr	1959-74		350 280	275 175	
F std prism blk	1959-74		400 320	285 200	
F early Photomic chr	1962-65		250 200	190 145	
F early Photomic blk	1962-65			230 190	
F Photomic T chr	1965-68			160 125	
F Photomic T blk	1965-68			200 160	
F Photomic Tn chr	1967-69			185 150	
F Photomic Tn blk	1967-69			200 160	
F Photomic FTn chr	1969-74		400 325	300 200	200 165
F Photomic FTn blk	1969-74		500 400	400 270	270 220
F2 no prism chr	1971-80			300 175	170 130
F2 no prism blk	1971-80			325 185	175 130
F2 (DE-1) chr	1972-80			340 280	
F2 (DE-1) blk	1972-80		450 400	425 300	
F2 Photomic (DP-1) chr	1972-77		450 380	360 275	265 230
F2 Photomic (DP-1) blk	1972-77		550 425	375 285	275 230
F2A (DP-11) chr	1977-80		600 470	450 350	
F2A (DP-11) blk	1977-80		650 550	450 350	300 250
F2AS (DP-12) chr	1977-80		865 650	650 525	
F2AS (DP-12) blk	1977-80		900 750	680 500	500 400
F2S (DP-2) chr	1973-77		450 400	395 325	300 240
F2S (DP-2) blk	1973-77		550 450	470 375	360 290
F2SB (DP-3) chr	1976-77		700 600	600 480	
F2SB (DP-3) blk	1976-77		850 750	700 580	

Nikon SLRs

Camera	Yrs. Made	New		Mint		Excellent		User	
F2T	1976-80			1400	1300	1200	900	875	750
F3	1980-84			600	475	490	400	420	360
F3AF (w/DX-1 finder)	1983-87			810	700	720	600		
F3HP	1983-	1350	1100	900	790	775	600	550	450
F3P	1987-89			1500	1125	1050	875	820	750
F3T	1983-	1600	1400	1125	900	850	700	650	470
F4 (MB-20)	1988-					1125	950		
F-4E (MB-23)	1988-	2200	1740						
F4s (MB-21)	1988-	2200	1900	1400	1295	1350	1000		
FA chr	1983-87			450	385	395	300	270	240
FA blk	1983-87			450	400	390	325	300	250
FE chr	1978-83			300	225	280	200	250	180
FE blk	1978-83			350	280	320	230	260	200
FE2 chr	1983-87			460	400	380	300		
FE2 blk	1983-87			480	425	400	350	360	280
FG chr	1982-87			200	165	175	130		
FG blk	1982-87			240	185	200	160		
FG20	1984-88			170	150	140	110		
FM chr	1977-83			280	240	225	175	180	165
FM blk	1977-83			285	250	250	200	200	165
FM2 chr	1983-85			295	250	250	225		
FM2 blk	1983-85			315	280	285	250		
FM2n chr	1985-	520	430	380	320	340	280		
FM2n blk	1985-	520	430	380	320	340	280	270	250
FM2T (titanium)	1994-	980	740						
Nikkormat EL chr	1972-77			250	200	195	150		
Nikkormat EL blk	1972-77			300	220	210	165	160	120
Nikkormat ELW chr	1976-78					250	170		
Nikkormat ELW blk	1976-78					270	190		
Nikon EL2 chr	1977-78			300	250	275	200	190	165
Nikon EL2 blk	1977-78			350	300	275	225		
Nikkormat FS	1965-69					150	100		
Nikkormat FT	1965-67					150	100		
Nikkormat FTN chr	1967-74			230	170	150	125	120	75
Nikkormat FTN blk	1967-74					190	140	120	80
Nikkormat FT2 chr	1975-78			250	220	200	140	120	80
Nikkormat FT2 blk	1975-78					230	160	165	120
Nikkormat FT3 chr	1977-78			275	220	250	175	155	130
Nikkormat FT3 blk	1977-78			325	250	275	190		
N50	1994-	440	365						
N70	1994-	780	675						
N90	1992-	870	775						
N90s	1994-	995	860						
N2000 (F301)	1985-90			250	215	240	195		
N2020 (F501)	1986-90			275	225	250	200		
N4004 (F401)	1987-89			230	210	190	165		
N4004s	1989-91			250	225	215	190		
N5005	1991-	475	380						
N6000	1990-	460	370						
N6006	1990-	550	400	380	330				
N8008 (F801)	1988-91			480	440	450	385		
N8008s	1991-	700	625						

Nikon Lenses

Since 1959, F-mount Nikon lenses have been available in only three mechanical meter coupling styles: Non-AI (the original), AI (for Auto Indexing), and AIs (AI lenses with an additional notch; the "s" stands for "shutter"). AF Nikkors, sporting an array of electrical contacts in addition to the AIs meter coupling, communicate aperture indexing information via these contacts to autofocus Nikons that require it. Some F-mount lenses, such as the Reflex Nikkors, have no meter coupling facility at all. In addition, Nikon has produced several variations of a single focal length in a given coupling style. The differences may be in the coating, or the size or material of the focusing ring or such, or may represent a totally redesigned lens. If the differences are minor, they usually affect the value only slightly, if at all, and are not listed separately. But when the difference does affect the value, each model is listed.

Non-AI Nikkor Lenses

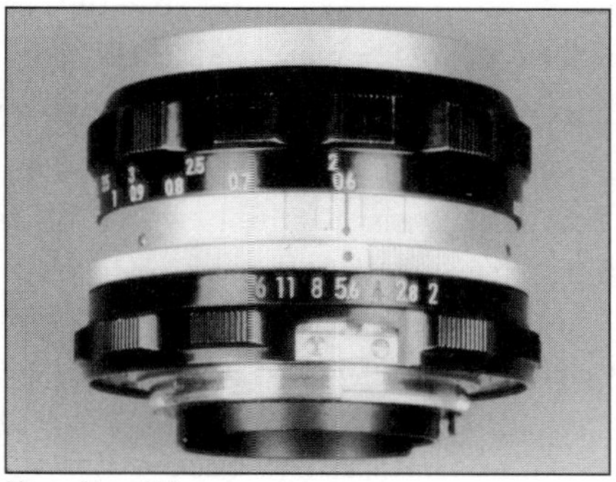

Nikon Non-AI lens

Non-AI lenses have the traditional meter coupling shoe located on the aperture ring, which engages the meter coupling post of earlier Nikon cameras. When mounting one of these or later lenses with a meter coupling shoes to pre-1977 Nikkormats or to Fs with pre-FTn finders, the aperture ring must be set to f/5.6 for the lens to couple with the meter properly. Even Fs with FTN finders and F2s with non-AI coupling posts will couple much easier if this procedure is followed.

There are only eight AI-coupling style Nikon cameras that will accept Non-AI lenses. These are the F2A, F2AS, F3, F4, FE, FM, and the EL2 and FT3 Nikkormats. All other AI, AIs, or AF-mount cameras will not take Non-AI lenses. Damage can result to the cameras if these lenses are mounted.

Before mounting a Non-AI lens on the F2A or F2AS, the AI coupling lever must be pushed up into the finder until it clicks in place. After dismounting the lens, the sliding switch above the lever is pushed and the lever snaps back into place. On all other models that accept Non-AI lenses, the meter coupling tab must be raised out of harm's way before mounting Non-AI lenses. Next to the tab is a small button. Depressing this button unlocks the tab, allowing it to be raised. Releasing the button then locks the tab in the raised position. With either arrangement, metering must be done via the stop-down method.

Non-AI lenses that have been "AI'd" by Nikon have had replacement AI aperture rings installed, which are designed specifically for these older lenses. Some older Non-AI lenses are not "AI-able" by Nikon, but can be AI'd by others. This method involves cutting a notch in the aperture ring for the AI coupling lever and adding a sticker showing the f/stops so that the Aperture Direct Readout scale will be visible within the viewfinders of cameras supporting that feature. It doesn't look as nice as a replacement ring (and the lens is still worth about the same as a Non-AI model), but it works just fine on most Nikon SLRs. (If you have a N4004, N4004s or N5005, see the warning regarding the use of these lenses following the above cameras' descriptions.) Only Non-AI lenses that have been AI'd by Nikon are included in the listings below.

The earliest Non-AI lenses are becoming collectible now, if they're in mint condition. These semi-collectible Nikkors have their focal lengths listed in centimeters, rather than millimeters. Price differences between these early Nikkors and their later Non-AI counterparts are still small, but they are growing.

AI Nikkor Lenses

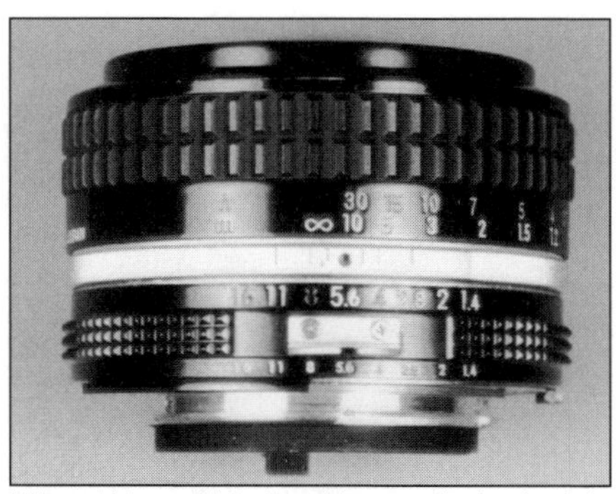

Nikon AI lens. Note the ridge on the back of the aperture ring that begins at f/8.

AI lenses retain the meter coupling shoe to insure backward compatibility for older Nikon SLRs, but also have a ridge on the back of the aperture ring that engages the AI coupling lever on 1977 and later Nikons.

AIs Nikkor Lenses

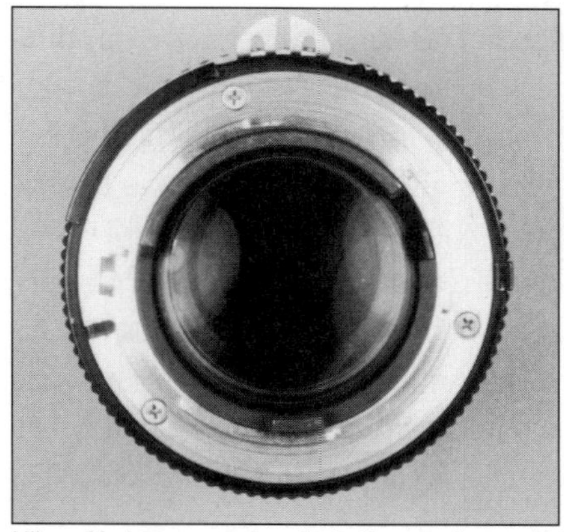

Nikon AIs lens, rear view. Note the small, rounded notch on the left side of the lens flange.

AIs lenses have an additional rounded notch machined into the rear of the lens mount (See illustration), which, along with other protrusions back there, communicates to certain cameras the focal length and maximum aperture of the lens that has been mounted. This notch matters only with the FA, N2000, N2020 and F4, and then its only purpose is to allow the camera to bias toward certain shutter speeds when used in program modes (e.g.: a long telephoto will cause the program mode to favor higher shutter speeds in order to reduce the possibility of camera shake).

Series E Nikon Lenses

Early Series E lenses are AI mount, later models are AIs. Neither have the meter coupling shoe for earlier model Nikons. Series E lenses were designed for amateur use and were originally introduced with the Nikon EM in 1979. Although less rugged in construction than their Nikkor equivalents, they are generally of high optical quality, and represent a good bargain. Certain Series E lenses are stand-outs in terms of both optical quality and price, most notably the three zoom lenses.

Autofocus Nikkor Lenses

Nikon's Autofocus lenses use the AIs mount and, like the Series E lenses, do not have the meter coupling shoes. They do, however, have tiny dimples on their aperture rings, showing where the screws that hold the shoes in place would be mounted if one felt the need to add them for his or her beloved old FTn (or F2 Photomic, or whatever). In addition, they have a series of electrical contacts that communicate various information electronically to Nikon autofocus cameras and to the N6000.

Pricing Strategies

Nikon announced the discontinuation of about twenty of its manual focus AIs lenses in 1990, and has been slowly dropping manual focus Nikkors since then. Some of these discontinued lenses are sold out and are no longer available new. Those still in dealer stock have skyrocketed in price. For example, the 80-200 f/4 Zoom-Nikkor was already pricey ($450 mail order) before being discontinued. Now if you want a new one, expect to shell out $200 to $300 more. In some instances, these pricing practices have affected the value of used lenses. This spike in prices will probably last only as long as dealer stocks of new lenses will. After they're gone, used prices probably will settle down to where they were before. Keep in mind, there is no shortage of manual-focus Nikkors on the used market.

AI and Non-AI lenses that have been AI'd by Nikon often sell for less on the used market than their AIs counterparts—probably just because they're older. Non-AI lenses and those that have been AI'd by someone other than Nikon are usually substantially less. This isn't a strict rule, however. In a few cases, AI lenses sometimes command higher prices than some of the latest model AIs lenses, no doubt because the earlier models are often sturdier in construction. Often the price differences are negligible between meter-coupling styles, especially with lenses that are in high demand. When major price differences exist, each coupling style is listed separately. Series E lenses are grouped with the manual focus lenses, but are always listed separately. AF Nikkors are grouped in their own listing.

Nikon Manual Focus Lenses

Lens	New		Mint		Excellent		User	
6mm f/2.8 fisheye	13000+		6700	5500				
6mm f/5.6 fisheye (w/finder)			695	450				
The 6mm f/2.8, with its incredible 220° angle of view, is available new only by special order with a very long wait. The 6mm f/5.6 has the same angle of view at a tiny fraction of the cost. The 6mm f/5.6, 7.5mm f/5.6, 8mm f/8, 10mm f/5.6 and 21mm f/4 lenses are very short back-focus designs, requiring they be used on Nikon SLRs with true mirror lock-up capability.								
7.5mm f/5.6 fisheye (w/finder)					500	350		
8mm f/2.8 fisheye	1795	1500	1000	895	875	700	740	600
8mm f/8 fisheye (w/finder)					500	350		
10mm f/5.6 fisheye (w/finder)					500	350		
13mm f/5.6			5000	4000				
15mm f/3.5	1995	1750	1430	1320	1300	1100		
15mm f/5.6 Non-AI			980	855	840	750		
16mm f/2.8 fisheye	825	690	525	500	500	425		
16mm f/3.5 fisheye AI					450	375		
16mm f/3.5 fisheye AI'd or Non-AI					425	325		
18mm f/3.5	1250	980	775	700	650	530	550	400
18mm f/4 AI					625	500		
18mm f/4 AI'd or Non-AI			650	600	575	400		
20mm f/2.8 AIs	660	550	495	430	460	400	370	270
20mm f/3.5 AIs (52mm)			485	440	450	380		
20mm f/3.5 AI (52mm)			370	325	350	275		
20mm f/3.5 Non-AI, AI'd (72mm)			325	250	270	200		
20mm f/4 AI			325	275	295	225		
20mm f/4 Non-AI			275	210	225	185		
21mm f/4 (w/finder)			350	325	300	195		
24mm f/2	775	580	445	380	420	370	375	300
24mm f/2.8	460	370	350	250	320	195	200	150
24mm f/2.8 Non-AI			240	200	215	180	165	150
28mm f/2	640	550	400	350	380	275		
28mm f/2 AI'd			380	300	300	200	180	150
28mm f/2 Non-AI			300	250	260	195		
28mm f/2.8	380	325	300	225	270	190	200	170
28mm f/2.8 AI'd or Non-AI			250	200	200	150		
28mm f/2.8 E			150	125	130	95		

Nikon Manual Focus Lenses

Lens	New		Mint		Excellent		User	
28mm f/3.5			150	140	130	110		
28mm f/3.5 AI'd					150	100		
28mm f/3.5 Non-AI			145	115	100	80	65	50
28mm f/3.5 PC	1095	930	750	700	680	595		
28mm f/4 PC Non-AI			625	500	540	480		
35mm f/1.4	800	600	485	400	400	340		
35mm f/1.4 Non-AI			380	340	330	250		
35mm f/2	440	330	270	225	215	175	165	120
35mm f/2 AI'd					215	160	150	120
35mm f/2 Non-AI			220	190	150	125		
35mm f/2.5 E			125	100	100	85	70	60
35mm f/2.8			160	125	150	100		
35mm f/2.8 AI'd			120	95	85	70	65	60
35mm f/2.8 Non-AI			100	85	80	60		
35mm f/2.8 PC	750	615	465	400	380	340		
35mm f/3.5 PC			370	330	340	300		
45mm f/2.8 GN AI, AI'd or Non-AI			150	120	130	100		
50mm f/1.2	520	410	325	275	250	225	220	160
50mm f/1.4	395	300	250	200	180	120		
50mm f/1.4 AI			160	125	130	85		
50mm f/1.4 AI'd					130	80	80	70
50mm f/1.4 Non-AI					85	50	55	40
50mm f/1.8 AI, early AIs			115	80	95	60		
50mm f/1.8N late AIs			95	75	70	60		
50mm f/1.8 E			60	40	50	30		
50mm f/2 AI or AI'd			100	75	75	55	55	45
50mm f/2 Non-AI			65	55	50	35	40	25
55mm f/1.2 AI, AI'd or Non-AI			220	180	170	125		
55mm f/2.8 Micro			280	210	250	190		
55mm f/3.5 Micro AI, AI'd or Non-AI			220	175	190	145	155	125
58mm f/1.2 Nocturnal	1645	1400	1200	985				
58mm f/1.4 Non-AI			150	100	95	60		
85mm f/1.4	850	690	600	550	530	440		
85mm f/1.8 AI			290	275	280	200		
85mm f/1.8 AI'd or Non-AI					220	140		
85mm f/2			270	225	240	200	200	150
100mm f/2.8 E			135	120	120	100		
105mm f/1.8	595	615	560	500	480	390		
105mm f/2.5	330	300	280	200	225	175	180	150
105mm f/2.5 AI'd			185	150	160	140		
105mm f/2.5 Non-AI			175	140	140	110	125	95
105mm f/2.8 Micro	600	490	500	450	435	390		
105mm f/4 Micro			400	330	350	300	290	240
105mm f/4 Micro Non-AI			330	300	300	225	200	170
105mm f/4 Bellows			450	400	375	290		
105mm f/4.5 UV (w/AF-1 & UR-2)	3000	2590						
120mm f/4 Medical Nikkor (LA-2/LD-2 req'd)	1200	1000	950	800				
135mm f/2	1050	800	720	650	650	500		
135mm f/2 AI'd or Non-AI					500	400		
135mm f/2.8	385	315	250	210	225	175	150	140
135mm f/2.8 AI'd			190	125	140	100		
135mm f/2.8 Non-AI			140	120	125	80		
135mm f/2.8 E			150	120	125	90		
135mm f/3.5			135	110	110	70		
135mm f/3.5 AI'd or Non-AI			100	85	80	50	50	45
135mm f/4 Bellows (w/BR-1 tube)			350	300	250	200		
180mm f/2.8 ED	1050	800	720	650	625	520		
180mm f/2.8 AI or AI'd			525	460	450	400	350	295
180mm f/2.8 Non-AI					400	250	225	200
200mm f/2 EDIF	4380	3970	3300	2900	2850	2300	2350	1895
200mm f/4	440	370	300	250	230	175	175	145
200mm f/4 AI'd			195	140	160	100	90	75
200mm f/4 Non-AI			140	110	125	90	80	65
200mm f/4 Micro IF	700	570	525	480	485	400		
200mm f/5.6 Medical Nikkor (w/LA-1)					450	350		

NIKON

Nikon Manual Focus Lenses

Lens	New	Mint	Excellent	User
300mm f/2 EDIF			25000+	

The 300mm f/2 EDIF was discontinued in 1989. At that time it was a special-order-only item with a list price of about $13,000. These lenses are still in very high demand within the motion picture industry and are currently commanding prices as high as $25,000.

Lens	New	Mint	Excellent	User
300mm f/2.8 EDIF		2800 2650	2695 2200	
300mm f/2.8 EDIF N		3500 2800		
300mm f/4.5 EDIF	1250 970	870 795	750 600	
300mm f/4.5 ED AI, AI'd or Non-AI			550 490	
300mm f/4.5	500 600	540 450	475 390	345 290
300mm f/4.5 AI'd		400 340	350 300	270 250
300mm f/4.5 Non-AI			300 250	220 170
400mm f/2.8 EDIF	6945 6400		4500 4000	
400mm f/3.5 EDIF	4350 4000	3650 3200	3150 2495	2280 2000
400mm f/4.5 (w/focusing unit)			750 650	
400mm f/5.6 ED			1000 850	
400mm f/5.6 EDIF	2495 2000	1600 1400	1300 1050	
400mm f/5.6 AI'd or Non-AI			495 450	
500mm f/4 EDIF P	4350 3800	3650 3400		
500mm f/5 Reflex		1350 1000	900 600	
500mm f/8 Reflex (latest)	810 690	650 575	550 400	
500mm f/8 Reflex (early)		385 350	350 270	285 220
600mm f/4 EDIF	7200 6450	5200 4600	4350 3800	
600mm f/5.6 EDIF	4895 4250	3800 3450	3320 2800	2650 2300
600mm f/5.6 (w/focusing unit)			1000 800	
800mm f/5.6 EDIF	6250 5500	4895 4480		
800mm f/8 (w/focusing unit)			1200 1000	
800mm f/8 ED		2150 2000		
800mm f/8 EDIF		2500 2300		
1000mm f/11 Reflex (early)		1000 880	850 750	
1000mm f/11 Reflex (late)	1950 1590	1350 1200	1180 950	
1200mm f/11 (w/focusing unit)		1500 1200		
1200mm f/11 ED		3000 2500		
1200mm f/11 EDIF		4000 3500		
2000mm f/11 Reflex			4000 3000	

The 2000mm f/11 Reflex Nikkor is huge and heavy, and was made in small numbers. Most imported into the USA were sold to the military. Although rare, they do appear on the used market from time to time.

Lens	New	Mint	Excellent	User
TC1 Non-AI		385 255	245 200	
TC2 Non-AI			250 200	
TC14 AI			330 300	
TC14A AIs	345 260		175 150	
TC14B AIs	610 530	450 400	385 300	
TC200 AI		170 150	150 120	130 95
TC201 AIs	325 260	220 200	190 140	
TC300 AI		350 275	300 225	
TC301 AIs	640 535	470 400	380 325	

Nikon Manual Focus Zoom Lenses

Lens	New	Mint	Excellent	User
25-50 f/4		450 370	390 320	
28-45 f/4.5 AI		250 200	220 190	175 140
28-45 f/4.5 AI'd			220 180	
28-45 f/4.5 Non-AI			175 125	
28-50 f/3.5		345 250	250 185	
28-85 f/3.5-4.5	480 500	480 400	425 300	
35-70 f/3.3-4.5	275 260	195 150	135 100	
35-70 f/3.5 (62mm)		425 360	375 325	
35-70 f/3.5 (67mm)		400 350	350 300	
35-70 f/3.5 AI or AI'd (72mm)		375 325	300 250	
35-105 f/3.5-4.5		350 280	320 250	

Nikon Manual Focus Zoom Lenses

Lens	New		Mint		Excellent		User	
35-135 f/3.5-4.5	585	490	440	380	360	300		
35-200 f/3.5-4.5	1100	800	700	650	635	500		
36-72 f/3.5 E			180	150	160	120		
43-86 f/3.5			175	140	140	120	130	110
43-86 f/3.5 AI'd or Non-AI			150	120	125	80	90	70
50-135 f/3.5			315	280	290	245		
50-300 f/4.5 ED	2995	2600	2200	1975	1850	1400	1320	1000
50-300 f/4.5 AI or AI'd			625	500	525	425		
50-300 f/4.5 Non-AI					450	375		
70-210 f/4 E			300	250	275	180	200	150
75-150 f/3.5 E			225	175	175	150	135	120
80-200 f/2.8 ED			1450	1300	1250	1100		
80-200 f/4	820	730	650	570	550	440	425	360
80-200 f/4.5 AI or AI'd			395	280	295	240	225	175
80-200 f/4.5 Non-AI					230	190	180	160
85-250 f/4-4.5 (Nikon's 1st Zoom)			280	225	240	150		
100-300 f/5.6	610	500	425	350	375	300		
180-600 f/8 ED			5200	4900	4800	4400		
200-400 f/4 ED			4275	3895	3450	3390		
200-600 f/9.5-10.5 (Nikon's 2nd Zoom)			985	750	650	485		
360-1200 f/11 ED					5000+			

The 360-1200 ED Zoom Nikkor was offered for only a short time and few were sold. The above price is probably the least you can expect to pay for one, assuming you can find one at all.

AF Nikkor Lenses

Lens	New		Mint		Excellent		User	
16mm f/2.8 D	950	710						
18mm f/2.8 D	1380	1130						
20mm f/2.8	700	525	450	370				
24mm f/2.8	500	350	300	220	250	200		
24mm f/2.8 D								
28mm f/1.4 D	2150	1700						
28mm f/2.8			150	140				
28mm f/2.8 D	295	210						
35mm f/2	460	330	270	230				
50mm f/1.4	320	240	200	180				
50mm f/1.8	130	85	65	50				
55mm f/2.8 Micro			270	250	245	200		
60mm f/2.8 Micro			295	260				
60mm f/2.8 D Micro	500	400						
80mm f/2.8 (F3AF)			250	200	180	150		
The AF 80mm f/2.8 will autofocus on the F3AF only, but can be used on any Nikon SLR.								
85mm f/1.8	470	335	280	240	240	200		
85mm f/1.8 D	440	350						
105mm f/2 DFC D	1090	860						
105mm f/2.8 Micro			450	420				
105mm f/2.8 D Micro	795	630						
135mm f/2.8 DFC	1140	910						
180mm f/2.8 EDIF N	895	715						
180mm f/2.8 EDIF (early)			500	460	480	435		
200mm f/3.5 ED (F3AF)			500	400				
The AF 200mm f/3.5 will autofocus on the F3AF only, but can be used on any Nikon SLR.								
200mm f/4 D Micro	1640	1300						
300mm f/2.8 EDIF D	5200	4500						
300mm f/2.8 EDIF N			3200	2650				
300mm f/2.8 EDIF (early)			2500	2350				
300mm f/4 EDIF	1140	925	825	750				
400mm f/2.8 EDIF D								
500mm f/4 EDIF D								
600mm f/4 EDIF D	9500	8700						
TC14E	545	450						
TC-16A			180	150	150	100		
TC-16AF (F3AF)			70	125	115	90		
TC-20E	640	520						

AF Nikkor Zoom Lenses

Lens	New	Mint	Excellent	User
20-35 f/2.8 D	2100 1750			
24-50 f/3.3-4.5	475 390	350 300		
28-70 f/3.5-4.5 Aspherical		270 235		
28-70 f/3.5-4.5 D	470 390			
28-85 f/3.5-4.5	495 400	360 320	330 250	
35-70 f/2.8		520 400	385 350	
35-70 f/2.8 D	810 675			
35-70 f/3.3-4.5	170 135	120 110	115 100	
35-80 f/4-5.6 D	150 120			
35-105 f/3.5-4.5	495 400	350 300	280 240	
35-135 f/3.5-4.5	520 430	360 300		
70-210 f/4		280 225	200 180	
70-210 f/4-5.6	280 210	210 170	190 140	
70-210 f/4-5.6 D	410 320			
75-300 f/4.5-5.6	650 530	480 420		
80-200 f/2.8 EDIF		695 650	675 625	
80-200 f/2.8 EDIF D	1225 980			

Nikon Motor Drives, Winders & Accessories

Item	New	Mint	Excellent	User
Generic Winder (FA/FE/FE2/FM/FM2)	65 35		30 25	
AW-1 (ELW/EL2)			120 75	
F-36 w/Remote Pack (F)			285 200	
F-36 Cordless (F)		425 350	295 250	
F-250 (w/back, batt pack & cassettes)			300 200	
MD-E (EM/FG/FG20)		120 100	100 65	
MD1/MB1 (F2)		400 300	325 250	
MD2/MB1 (F2)		600 525	500 350	320 280
MD3/MB2 (F2)		340 290	275 200	

The MB1 battery pack will power either the MD1, MD2 or MD3 to 4 frames per second or so (about 5.5 fps w/NiCads). The MB2 is good for only 2 ½ fps. Expect to pay $50-70 more for the MD3/MB1 combination than the MD3/MB2 combination listed above.

Item	New	Mint	Excellent	User
MD4 (F3)	495 400	380 320	340 280	
MD4/MN2 (F3)			380 330	
MD11 (FA/FE/FE2/FM/FM2)		150 140	140 100	110 90
MD12 (FA/FE/FE2/FM/FM2)	350 280	250 220	200 180	

Although the MD-11 and MD-12 are interchangeable and may look the same, there are a couple of important differences: the MD-11 has a nasty habit of draining its batteries if the power switch is left on when not in use. Nikon corrected this problem with the MD-12. While they were at it, they gave the MD12 a new electric motor with more torque.

Item	New	Mint	Excellent	User
MD14 (EM/FG/FG20)		180 130	140 115	
MD15 (FA only)		300 230	240 175	160 140
MB-20 (F4)	55 45	40 25		
MB-21 (F4)	200 140			
MB-22 (F4) External Power Regulator	300 260			
MB-23 (F4 - High Output)	415 340			
MH-1 Charger for MN-1			50 40	
MN-1 Nicads for MD1,MD2 (pair, refurbished)		125 100		
MH-2 Charger for MN-2	210 140	125 85	75 60	
MN-2 Nicads for MD4	150 115	110 80	90 60	
MH-20 Charger for MN-20	300 240			
MN-20 Nicads for MB-23	130 115			
F Bulk Film Cassette	15 10			
AM-1 36 exp reloadable cassette (F2)			15 10	
MZ-1 Bulk Film Cassette (All 250s)	50 45		40 30	
Bulk Film Loader	220 210	180 150	140 125	
AH-2 or 3 Tripod Adapter	30 25	25 20		
AH-4 Tripod Adapter	65 55			
AP-2 Panoramic Head	120 85			
MK-1 Firing Rate Converter	190 140	90 65		
MR-2 Aux shutter release		20 15		
MR-3 Aux shutter release	40 30			
ML-1 Modulite Remote Control Set		220 180	195 150	
ML-2 Modulite Remote Control Set	385 300			

Nikon Motor Drives, Winders & Accessories

Item	New	Mint	Excellent	User
MW-1 Remote Control Set			780 620	
MW-2 Remote Control Set	1520 1300	1175 1000		
MT-1 Intervalometer			650 500	
MT-2 Intervalometer	1000 825			
Pistol Grip			30 25	
Pistol Grip 2	50 40	40 25		

Nikon Backs

Item	New	Mint	Excellent	User
MF-1 (250 exp for F2)		290 200	250 180	
MF-3 (Stops film rewind w/MD2)		125 90	95 60	
MF-4 (250 exp for F3)	1075 950	750 700	700 500	
MF-6B (Stops film rewind w/MD4)	100 85	60 50	45 35	
MF-11 (Data back for MF-1)			175 150	
MF-12 (FE/FM)			100 60	
MF-14 (F3)	210 160	140 120	110 70	
MF-15 (FG)		100 80	90 60	
MF-16 (FA/FE2/FM2)	230 170	160 130	120 80	
MF-17/MF-4 set	3800 3500			
MF-18 (F3)	285 250	225 200	180 150	
MF-19 (N2000/N2020)	280 190	170 150	140 100	
MF-20 (N8008/s)	120 75	70 60		
MF-21 (N8008/s)	210 155	140 125		
MF-22 (F4)	170 130	110 75		
MF-23 (F4)	590 440		365 300	
MF-24 (F4)	4895 4500			
MF-25				
MF-26				
Speed Magny RF (F)			700 600	
Speed Magny 45 (F)			600 450	
Speed Magny 45-2 (F2)			700 600	
Speed Magny 100 (F)			350 200	
Speed Magny 100-2 (F2)			400 250	
Speed Magny 100-3 (F3)			1200 800	
Forscher or NPC Polaroid Back *(various models)*	720 600		585 450	
Datalink Introductory Package (AC-1E w/MC-27 & Sharp Wizard 8200s)	600 500			
AC-2E for above package (N90s)	240 195			

Nikon Finders and Finder Accessories

Item	New	Mint	Excellent	User
F Eye Level Prism (blk or chr)		175 150	150 95	60 40
F Waist Level Finder (blk or chr)		100 70	70 60	
F Sportfinder (blk or chr)		295 250	250 165	
F Photomic (non-TTL) (blk or chr)			60 50	
F Photomic T (blk or chr)			60 50	
F Photomic TN (blk or chr)			70 55	
F Photomic FTN (blk or chr)		250 190	185 140	125 85
DA-1 Sportfinder (F2)		250 195	190 150	
DA-2 Sportfinder (F3)	420 290	250 200	225 175	
DA-20 Sportfinder (F4)	650 550			
DE-1 Eye Level Prism (F2)		140 125	120 90	
DE-2 Eye Level Prism (F3)		100 90	80 75	80 70
DE-3 High Eye Point Prism (F3)	275 200	200 150	140 100	
DG-2 2X Eyepiece Magnifier	60 40	35 30	35 25	
DP-1 (F2 Photomic)		190 150	170 120	110 90
DP-2 (F2S)		210 170	175 140	135 100
DP-3 (F2SB)		400 325	310 260	

Nikon Finders and Finder Accessories

Item	New	Mint	Excellent	User
DP-11 (F2A)			270 200	180 160
DP-12 (F2AS)		450 395	410 355	330 295
DP-20 (F4)	520 425			
DR-2 Right Angle Finder			45 40	
DR-3 Right Angle Finder	125 75			
Right Angle Finder (early)		35 30	30 20	
DS-1 Servo EE (w/DH1 chgr & DN1 NiCads)			150 100	
DS-2 Servo EE (w/DH1 chgr & DN1 NiCads)			190 125	
DS-12 Servo EE (w/DH1 chgr & DN1 NiCads)			270 200	220 150

Addition of the DS-1 or DS-2 Servo EE unit to a Nikon F2S or F2SB allows the camera to operate in shutter-priority AE. The DS-2 is identical to the DS-1, but has a PC connector. The PC connector on the front of the camera is sacrificed with the DS-1, since the connector's threads are the main attachment point. Even though the AS-1 flash adapter can still be used for flash work with the DS-1, the DS-2 (with a built-in PC connection) is the non-AI model most everyone wants. The DS-12 is the AI version of the DS-2 and works with the F2AS only.

Item	New	Mint	Excellent	User
DH-1 Charger for DN-1		95 75	85 50	
DN-1 Nicads for DS-1/2/12	35 30			
DW-1 (F2 waist level)		110 80	80 50	
DW-2 (F2 6X)		250 175	200 125	120 85
DW-3 (F3 waist level)	120 80	70 50	50 40	
DW-4 (F3 6X)	280 180	165 100		
DW-20 (F4 waist level)	230 160		120 100	
DW-21 (F4 6X)	360 300			
DX-1 (AF finder for F3AF)		200 185	160 125	

The DX-1 can be used on a non-autofocus F3. The camera won't autofocus, but it does provide focus direction and confirmation with manual and auto-focus lenses that are f/3.5 or faster.

Nikon Close-up Accessories

Item	New	Mint	Excellent	User
Bellows 2		125 90	85 70	
Bellows 3		150 100	120 75	
PB-4 Bellows		300 250	280 200	
PB-5 Bellows		150 120	125 100	
PB-6 Bellows	300 220	200 140		
Slide Copier 2 (fits Bellows 2)		110 75	80 75	
PS-4 Slide Copier		100 90	90 80	
PS-5 Slide Copier		50 40	35 20	
PS-6 Slide Copier for PB-6	195 135	115 80	80 70	
PB-6D Spacer (2 req'd), each	70 50			
PB-6E Bellows Ext for PB-6	220 145	120 100		
PB-6M Macro Stage	75 45		25 20	
PF-2 Stage		40 30		
PF-4 Repro Copy Outfit	595 500		295 250	
PG-2 Focusing Stage	220 170			

The PB-4 Bellows provides Tilt-Shift capability, whereas the PB-5 and PB-6 do not. The PB-6 has the socket for the double cable release built in to the front standard for convenient auto-aperture stop-down. To achieve the same result with the PB-4 or PB-5, the BR-4 ring (equipped with a cable release socket) must be used between the lens and the front standard. The PS-4 or PS-5 Slide Duplicators can be interchanged between the PB-4, PB-5 and most other early Nikon bellows. However, the PS-4 and PS-6 allow up/down/sideways movement of the slide for cropping, whereas the PS-5 does not. The PB-6E is an extension unit that fits onto the end of the PB-6 allowing a total extension of 438mm.

Item	New	Mint	Excellent	User
M or M2 Ext Tube (1:1 w/55mm Non-AI Micro)			25 20	
PK-2 Ext Tube			25 20	
PK-3 Ext Tube		40 35	35 30	
PK-11 Ext Tube		40 25		
PK-11A Ext Tube (AIs)	80 60	50 40		
PK-12 Ext Tube (AI-14mm)	80 60	50 40		
PK-13 Ext Tube (AI)	80 60	50 40		
PN-1 Ext Tube (Non-AI)		75 70		
PN-11 Ext Tube (AI)	175 105	100 75		
Ext. Ring Set K		60 50	40 30	

The PN-11, when used with the 105 AI/AIs Micro, provides from 1:2 to 1:1 image size. The PN-1 is the non-AI version. The PK-13 does the same thing, but for the 55 AI/AIs Micro. The PK-11A, while providing full function with any AI camera/lens, was designed to clear the contacts on the N2020 (and, presumably, will clear the contacts on other autofocus Nikons as well). The Extension Ring Set K is a set of five rings which can be used separately or in combination.

Nikon Close-up Accessories

Item	New		Mint		Excellent		User	
BR-2/2A Reversing Ring (52mm)	40	25	20	10				
BR-3 Reversing Ring	40	25			15	10		
BR-4 Reversing Ring (Auto Diaphragm)	65	45	40	25	30	20		
BR-5 Reversing Ring (for 20 f/2.8)	40	25			10	10		
BR-6 Reversing Ring	70	55	35	25				
E2 Extension Ring (Diaphragm)					25	20		
AR-4 Double Cable Release	60	35	35	25				
AR-7 Double Cable Release	60	35	35	25				
AR-10 Double Cable Release	80	65						

Nikon Speedlites and Speedlite Accessories

Item	New		Mint		Excellent		User	
SB-E (EM)			40	30	25	20		
SB-1 w/batt pack (Handle-mount)					75	50		
SB-2 (F/F2)			110	90				
SB-3 (ISO shoe)					60	50		
SB-5 (Handle-mount)					275	250		
SB-6 (F/F2 or ISO w/adapter)			1450	1400				
SB-7E (F/F2)			110	95				
SB-8E (ISO shoe)			65	60				
SB-9 (ISO shoe)			45	35	35	25		
SB-10 (FE)			50	40	45	35	30	25
SB-11 (Handle-mount - F3 TTL)			200	160	180	145		
SB-12 (F3 TTL)			60	50	50	25		
SB-14 (Handle-mount - F3 TTL)			300	250	200	130		
SB-15 (TTL ISO shoe)			135	90	120	85		
SB-16A (F3 TTL)	320	280	250	225	230	180	150	130
SB-16B (TTL ISO shoe)	300	260	240	210	200	160		
SB-17 (F3 TTL)	215	185	150	135	120	85		
SB-18 (TTL ISO shoe)			60	50	40	35		
SB-19 (ISO - FG20/EM)			50	40				
SB-20 (TTL ISO/AF)	260	210	190	165	150	120		
SB-21A Macrolite (F3 TTL)	500	410	360	325				
SB-21B Macrolite (TTL ISO shoe)	485	415	365	325				
SB-22 (TTL ISO/AF)	185	135	120	85				
SB-23 (TTL ISO/AF)	120	105	80	60	70	50		
SB-24 (TTL ISO/AF)			225	175	165	145		
SB-25 (TTL ISO/AF)	395	295						
SB-26 (TTL ISO/AF)	480	380						
SM-1 Macro Ringlite					55	45		
SM-2 Macro Ringlite			225	150				
SR-1 Macro Ringlite					50	40		
SR-2 Macro Ringlite			180	160				
LA-1 AC Unit (SM-2/SR-2)			125	100				
LA-2 AC Unit (120mm Med Nikkor)	300	230						
LD-1 DC Batt Pack (SM-2/SR-2)			125	110				
LD-2 DC Batt Pack (SB-21/120mm Med Nikkor)	200	140						

The SM-1 and SM-2 attach to reverse-mounted Nikkors. The SR-1 and SR-2 thread into the 52mm front filter threads. The SM-1 and SR-1 draw power from another flash unit's power supply, such as the SB-1 or SB-7. The SM-2 and SR-2 are powered by the LD-1 battery pack or the LA-1 AC power supply.

Item	New		Mint		Excellent		User	
SD-7 Batt Pack (SB-14)	150	100						
SD-8 Hi-Perf Batt Pack (SB-11/20/22/24)	150	100	100	85				
SK-6 Power Bracket	300	260						
AS-1 (ISO foot to F/F2 shoe)	30	25			20	15		
AS-2 (F/F2 foot to ISO shoe)	30	20			15	10		
AS-3 (F/F2 foot to F3 shoe)	35	20			20	15		
AS-4 (ISO foot to F3 shoe)	30	25			20	15		
AS-5 (F3 foot to F/F2 shoe)	40	25						
AS-6 (F3 foot to ISO shoe)	45	40			25	20		
AS-7 (F3/ISO foot to F3 shoe)	90	70			60	50		

Nikon Speedlites and Speedlite Accessories

Item	New	Mint	Excellent	User
AS-8 (F3 foot for SB-16)	150 ... 125	90 ... 75	80 ... 70	
AS-9 (ISO foot for SB-16)	130 ... 90		65 ... 50	
AS-10 (ISO TTL Multi-flash adapter)	40 ... 35	30 ... 20		
AS-11 (F3 foot tripod adapter)	40 ... 35		25 ... 15	
AS-12 (F3 foot for SB-21)	230 ... 220	180 ... 150		
AS-14 (ISO foot for SB-21)	250 ... 215	180 ... 150	155 ... 125	
AS-15 (PC adapter for N8008)	25 ... 20			

The AS-7 Flash Coupler is designed to allow the flash to stand off from the F3 camera body, permitting film rewind/removal without having to dismount the flash. It also permits the use of flashes with either the F3 foot or the standard ISO foot. TTL flash is still posible with flashes that have the F3 foot, but not for flashes with the standard ISO foot, even if they provide TTL flash on other Nikons. TTL flash is also lost when using the AS-4 or AS-6. The only way around this is to buy a base for each shoe type. But this option exists only for the SB-16 (AS-8/AS-9) and SB-21 (AS-12/AS-14), and it's an expensive one.

Item	New	Mint	Excellent	User
SC-6 (3 Prong to PC)	30 ... 25			
SC-10 (ISO foot to PC)	25 ... 20			
SC-11 (SB11/14 sync cord)	25 ... 20		10 ... 10	
SC-12 (F3 TTL to SB11/14)	170 ... 140			
SC-13 (Remote sensor cord - SB11/14)	120 ... 90			
SC-14 (F3 TTL)	75 ... 60		40 ... 30	
SC-15 (PC to PC)	25 ... 20			
SC-17 (ISO TTL)	50 ... 55		40 ... 30	
SC-18 (TTL Multi-flash - 5 ft)	40 ... 30			
SC-19 (TTL Multi-flash - 10 ft)	55 ... 30	25 ... 20		
SC-21 (120mm Medical Nikkor to SB-21 A/B)	60 ... 40			
SC-23 (ISO TTL to SB11/14)	150 ... 115			
SC-24 (TTL cord - F4)	65 ... 55			

What's all this "foot" and "shoe" business, you ask? Simple. The thingy on the bottom of your flash is called the foot. The doohickey on the camera that a flash fits into is called the shoe. So, if the thingy on the bottom of your flash doesn't fit on to the doohickey on your camera, perhaps you need one of the above adapters. An ISO foot/shoe is the square flash base/receptacle that is of standard dimensions, regardless of the brand of camera or flash — hence the designation ISO (International Standards Organization).

Olympus

Olympus' OM-Series SLRs

Olympus' OM-series cameras have many strong points. Most often extolled are their compactness and light weight. But there are other notable advantages. Almost any OM camera will accept almost any OM accessory. For example, both Motor Drives 1 & 2 will work with the OM-1MD, OM-1N, OM-2, OM-2N, OM-2S, OM-3, OM-4, OM-4T, OM-G & OM-F. Most OM cameras have interchangeable focusing screens and it doesn't matter which camera you have, either. Any OM screen will fit any OM camera that has that capability. Another characteristic of the OM system is a depth-of-field preview button located on OM lenses, which means all OM-mount cameras support this feature.

In the following listings, the only current OM camera is the OM-4T, Olympus' highly regarded professional model. Apparently, Olympus' brief foray into the AF interchangeable-lens SLR market met with little success. Not only has Olympus discontinued the OM-77 and OM-88, but its entire line of AF lenses has met with the same fate. The explanation given to me by an Olympus representative was that the IS-1 has become so popular that the company sees no reason to market amateur-level interchangeable-lens AF SLRs at this time. He also indicated that Olympus has no plans to replace the OM-4T with a professional-level AF SLR. We'll see.

Olympus M-1/OM-1, OM-1MD & OM-1N

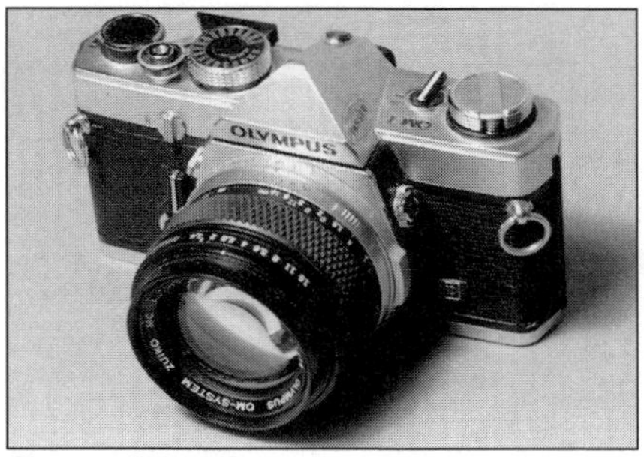

Olympus OM-1 MD

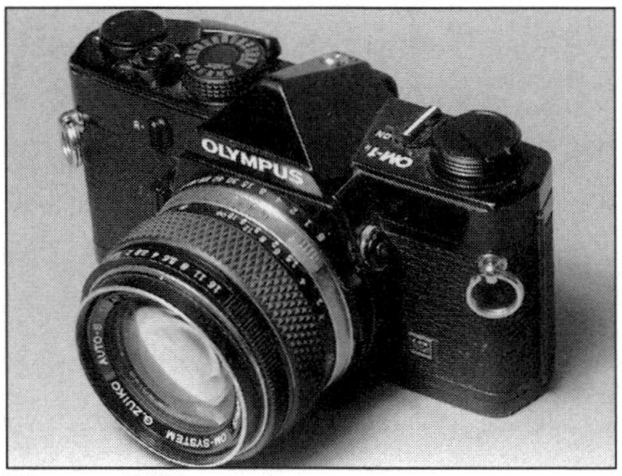

Olympus OM-1n

The M-1, actually the first OM camera and identical to the OM-1, was marketed for a short time before Leica protested the designation. Though it is somewhat rare, I've listed it below because it isn't particularly expensive.

The OM-1 is a compact, mechanical, manual exposure SLR. Its TTL meter provides centerweighted, center-the-needle metering. Shutter speeds range from 1 second to 1/1000, plus B, with flash sync at 1/60. Other features include a self-timer, mirror lock-up and provisions for the attachment of an accessory hot shoe.

Introduced a couple of years later, the OM-1MD can use a winder or a motor drive (The MD stands for Motor Drive). Otherwise, it's the same camera. Most OM-1MDs have a label that says MD on the front, but not all do. If in doubt, turn the camera over and look at the baseplate. The standard OM-1 will have one port for the batteries. The MD model will have an additional port for the motor drive.

The OM-1N was the last of the OM-1 series. With the accessory Shoe 4 and a dedicated flash unit, the OM-1N has a ready light that will appear in the viewfinder.

Olympus OM-2, OM-2N & OM-2S Program

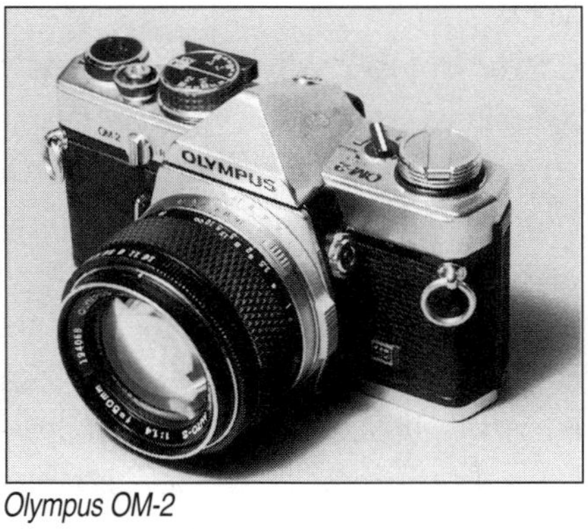

Olympus OM-2

The OM-2 series cameras feature Olympus' off-the-film (OTF) method of determining exposure, and are renowned for their super-long, auto-exposure capability for truly amazing low-light results. The OM-2's exposure modes are aperture-priority AE and metered manual. Manual shutter speeds range from 1 second to 1/1000, plus B, with flash sync at 1/60. In aperture-priority, the OTF metering system is active and, while the viewfinder may show a certain speed, the OTF system may select another. If the camera deems it necessary, speeds can time out to well over one minute. I've read of one photographer who claims to take low-light photos of up to 30 minutes and longer with an original OM-2 on the auto setting. Other features include mirror lock-up, a self-timer and compatibility with the long list of OM accessories.

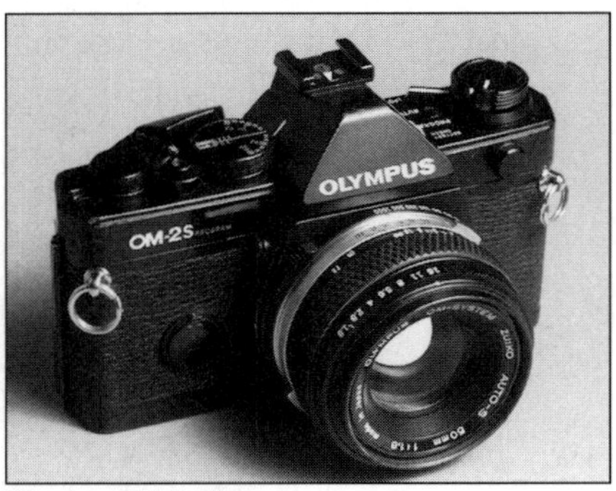

Olympus OM-2s Program

The OM-2N features TTL (OTF, I presume) flash. Olympus changed the main computer chip with this model, which resulted in shortening its low-light exposure times, but they're still plenty long.

The OM-2s Program is a completely redesigned camera. Exposure modes are program, aperture-priority, metered manual and TTL flash. The standard centerweighted metering pattern is used in the AE modes. In the manual mode, the user has a choice between centerweighted and spot metering patterns. In program or aperture-priority, the camera meters the film plane during exposure and shutter speeds can range from about 1 minute to 1/1000 second. In manual, the standard range of shutter speeds is available, plus B, with X sync at 1/60. Other features include exposure compensation, a self-timer and all the other accessories that are part of the OM system.

Olympus OM-3

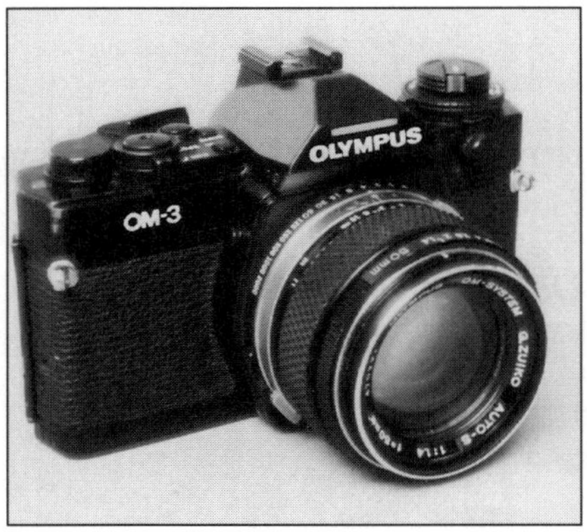

Olympus OM-3

The OM-3 saw a somewhat brief production history, due perhaps to lackluster sales. Since its discontinuation, however, it has become the most highly sought-after camera of all OM models. Clean examples often command higher prices than new OM-4Ts. Something of a high-tech return to basics, the OM-3 is a manual-exposure-only camera that features two metering patterns: center-weighted averaging and spot. The mechanical shutter provides speeds ranging from 1 second to 1/2000, plus B. Other features you'd expect, such as interchangeable focusing screens, a self-timer, and compatibility with most all OM accessories round out the capabilities of this camera.

Olympus OM-4 & OM-4T

The only current OM camera at the date of this writing is the OM-4T, successor to the original OM-4. The original OM-4 features two exposure modes, aperture-priority AE and metered manual. Either centerweighted metering or spot can be employed. The spot function will allow up to eight readings to be stored and averaged for critical exposure control. Other exposure features are a highlight/shadow bias function, exposure compensation and TTL flash with dedicated flash units. Shutter speeds in the aperture priority mode range from 4 minutes to 1/2000, plus B, with X sync at 1/60. In manual mode, shutter speeds range from 1 second to 1/2000.

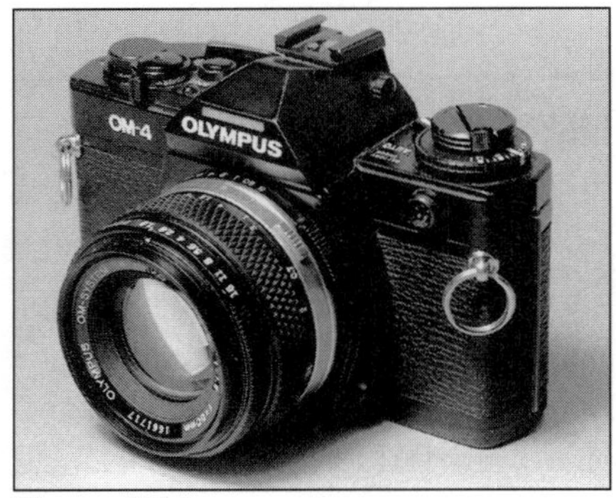

Olympus OM-4

The OM-4T is much the same camera with a few very nice improvements. For starters, it is housed in titanium (hence the T). It is well-gasketed against dust and moisture intrusion. A diopter adjustment was added. But the most interesting new feature of the OM-4T is its flash capability. When coupled with the Full Synchro Flash F280 strobe, it's possible to take flash pictures at any shutter speed — all the way up to the OM4-T's top shutter speed of 1/2000. While this is the fastest flash sync on the market, power consumption of the F280 flash is prodigious and output is somewhat low. Of course, the OM-4 and OM-4T are compatible with the entire array of OM accessories, from focusing screens to motor drives.

Olympus OM-10, OM-G & OM-F

Designed as an entry-level camera, the OM-10 meets most photographic situations with a minimum of fanfare, yet performs its job quite capably. A single exposure mode, aperture priority AE, is available standard. With the installation of the Manual Adapter, metered manual is also available. Shutter speeds range from 2 seconds to 1/1000, plus B. TTL OTF flash is available with dedicated flash units. Other features include a self-timer, a winder option and compatibility with most OM accessories.

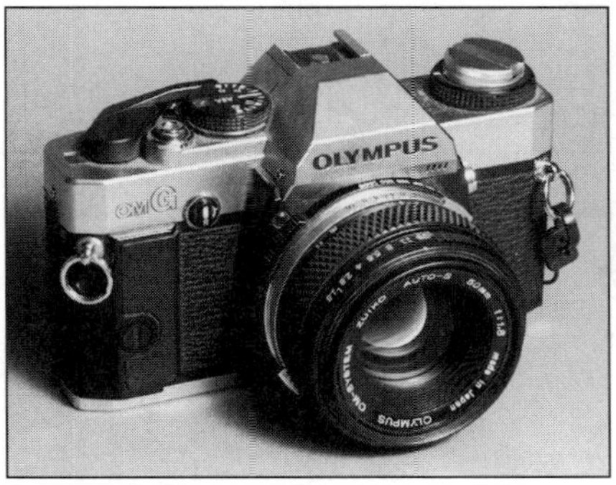

Olympus OM-G

The OM-G is essentially an OM-10 with the manual mode built in. The OM-F is an OM-G with a focus assist feature, the direct predecessor, and the next best thing to autofocus. This feature is particularly useful to those folks whose eyes 'ain't what they used to be', but who may balk at the idea of buying into an autofocus system. The OM-F offers a very serviceable alternative.

Olympus OM-PC

The OM-PC was the first Olympus to feature its ESP (Electro Selective Pattern) metering system. ESP employs a comparative recognition system that monitors the contrast levels of a scene and spots difficult lighting situations. The camera then adjusts the shutter speed and/or aperture to produce the best possible exposure, then continues to monitor the scene during exposure via the OTF metering method. TTL OTF flash automation is also available with dedicated flash units.

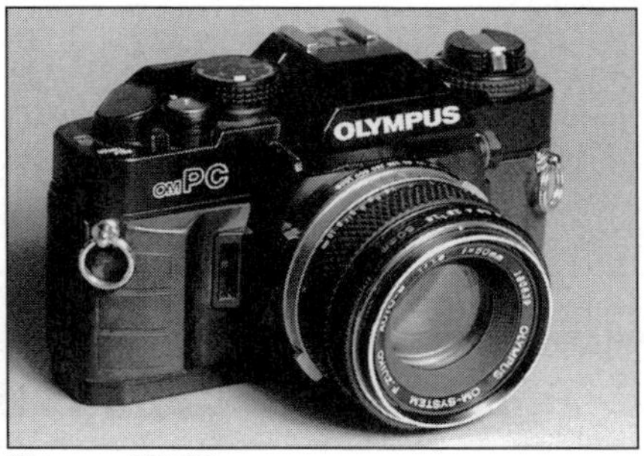

Olympus OM-PC

Shutter speeds range from 2 seconds to 1/1000, plus B (1 second to 1/1000 in manual). The OM-PC's exposure modes are program, aperture-priority AE and metered manual. Other features include a self-timer, DX film coding with manual override, and use of virtually the full line of Olympus accessories.

Olympus OM-77AF

The OM-77AF's autofocus modes are single shot (Focus priority) and continuous (servo). It will manual-focus AF lenses in the "Power Focus" mode only. Exposure options include a program mode, which adjusts for lens focal length, a shift function, aperture-priority AE and AE lock. Shutter speeds range from 2 seconds to 1/2000, with X sync at 1/100. When using the F280 Full Synchro Flash, flash photography is possible at all shutter speeds. Other features include an integral motor drive with continuous speeds up to 1.5 fps, auto film loading and rewind, and DX film coding with no override.

Either autofocus or manual focus lenses can be used. With the latter, only aperture-priority AE is possible.

Olympus OM-88

The Olympus OM-88 is unique in that it is neither a manual-focus camera, nor is it an autofocus camera— it's an almost autofocus camera, using a system Olympus called "Power Focus." The camera accepts PF (Power Focus), AF and manual focus lenses. When using PF or AF lenses, the user pushes a button to focus the lens. This activates a motor that drives the lens in the focus direction desired — an interesting novelty, but not interesting enough, it would seem. The OM-88 was discontinued in 1991.

The OM-88's exposure options include program, aperture-priority AE (when using manual focus lenses) and metered manual (with Manual Adapter 2). Shutter speeds range from 2 seconds to 1/2000, plus B (when using the optional Manual adapter 2), with X sync at 1/80. TTL flash is possible with dedicated flash units. Other features include a backlight control, a built-in single- frame-only motor drive, auto film loading and rewind, DX film coding with no override, a dedicated hot shoe and a self-timer.

Olympus OM-series SLRs

Camera	Yrs. Made	New	Mint	Excellent	User
M-1	1972			350 275	
OM-1 chr	1973-79		180 145	160 125	130 100
OM-1 blk	1973-79			200 140	
OM-1MD chr	1975-79			175 140	
OM-1MD blk	1975-79		260 220	200 150	
OM-1N chr	1979-87		225 175	180 150	150 120
OM-1N blk	1979-87		250 220	200 160	170 130
OM-2 chr	1975-79		210 175	200 150	
OM-2 blk	1975-79		260 200	220 170	
OM-2N chr	1979-84		220 195	200 165	
OM-2N blk	1979-84		300	225 180	190 160

Olympus OM-series SLRs

Camera	Yrs. Made	New		Mint		Excellent		User	
OM-2S	1984-88			350	300	275	225	200	165
OM-3	1983-86			700	500	450	350	300	260
OM-4 chr	1984-87			450	400	400	315		
OM-4 blk	1984-87					400	350	325	300
OM-4T chr	1987-	900	750	500	460	475	395		
OM-4T blk	1990-	900	750	520	490				
OM-10	1979-87			130	75	85	65		
OM-10 Quartz	1984-87			120	90				
OM-F (Focus Assist)	1983-87			180	150	150	120		
OM-G	1983-87			240.	215	100	85		
OM-PC	1985-87			220	150	165	125		
OM-77AF	1986-91			180	150	155	125		
OM-88 w/50 PF	1988-91			175	160	150	135		

Zuiko Manual Focus Lenses

Lens	New		Mint		Excellent		User	
8mm f/2.8	1700	950	870	800	820	600		
16mm f/3.5	800	600	550	500	520	400		
18mm f/3.5	860	550	500	450	450	390		
20mm f/2 Macro (Bellows)	330	250	200	180	175	140		
20mm f/3.5 Macro (Bellows)			125	100				
21mm f/2	710	500	450	380	340	290		
21mm f/3.5	380	300	225	200	200	150		
24mm f/2	510	380	340	280	270	250		
24mm f/2.8	320	290	250	220	200	180	185	160
24mm f/3.5 PC	1160	1000	940	890	850	700		
28mm f/2	500	350	325	265	275	230		
28mm f/2.8	210	170	145	120	120	95		
28mm f/3.5			95	80	80	65		
35mm f/2	280	230	195	170	180	130		
35mm f/2.8	190	140	115	80	90	65		
35mm f/2.8 PC	685	500	450	400				
38mm f/2.8 Macro (Bellows)	300	220						
38mm f/3.5 Macro (Bellows)			175	125				
40mm f/2			100	85	90	75		
50mm f/1.2	325	285	250	225	225	190		
50mm f/1.4	220	180	160	95	100	80		
50mm f/1.8	80	75	50	40	45	35		
50mm f/2 Macro	480	390	325	280	250	200		
50mm f/3.5 Macro	270	210	180	150	160	125		
80mm f/4 Macro (Bellows)	410	200	200	170	180	150		
85mm f/2	350	290	250	235	230	190		
90mm f/2 Macro	585	490	450	400	400	350		
100mm f/2	520	450	400	375	380	325		
100mm f/2.8	260	230	200	170	160	125		
135mm f/2.8			150	125	135	90		
135mm f/3.5			85	50	55	45		
135mm f/4.5 Macro (Bellows)	400	220	200	190	170	150		
180mm f/2	3300	2500	2200	1850				
180mm f/2.8	750	570	520	470	425	350		
200mm f/4	270	245	200	140	150	120		
200mm f/5					120	90		
250mm f/2	4250	3800			2950	2500		
300mm f/4.5	525	460	420	375	350	300		
350mm f/2.5 ED			3700	3200				
350mm f/2.8	4450	4000	3650	3000	3100	2750		
400mm f/6.3	1500	1100	1000	900	850	700		
500mm f/8	625	470	450	400	390	300		
600mm f/6.5	2200	1700	1450	1380	1350	1200		
1000mm f/11	2100	1500	1350	1250	1200	950		
1.4X-A	360	270	240	200	200	150		
2X-A	295	160	140	110	90	75		

Zuiko Zoom Lenses

Lens	New	Mint	Excellent	User
28-48 f/4			180 120	
35-70 f/3.5-4.5		160 100	100 80	
35-70 f/3.6		300 240	270 200	
35-70 f/4		160 125	145 90	
35-70 f/4 AF		160 120		
The 35-70 f/4 AF will autofocus on any Olympus OM-series SLR.				
35-105 f/3.5-4.5		235 220	210 150	
50-250 f/5	735 600	550 485	450 350	
65-200 f/4	395 310	250 200	200 145	
75-150 f/4		150 100	120 85	
85-200 f/4			170 150	
85-250 f/5			290 225	
100-200 f/5		150 70	85 60	

Olympus Autofocus Lenses

Lens	New	Mint	Excellent	User
24mm f/2.8		150 125	105 85	
28mm f/2.8		70 50		
50mm f/1.8		40 35		
50mm f/2 PF (OM-88)		50 40		
50mm f/2.8 Macro		190 175		
28-85 f/3.5-4.5		120 100		
35-70 f/3.5		90 85		
35-70 f/3.5 PF (OM-88)		90 80		
35-105 f/3.5-4.5		140 100		
70-210 f/3.5-4.5		170 140		
70-210 f/3.5-4.5 PF (OM-88)		200 150		

Olympus Motor Drives, Winders & Accessories

Item	New	Mint	Excellent	User
Motor Drive 1 (w/18v Control Grip 1)			185 150	
Motor Drive 2	480 360	230 180	170 150	
Requires M15 NiCad Control Pack or M18V Control Grip 2 - not included.				
Motor Drive 2 w/18V Control Grip		320 280	300 250	
Motor Drive 2 w/M15 Pack & chgr	725 545		360 300	
M18V Control Grip 2		100 70		
M15 Nicad Control Pack w/chgr	250 170			
Winder 1		80 70	75 50	
Winder 2	165 100	100 85	90 65	
Generic Winder	55 40		35 25	
Motor AC Control Box 1	380 270	220 190		
M Quartz Remote Control Intervalometer	200 140			
Manual Adapter (OM10)	30 25			
Manual Adapter 2 (OM88)	30 25			

The Motor Drive 1 and 2 fit OM-1MD/1N, OM-2/2N/2S, OM-3, OM-4/4T, OM-G, OM-F, OM-PC — but not the OM-10. The Motor Drive 2 features power film rewind. The Winder 1 and 2 fit all of the above and the OM-10.

Olympus Backs

Item	New	Mint	Excellent	User
250 Exp Back (OM-1/MD/N/OM-2/N)	790 570		225 180	
250 Exp Back (OM-2S/3/4/4T)	790 570		350 250	
250 Film Magazine (2 req'd)	70 40			
250 Bulk Film Loader	180 110			
Recordata Back 1		45 40		
Recordata Back 2		125 80	65 50	
Recordata Back 3			110 75	
Recordata Back 4	180 130		60 50	
Recordata Back 100 (OM-77)	50 40			
Recordata Back 200 (OM-88)	60 45			
Forscher or NPC Polaroid Back	700 620		550 450	

Olympus Close Up Accessories

Item	New	Mint	Excellent	User
Telescopic Auto Tube (65-116mm)	220 170	150 125	115 85	
Auto Extension Tube 7mm	50 40			
Auto Extension Tube 14mm	50 40			
Auto Extension Tube 25mm	50 40			
Auto Extension Tube Set	125 100			
Auto Bellows	250 130	100 90	90 80	
Double Cable Release for above	25 20			
Slide Copier	80 65			
Focusing Rail & Stage	180 100			
Right Angle Finder		45 35		
Varimagni Finder	160 125			

Olympus Flashes & Accessories

Item	New	Mint	Excellent	User
Auto 310			50 35	
F-280	210 160	150 120	115 100	
T-8 Ring Flash 2	170 145			
T-10 Ring Flash 1	130 80			
T-18		50 40		
T-20	100 85	65 50	50 40	
T-28 Macro Single 1	95 60			
T-28 Macro Twin 1	160 110	90 80		
T-32	220 185	150 125	120 70	
T-45	350 250	220 175		
T-45 w/NiCads, chgr	470 370	320 280		
T-45 Nicads & chgr	170 120			
T Power Control 1	175 130			
6V Power Pack 2	80 35			
Bounce Grip 1		90 60	55 40	
Bounce Grip 2 (T-20, T-32)	165 115	110 90	90 70	
Shoe 1 (OM-1/2)	25 20		15 10	
Shoe 2 (OM-2 w/310 Flash)	25 20		15 10	
Shoe 3 (OM-2 w/T series Flash)	25 20		15 10	
Shoe 4 (OM-1N/2N)	25 20		15 10	

The T-8 Ring Flash 1 & 2, T-10 Ring Flash 1, T-28 Macro Single and Twin Flash 1's all require either the T Power Control 1 or the 6V Power Pack 2. The 6V Power Pack 2 also powers the Winders 1 and 2.

Olympus Pen

The Olympus Pen SLR, in its various models, is another one of those cameras that is regarded by some people as collectible and by others as a great "user". It has the distinction of being the world's first half-frame 35mm SLR camera. Instead of using a bulky pentaprism, Olympus elected to employ the porroprism method of reflecting light rays, which allowed the design of an almost flat top plate.

All Pen SLRs use a rotary, metal focal-plane shutter that provides speeds from 1 second to 1/500, plus B, and flash sync at all speeds.

Olympus also produced several models of rangefinder Pens with fixed lenses. These are not listed. For more detailed information about Pen SLRs, I highly recommend Peter Dechert's 1988 series on these cameras in *Shutterbug* magazine.

Olympus Pen F

Olympus' first 35mm SLR, the Pen F, is the least desirable of the four Pen models from a user standpoint, though it is the camera that founded the Pen's solid reputation. It's the least desirable as a user camera for a couple of reasons: first, it is the oldest of the four models and most likely to be thrashed; second, the FT has a double-stroke film advance mechanism that is prone to mechanical problems. Clean examples remain popular on the used market, mostly due to their collectible value.

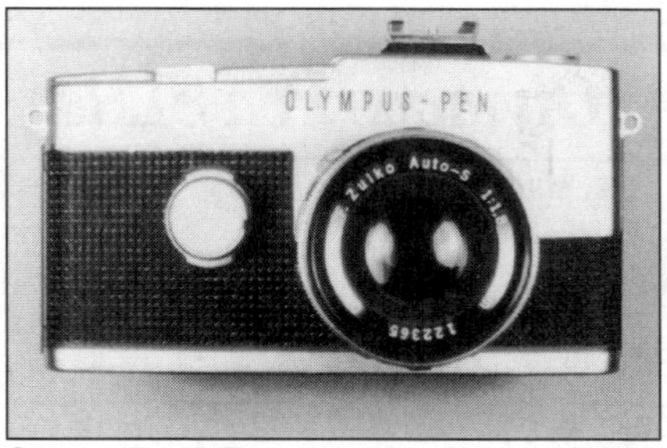

Olympus Pen F. The only model with the gothic F.

The Pen F will accept an accessory exposure meter, which clips to the front of the shutter speed dial for non-TTL metering. Flash photography is possible with strobe units only (X sync).

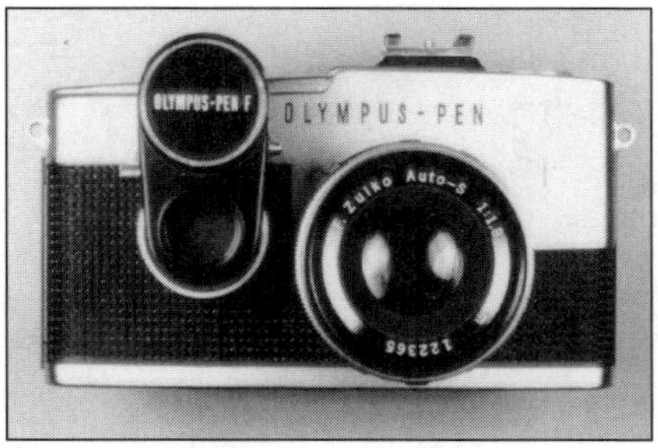

Olympus Pen F with external meter.

Olympus Pen FT

The Pen FT is the only Pen SLR with a TTL exposure meter. The meter cell is located behind the mirror, which is half-silvered to allow a portion of the light to pass through to the cell. A dimmer viewfinder image is an unavoidable result of this arrangement.

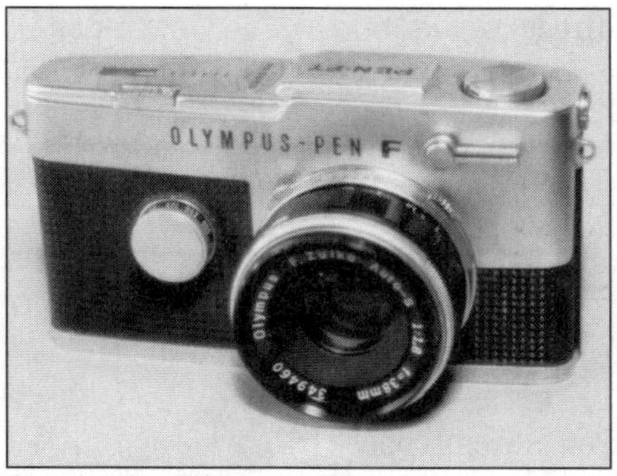

Olympus Pen FT. Note the FT designation on the top plate and the self-timer lever.

The FT's meter window in the viewfinder has a numerical readout, numbered from 0 to 7. Lenses produced after the release of the FT have a dual aperture scale. One scale has the normal aperture numbers you'd expect to find, the other has the numbers that correspond to those in the viewfinder. By pulling the aperture ring out and rotating it 180 degrees, the user can switch from one scale to another. Earlier lenses will work on the FT, but since they don't have these special numbers engraved on them, the user must resort to guestimation. Your average serious Pen user will ignore the on-board meter and use a hand-held meter instead, since the FT's built-in meter wasn't particularly good even when new and is probably much less than that now. Having said that, though, the prices for the FT listed below are for FTs with working meters. If the meter is inoperative, you should be able to purchase the camera for 25-50% less.

Other features new to the FT were a single-stroke film-advance lever, a self-timer and an additional connector for M-class flash bulbs.

Olympus Pen FV

The FV is the same basic camera as the FT, the most important difference being that it doesn't have a built-in meter. This alleviated the necessity of using a half-silvered mirror, so as a direct result the FV's viewfinder is much brighter. Like the F, the FV will accept the clip-on accessory meter. Also like the F, the FV has X sync only.

Olympus Pen F Microscope

As its name suggests, the Pen F Microscope was intended for scientific use. Since the company's inception back in 1920 or so, Olympus has manufactured microscopes. In fact, Olympus started out as a microscope maker exclusively, and was Japan's first. It shouldn't surprise anyone, then, that a maker of microscopes, which also happens to make cameras, would make a microscope camera.

The F Microscope, like the FV, lacks a meter, but like the FT, can use both strobe flash and M-class bulbs. It will take the clip-on accessory meter. It does not have a self-timer. Unique among the Pens, the F Microscope has a focusing screen designed for high-magnification photography, consisting of a plain ground glass screen with a clear center spot. Within the center spot is a fine cross hair.

In the lens listings below, no distinction has been made between F and FT lenses. Price differences range from nonexistent to minor.

While the following camera prices are for bodies without lenses, often you'll find them for sale only with normal lenses, most typically the 38mm f/1.8. Expect to pay $20 to $40 more for a body with lens than the prices listed below.

Olympus Pen SLRs

Camera	Yrs. Made	Mint	Excellent	User
Pen F	1963-66	200 ... 150	125 ... 90	70 ... 50
Pen FT	1966-72	250 ... 200	185 ... 125	
Pen FV	1967-70		200 ... 150	
Pen F Microscope	1966-72		170 ... 140	

Olympus Pen Lenses

Lens	Mint	Excellent	User
20mm f/3.5	300 ... 250	175 ... 125	
25mm f/2.8	200 ... 175	175 ... 125	
25mm f/4	230 ... 140	160 ... 100	
38mm f/1.8	60 ... 40	50 ... 25	
38mm f/2.8 Compact	250 ... 200	230 ... 160	
38mm f/3.5 Macro		250 ... 180	
40mm f/1.4		100 ... 50	
42mm f/1.2	330 ... 180	150 ... 120	
60mm f/1.5		250 ... 170	
70mm f/2	220	175 ... 125	
100mm f/3.5		130 ... 80	60
150mm f/4	200 ... 170	150 ... 100	
250mm f/5		375 ... 300	
400mm f/6.3		1000+	
800mm f/8 Mirror		1000+	
Both the 400mm and 800mm lenses are rare. The above prices are indicative of this and are estimates, based entirely upon their rarity and collectible value.			
50-90 f/3.5 FT	225 ... 190	200 ... 125	
100-200 f/5		290 ... 200	
2X Teleconverter (Vivitar)		50 ... 40	

35 MM

Pen F Accessories

Item	Mint		Excellent		User
Accessory Shoe			25	15	
External Meter (F & FV)		80	60	40	
Angle Finder	75	50	50	35	
Bellows	100	70	75	40	
Bellows 2	150	125	125	90	
Ext Tube Set			50	35	
Focusing Rail			30	20	
Pen F Camera Slider #2			30	20	
Slide Copier	75	50	30	20	
OM to Pen Adapter			35	25	
T-Mount			30	20	

Pentax 35mm

Asahi Optical Company's modern 35mm SLRs have employed two basic lens mount designs, the 42mm screw-mount design originated by Praktica and, beginning in the early 1970's, its own bayonet-mount design. Both designs have become somewhat universal since their introduction. In fact, the Pentax/Praktica 42mm threaded mount is often referred to today as Universal Screw mount.

Several lesser-known camera manufacturers have used both these mounts. I haven't listed any of these cameras, but a few of the more frequently seen names are Chinon, Cosina, Ricoh, Yashica (screw-mount only) and Zenit (screw-mount only). The going used prices for these cameras in good operating condition with normal lenses are usually between $50 and $75. Exceptions would be later model Ricoh and Chinon K-mount SLRs, the top models of which often contain hosts of features, including multiple auto-exposure and metering modes. Sophisticated cameras they are, but even when new, these top-of-the-line models seldom sell for more than about $200 (discount), and when used they often sell for much less.

Asahi Optical Company's earliest SLRs, the Asahiflexes, are not listed either. These cameras are of limited usefulness to the practicing photographer, mostly because they employ a non-standard screw-mount thread, but also because they are becoming uncommon due to collecting activity in recent years. Their escalating prices are a reflection of this. Neither have I listed the original Pentax of 1957 or the Pentax K of 1958. They are neither especially common nor collectible, and are of limited usefulness to the practicing photographer these days. Either model is worth about the same as the original Spotmatic in equivalent condition.

Pentax screw-mount cameras and lenses are listed first, followed by the K-type bayonet-mount cameras and lenses.

Pentax Screw-Mount SLRs

The various Pentax screw-mount cameras and Takumar lenses have a loyal — bordering on fanatical — following. Many a crusty old aficionado would be happy to take you aside and deliver an impromptu lecture on the superior nature of both the cameras and their optics, and will inform you in no uncertain terms that the screw-mount Takumars were the sharpest lenses ever made—by anybody. I say this because I have been the subject of such harangues more than once. Well, I'm still not going to take sides, but I can say with confidence that a screw-mount Takumar will give any modern, computer-designed lens a run for the money in sharpness and contrast — especially the later SMC Takumars. And when these folks talk in glowing terms about their beloved Spotmatics, I can't blame them. The Spotmatic, in its various forms, is probably *the* original workhorse and is as reliable as they come.

Screw-mount Pentax cameras officially imported into the U.S. bore the inscription "Honeywell Pentax," and sometimes "Honeywell Heiland Pentax," as a result of a marketing agreement between Asahi Optical Company and Honeywell. Those marketed outside the US were labeled Asahi Pentax.

Pentax H1, H1a, H2, H3 & H3v

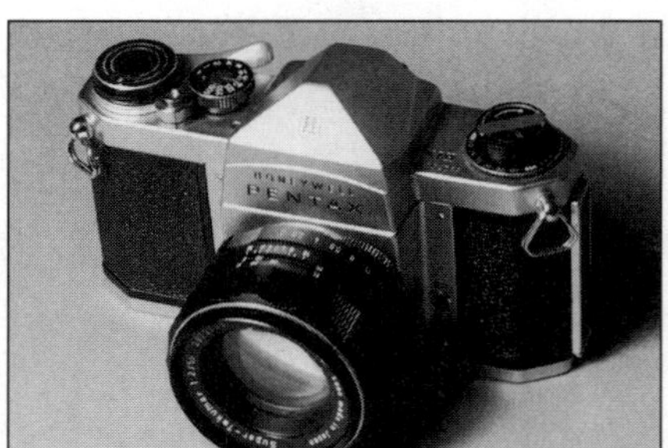

Pentax H1a

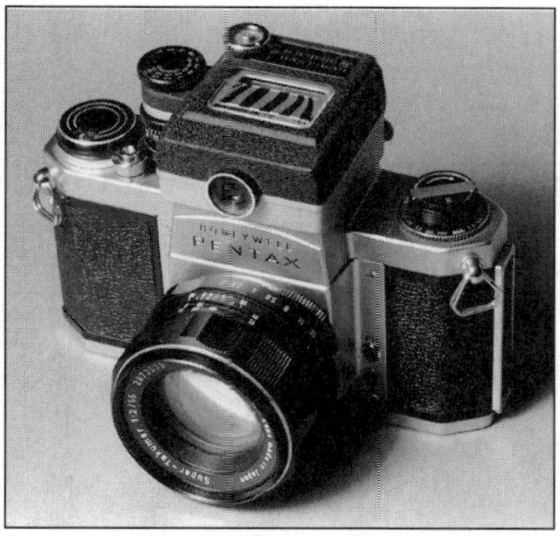

Pentax H1a with non-TTL accessory meter attached

The **H2** preceded both the H1 and H1a models. It features a semi-automatic diaphragm and shutter speeds from 1 second to 1/500. The **H3** closely resembles the H2 and was the first Pentax with auto diaphragm operation. The top shutter speed was increased to 1/1000. The **H3v** superceded the H3. It's the same camera, but has a self-timer and an automatic-reset film counter. The **H1** was released simultaneously with the H3 and also featured an automatic diaphragm. Like the H2, its top shutter speed is only 1/500. The **H1a** is an updated model with an automatic reset film counter.

Note: Outside the U.S., these cameras were marketed with "S" prefixes to their model numbers, instead of the "H" prefixes.

The Pentax Spotmatics

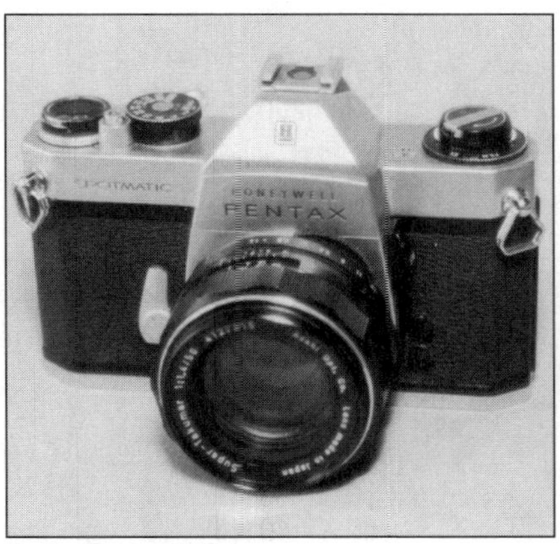

Pentax Spotmatic II

The Spotmatic saw a long and successful ten-year production run. The models listed below are the original Spotmatic, the SP500 and SP1000, the Spotmatic II and IIa, the Spotmatic F and the Spotmatic Motor Drive.

The Spotmatic was the first Pentax with a TTL meter. Contrary to what the name seems to imply, it uses a centerweighted averaging system rather than a spot meter. Employing a CdS cell, the scene is metered at taking apertures by moving a sliding lever on the left side of the camera next to the lens mount. This action both stops down the lens and activates the meter. Shutter speeds range from 1 second to 1/1000, plus B, with X sync at 1/60.

The **SP500** is the same basic camera as the Spotmatic, but with a top shutter speed of 1/500 and no self-timer. The **SP1000** is the same as the SP500, but has a 1/1000 top shutter speed.

The **Spotmatic II** is the same as the Spotmatic, but has a hot shoe. The **Spotmatic IIa** was sort of an oddball update, with a round flash sensor on the front of the camera, below the rewind lever. The flash sensor was designed to be used with a dedicated Honeywell strobe, but the idea never caught on.

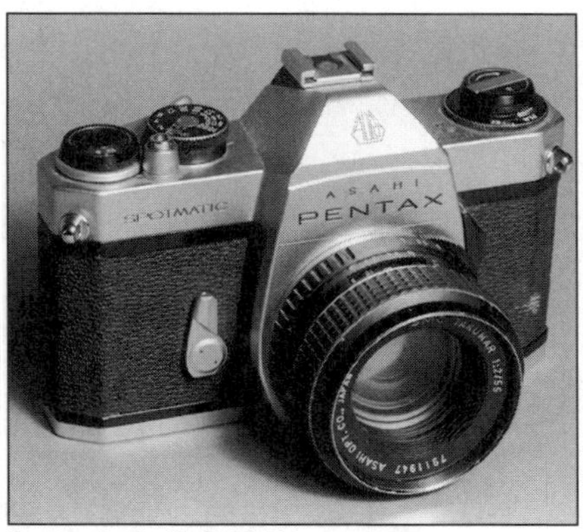

Spotmatic F with SMC Takumar lens

The **Spotmatic F** has all the features of the Spotmatic II, with one big difference: full-aperture metering is possible with SMC Takumar lenses.

The Spotmatic Motor Drive camera is an SP1000 that was factory modified to take the Spotmatic Motor Drive, which powers film advance at speeds up to 2 fps. Incidentally, the motor drive for the Pentax KX and KM Motor Drive cameras can be used on this camera as well.

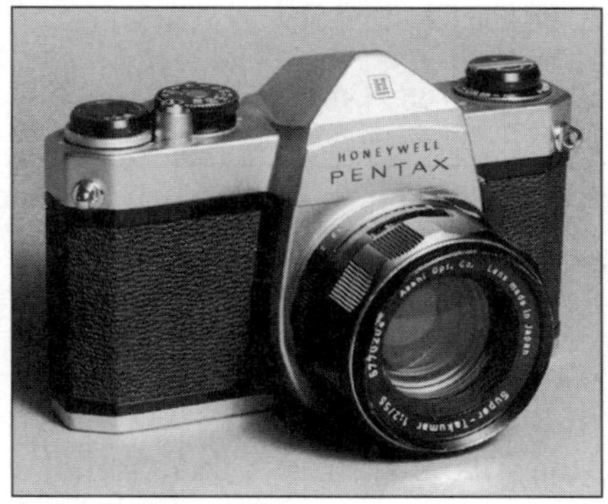

Pentax Spotmatic 1000

Pentax ES and ES-II

The **ES** (Electro Spotmatic) was introduced in 1972. It was arguably the first SLR to use integrated microcircuitry. The ES has two exposure modes: Aperture-priority and non-metered manual. Shutter speeds range from 8 seconds to 1/1000 in auto. In manual, only the 1/60-1/1000 mechanical speeds are available. Other features include depth-of-field preview and exposure compensation. The ES provides full aperture metering with SMC Takumar lenses. Earlier Takumars can be used, but metering must be done via the stop-down method.

The **ES II** is the same as the ES with a few improvements. The battery was relocated to the baseplate. This allowed the addition of a self-timer. An eyepiece shutter was added.

Pentax Screw-Mount SLRs

Often, these cameras are sold with normal lenses (although the prices shown are for bodies only) and are not available separately. However, it is not unusual to find screw-mount Pentaxes with normal lenses at close to these same prices.

Camera	Yrs. Made	Mint		Excellent		User	
ES	1972-74	220	180	150	100		
ES II	1973-74	290	225	220	150		
H1	1960-63			100	75		
H1a	1963-71			100	75		
H2	1959-61			100	60		
H3	1960-63			100	60		
H3v	1963-68			125	65		
SP 500	1972-74			125	85		
SP 1000	1974-78			150	100		
Spotmatic	1964-67	175	150	140	100	80	70
Spotmatic II	1971-74	180	150	150	100	85	75
Spotmatic IIa	1972-74			150	100		
Spotmatic F	1972-74	200	165	175	125		
Spotmatic Motor Drive *w/motor drive, grip, cord*	1972-74			500	350		

Takumar Screw-Mount Lenses

In the lens listings below, the following abbreviations are used: AT = Auto Takumar; T = Takumar; TT = Tele Takumar; ST = Super Takumar; SMCT = Super Multi Coated Takumar. Auto Takumar lenses have a semi-automatic diaphragm; it closes when the exposure is made, but must be manually reset. Takumar lenses and early Tele Takumar have either manual or preset diaphragms. Later Tele Takumars and all Super Takumars use a single diaphragm actuating pin that provides auto diaphragm coupling with cameras that support the feature. The SMC Takumars have two additional registration extensions at the rear of the lens mount. These extra projections communicate the necessary information to those cameras that perform full-aperture metering (the Spotmatic F, ES and ES II). Because the SMC Takumars are the most useful of the Pentax screw-mount lenses, especially when used with the Spotmatic F, ES, or ES II, they often command noticeably higher prices.

Takumar Screw-Mount Lenses

Lens	Mint		Excellent		User	
15mm f/3.5 SMCT			400	300		
17mm f/4 Fish Eye ST			250	200		
17mm f/4 Fish Eye SMCT	300	270	260	220		
18mm f/8 Fish Eye		400	250	200		
18mm f/11 Fish Eye ST-M			200	150		
20mm f/2.8 SMCT	350	300				
20mm f/4.5 ST	300	260	270	200		
24mm f/2.8 T			200	200		
24mm f/3.5 ST	160	135				
24mm f/3.5 SMCT			170	125		
28mm f/3.5 ST	90	80	80	65		
28mm f/3.5 SMCT	120	85	100	70		
35mm f/2 ST	150	125	125	90		
35mm f/2 SMCT	200	160	170	125		
35mm f/2.3 AT			100	75		
35mm f/3.5 ST			70	55		
35mm f/3.5 SMCT			90	70		
35mm f/4 T			55	40		
50mm f/1.4 T			50	30		
50mm f/1.4 ST	65	50	60	40		
50mm f/1.4 SMCT	95	75	75	55		
50mm f/4 T Macro			140	120		
50mm f/4 ST Macro			170	135		
50mm f/4 SMCT Macro	250	200	180	140		

35 MM

Takumar Screw-Mount Lenses

Lens	Mint	Excellent	User
55mm f/1.8 T		35 25	
55mm f/1.8 ST		45 30	
55mm f/1.8 SMCT		50 30	
55mm f/2 T		30 20	
55mm f/2 ST		35 25	
55mm f/2 SMCT		45 35	
85mm f/1.8 SMCT		250 200	
85mm f/1.9 ST		225 175	
85mm f/1.9 SMCT		250 200	
85mm f/4.5 Ultra-Achromat T		450 300	
100mm f/4 SMCT Macro		250 200	
100mm f/4 T Macro Preset (Bellows)		150 100	
100mm f/4 SMCT Macro Preset (Bellows)		175 125	
105mm f/2.8 T	140 120	110 90	
105mm f/2.8 ST		130 100	90 70
105mm f/2.8 SMCT		125 100	
120mm f/2.8 SMCT	170 150	130 100	
135mm f/2.5 T	100 60	80 50	
135mm f/2.5 ST	130 120	100 70	
135mm f/2.5 SMCT	150 120	130 90	
135mm f/2.8 SMCT		150 150	
135mm f/3.5 T		40 30	
135mm f/3.5 ST	70 55	50 35	
135mm f/3.5 SMCT	75 60	65 50	
150mm f/4 T		90 75	
150mm f/4 ST	150 110	120 90	85 40
150mm f/4 SMCT	150 125	125 100	
200mm f/3.5 T Preset		85 65	
200mm f/4 ST	200 160	120 85	
200mm f/4 SMCT	150 120	125 95	
200mm f/5.6 T Preset		100 70	
300mm f/4 T		290 220	
300mm f/4 ST		300 235	
300mm f/4 SMCT	430 325	325 240	
300mm f/6.3 TT	280	125 85	
400mm f/5.6 TT		350 275	
400mm f/5.6 SMCT		375 300	
500mm f/4.5 T		460 400	
500mm f/4.5 SMCT		500 440	
500mm f/5 T	500 450	425 385	
1000mm f/8 TT		1200 875	
1000mm f/8 SMCT		1450 1025	

Takumar Screw-Mount Zoom Lenses

Lens	Mint	Excellent	User
28-80 f/3.5		120	
45-125 f/4 SMCT	160 125	130 90	
70-150 f/4.5 ST	200	160 130	
85-210 f/4.5 SMCT	350 250	260 180	
135-600 f/6.7 SMCT	1275 950		

Spotmatic Accessories

Item	Mint	Excellent	User
Spotmatic Motor Drive *For Spotmatic, KM and KX Motor Drive cameras only*		250 ... 150	
Spotmatic 250 Exposure Back		200 ... 180	
Auto Bellows (Screw Mount)		100 ... 80	
Bellows II	80 ... 70		
Slide Copier for Bellows II	50 ... 40		
Screw Mount Auto Ext Tube Set	25 ... 20	20 ... 15	
Screw to Bayonet Adapter	25 ... 15		
Right Angle Finder (K-series, Spotmatic)		55 ... 50	
Magnifier (K-series, Spotmatic)	35 ... 25		
Magnifier 1 (K-series, Spotmatic)	60 ... 40		
Magnifier 2 (K-series, Spotmatic)	75 ... 50		

Pentax K-Mount SLRs

In 1973 Pentax released three new camera models, the KM, the KX and the K2, with the advent of their bayonet-mount lens line. This new line of cameras and lenses was produced concurrently with the screw-mount line for about a year before the lastwas discontinued. K-mount cameras have evolved steadily since then, while always maintaining their backward compatibility. Pentax's latest autofocus, picture-taking computers still accept 1973-vintage K-mount lenses. Only Nikon can make a similar claim. And, while Nikon has made backward compatibility a big selling point for its top-of-the-line F4, this is the only Nikon AF camera that can use early Nikon lenses unmodified. Pentax AF cameras have no such limitations, although some auto-exposure functions are lost when using early lenses.

The following listings are in rough chronological order.

Pentax KM & KM Motor Drive, KX & KX Motor Drive

The KM is a Spotmatic F with a bayonet lens mount. Basic features include full-aperture centerweighted TTL metering, shutter speeds from 1 second to 1/1000, plus B, X sync at 1/60, a depth-of-field preview feature, a hot shoe and a self-timer.

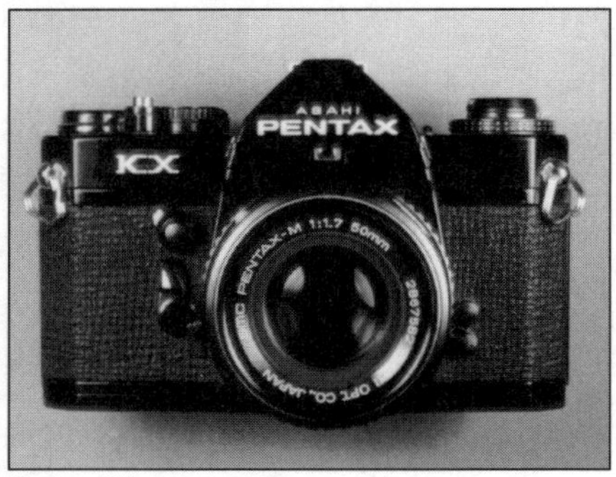

Pentax KX

Intended for the advanced amateur and professional, the KX was the forerunner to the Pentax LX, which inherited a few of its features. Improvements over the KM offered by the KX are such niceties as match-needle metering with full exposure information in the viewfinder and mirror lock-up. All other features of the KM are included on the KX.

Both a KM Motor Drive camera and a KX Motor Drive camera were produced. Both took the same, detachable motor drive. This dedicated motor drive will not work on the standard KM or KX. It provides continuous film winding speeds up to 3 fps. The Spotmatic Motor Drive can be used on these cameras, also.

Pentax K2 & K2DMD

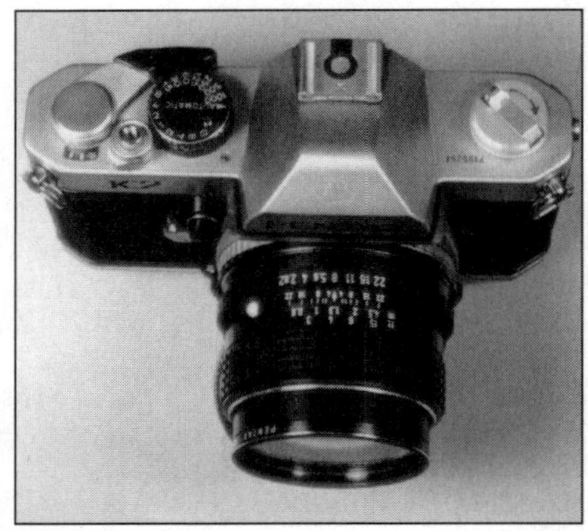
Pentax K2

The K2 was an all-new design for Pentax when it was released. For those who were already familiar with the Nikkormat EL, which hit the market the year before, the similarities must have been startling. The K2 is, for all practical purposes, a Nikkormat EL that takes K-mount lenses.

The K2 has two exposure modes: aperture-priority AE and match-needle manual. Electronically-governed shutter speeds range from 8 seconds to 1/1000, plus B, with X sync at 1/125 (B and X sync are mechanical). Other features include exposure compensation, depth-of-field preview, mirror lock-up, a self-timer and a hot shoe.

The K2DMD is a K2 that was designed especially for the K2DMD Motor Drive. It was usually sold as an outfit, which included a bulky watch databack and the motor. This motor drive will not interchange with the K-series motor drive (for the KM or KX Motor Drive cameras), nor can it be used on a standard K2. The motor provides film advance speeds of 2 fps, 1 fps and 1 frame every two seconds. Clean, used examples of the complete outfit are pricey. With a discount retail price with motor running close to $1,000 when it was introduced in 1976, this was by far Pentax's most expensive camera. This may be why the camera never sold very well.

Pentax K-1000

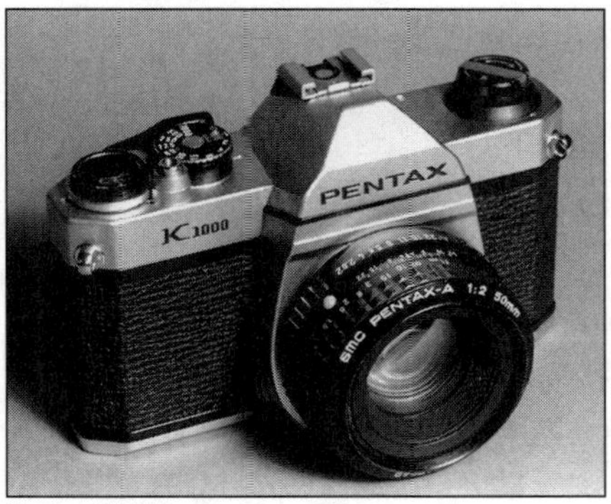

Pentax K1000

The venerable Spotmatic continues to live on, albeit in a somewhat disguised form. The K-1000, like the KM, is a Spotmatic F with a bayonet mount, but with a couple of omitted features: it has no self-timer or depth-of-field preview. Entering its fourteenth year of production and still going strong, the K-1000 is one of the very last of a vanishing breed: a rugged, mechanical, manual exposure only camera. The K-1000 has probably started more beginners down the road toward careers in photography during the past couple of decades than any other camera. Pentax claims it has no intentions of discontinuing the K-1000 as long as sales justify its continued production.

Pentax LX

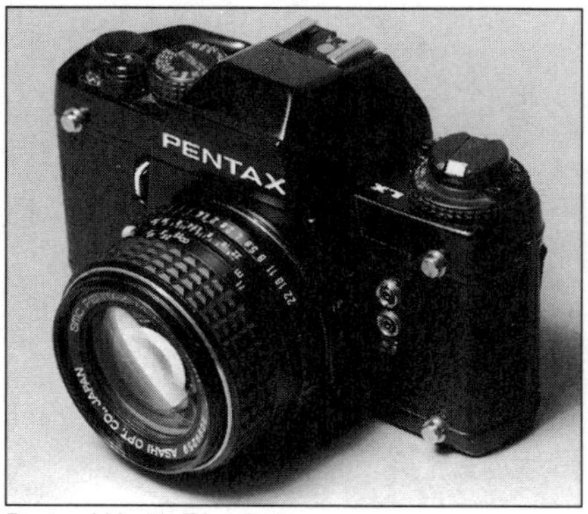

Pentax LX with FA-1 finder

The LX is Pentax's current flagship model and sometimes goes overlooked when professional quality SLRs are discussed. Its design is simple, straightforward — in a word, elegant. Although compact, it features stout construction and the full array of attributes associated with a professional camera.

The LX offers a unique system of interchangeable finders, which is just as effective, but much more economical than the traditional accessory finder options offered by Canon and Nikon. Rather than having a different finder for each use, the LX has a system finder base, called the FB-1, to which an action eyepiece, a magnifier eyepiece, or a standard eyepiece can be fitted. For the purists, however, a more traditional magnifier finder and a waist level finder are also available.

The LX has two exposure modes, aperture-priority AE and metered manual, using the centerweighted metering method. The LX can meter down to an extraordinarily dim -6.5 EV — that's 2 *minutes* at f/1.2 using ISO 100 film! In aperture-priority AE, the LX uses OTF (Off The Film plane) metering, so any change in lighting conditions during long exposures will be factored into the exposure.

The LX is an electro-mechanical hybrid, having electronically controlled shutter speeds from 2 minutes to 1/2000 and mechanically controlled speeds from 1/75 to 1/2000. So if the battery should fail, the user still has shutter speeds from 1/75 (flash sync) to 1/2000 and B at his or her disposal. In the manual mode, speeds from 4 seconds to 1/2000 can be selected.

Other features include TTL flash with dedicated strobe units, interchangeable focusing screens, eyepiece diopter adjustment, depth-of-field preview, mirror lock-up, multiple-exposure capability and a self-timer. The LX will accept either the Motor LX or Winder LX. Either accessory offers motorized film rewind.

Pentax ME, ME-F & ME Super

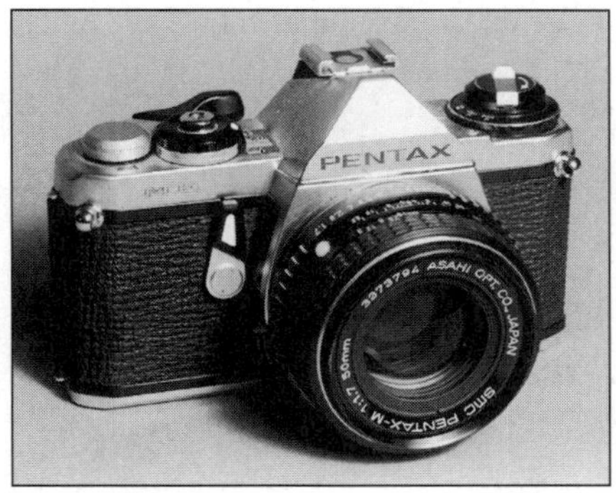

Pentax ME

The ME (with the simultaneously-released MX) was Pentax's first entry into the category of downsized SLRs essentially created by Olympus with the release of the OM-1 some five years before. Even smaller than the OM-1, the ME is extremely compact and light, even by today's standards. It has one exposure mode, aperture-priority AE, and exposure compensation. Shutter speeds range from 8 seconds to 1/1000, plus B, with X sync at 1/100 (the latter two are mechanical). Other features include interchangeable focusing screens, a self-timer, a hot shoe and an optional winder for film advance speeds up to 2 fps.

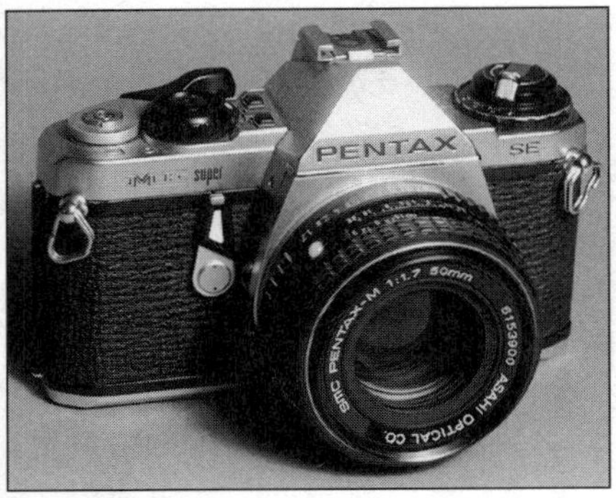

Pentax ME Super

The ME Super has all the above features, plus a few: manual exposure control, a shutter speed range from 4 seconds to 1/2000, flash sync at 1/125 and limited flash AE (auto setting of shutter speed) with dedicated flash units. The addition of these features made the ME Super a very popular camera and it continues to be a good seller on the used market.

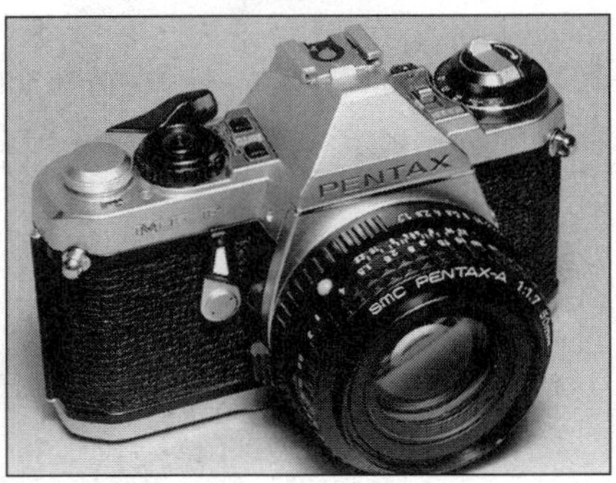

Pentax ME-F

The ME-F is an ME Super with a focus-assist feature, a manual precursor to autofocus technology. When a subject is in focus, a focus confirmation light appears in the viewfinder and, if activated, an alarm will sound.

Pentax MV & MV-1

The MV is essentially a simplified ME. Like the ME, it has aperture-priority AE with no manual mode, but it differs from the ME in that it lacks exposure compensation and winder capability. The MV accepts dedicated flash units for limited flash AE. X sync is a mechanical 1/100. The MV-1 is an MV with a self-timer.

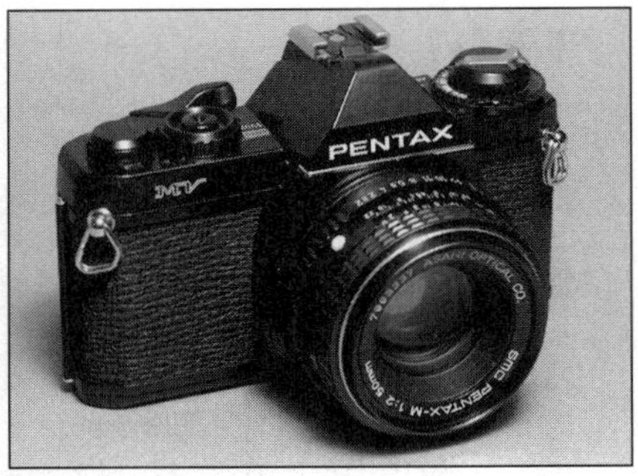

Pentax MV

Pentax MX

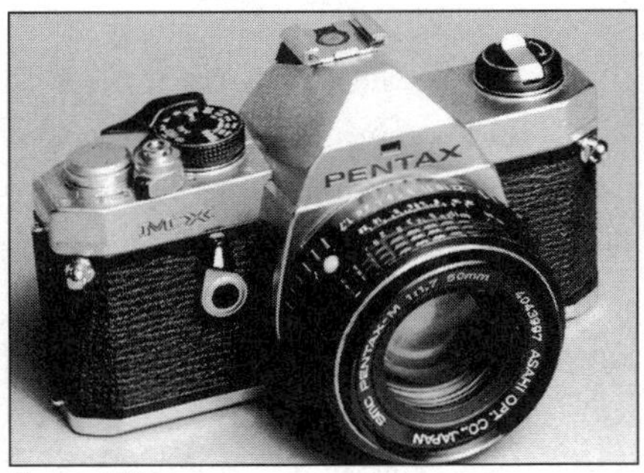

Pentax MX

The MX is the same size as the ME, but is a completely different camera. Designed for the serious student, the advanced amateur, or as a second camera for the working professional, the MX is a lightweight, but durable photographic tool and continues to be a top seller on the used market.

The MX provides manual exposure only, using a counterweighted meter with a match-diode display. The mechanical shutter speeds range from 1 second to 1/1000, plus B, with X sync at 1/60. Other features include interchangeable focusing screens, a self- timer, depth of field preview, a hot shoe and either a winder or motor drive option.

Pentax Program Plus & Super Program

The Super Program features six exposure modes: a standard program mode, aperture-priority and shutter-priority AE, metered manual, TTL flash with dedicated units and Programmed Auto Flash (non-TTL). Shutter speeds range from 15 seconds to 1/2000, plus B, with X sync at 1/125 (the latter is the only mechanical shutter speed). Other features include exposure compensation, interchangeable focusing screens, a self-timer, depth-of-field preview, and both a winder and a motor drive option.

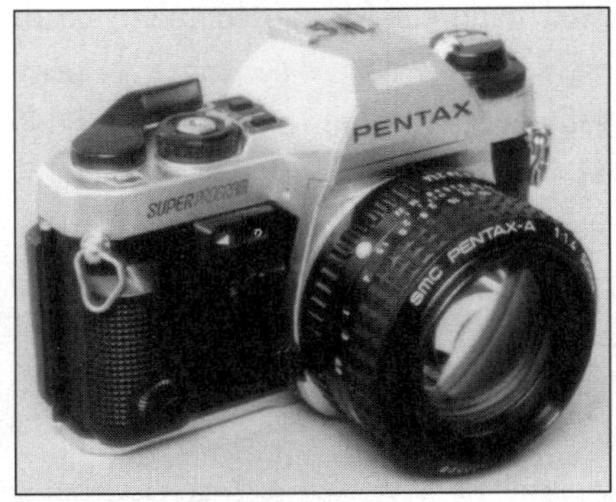

Pentax Super Program

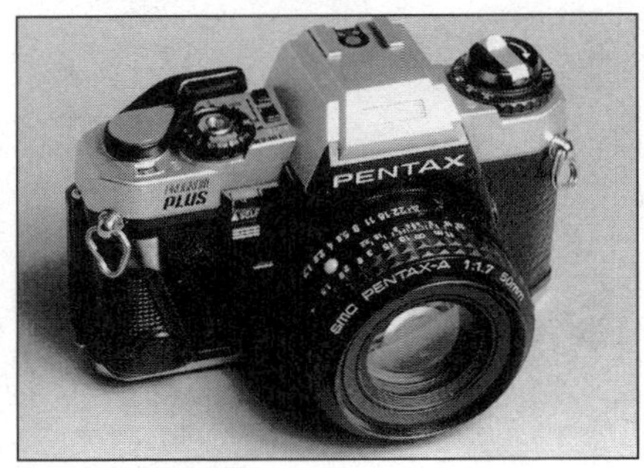

Pentax Program Plus

The Program Plus lacks shutter-priority AE and TTL flash capability, but retains the Programmed Auto Flash feature. Shutter speeds range from 15 seconds to 1/1000, plus B, with X sync at 1/100. Other features include exposure compensation, a self-timer, and depth-of-field preview. It has the same winder and motor drive options as the Super Program.

Pentax K-A or later lenses must be used on both the above cameras to engage the program mode, or to engage the shutter-priority mode on the Super Program.

Pentax A3000

The A3000 was designed for people who would rather take pictures than think about taking pictures. Its exposure system features a program mode and aperture priority AE, as well as Programmed Auto Flash (non-TTL). Shutter speeds range from 2 seconds to 1/1000, plus B, with 1/60 flash sync. Other features include exposure compensation, DX film loading with manual override, a self-timer and a built-in motor drive that provides auto film loading and film winding speeds up to 1.5 fps.

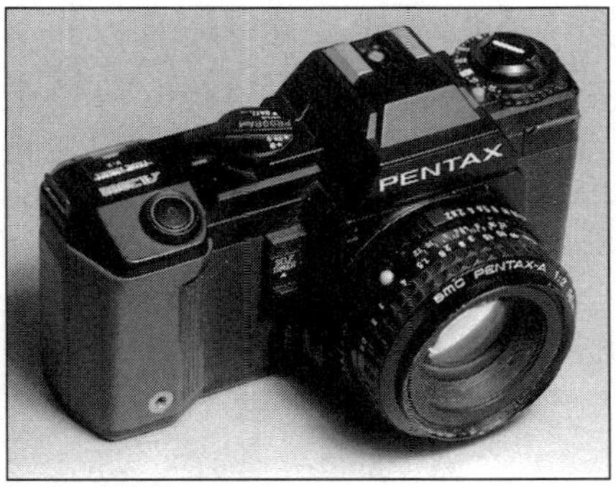

Pentax A3000

Pentax K-A or later lenses must be used to engage the program mode.

Pentax P3 & P3n

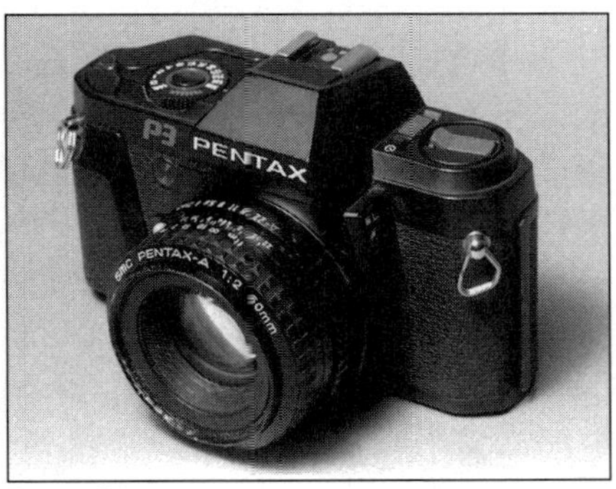

Pentax P3n

The Pentax P3, now superceded by the P3n, is a lot of camera for not a lot of money. Instead of adding a built-in motor (and cost), Pentax elected to leave the P3 and P3n as manual-wind cameras. The P3 has two exposure modes: standard program and metered manual. Shutter speeds range from 1 second to 1/1000, plus B, with X sync at 1/60. Programmed Auto Flash (non-TTL) is available with dedicated strobe units. Other basic features include an AE lock, depth-of-field preview and DX film coding.

The P3n has, in addition to the above features, an aperture-priority AE mode, plus a rubberized body.

Pentax K-A or later lenses must be used to engage the program modes on the above cameras.

Pentax SF-1 & SF-1n

Pentax's first Autofocus camera, the SF-1 offers a choice of two autofocus modes: single-shot (focus priority) or continuous (servo), plus AF lock.

Exposure modes include a standard program mode, a high speed program mode, a depth of field program mode, aperture and shutter-priority AE, and metered manual. Other exposure features include exposure compensation, autobracketing and an AE lock. TTL flash and auto fill flash are available via the built-in flash unit (GN 14 @ ISO 100) or dedicated accessory strobe units.

Shutter speeds range from 30 seconds to 1/2000 (manually set speeds from 1 second to 1/2000), plus B, with X sync at 1/100 (1/60 with non-dedicated units).

Other features include interchangeable focusing screens, built-in diopter adjustment, DX film coding, a self-timer with a one to three shot option and a built-in motor that provides auto film loading, advance speeds up to 1.8 fps and auto film rewind.

The Pentax SF-1n is the same camera with souped up shutter speeds. The top shutter speed is 1/4000 and flash sync was boosted to 1/250.

Either the SF-1 or SF-1n can use any K-mount lens. Focus confirmation is provided for with non-AF lenses that have maximum apertures of f/5.6 or greater. All program modes will function with manual focus K-A lenses. When using K-M lenses, only manual and aperture-priority AE are available.

Pentax SF-10

Essentially a scaled down SF-1, the SF-10 offers one autofocus mode: single-shot (focus priority). Exposure modes include program, aperture and shutter-priority AE and metered manual. TTL flash automation and auto fill flash are available with the built-in flash (GN 12 @ ISO 100) or with more powerful, optional dedicated strobe units. Shutter speeds range from 30 seconds to 1/2000 (1 second to 1/2000 in manual), plus B, with X sync at 1/100.

Other features include interchangeable focusing screens, DX film coding and an integral winder that provides auto film loading and rewind. The same restrictions regarding use of non-AF lenses on the SF-1 and SF-1n apply to the SF-10.

Pentax PZ-1

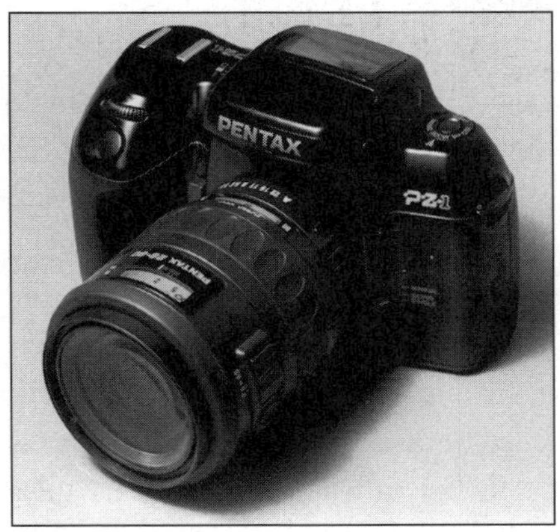

Pentax PZ-1

Probably the most notable feature that sets the Pentax PZ-1 (and the PZ-10) apart from the SF models is its power zoom feature. When one of the Pentax Intelligent Power Zoom lenses is mounted, four zooming options are available. A slight rotation of the zoom collar causes the lens to zoom from one focal length to another at a slow rate —

a useful feature for small framing adjustments. Rotate the zoom collar a little further and the lens zooms at a slightly faster rate. By turning the collar all the way to its stop, the lens zooms at its fastest—useful when quick changes in focal length are desired. Finally, by pulling the zoom collar toward the camera and then turning it, manual zooming is possible.

Several other power-zooming functions are available, including Image-Size Tracking and Zoom Clip. Image-Size Tracking does exactly what the name implies. When this mode is engaged, the lens will track a moving subject and zoom in or out to maintain a constant image size. Zoom Clip allows the user to store up to two predefined focal lengths — a handy feature when concentrating on separate areas of interest, such as home plate and second base at a baseball game. Still another feature is the Zoom Effect mode in which the camera will zoom the lens from one extreme to another during exposure for smooth and spectacular zoomed exposures.

The PZ-1 offers a choice of two autofocus modes: focus-priority (single shot) and continuous (servo). In the continuous mode, focusing switches to predictive focus automatically when subject movement warrants it. Manual focusing with focus confirmation is also available. When using manual-focus lenses, still another focusing option is available, called Snap-in Focus (also known as Trap Focus). In this mode, the lens is focused on a stationary subject, the shutter button is locked down (with the optional Cable Switch F), and the camera will automatically fire when a moving subject enters the frame at the point of focus.

Exposure modes include a unique feature called Hyper Manual Mode. This can be a manual-exposure mode with full control via the thumb and forefinger driven wheels (one for aperture, one for shutter speeds), or, with the touch of the IF (Interactive Function) button, you can switch to full program mode, called Hyper Program AE. Touching another button activates Memory Lock, which is actually a program shift feature. With the lens moved from the A position, manual exposure is still available, but with depth-of-field preview, if desired. Aperture-priority AE is also available at this setting by touching the IF button. Shutter-priority AE is another option, as is a standard program mode, plus program modes that bias toward high shutter speeds or small apertures. Still another mode, called MTF (for Modular Transfer Function), is available, which first selects the lens' optimum aperture by measuring its highest contrast and then selects a matching shutter speed.

The PZ-1's metering modes include a standard eight-zone evaluative pattern, centerweighted and spot, and will switch automatically depending on lighting conditions. Manual selection of the different patterns is also available.

Shutter speeds range from 30 seconds to 1/8000, plus B, with a maximum X sync of 1/250. Other features include a built-in pop-up TTL flash (GN 45 @ ISO 100), multiple-exposure capability, motorized film advance (up to 3 frames per second) with auto film-loading and rewind, exposure compensation, interchangeable focusing screens, DX film setting with override, an intervalometer and a three-speed self-timer. Additionally, the PZ-1 comes with 18 "Pentax Functions" that allow the user access various custom settings for further fine tuning of camera operations.

Pentax PZ-10

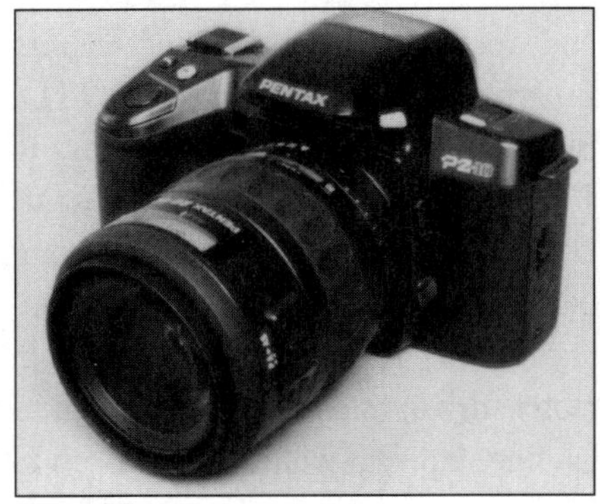

Pentax PZ-10

The PZ-10 reached the market several months before the PZ-1, but is its less full-featured sibling. It supports the same automated zoom modes found on the PZ-1. Autofocusing modes include the now-standard array of predictive, single-shot and continuous modes. Auto exposure is calculated using a six-segment matrix metering method; centerweighted and spot metering are also available.

Exposure modes include multi-program AE, program AE, shutter-priority AE, and manual. Shutter speeds range from 30 seconds to 1/2000, plus B. The PZ-10 has a built-in pop-up flash that fires automatically when necessary. Dedicated TTL accessory flash units can also be used.

Other features include DX film coding with no override, auto film loading and rewind with the built-in winder, a self-timer, exposure compensation, and an eyepiece with built-in dioptric correction.

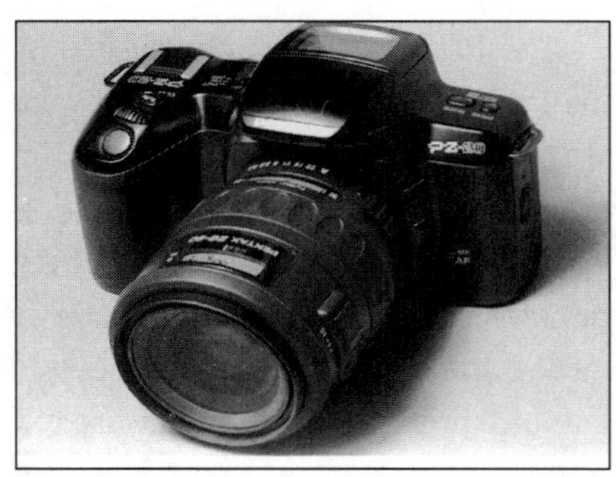

Pentax PZ-20

Pentax K-Mount SLRs

Camera	Yrs. Made	New		Mint		Excellent		User	
A3000	1985-87			160	140	150	120		
K2	1973-82			270	245	150	130	130	120
K2DMD (w/motor and grip)	1976-80					550	500		
K1000	1977-	200	160	120	100	95	65		
K1000SE				125	100	100	85		
KM	1973-78			150	125	120	90		
KM Motor Drive (w/motor)	1973-78					350	300		
KX	1973-78			225	180	185	150		
KX Motor Drive (w/motor)	1973-78					550	400		
LX (w/FA-1 finder)	1980-	1100	900	825	795	750	650		
ME, ME SE	1977-81			150	100	100	80		
ME-F						160	120		
ME Super	1979-87			200	180	150	100	110	70
MG				100	75	75	65		
MV	1979-82			125	100	100	80	90	55
MV-1						100	75		
MX	1977-85			220	175	195	150	150	120
P3	1985-89			125	105	125	90		
P3N	1989-	195	140	125	100				
P30T	1991-	225	160						
P5	1988-1989			175	150	140	100		
PZ-1	1991-	600	450						
PZ-10	1991-	320	200						
PZ-20	1994-	350	265						
Program Plus	1983-86			225	175	175	145		
Super Program	1983-88			290	200	225	150		
SF-1	1988-89			200	175	200	150		
SF-1N	1989-91			250	200	225	170		
SF-10	1988-91			200	180	180	150		

Pentax K-Mount Lenses

When Pentax introduced its line of bayonet-mount cameras, the line of lenses made to fit these cameras were called SMC-Pentax in an effort to distinguish them from the screw-mount SMC-Takumars. Later, the SMC-Pentax lenses were superceded by the SMC-Pentax M lenses, which were then superceded by the SMC-Pentax A lenses when Pentax introduced the Super Program and Program Plus. Actually, the above statement is an over-simplification, since as late as 1985 Pentax was still producing several models of SMC-Pentax and SMC-Pentax M lenses concurrent with its line of SMC-Pentax A lenses. And, just to make things really confusing, a few very late A lenses carry a T suffix in the listings below, short for Takumar-A (it would seem Pentax has come full circle). Of the three above lens styles, only the A lenses have an AE setting, the use of which is necessary to engage the shutter-priority and program modes on Pentax SLRs with such features.

To sort out the confusion, the following abbreviations are used in the manual-focus lens listings: A, M, P & T. A = SMC-Pentax A, M = SMC-Pentax M, P = SMC-Pentax and T = a few late-model SMC-Pentax A lenses. A and M lenses with an asterisk after the letter (e.g. A*) incorporate low-dispersion (ED) glass; later A lenses which use low-dispersion glass are labeled A* ED, or, if they have internal focusing, A* EDIF. Lenses are listed separately only when price differences are significant between the various models.

Pentax autofocus lenses exist in two basic styles, the F-series and FA-series. Both styles are fully compatible with the standard Pentax K-mount and will function as SMC-Pentax A lenses on cameras that support A lens' features. The biggest difference between F and FA lenses is that FA lenses, when used on the Pentax PZ cameras, will support their power-zooming feature.

Pentax K-Mount Manual-Focus Lenses

Lens	New		Mint		Excellent		User	
15mm f/3.5 A/P	750	680	600	540				
16mm f/2.8 A	540	480						
17mm f/4 Fish-Eye P			275	250	250	200		
18mm f/3.5 P			275	250	225	180		
20mm f/2.8 A	420	600	350	300	290	225		
20mm f/4 M			280	250	200	150		
24mm f/2.8 A					225	180		
24mm f/2.8 P			200	185	170	125		
24mm f/3.5 P			160	140	150	100		
28mm f/2 A	525	400	350	300	275	200		
28mm f/2 M			225	200	225	150		
28mm f/2.8 A			180	100	120	90		
28mm f/2.8 M			125	100	100	80		
28mm f/2.8 T			110	80				
28mm f/3.5 P			75	60	60	45		
28mm f/3.5 Shift	1050	750	675	600	575	450		
30mm f/2.8 P					100	75		
35mm f/2 A			200	170	185	140		
35mm f/2 M					170	130		
35mm f/2.8 A					130	75		
35mm f/2.8 M					90	65		
35mm f/3.5 P					50	35		
40mm f/2.8 M			260	150	170	120		
50mm f/1.2 A/P	550	470	350	300	320	250		
50mm f/1.4 A/M	225	170	150	100	120	90		
50mm f/1.7 A/M			60	50	50	40		
50mm f/2 A/M	60	45	45	40	30	25		
50mm f/2.8 A Macro			275	175	170	150		
50mm f/4 M Macro			200	170	165	125		
75mm f/2.8 A			160	125				
85mm f/1.4 A*					450	375		
85mm f/2 M			250	150				
85mm f/2.2 A Soft Focus			200	150				
100mm f/2.8 A/M			190	125	125	100		
100mm f/2.8 A Macro			325	300	230	230		
100mm f/4 A Macro			270	225	220	190		
100mm f/4 M Macro			275	200	210	180		
100mm f/4 Bellows			170	125				
120mm f/2.8 M/P			150	100				
135mm f/1.8 A*			520	450				
135mm f/2.5 P			100	80	75	60		
135mm f/2.8 A			100	80				
135mm f/3.5 M			100	80	40	25		
150mm f/3.5 M			120	100	80	60		
200mm f/2.5 P			450	350	350	270		
200mm f/2.8 A* ED	1000	870	790	675	650	500		
200mm f/4 A			160	140	130	100		
200mm f/4 M			170	120	125	90		
200mm f/4 A ED Macro	950	800						
300mm f/2.8 A* EDIF	4700	4100						
300mm f/4 A*			550	450				
300mm f/4 M*			500	400				
300mm f/4 P			360	275				
400mm f/2.8 A* EDIF	5575	5000	4450	4000				
400mm f/5.6 A/M	680	575	500	450				

Pentax K-Mount Manual-Focus Lenses

500mm f/4.5 P	1450 1100	900 750		
600mm f/5.6 A* EDIF		2690 2500	2200 1950	
1000mm f/8 P		1300 1150		
1000mm f/11 Reflex		1000 750		
1200mm f/8 A* EDIF	7200 6700	6200 5850	5750 5000	
2000mm f/13.5 Reflex		5400 5000	4870 4300	
1.4X-S	225 175		125 100	
1.4X-L	340 270	220 180		
2X-A	50 35	35 25		
2X-S	175 120	125 75		
2X-L	340 270	220 180		

Pentax K-Mount Manual-Focus Zoom Lenses

Lens	New	Mint	Excellent	User
24-35 f/3.5 M		160 140		
24-48 f/3.5		180 150		
24-50 f/4 A/M		150 125		
28-50 f/3.5-4.5 M		135 105	115 100	
28-80 f/3.5-4.5 A		125 90		
28-80 f/3.5-4.5 T				
28-135 f/4 A		450 325	300 250	
35-70 f/2.8 AF		150 100	120 100	
The 35-70 f/2.8 AF provides autofocus with the ME-F only				
35-70 f/2.8-3.5 M			150 140	
35-70 f/3.5-4.5 A		130 110	125 100	
35-70 f/4 A			150 120	
35-80 T		120 85		
35-105 f/3.5 A		225 200	200 145	
35-135 f/3.5-4.5 A		250 200		
35-210 f/3.5-4.5 A		350 300		
40-80 f/2.8-4 M		170 100	105 90	
45-125 f/4 P		160 125	130 90	
70-200 f/4 T		125 90		
70-210 f/4 A		210 185	170 125	
75-150 f/4 M		175 150	140 100	
80-200 f/4.5 M		170 150	150 120	
80-200 T		140 100		
135-600 f/6.7 P		1275 950	1025 700	
400-600 f/8-12 Reflex		650 600	550 500	

Pentax F-Series Autofocus Lenses

Lens	New	Mint	Excellent	User
28mm f/2.8		110 90		
50mm f/1.2		250 200		
50mm f/1.4		125 100		
50mm f/1.7		55 50		
50mm f/2.8 Macro		225 185		
85mm f/2.8 Soft Focus		240 200		
100mm f/2.8 Macro		275 250		
135mm f/2.8		125 100		
300mm f/4.5 EDIF		550 500		
600mm f/4 EDIF		3800 3200		
1.7X (Autofocus w/K-A lenses)		90 50		

Pentax F-Series Autofocus Zoom Lenses

Lens	New	Mint	Excellent	User
24-50 f/4		250 200		
28-80 f/3.5-4.5 T		130 100		
28-80 f/3.5-4.5		220 200		
28-85 f/4		250 225		
35-70 f/3.5-4.5		100 80		
35-80 f/4-5.6	170 120			
35-105 f/3.5-4.5		160 130		
35-135 f/3.5-4.5		225 200		
35-210 f/4-5.6		360 325		
70-200 f/4.5 T		125 100		
70-210 f/4.5-5.6		160 125		
250-600 f/5.6 EDIF		4000 3650		

Pentax FA-Series Autofocus Lenses

Lens	New	Mint	Excellent	User
24mm f/2 Aspherical	455 410			
28mm f/2.8	240 210			
50mm f/1.4	210 165			
50mm f/1.7	150 115			
50mm f/2.8 Macro	385 315			
85mm f/1.4	950 800			
100mm f/2.8 Macro	595 500			
135mm f/2.8	420 305			
200mm f/2.8	1350 1100			
300mm f/2.8	4980 4400			
300mm f/4.5 ED	945 800			
600mm f/4 EDIF	6200 5500			
1.7X Teleconverter PZ	100 70			
2X Teleconverter PZ	110 80			

Pentax FA-Series Autofocus Zoom Lenses

Lens	New	Mint	Excellent	User
28-70 f/2.8	1380 1120			
28-80 f/3.5-4.5	250 175			
28-105 f/4-5.6	395 330			
70-200 f/4-5.6	325 250			
80-200 f/2.8	2250 1700			
100-300 f/5.6	410 340			
250-600 f/5.6 EDIF	7200 6400			

Pentax LX System Accessories

Item	New	Mint	Excellent	User
FA-1 Finder	225 200		60 50	
FA-1W Finder	225 200			
FA-2 Finder	65 30			
FB-1 System Finder	200 170	100 70		
FC-1 Action Eyepiece	85 60	50 40		
FD-1 Magni-Eyepiece	90 65	50 40	45 35	
FD-2 Standard Eyepiece	45 25	30 25		
FE-1 Magni-Finder	130 100	85 60	70 50	
FF-1 Waist Level Finder	75 65	60 50		

Pentax LX System Accessories

Item	New	Mint	Excellent	User
Motor Drive LX (w/cord)	890 800	295 250	250 230	
Motor Drive LX (w/NiCads/chgr/cord)	1100 1000	450 350	340 300	
Winder LX	495 450	180 150	150 120	
LX Grip				
Remote Cord (Wndr/MD LX)				
Nicad Batt Pack LX (w/chgr)		120 95		
Dial Data Back		75 50		
Watch Data Back		195 160		
LX 250 Exp Back		350 250	280 180	

Other Pentax Accessories

Item	New	Mint	Excellent	User
Generic winder (not Pentax)	60 50	35 30		
K-series Motor Drive (w/grip)			250 150	
For KM, KX and Spotmatic Motor Drive cameras only				
K2DMD Motor Drive (w/grip)			275 200	
(For K2DMD camera only)				
Motor Drive A		200 140	150 110	
For Program Plus, Super Program				
MD Grip II			35 25	
ME Winder		90 60	55 50	
ME II Winder			95 75	
Fits ME, ME Super, MEF, MG, MV1, Program Plus, Super Program				
MX Motor			275 225	
MX Winder		140 95	125 80	
MX 250 Exp Back		250 200	200 150	
Dial Data Back (ME, MX)			60 50	
Digital Data Back M	130 110	100 80		
Fits ME Super, ME-F, MG, Super Program, Program Plus				
Interval Data Back F (SF-1/1N/10)	260 200	125 100		
Data Back F (SF-1)	135 85	100 80		
Data Back FB (SF-1/1N/10)	110 90			
Data Back FC	110 90			
Data Back FD	110 90			
Data Back FE	110 90			
IR Remote Control Set		175 150		
K-Mount Ext Tube Set	70 55			
Auto Ext Tube Set		95 75		
Auto Bellows A	250 200	170 140		
Slide Copier A	100 80			
Macro Focusing Rail III	150 130			
Right Angle Finder A	120 110	85 70		
Right Angle Finder (K series, Spotmatic)			55 50	
Magnifier (K-series, Spotmatic)		35 25		
Magnifier 1 (K-series, Spotmatic)		60 40		
Magnifier 2 (K-series, Spotmatic)		75 50		
Magnifier F (SF-1/SF-1n/SF-10)	55 50			
Magnifier M (M-series, Prog +, Sup. Prog)			45 35	
Stereo Adapter & Viewer	250 200			
Screw-Mount lens to K-Mount adapter	35 25			
Pentax 6x7 lens to K-Mount adapter	120 100			

PENTAX

Pentax Flashes

Item	New		Mint		Excellent		User
AF-14		15					
AF-080C Macro Flash	350	290	175	150			
AF-140 C Macro Flash	440	380					
AF-160					30	15	
AF-160S					20	15	
AF-160SA	40	30	20	15			
AF-200S			40	30			
AF-200SA	120	80	50	40	40	30	
AF-200T	90	70	75	60	65	50	
AF-240FT (Autofocus)	120	105					
AF-240Z	75	65	50	30			
AF-260 SA	95	60					
AF-280T	140	120	100	80	90	70	
AF-330FTZ	165	140					
AF-400FTZ (Autofocus)	295	250	180	150			
AF-400T Set	390	300	260	225			
510v Power Pack (AF-400T)	180	130					
Transistor Power Pack (AF400T)	165	120					
AF-500 FTZ (Autofocus)	350	280					

Underwater Cameras and Equipment

Nikonos

The forerunner to the Nikonos was developed by Jacques Cousteau and was called, appropriately enough, the Calypso. The Calypso was the first camera designed for underwater use without a housing. Nikon liked Cousteau's design so much, they bought the company. Enter the Nikonos I, which was basically the same camera and which led to Nikon's domination of the underwater camera market. The Calypso is not included in these listings, since it isn't really a Nikon and because it's an uncommon camera. According to the collector guides, the Calypso with an original lens should sell for about the same as a Nikonos I with lens, which in my estimation is underpriced. If you run across a clean Calypso for a reasonable price, buy it and stash it away. It'll be better than money in the bank at today's interest rates.

Mechanical Nikonos Cameras

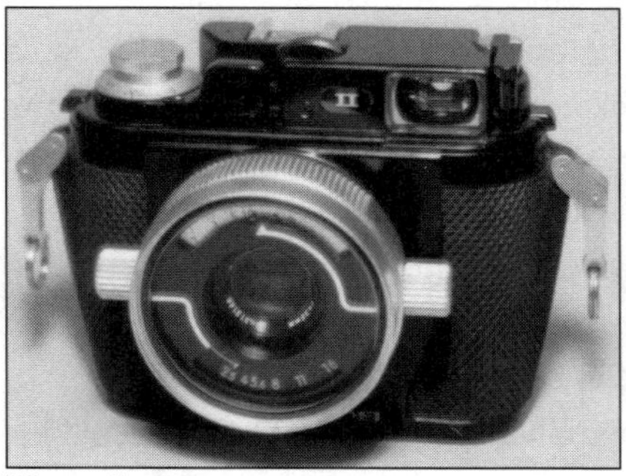

Nikonos II

The Nikonos models I, II and III are mechanical cameras. The Nikonos I is essentially a Calypso, but rather than using any of the several French-made optics available, Nikon developed its own lenses for this camera. The Nikonos II features minor improvements over the I, mostly in the way the film is rewound. The Nikonos III is the most popular, by far, of these three and remains in high demand. It features a single-stroke film advance mechanism (the previous models were double-stroke) and an improved film loading design. Non-TTL flash automation is possible with the model III when using the SB-102 underwater strobe and the SU-101 sensor unit.

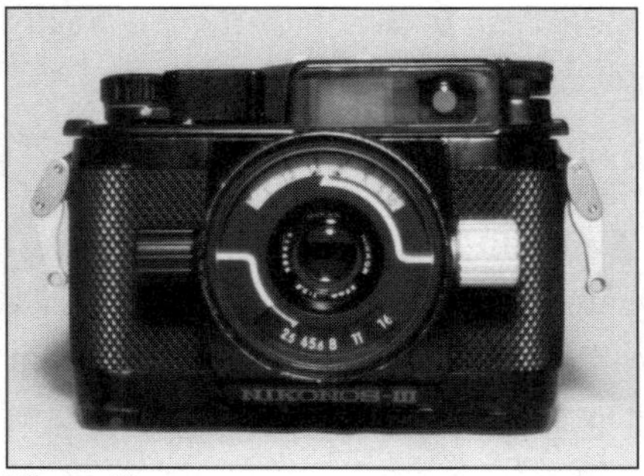

Nikonos III

Electronic Nikonos Cameras

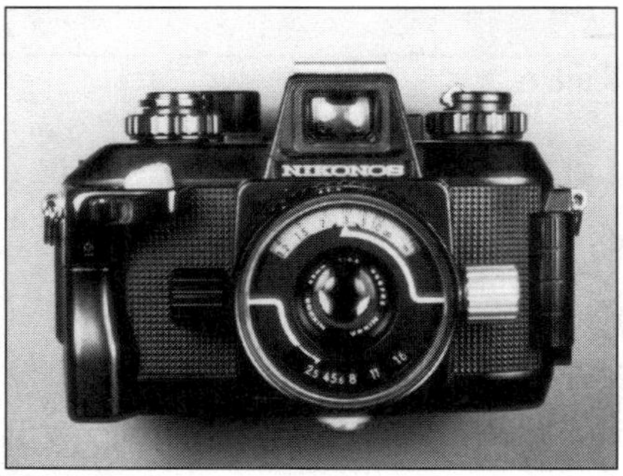

Nikonos IVa

The Nikonos IVa is the first electronic Nikonos and is battery-dependent. It has a TTL light meter and offers aperture-priority exposure only. Non-TTL flash automation is possible when using the SB-101 or the SB-102 strobes with the SU-101 sensor unit. The Nikonos V is an electronic, battery-dependent camera also, but has a manual mode in addition to aperture-priority AE and provides TTL flash metering when used with the SB-102 or the SB-103.

Nikonos RS

I guess anyone involved with underwater photography knew it had to happen. For the last thirty years, the state of the art of underwater photography has been defined by the Nikonos — a camera with no rangefinder coupling between body and lens, primitive image framing, no motorized film transport and a paucity of exposure options. For the fortunate few who can afford to invest in a system that would make Hasselblad owners gag, there is finally an alternative.

If the RS were designed for above-water use it would be just another autofocus SLR. But because it is an underwater camera, its features set it in a category by itself. Like many current above-water SLRs, the RS features ergonomic styling, but unlike the others its styling was designed specifically with underwater use in mind. Its large, contoured, O-ring-sealed body can withstand depths to 300 feet. All control knobs are oversized and can be operated easily with gloved hands. The viewfinder an action finder type, which provides 60mm of eye relief at a nine degree offset angle for easier viewing through a diver's mask.

Five separate focusing modes are available, four of which are selected by rotating a knob on the viewfinder. The modes are: Single-Servo Autofocus (S) with focus lock, Continuous-Servo Autofocus (C), Power Manual Focus (P), Freeze Focus (F), and Focus Tracking (activated in S & C modes).

Like the Nikonos V, the RS has two exposure modes: aperture-priority AE and manual, but that's where the similarity ends. The RS employs Nikon's tried-and-true five-segment matrix metering pattern in the aperture-priority mode, and 75/25 centerweighted metering in the manual mode, plus exposure compensation. When using the SB-104 strobe (GN of 105 above water, 53 below water, @ ISO 100), a variety of flash-exposure options are available, including matrix-balanced fill-flash, centerweighted TTL flash, variable-power manual flash and second-curtain flash sync (when set for centerweighted TTL).

Shutter speeds range from 1 second to 1/2000, plus B, with X sync at 1/125. The RS' integral single-shot film winder offers auto film loading and manually-activated rewind. DX film coding is available, as is the ability to override it.

Currently only three lenses are available for the RS: a 28mm f/2.8, a 50mm f/2.8 Micro and a 20-35 f/2.8 zoom. These lenses use a new double-bayonet mount that is both airtight and watertight, and which is not compatible with any other Nikon mount. Each lens has a permanently-attached rubberized hood, but lacks both the aperture and focusing knobs found on other underwater Nikkor lenses. Apertures are set on the camera body, and manual focusing is done by moving a sliding lever below the shutter release. The 28mm and the 20-35mm zoom are underwater lenses only; the 50mm Micro can be used both above and under water.

Does the advent of the RS and its impressive line of lenses and accessories spell the demise of the Nikonos V? Hardly. This is a very expensive and very *large* system. The camera body alone weighs over 4 ½ pounds and makes the Nikon F4 seem lightweight by comparison. Demand for the much smaller and cheaper Nikonos V should continue to remain strong as it appeals to photographers who don't need the extensive capabilities of the RS system.

Nikonos Cameras

Camera	Yrs. Made	New	Mint	Excellent	User
I	1963-68			115 90	
II	1968-75		200 175	180 150	
III	1975-81		420 375	385 310	
IVa	1980-85			250 210	
V	1984-	620 510	450 400	395 325	
RS	1992-	3100 2600			

Nikonos Cameras with Lenses

Camera	New		Mint		Excellent		User	
I w/35mm f/2.5					200	150		
II w/35mm f/2.5			300	275	250	175		
III w/35mm f/2.5					485	350		
IVa w/35mm f/2.5			400	350	325	275		
V w/35mm f/2.5	740	660	600	550	500	425		

Nikonos Lenses & Accessories

The 15mm and 20mm lenses are for underwater use only. The 28mm focal length exists in both an above-water (LW) and a below-water (UW) design. The 35mm and 80mm lenses can be used either above or below water.

Item	New		Mint		Excellent		User	
15mm f/2.8 w/DF-11 Finder	1600	1380	1270	1200				
20mm f/2.8	780	670	625	580				
28mm f/2.8 LW			320	250				
28mm f/3.5 UW	410	340						
35mm f/2.5	180	150	125	95	85	75		
80mm f/4	420	330	290	250	230	180		
15mm Optical Finder	440	380						
DF-10 Optical Finder (80mm)	110	80	60	50				
DF-11 Optical Finder (15mm)	350	275						
DF-12 Optical Finder (20 & 28mm)	240	175	150	125				
28mm Frame Finder	20	15						
35mm/80mm Frame Finder	25	20						
SB-101 Speedlight			250	195				
SB-102 Speedlight	1100	950						
SB-103 Speedlight	600	440						
SB-105 Speedlight								
SU-101 Sensor	165	120						
Double Bracket Set #10201 (SB102/3)	380	300						
Sensor Holder #10202 (SB102/3)	80	65						
Extension Arm Set #10203 (SB102/3)	185	135						
Double TTL Sync Cord #10204 (SB102/3)	165	135						
On-Land TTL Sync Cord #10205 (SB102/3)	95	85						
Single Sync Cord (SB102/3)	90	80						
Nikonos Close-up Outfit w/case	340	260	240	200				

Nikonos R-UW AF Nikkor Lenses and RS Accessories

Item	New		Mint		Excellent		User	
13mm f/2.8	2450	2100						
20-35 f/2.8	3550	2995						
28mm f/2.8	850	750						
50mm f/2.8	1400	1250						
SB-104 Speedlight	1400	1250						
SK-104 Bracket System (for SB-104)	220	170						
SK-104W Double Bracket System (for SB-104)	280	200						
SH-104 Quick Charger (for SN-104 NiCad Pack)								
SN-104 NiCad Pack (for SB-104)								

Ikelite Accessories for Nikonos

Item	New		Mint		Excellent		User	
Ikelite Ext Tube set	110	90						
Ikelite Optical Finder #5002	110	95						
3942.35 Substrobe MS Kit	250	210						
3942.42 Substrobe MV Kit	340	290						
3945.42 Substrobe MV Kit	400	340						

Ikelite Accessories for Nikonos

Ikelite has been making underwater accessories for years. Probably best known for their sturdy acrylic underwater housings, they are also makers of high-quality underwater strobes. The strobes listed below are the same as those in the Ikelite listings, but are in complete kits for use with Nikonos cameras. For detailed information on these strobe units, refer to the descriptions under the separate Ikelite listing by name rather than model number (e.g., Substrobe MS or Substrobe 225 NiCad).

Item	New	Mint	Excellent	User
3945.46 Substrobe AI Kit	590 495			
3945.47 Substrobe AI/N Kit	580 490			
3945.48 Substrobe 100 Alkaline	620 525			
3945.49 150 D Kit	700 570			
3945.52 150 Nicad Kit	850 695			
3945.56 225 Nicad Kit	920 775			
3945.56 Substrobe 300 Kit	995 860			
3945.57 Substrobe 300 Kit	985 850			

Sea & Sea Accessories for Nikonos

Sea & Sea makes four prime lenses for Nikonos cameras, as well as a 16mm conversion lens that will fit on to the front of the Nikonos 35mm f/2.5, and strobes for Nikonos. The strobes must have adapters for Nikonos in order to be used. The YS 50TTL will provide TTL flash automation with the Nikonos V and a TTL flash adapter.

Item	New	Mint	Excellent	User
SWL-16 16mm Conversion Lens	450 315			
12mm f/3.5 Fisheye	1135 950			
WL-15 15mm f/3.5	750 620			
WL-17 17mm f/3.5	690 520			
WL-20 20mm f/3.5	280 230			
Optical FInder (15mm)	150 115			
Optical Finder (16mm, 17mm, 20mm)	125 85			
28mm 1:2 Extension Tube	85 75			
35mm 1:1 Extension Tube	100 85			
35mm 1:2 Extension Tube	95 80			
35mm 1:3 Extension Tube	90 75			
YS 50TTL Strobe	470 430		200 175	
YS 200 Strobe	660 530			
YS 300 Strobe	1425 1200			

Other Accessories for Nikonos

Item	New	Mint	Excellent	User
Close-Up Kit (various makes)			190 150	
Sunpak Marine 32 Strobe		150 100		
Sunpak Marine 2400 Strobe	300 350			

Sea & Sea

A relative newcomer to the underwater game, Sea & Sea is making inroads into territory previously enjoyed almost exclusively by the champ, Nikonos. The Motormarine cameras are not as full-featured in some respects as the Nikonos, but they do pack a lot of capabilities into small, easy-to-use packages. And, when comparing their prices and features to Nikonos, they become very tempting alternatives, indeed.

The discontinued **Motormarine I** was made in two versions. The standard Motormarine I features an integral film winder, a built-in 35mm f/3.5 lens, a built-in flash and aperture-priority AE. The deluxe version has a bulkhead flash connector for attaching auxiliary flash units. The **Motormarine II** offers all the features of the deluxe Motormarine I, plus a built-in close-up lens, TTL flash exposure with the built-in flash and with the YS-50TTL optional flash unit, manual exposure control and DX film coding. It has a fixed shutter speed of 1/100 second and apertures ranging from f/3.5 to f/22. The latest Motormarine camera, the **Motormarine MX-10**, replaces the Motormarine I. It features aperture-priority AE, a fixed 32mm f/4.5 lens, motorized film advance and rewind, a built-in flash, and a unique wireless infrared connector for the handle-mount YS-40 flash. It has a fixed shutter speed of 1/100 and an aperture range of f/4.5 to f/22.

Sea & Sea Cameras, Lenses & Accessories

In the following descriptions, (I), (II) and (MX10) indicate which cameras they fit.

Item	New	Mint	Excellent	User
Motormarine I		180	150	
Motormarine I (w/bulkhead)		200	175	
Motormarine I 35 SE	270	210		
Motormarine II	475	350		
Motormarine II Explorer Kit	1395	1170		
Motormarine II Endeavor Kit	1895	1650		
Motormarine II 35S E	470	340		
Motormarine MX-10	390	230		
Motormarine MX-10 w/YS-40 flash	485	375		
Close-Up Lens (I)		50	45	
Macro Lens (I)		80	70	
Macro Lens (II)	140	95		
SWL-16 16mm Conversion Lens (I)	255	255		
SWL-16-II 16mm Conversion Lens (II)	410	320		
SWL-20-II 20mm Conversion Lens (II)	395	315		
20mm Conversion Lens (MX20)	250	190		
Optical Finder (15mm/20mm/35mm)	295	230		
Optical Finder (20mm/28mm/35mm)	135	195		
YS 20 Strobe (I)	235	180		
YS 40 (MX10)	210	150		
YS 50ms w/arm, tray (I)		250	200	
YS 50TTL-II w/arm, tray (II)	470	400		
YS100				
YS150				
YS 200m III (II)	700	550		
YS 300	995	850		

Ikelite Underwater Housings and Strobes

If you're interested in underwater photography and you already have a favorite 35mm camera and a nice array of lenses, the acrylic underwater housings Ikelite makes may be just what you're looking for. A typical Ikelite underwater housing is tailored for a specific camera make and model and is good for depths up to 150 feet. It's designed so that the camera will fit snugly within and couple to the exterior via a collection of linkages and gears. Ikelite also makes a universal model underwater housing that can be adapted for use with most SLRs. All normal operation is retained, such as focusing, aperture and shutter-speed selection, film advance and, of course, shutter release.

Underwater strobes built by Ikelite are offered in a wide variety of models to suit most any underwater photographic need. Following is a brief explanation of current models and their features. Most all the following models are also available in kits tailored specifically for use with Nikonos cameras (see Ikelite listings under Nikonos). All guide numbers are given in feet at ISO 100.

The 4038.7 Substrobe S is a Slave unit for use with the Sea & Sea Motormarine I (bulkhead model). The 4040.5 Substrobe MS is a Manual strobe with Slave (hence the MS) with a surface guide number of 92 and an underwater guide number of 24. The 4042 Substrobe MV is almost the same unit as the Substrobe MS, with the same light output, but it features TTL flash operation with the Nikonos V, the Sea & Sea Motormarine II and TTL SLRs. The 4046 Substrobe AI features TTL and manual flash for the above-mentioned cameras, with an adjustable coverage angle. It's rated at a surface guide number of 105-120 and an underwater guide number of 28-34, depending on the selected coverage angle. The 4049 Substrobe 150 D and the 4050 Substrobe 150 NiCad are the same strobe units with different power supplies. Both feature a surface guide number of 120 and an underwater guide number of 34, and a modeling light, TTL flash operation with the Nikonos V, the Sea & Sea Motormarine II and TTL SLRs, plus manual and slave operation. The 4056 Substrobe 225 NiCad has all the features of the Substrobe 150 with a boosted light output. The surface guide number is 145 and the underwater guide number is 40.

Lens coverages for the some of the above-mentioned strobes are: down to 28mm for the Substrobe MS and MV; down to 15mm with a Nikonos or 20mm with SLRs for the Substrobe AI; down to 15mm with the Nikonos or 18mm with SLRs for the Substrobe 150D, 150 NiCad or 225 NiCad.

UNDERWATER

Ikelite Underwater Housings & Strobes

Item	New	Mint	Excellent	User
Most Housings w/Super Eye	430	400	250	150
Most Housings w/Dome Kit	560	510	350	250
4038.7 Substrobe S	150	100		
4040.5 Substrobe MS	200	135		
4042 Substrobe MV	225	165		
4046 Substrobe AI	370	315		
4047 Substrobe AI/N	390	330		
4048 Substrobe 100	345	285		
4049 Substrobe 150 D	450	380		
4050 Substrobe 150 Nicad	575	490		
4056 Substrobe 225 Nicad	640	560		
Substrobe 300 Nicad	780	670		
3949.46 Substrobe AI Kit	500	400		
3949.47 Substrobe AI/N	490	430		
3949.48 100 Alkaline Kit		440		
3949.49 150 D Alkaline Kit	550	500		
3949.52 150 Nicad Kit	630	580		
3949.56 225 Nicad Kit	730	665		

Aftermarket Lenses

The listings below have been confined to independently manufactured lenses that are considered to be close to, as good as, and in some cases superior to lenses produced or marketed by camera manufacturers. One usually pays a premium for lenses that carry the same brand name as that of his or her camera. For those less label-conscious individuals, optics produced by the better independents can represent a real value.

Angenieux

I've chosen these lenses from Angenieux because of Angenieux's long-standing reputation as a producer of superb optics. These lenses are uncommon and expensive. The 180 f/2.3 and 200 f/2.8 are available in mounts for Leica, Nikon, Canon and Contax/Yashica only. The zooms are available for Leica, Nikon, Canon, Contax/Yashica, Minolta, Olympus and Pentax K. Expect to pay a $200 to $300 premium for new lenses with mounts for R-series Leicas.

Angenieux Lenses

Lens	New	Mint	Excellent	User
180mm f/2.3 APO	1500 1300	1200 950		
200mm f/2.8 ED	1000 800			
28-70 f/2.6	1500 1300			
35-70 f/2.5-3.3		725 650	600 400	
70-210 f/3.5	1300 1000	850 650	600 495	

Century Precision Optics

Something of a rarity today, Century Precision Optics is a company that offers lenses manufactured right here in the U.S. Shortly after World War II, Century Precision Optics began to manufacture telephoto lenses for 16mm movie cameras and offer a wide variety of custom work for the motion picture industry. The demand for Century optics and services grew steadily during the 1950's and 1960's, and as the demand grew they began to offer a progressively more extensive line of high-quality lenses for 16mm and 35mm movie cameras.

Meanwhile, a few wildlife and surf photographers, who were looking around for high-quality, long telephoto lenses to use on 35mm SLRs, stumbled upon the Century telephotos. Back in the 1960's and early-to-mid 1970's, super telephotos were scarce and expensive commodities. In those days, Century's line of long telephotos was optically second to none, but priced very competitively. What followed was a word-of-mouth, sideline business that has continued to this day in which Century sells their telephotos on a factory-direct basis to still photographers.

A Century telephoto lens consists of a coated, well-corrected achromatic doublet, mounted in a sturdy, aluminum tube. There is no linkage between lens and camera, so TTL metering must be done using the stop-down method. All Century telephotos employ the T-mount system, and can be used on any camera for which a T-mount is made. They come in two styles, the Tele-Athenar and the Tele-Athenar II. The main difference between the two is that the standard Tele-Athenar uses a rotating focusing mechanism (the entire tube forward of the focusing collar rotates), whereas the Tele-Athenar II employs the more traditional (for us still photographers) non-rotating focusing mechanism.

Either will work for 35mm applications, but the Tele-Athenar II is better suited for still photography.

Tele-Athenar II's come in a wide range of focal lengths and f/ratios, from a 230mm f/2.8 to a 1200mm f/6.8. While the entire line of Tele-Athenar II's is listed below, those best suited for 35mm still photography have asterisks following their aperture numbers.

The new prices listed below are factory-direct. The lenses are available on a special-order basis through camera dealers, but only one new price is shown for each focal length because Century offers only small discounts to dealers. The used prices were based on a discussion with Bill Turner, Century's executive vice-president, who estimates that these lenses usually resell at about 25% to 50% of their new prices. If you would like more information about Century's full line of lenses and custom services for both still and movie applications, their address is 10713 Burbank Blvd., North Hollywood, CA 91601. Their phone number is (818) 766-3715.

Lenses in black finish are made for civilian applications; those in a white finish were sold originally for government use.

Century Tele-Athenar II Telephotos

Lens	New	Mint	Excellent	User
230mm f/2.8	1750		875 440	
300mm f/3.2 *	1750		875 440	
385mm f/4.5 *	925		465 230	
500mm f/3.8	2950		1500 740	
500mm f/5.6 *	950		480 240	
600mm f/4.5	2750		1375 690	
650mm f/6.8 *	975		490 245	
800mm f/4.7	4500		2250 1125	
1000mm f/5.6	4750		2375 1190	
1000mm f/8 *	2850		1425 715	
1200mm f/6.8	4950		2480 1240	

KIRON

You may already be aware that Kiron is one of the manufacturers that makes lenses for Vivitar. This doesn't mean that a Kiron lens and a Vivitar lens of equivalent focal lengths are the same; they are not — or at least they're not supposed to be. Kiron makes lenses for Vivitar as per Vivitar's own exacting specifications.

Kiron lenses are no longer officially imported into the United States. Speculation is that a somewhat severe conflict of interests on Kiron's part (that is, some of their lenses were becoming a little too similar to Vivitar's) led to this cessation. Having said that, though, lenses that were marketed under their own trademark were generally high quality optics.

Kiron Lenses

Lens	New	Mint	Excellent	User
24mm f/2		100 80		
28mm f/2			110 75	
105mm f/2.8 Macro		185 160	175 150	
28-70 f/3.5-4.5		125 80	90 60	
28-85 f/2.8-3.8		140 100		
28-105 f/3.2-4.5		160 125	110 80	
28-210 f/4-5.6		150 125	110 85	
30-80 f/3.5-4.5			75 50	
35-105 f/3.5-4.5			110 85	
35-135 f/3.5-4.5			140 90	
70-150 f/4		75 50		
70-210 f/4		140 100	120 80	
80-200 f/4			100 65	
80-200 f/4.5		70 60	55 40	
1.5X		40 30		
2X			30 25	
2X 7-Element		80 50		

Sigma

Sigma lenses, especially those in the APO line, have always been a good value. The APO Sigmas are reported to be tack sharp, providing great color and contrast. (APO stands for apochromatic, a design which eliminates chromatic and other unwanted aberrations).

Sigma Manual Focus Lenses

Lens	New	Mint	Excellent	User
8mm f/4	550 475	295 200	185 150	
12mm f/8			150 120	
14mm f/3.5	620 550			
15mm f/2.8	480 400			
16mm f/2.8		220 200	190 150	
18mm f/2.8			200 160	
18mm f/3.2			125 100	
18mm f/3.5	350 295			
24mm f/2.8	220 150		100 80	
28mm f/1.8 Aspherical	275 210			
28mm f/2.8	110 85	70 50		
35mm f/2.8			40 30	
50mm f/2.8 Macro	220 190	170 140		
90mm f/2.8 Macro	350 295	250 220		
135mm f/2.8		50 35		
135mm f/3.5		40 25		
180mm f/2.8 APO Macro	870 780			
180mm f/5.6 APO Macro	360 300			
200mm f/2.8			140 100	
200mm f/3.5			60 50	
200mm f/4		55 50	45 40	
300mm f/2.8 APO	2400 2100			
400mm f/5.6		200 150		
400mm f/5.6 APO	570 485	420 390		
400mm f/5.6 Mirror		190 170		
500mm f/4 Mirror		600 550		
500mm f/4.5 APO	3450 3000		2400 1950	
500mm f/7.2 APO	610 520			
500mm f/8 Mirror			150 125	
600mm f/8 Mirror	420 350	310 280	260 230	
1000mm f/8 APO		2200 1750		
1000mm f/13.5		275 250		
18-35 f/3.5-4.5	520 415			
21-35 f/3.5-4.2	445 380	280 240	225 180	
24-50 f/4-5.6	220 175			
24-70 f/3.5-5.6	220 150			
28-70 f/2.8	390 295			
28-70 f/3.5-4.5		95 85		
28-70 f/3.5-4.5 UC	145 110			
28-80 f/3.5-4.5			125 75	
28-85 f/3.5-4.5			85 70	
28-105 f/4-5.6 UC	285 200			
28-200 f/3.8-5.6 UC	335 240			
28-200 f/4-5.6		175 140		
35-70 f/2.8-4		100 80	75 60	
35-70 f/3.5-4.5		75 50		
35-70 f/3.5-4.5 UC		100 85		
35-80 f/4-5.6	130 90			
35-105 f/3.5-4.5			90 75	
35-135 f/3.5-4.5	160 130	110 90	95 60	
35-135 f/4-5.6 UC	210 155			
35-200 f/4-5.6		140 120		
39-80 f/3.5		80 50		
50-200 f/3.5 APO		185 150		
50-250 f/3.5-4.5 APO		215 190		
55-200 f/4-5.6		120 100		

Sigma Manual Focus Lenses

Lens	New	Mint	Excellent	User
60-200 f/4-5.6		90 75		
70-150 f/3.5		80 65		
70-210 f/2.8 APO	695 600			
70-210 f/3.5-4.5		120 110		
70-210 f/3.5-4.5 APO	260 190		170 125	
70-210 f/4-5.6		85 70		
70-210 f/4-5.6 APO UC	260 190			
70-210 f/4-5.6 UC	160 110			
70-210 f/4.5-5.6		100 80	75 60	
70-230 f/4.5			80 70	
70-300 f/4-5.6 APO "DL"	395 285			
75-150 f/3.5			65 45	
75-200 f/2.8-3.5	220 180	150 125		
75-200 f/3.8	150 130			
75-200 f/4		125 85		
75-210 f/3.5-4.5		100 70		
75-250 f/4			120 100	
75-250 f/4.5		120 100		
75-300 f/4-5.6 DL	250 165			
75-300 f/4-5.6 APO UC	315 235			
75-300 f/4.5-5.6 APO	285 215			
75-300 f/4.5-5.6	195 175		120 90	
75-300 f/4.5-5.6 DL	240 180			
80-200 f/3.5			75 50	
80-200 f/3.5-4			70 45	
80-200 f/4.5-5.6		90 75		
100-200 f/4.5		100 80	75 45	
100-500 f/5.6-8 APO	1600 1295	1250 1000		
350-1200 f/11 APO		3800 2900		
2X Macro Teleconverter	100 85	70 65		

Sigma Autofocus Lenses

Sigma autofocus lenses sell for different prices depending upon which mount is offered. Lenses to fit EOS, for example, have built-in micro motors, while other mounts don't. It's no coincidence then that lenses made for the EOS mount cost more than the others do. To take these price differences into account, the New range of prices shows what to expect when buying from one of the large mail order houses. The low price is usually for either Nikon or Minolta mount, and the high end of the range is EOS unless the lens is not made for EOS. If you're not buying from one of the large mail order outfits, prices probably will be higher than those I've shown.

All Sigma AF lenses are available for Maxxum. Most are available for Canon and Nikon. Just a few are available for Olympus, Pentax or Yashica.

Sigma Autofocus Lenses

Lens	New	Mint	Excellent	User
14mm f/3.5	530 530			
18mm f/3.5	330 295			
24mm f/2.8	190 130			
28mm f/1.8 Asph	210 190			
50mm f/2. 8 Macro	240 170			
90mm f/2.8 Macro	330 285			
180mm f/2.8 APO Macro	775 740			
180mm f/5.6 APO Macro	335 285			
300mm f/2.8 APO	2200 2150	1750 1600		
400mm f/5.6	350 230		180 150	
400mm f/5.6 APO	520 430		300 250	
500mm f/4.5 APO	3100 3000			
500mm f/7.2 APO	550 515			
600mm f/8 Mirror (Manual Focus)	350 350			
800mm f/5.6 APO	5520 5310			
1000mm f/8 APO	4280 4130			
18-35 f/3.5-4.5	445 415			

Sigma Autofocus Lenses

Lens	New	Mint	Excellent	User
21-35 f/3.5-4.2	335			
24-50 f/4-5.6	190 155			
24-70 f/3.5-5.6	180 150			
28-70 f/2.8	300 270			
28-70 f/3.5-4.5		90 75		
28-70 f/3.5-4.5 UC	140 115			
28-70 f/3.5-4.5 Power Zoom	175 135			
28-80 f/3.5-4.5		125 100		
28-105 f/4-5.6 UC	220 190			
28-200 f/3.8-5.6	235 215			
28-200 f/4-5.6		200 175		
35-70 f/3.5-4.5		100 75		
35-70 f/3.5-4.5 UC		85 75		
35-80 f/4-5.6	105 95			
35-105 f/3.5-4.5		100 80		
35-135 f/3.5-4.5	175 150	125 90		
55-200 f/4-5.6		150 125		
60-200 f/4-5.6		95 75		
70-210 f/2,8 APO	660 640			
70-210 f/3.5-4.5 APO	310 250			
70-210 f/4-5.6		100 85		
70-210 f/4-5.6 APO	200 180			
70-210 f/4-5.6 UC	145 105			
70-210 f/4-5.6 Power Zoom	225 195			
75-200 f/2.8-3.5		170 140	140 125	
75-200 f/3.8		150 125	120 80	
75-300 f/4-5.6 APO UC	260 235			
75-300 f/4-5.6 DL	190 175			
75-300 f/4.5-5.6	230 220	170 150		
75-300 f/4.5-5.6 APO	280 220			
1.4X Teleconverter	190 165			

TAMRON

Tamron lenses have long been known for their interchangeable lens mounts. In fact, the term "T-Mount" came from — you guessed it — Tamron. Some early Tamron lenses used an interchangeable mount that provided auto-diaphragm control called the Adaptamatic. In reality, it was interchangeable only with considerable difficulty. Later, Tamron introduced the Adaptall system, which made changing mounts a lot easier, although for some lens/mount combinations it could still be a bit tedious, requiring adjustments. Finally, the Adaptall-2 system made changing lens mounts a breeze. This interchangeability between camera systems provides a real boon for photographers who either find themselves using more than one system or who decide to change from one system to another.

Tamron has built a reputation for producing outstanding lenses at competitive prices. The premium quality zooms and fixed focal length telephotos, designated SP for Super Performance, such as the 80-200 f/2.8 and 300 f/2.8 (both which incorporate low-dispersion glass elements), are excellent optics and compare very favorably with equivalent lenses produced by camera manufacturers. In the listings below, LD stands for Low Dispersion Glass, and IF stands for Internal Focusing.

New prices are for the lens only and do not include the Adaptall-2 mount ($20-30 more. Contax or Leica: $40-55 more).

Tamron Manual Focus Lenses

Lens	New	Mint	Excellent	User
SP17mm f/3.5	390 335			
21mm f/4			150 100	
24mm f/2.5	295 225	200 180	150 125	
24mm f/3.5			50 40	
28mm f/2.5	95 80		50 40	
SP90mm f/2.5 Macro (early)			180 150	
SP90mm f/2.5 Macro (late)	270 245	220 190		
1:1 Tube for above	60 40	30 25		

AFTERMARKET LENSES

Tamron Manual Focus Lenses

Lens	New		Mint		Excellent		User
135mm f/2.5					130	85	
135mm f/2.8 Auto (early)					40	30	
135mm f/2.8			115	95	90	65	
135mm f/3.5			50	40			
SP180mm f/2.5 LDIF	850	700	600	500	490	440	
200mm f/3.5					110	85	
SP300mm f/2.8 LD (early)					950	800	
SP300mm f/2.8 LDIF w/1.4x	2350	1900	1600	1400	1500	1300	
SP300mm f/2.8 LDIF (latest—no 2X)	2500	2100					
SP300mm f/5.6 Tele Macro					185	160	
SP350mm f/5.6 Mirror					175	150	
SP400mm f/4 LDIF			1750	1600			
SP500mm f/8 Mirror	395	335	290	270	260	225	
SP24-48 f/3.5-3.8			320	280	285	240	
28-50 f/3.5-4.5			150	125			
28-70 f/3.5-4.5	175	150	125	90			
SP28-80 f/3.5-4.2			245	180			
28-85 f/?					115	95	
SP28-135 f/4-4.5			325	285			
28-200 f/3.8-5.6	385	290					
35-70 f/3.5					100	75	
SP35-80 f/2.8-3.8			270	225	240	180	
SP35-105 f/2.8 Aspherical	645	560					
35-135 f/3.5-4.2	335	270	240	200	210	160	
SP35-210 f/3.5-4.2			290	240	220	170	
SP60-300 f/3.8-5.4	410	320	280	260			
70-150 f/3.5					150	100	
70-150 f/2.8 Soft Focus					175	140	
SP70-210 f/3.5	385	315	280	250	240	200	
SP70-210 f/3.5-4					175	125	
70-210 f/3.8-4					160	125	
70-210 f/4 AF (IF)			120	100			
The 70-210 AF will autofocus on any SLR for which an Adaptall-2 mount is made.							
70-210 f/4-5.6	190	150	120	100			
SP70-350 f/4.5					525	450	
75-250 f/3.8-4.5					175	125	
SP80-200 f/2.8 LD			700	650	650	500	
80-200 f/4.5					80	70	
80-210 f/3.8-4			150	130	130	90	
80-250 f/3.8					125	80	
85-210 f/4.5					75	60	
SP200-500 f/5.6			1000	900	890	700	
200-500 f/6.9			595	500	450	400	
1.4X Custom Converter			120	100	105	75	
2X Flat Field	150	120			75	60	
Adaptall-2 Mount	40	30					
Leica and Contax Adaptall-2 mounts are higher							

Tamron Autofocus Lenses

Tamron makes autofocus lenses for Minolta Maxxum, Nikon, Canon EOS and Pentax autofocus cameras. Only three lenses, the 300mm f/2.8 LD, the 28-70 f/3.5-4.5 and the 70-210 f/4-5.6, are not made for the EOS. Only one lens, the 28-200 f/3.5-5.6 is made for Pentax. All focal lengths listed are made for Maxxum and Nikon. These lenses do not have interchangeable mounts.

Lens	New		Mint		Excellent		User
90mm f/2.5 Macro	385	300					
300mm f/2.8 LD IF	2850	2530					
20-40 f/2.7-3.5	750	670					
24-70 f/3.3-5.6	235	235					
28-70 f/3.5-4.5	175	140					
28-200 f/3.8-5.6	375	290					
35-90 f/4-5.6			100	85			

Tamron Autofocus Lenses

Lens	New	Mint	Excellent	User
35-105 f/2.8 Aspherical	795 700			
35-135 f/3.5-4.5		150 125		
70-210 f/2.8 LD	995 875			
70-210 f/3.5-4.5		150 125	130 100	
70-210 f/4-5.6	200 140			
70-300 f/4-5.6	340 255			
90-300 f/4-5.6		150 130		
1.4X Teleconverter	120 90			
2X Teleconverter	140 120			

TOKINA

Tokina has offered a bewildering variety of lens styles (many for the same focal length) over the years. It has offered manual-focus lenses in the following series, listed more or less in order of quality: ATX, SMZ, SZX, SZ, EMZ and ELZ. Except for the ATX series, I've listed the series names of lenses only if more than one type was made for the same focal length (as an example, see the listings below for 80-200 zooms).

Tokina lenses are generally well made, the stand-outs being those ATX lenses that incorporate SD and HLD glass. These lenses are outstanding values. In the listings below, SD stands for Super-low Dispersion; HLD stands for High-refractive, Low Dispersion. Lenses with these suffixes incorporate special low-dispersion glass elements for improved sharpness and color rendition.

Tokina Manual Focus Lenses

Lens	New	Mint	Excellent	User
17mm f/3.5 SL	270 200		150 125	
24mm f/2.8 SL		100 80		
28mm f/2.8 SL or ELF	110 80	65 50	50 30	
90mm f/2.5 Macro ATX w/1:1	380 305	225 205		
300mm f/2.8 SD ATX	1750 1500	1295 1220		
400mm f/5.6		160 125		
400mm f/5.6 SD	310 235			
400mm f/6.3 Preset?			100 75	
500mm f/8 Mirror	320 225	195 175	180 140	
600mm f/8 SL Preset			400 350	
800mm f/8 SL Preset			550 425	
24-40 f/2.8 ATX	300 250		170 140	
24-70 f/3.5-4.8 SZX	285 200			
25-50 f/4			100 85	
28-70 f/2.8-4.3 SZX		110 100	100 85	
28-70 f/3.5-4.5 EMZ		80 70		
28-70 f/3.5-4.5 SZX	145 110			
28-70 f/4 SZ		115 80		
28-85 f/3.5-4.5 ATX		150 110	125 80	
28-85 f/4		150 100	120 80	
28-105 f/3.5-4.5 SZX	285 200			
28-105 f/3.8-4.3			150 125	
28-105 f/4-5.3 SZX		130 100		
28-135 f/4-4.6 ATX			200 150	
28-200 f/3.5-5.3 SZX	250 180	150 120		
35-70 f/2.8 ATX		190 150		
35-70 f/3.5-4.5 SZX	125 100			
35-70 f/4 SZ			80 60	
35-105 f/3.5-4.3		150 125	120 85	
35-135 f/3.5-4.5		150 125	115 85	
35-135 f/4-4.5		120 110	90 75	
35-200 f/4-5.6 SZX		180 160	165 140	
35-200 f/3.5-4.5 ATX		220 180		
50-200 f/3.5-4.5 SMZ		180 150		

Tokina Manual Focus Lenses

Lens	New	Mint	Excellent	User
50-250 f/4-5.6 ATX		225 175	170 140	
60-120 f/2.8 ATX		160 140	125 100	
60-300 f/4-5.6 SZX	255 190			
70-210 f/3.5 SZ			140 125	
70-210 f/4 SMZ		100 80		
70-210 f/4.5 EMZ		90 70		
70-210 f/4-5.6 SZX	160 110	80 60		
75-150 f/3.8		100 80		
80-200 f/2.8 SD ATX	490 395	350 325	330 250	
80-200 f/3.5-4.5 SMZ		100 90		
80-200 f/4.5-5.6 SZX	135 95	75 50		
80-200 f/4 ELZ (no macro)		90 80	80 60	
80-200 f/4 EMZ (w/macro)		120 100		
80-200 f/4.5			75 50	
100-300 f/4 ATX SD	500 410	365 340	350 300	
100-300 f/5.6 SZ		120 100	100 85	
150-500 f/5.6 SD ATX	1250 930	850 800		
2X (4 element)	45 40		25 20	
2X (7 element)	110 80	70 50	50 40	

Tokina Autofocus Lenses

Currently, Tokina makes autofocus lenses for EOS, Maxxum, Nikon AF and Pentax AF. Not all of the following lenses will fit the above-mentioned systems, so I've included in parentheses the initial of the AF mounts available. Lenses to fit EOS are priced substantially higher than the other mounts because of their integral focusing motors. Expect to pay closer to the high end of the New range, even when buying from deep-discount retailers.

Lens	New	Mint	Excellent	User
17mm f/3.5 (E,M,N)	470 360			
100mm f/2.8 Macro (E,M,N)	425 380			
300mm f/2.8 ATX SD (M,N)	2500 2050			
400mm f/5.6 ATX SD (E,M,N,P)	475 380			
20-35 f/3.5-4.5 ATX HLD (E,M,N)	370 240			
24-40 f/2.8 ATX (E,M,N)	530 450			
28-70 f/2.6-2.8 PRO (E,M,N,P)	550 460			
28-70 f/2.8 ATX HLD (E,M,N,P)	400 290			
28-70 f/2.8-4.5 SD (E,M,N,P)	190 120			
28-70 f/3.5-4.5 (M,N,P)		90 80		
28-80 f/3.5-4.5 (M,P,N)		100 100		
28-200 f/3.5-5.3 (M,N)	300 225			
35-70 f/3.5-4.6 (M,N,P)		100 80		
35-200 f/4-5.6 (M)		160 135		
60-300 f/4-5.6 SZX	300 210			
70-210 f/4-5.6 (E,M,N)	180 110			
70-210 f/4.5 (N,P)		115 85		
75-300 f/4.5-5.6 (M,N)		180 150		
80-200 f/2.8 ATX SD (E,M,N)	550 480			
100-300 f/4 ATX SD (M,N)	940 610			

VIVITAR

Vivitar has been designing lenses for 35mm SLRs for almost as long as 35mm SLRs have been around. Although primarily an aftermarket producer of lenses and electronic flashes, Vivitar has long been a pioneer in photo technology. The famous Series 1 line of lenses (abbreviated below as S1) exhibit outstanding sharpness, color and contrast. Series 1 zooms come very close to rivaling the very best fixed focal length lenses in image quality.

35 MM

Vivitar Manual Focus Lenses

Lens	New		Mint		Excellent		User	
17mm f/2.8			150	130				
17mm f/3.5			125	100				
19mm f/3.8	140	100						
20mm f/3.8					120	80		
24mm f/2			100	90	80	60		
24mm f/2.8	100	70			50	40		
28mm f/1.9 (IF) S1			150	130	125	85		
28mm f/2			100	85	80	60		
28mm f/2.5			80	60	70	50		
28mm f/2.8	80	60	50	40	45	35		
35mm f/1.9			130	100	75	50		
35mm f/2.5					40	30		
35mm f/2.8			60	50				
55mm f/2.8 Macro			140	130	125	100		
90mm f/2.5 S1 Macro (w/1:1)			225	215	200	170		
90mm f/2.8 Macro			195	170				
100mm f/2.8 Macro					180	150		
105mm f/2.5 S1 Macro	380	295			220	180		
105mm f/2.8					65	50		
135mm f/1.5 Professional (T-Mt Preset)					325	250		
135mm f/2.3 S1			180	125	130	95		
135mm f/2.5 TX or dedicated					70	50		
135mm f/2.8 T-4 or dedicated			60	45	50	35		
135mm f/3.5					40	30		
200mm f/3 S1			225	180	175	125		
200mm f/3.5					80	60		
200mm f/3.5 AF (on any SLR)			180	140				
300mm f/5.6			90	75				
400mm f/5.6 Preset			160	140	150	125		
400mm f/5.6					200	130		
450mm f/4.5 S1 Mirror			450	350				
500mm f/6.3 Preset					95	70		
500mm f/8 Mirror	200	130						
600mm f/8 S1 Mirror			550	450	380	350		
600mm f/8 Preset					350	300		
800mm f/8 S1 Mirror					600	500		
800mm f/11 S1 Mirror			550	495				
17-28 f/4-4.5	220	130						
24-48 f/3.5 S1			195	150	180	120		
24-70 f/3.8-4.5 S1	230	155						
28-50 f/3.5-4.5			110	100	80	65		
28-70 f/3.5-4.8 AF (on any SLR)			150	100				
28-70 f/3.5-4.8			75	60				
28-80 f/3.5-5.6	140	100						
28-85 f/2.8-3.8			140	100	95	80		
28-85 f/3.5-4.5			95	75				
28-90 f/2.8-3.5 S1			190	150	170	120		
28-105 f/2.8-3.8 S1	260	225	200	180	170	140		
28-105 f/3.5-4.5	200	160	140	120				
28-135 f/3.5-4.5			170	120				
28-200 f/3.5-5.3			160	150				
28-210 f/3.5-5.6			140	120	130	70		
35-70 f/2.8-3.8			125	115	95	60		
35-85 f/2.8 S1			200	165	175	125	120	90
35-105 f/3.2-4			125	100	85	60		
35-200 f/3.0-4.5			135	120				
55-135 f/3.5					80	55		
70-150 f/3.5			100	80	90	75		
70-210 f/2.8-3.5 S1			150	140	130	95		
70-210 f/2.8-4 S1	295	220	190	160	150	120		
70-210 f/3.5 S1 (67 & 62mm filter)			175	130	140	125		

Vivitar has made four different Series 1 70-210's. The original is the 70-210 f/3.5 with a 67mm front filter size — big and heavy, but built like a tank. The second, often considered the best, is the f/3.5 model with a 62mm front filter size (while I've combined prices for the two models into one listing, expect to pay a little more for the second one). It's considerably lighter, just as sharp, and has an easier-to-engage macro mode. Next came the f/2.8-3.5, followed by the f/2.8-4, which is the current model.

AFTERMARKET LENSES

Vivitar Manual Focus Lenses

Lens	New		Mint		Excellent		User	
70-210 f/4.5			85	65	80	60		
70-210 f/4.5-5.6			85	50	60	40		
70-300 f/4.2-5.8			140	120				
75-150 f/3.8 close focus					75	60		
75-200 f/4.5			120	100				
75-200 f/4.5 AF (on any SLR)			150	120				
75-205 f/3.5-4.5					90	70		
75-205 f/3.8 2-Ring			75	65	70	50		
75-205 f/3.8 (add for matched 2X)			130	100	90	60		
75-260 f/4.5 TX					85	65		
75-300 f/4.5-5.6					140	100		
80-200 f/4					100	80		
80-200 f/4.5			100	95	85	60		
85-205 f/3.8			100	85	75	50		
90-180 f/4 Flat Field Macro			300	250	225	175		
100-200 f/4					60	40		
100-300 f/5 CF					115	85		
100-300 f/5.6			125	125				
100-500 f/5.6-8 S1	540	425	400	350				
120-600 f/5.6-8			450	400	400	350		
1.5X			40	25				
2X Macro (7 element)	130	90			65	50		
2X	50	35			25	20		
3X			50	40	35	25		

Vivitar Autofocus Lenses

Vivitar's autofocus lenses are available in mounts to fit EOS, Maxxum, Nikon and Pentax AF. Not all focal lengths are made for each mount, however. Check the abbreviations after each lens description.

Lens	New		Mint		Excellent		User	
28-70 f/2.8 S1 (E,M,N,P)	350	310						
28-70 f/3.5-4.5 (M,N,P)	160	110			85	65		
28-105 f/4-5.6 S1 (E,M,N,P)	235	220						
28-200 f/3.8-5.6 (M,N,P)	240							
28-210 f/3.5-5.6 (M)	200							
35-70 f/3.5-4.6 (M,N,P)	140	90						
28-200 f/3.5-5.6 S1 (E,M)	340	290	180	150				
70-210 f/2.8 S1 (E,M,N,P)	710	670						
70-210 f/4.5-5.6 (M,N,P)	185	115						
60-300 f/4-5.6 (M)	265	200						

Miscellaneous Lenses of Interest

Below is a selection of lenses, which, for various reasons, captured my interest. If you have a favorite oddball or unusual lens, available in mounts for popular cameras, that isn't included here, drop me a line describing it. In order to include it in this listing, I'll need verifiable pricing info.

Generic 135mm f/1.8

This lens is more or less a generic Japanese-made optic that can be found under an assortment of brand names, such as Spiratone, Soligor, 5 Star, Rexatar and others. It's big and heavy, sporting an impressive 82mm front element. Sharpness and contrast are acceptable, but this lens is still a bargain considering its maximum aperture. One early version of the lens featured mount interchangeability via the YS system. Later versions had dedicated non-interchangeable mounts.

Lens	Mint	Excellent	User
135mm f/1.8		175 ... 125	

Kalimar

Why do I list an off-brand Korean-made lens like a Kalimar? Well, it's the only wide-angle to long-telephoto zoom I've seen that has a constant maximum aperture. Every other 28-200 (or 28-210 or 35-200 or whatever) I've seen or read about has a variable aperture in the neighborhood of f/4-5.6. I've used this lens. It's a little heavy, but it's not bad at all. Unfortunately, Kalimar has discontinued this lens, replacing it with a more compact and lighter weight model that has a variable aperture like everyone else's.

Lens	Mint	Excellent	User
Kalimar 28-200 f/3.9	140 ... 100		

Kilar Macro Lenses

Kilar lenses were produced by the German company Killfit. The Kilar 40mm f/2.8 was the first true macro lens made. The Kilar 90mm f/2.8 is a beautiful lens that focuses all the way down to 1:1 without an extension tube. Both employ the preset style of aperture selection. These lenses are most frequently found in Exacta mount, but I've seen them in others, such as Nikon, Canon and Pentax screw.

Lens	Mint	Excellent	User
Kilar 40mm f/2.8 Macro		150 ... 125	
Kilar 90mm f/2.8 Macro		385 ... 350	

Schneider

The name Schneider is often associated with top-quality large format and medium format lenses, but the company does make a few for smaller formats. The two listed below are Perspective Control lenses, which are used in architectural photography and other special situations where converging vertical lines would detract from the shot. These lenses are pricey, but of extremely high quality.

Lens	New	Mint	Excellent	User
28mm f/2.8 PC	2350 ... 1990			
35mm f/4 PC	1580 ... 1320			

Spiratone

While Spiratone didn't manufacture the lenses it sold over the years, it offered a few with interesting focal lengths, especially ultra-wide angles and fisheyes, which are the ones I've chosen to list. All are generally of high optical quality.

Lens	Mint	Excellent	User
Spiratone 7.5mm f/5.6		160 ... 100	
Spiratone 12mm f/8		125 ... 80	
Spiratone 18mm f/3.5		150 ... 100	
Spiratone 20mm f/2.8	140 ... 100	120 ... 90	
Spiratone 24-40 f/3.5	200 ... 160		

Miscellaneous Mirror Telephotos

Most photographers have seen or shot with the ubiquitous 500mm f/8 CAT mirror at one time or another. It remains popular because of its light weight, close-focus capability, and generally good optical performance. The 300mm is surprisingly small, about the size of a typical 50mm lens. The lenses made by Bausch & Lomb, Celestron, Meade and Questar can be found configured as lenses, spotting scopes or telescopes. For example, the Celestron 1000mm f/11 is also known as the C90 telescope. The basic optics are the same, only the way accessories attach is different. The 500-800mm zoom is marketed by Cambridge Camera in New York City. It's a good performer optically, although somewhat large and heavy, and is one of only two mirror zoom lens I've run across designed specifically for photographic use (the other is a Pentax). All the lenses in this group adapt to cameras via T-mount adapters, so if you run across one and it intrigues you enough to buy it, chances are you won't have to worry about getting it to fit your camera. Prices for the B&L, Celestron and Meade lenses include camera adapters and T-mounts.

Lens	New	Mint	Excellent	User
Generic 300mm f/5.6			125 75	
Generic 500mm f/8			175 125	
B&L Criterion 1000mm f/11			300 200	
Cambron 500-800 f/8-12			350 325	
Celestron 300mm f/5.6			190 150	
Celestron 500mm f/5.6 (old style)			350 275	
Celestron 500mm f/5.6 (new style)	450 340			
Celestron 750mm f/6			600 500	
Celestron 1000mm f/10	370 300		350 250	
Celestron 1000mm f/11			350 250	
Celestron 1250mm f/10			550 400	
Meade 1000mm f/11			350 250	
Pro Optic 500mm f/5.6	320 250			
Questar 700mm f/8			1500 1300	

Miscellaneous Refractor Telephotos

The first two telephotos listed are found under a wide variety of house brand names. They are simple, economical telephotos that give surprisingly good results. The Novoflex lenses are made in Germany and are of very high optical quality — with prices to match. The Russian made Zenit Photo Sniper Outfit consists of a Zenit E camera with a 58mm f/2 normal lens, a 300mm f/4.5 telephoto and a gunstock, all of which fits snugly in a nice metal case. The prices shown for the Photosniper are for the complete outfit.

Lens	New	Mint	Excellent	User
400mm f/6.3 Preset	120 100		60 50	
500mm f/8 Preset	140 120		75 60	
Novoflex 400mm f/5.6	1400 1000	850 800		
Novoflex 400mm f/8			450 270	
Novoflex 600mm f/8			750 600	
Novoflex 640mm f/9			550 500	
Zenit Photo Sniper Outfit		350 275	250 175	

Panoramic Cameras

Panoramic photography has been a source of fascination for photographers for just about as long as they've been exposing silver halide crystals to light. Because these cameras have been around for so long, a tremendous variety exists. This section is devoted specifically to those using the rotating lens turret design popularized by Widelux. Other panoramic cameras are included as well, such as the Korona large format banquet cameras and the Fuji G-617, but are found in their respective sections. Some of the more unusual panoramics, such as the full 360-degree models, may be included in a later edition if demand and interest warrants inclusion.

Bogen Horizon 202

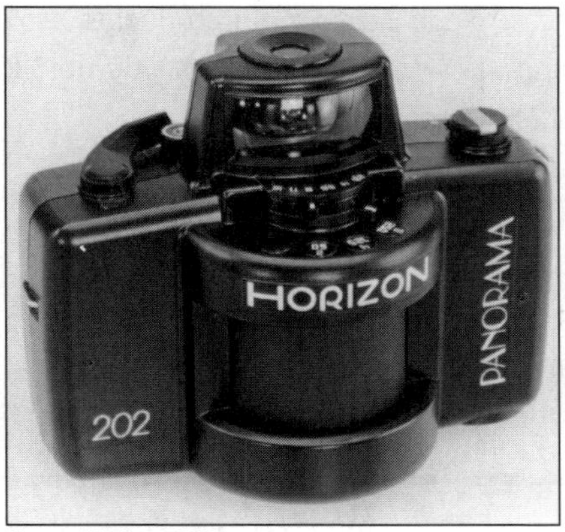

Bogen Horizon 202

Manufactured in Russia by Horizon KMZ, the Horizon 202 employs a rotating turret-mounted 28mm f/2.8 lens to render 24mm x 58mm images on 35mm film. This system provides the user with a 120 degree angle of coverage and up to 23 exposures on a conventional 36-exposure roll of film. The Horizon 202 is a simple, bare-bones panoramic camera: it has no meter and no battery. The camera's operation is entirely mechanical. It allows exposure times of 1/250, 1/125, 1/60, 1/8, ¼ and ½ seconds by combining three exposure aperture widths with two panning speeds. Selectable apertures are f/2.8, f/4, f/5.6, f/8, f/11 and f/16. The top-mounted viewfinder provides a 110 degree field of view. Mounted on it is a bubble spirit level, visible from within the viewfinder, to insure the camera has been placed true to horizontal.

Bogen Horizon 202

Camera	New	Mint	Excellent	User
Horizon 202	1000	850		

Noblex

All Noblex models are medium format roll-film cameras. The Pro 150, Pro 150S and Pro 150HS are "focus-free" cameras with the lenses' focus preset from 30 feet to infinity. The Pro 150 F (the F stands for Focusing) allows the user to focus the camera.

Specifications for all models are as follows: the negative size is 2.25" x 5", the angle of view is 146°, the top-mounted viewfinder provides you with a 90% field of view, the Accu Drive DC drive motor (no springs here) uses 4 AA batteries, the non-interchangeable lens is a 50mm Tessar with an aperture variable from f/4.5 to f/22, and multi-exposure capability. Each camera also comes with a bubble spirit level to aid the user in level placement of the camera.

The Pro 150, Pro 150S and Pro 150F have four shutter speeds: 1/30, 1/60, 1/125 and 1/250. The Pro 150HS has speeds ranging from 1/125 to 1/1000. A Pro 150 slow-speed retrofit is also available, with a full range of speeds from ½ second to 1/250 second.

The Pro 150S is a camera designed primarily for architectural work (the S stands for Shift), which allows the user to keep parallel lines from giving the appearance of converging.

PANORAMIC

Noblex

Camera	New	Mint	Excellent	User
Pro 150	2595	2250		
Pro 150F	3300	3095		
Pro 150HS	3550	3200		
Pro 150S	3300	3095		

WIDELUX

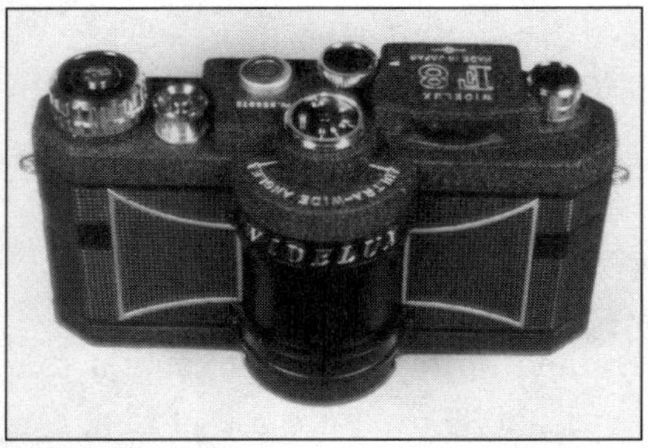

Widelux F8

Widelux cameras are made by the Japanese manufacturer Panon. Since the early 1950's this tiny company has been producing rotating lens panoramic cameras for the smaller film formats. A number of 35mm Widelux models have been made over the years, such as the FV, F6, F7 and the current model, the F8. Panon also produces the model 1500, which takes 120 film. Earlier models of their 120 film cameras were the Panon Wide Angle Camera and the Panophic. All models provide an effective 140° angle of view. The 35mm models provide 24mm x 55mm images, and the 120 models provide 60mm x 120mm images.

The Widelux F8 has a 26mm f/2.8 lens and offers shutter speeds of 1/15, 1/125 and 1/250. The F7 is essentially the same camera with only minor cosmetic differences. The 1500 has a 50mm f/2.8 lens and shutter speeds of 1/8, 1/60 and 1/250. Earlier model Wideluxes, while not listed, should sell for proportionally less than those shown below.

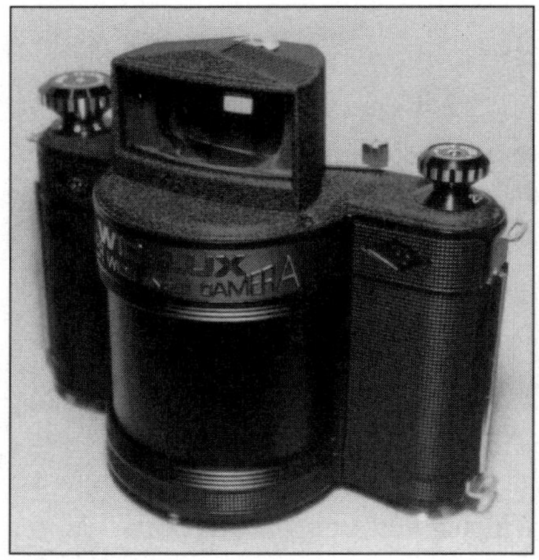

Widelux 1500

Widelux

Camera	New	Mint	Excellent	User
Widelux F6 (35mm)			800	700
Widelux F7 (35mm)			950	870
Widelux F8 (35mm)	1675	1400		
Model 1500 (120 film)	2825	2500		

Medium Format Cameras

Most of the medium format cameras listed in the following pages are SLRs. Despite the often hefty prices of medium format SLRs and lenses, their popularity has risen steadily. Unlike 35mm cameras, medium format cameras come in a variety of image sizes. Whereas most all 35mm cameras have an image size of 24mm x 36mm, medium format cameras come in sizes of 6cm x 4.5cm, 6cm x 6cm, 6cm x 7cm, 6cm x 8cm, 6cm x 9cm, and even wider in a few cases. By far, the most popular are 6cm x 4.5cm, 6cm x 6cm and 6cm x 7cm sizes.

Frequently, medium format cameras are offered for sale, both new and used, as outfits. Typically, a medium format outfit will consist of a camera body, a finder (usually waist-level), a roll-film back and a lens. All this can be purchased separately, of course, if buying new equipment, but it isn't always an option when buying used. So, I've included prices for some of the more common outfits in the following section.

Speaking of price, 6x4.5 systems are generally the most economical. Except for Hasselblad and Rollei, 6x6 systems are usually somewhat cheaper than 6x7 systems. And then there is the Pentax 6x7, which rivals the 6x4.5 systems in economy, and the heavyweights in quality.

A caveat for buyers of used equipment: medium format cameras tend to fall into two categories: heavily used and hardly used. Professionals often trade in their cameras for new ones every few years because of the heavy use to which they subject their equipment. Others, such as former "serious amateurs" may decide to sell their systems because they don't use them enough anymore to justify the investment. So, when considering a used system, inspect it for wear as thoroughly as possible and, if possible, try to find one that obviously didn't get much use.

Bronica

Did you know that Bronica cameras owe their name to the Kodak Brownie? As the story goes, the Japanese still refer to 120 size film as "Brownie size," (Though I've heard Japanese folks call it *roku-roku*, which means 6-6). So, if your camera uses Brownie size film, then it's a Brownie camera, right? Or a Brownie-camera...Brownieca...Bronica! More likely, though, the name is derived from Bronica's founder, whose surname was Zenzaburo. In Japanese, *Zenzaburo no nica* approximates Zenzaburo's camera. Recombining a few of the syllables then gives us Zenza Burononica, which can be contracted further to Zenza Bronica quite easily. Though the first explanation is the more interesting, the latter is more likely.

Early Bronica SLRs

Bronica's first medium format cameras (the C, D and S) had lousy reputations for durability — *hanger queens,* as one photographer/pilot I know calls them. They were noisy, plagued by excessive vibration and particularly prone to shutter problems. By now, most have died and gone to Brownie heaven. So, needless to say, they aren't listed. If you should run across one, chances are its broken. But if by some miracle it's still working, and you're in a particularly masochistic mood, the going price for one of these cameras in clean condition with a finder, a back (where applicable) and a normal lens is from $250 to $350.

Bronica S2 & S2A

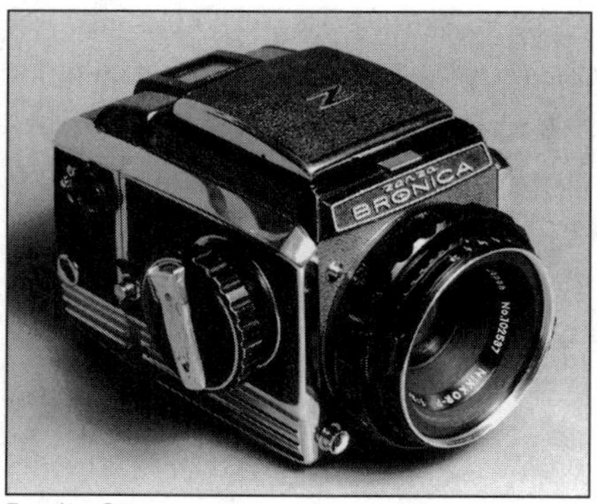

Bronica S2

The Bronica S2 was the first of the early Bronicas that employed the removable helical-focusing mount, which goes between the body and the lens, and was the first Bronica SLR to show some semblance of reliability. Outward appearances between the S2 and S2A are almost identical, but inward differences are more significant. The S2 employs brass gears in the shutter-cocking mechanism, which, after being subjected to heavy use are prone to stripping. The shutter cocking mechanism in the S2A uses stainless steel gears and is much more resistant to wear. To tell the difference between an S2 and S2A, look at the top of the camera body, behind the finder. If the camera is an S2A, it'll say so next to the serial number.

While the S2 is capable of rendering many years of reliable service if not abused, the S2A was the best model in Bronica's line of mechanical, square-format, focal-plane shutter cameras. It's sturdy and reliable and has proven itself over the past twenty years to be capable of withstanding the demands to which medium format equipment is often subjected.

Models prior to the S2 focused by turning a knob on the side of the camera, which racked the lens mount in or out of the camera body, much as is done with a typical twin-lens reflex. For the S2 Bronica abandoned this design in favor of a removable, focusing helical adapter that goes between the body and the lens, and allows the lens to be focused by rotating the helical's focusing collar.

The S2/S2A is a modular system that accepts interchangeable finders, backs and a large assortment of lenses. It features a mechanical, focal-plane shutter with speeds ranging from 1 second to 1/1000, plus B. X sync is 1/60. While 120 backs made for earlier vintage Bronicas will work just fine on the S2 or S2A, the later backs will accept either 120 or 220 film and provide multiple exposure capability.

Bronica EC & EC-TL

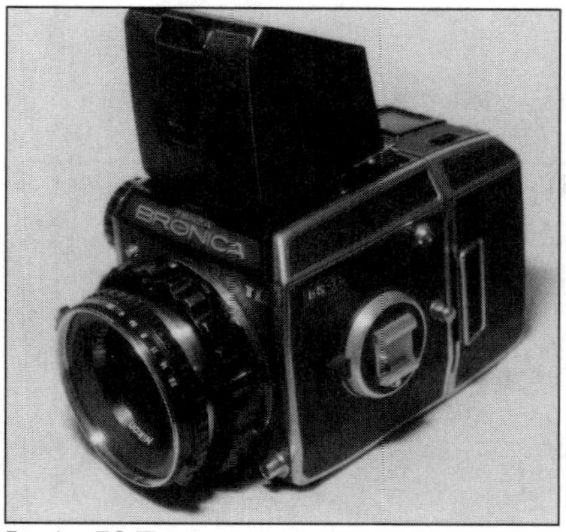

Bronica EC-TL

The EC and its update, the EC-TL, are somewhat similar in appearance to the S2A and its predecessors, but are entirely different cameras. Like the mechanical models, they are square-format, focal-plane shutter cameras. Unlike earlier models, however, they are battery dependent, having electronically-controlled shutter speeds from 4 seconds to 1/1000, plus B, with X sync at 1/60. Only B and X-sync will work without a battery. Both the EC and EC-TL have mirror lock-up and multiple-exposure capability, and accept the same removable focusing helicals and lenses as earlier Bronicas (Except the 105mm f/3.5 leaf-shutter Nikkor; this lens will work with the S2, S2A and EC only — not the EC-TL.), but their finders and backs will not interchange with those intended for the S, S2 and S2A.

Incorporated into the EC-TL's body is a selective-area TTL exposure meter, with an LED readout in the viewfinder. The metered portion of the image, which is approximately 10%, is indicated by a circle scribed in the focusing screen. Set the shutter speed dial to "A" and you have an aperture-priority auto exposure camera — a rarity among medium format cameras even to this day.

Here's a little tip for you EC-TL users who may have bought your cameras second hand without instruction books, or who may have lost your instruction books. Have you ever wondered what those different colored dots next to the ASA setting are for? Wonder no more: The white dot is the setting for 40mm to 100mm lenses, the yellow dot is the setting for 135mm to 200mm lenses, and the red dot is the setting for 300mm to 1200mm lenses. A large variety of lenses were made for the Bronica S and EC-series cameras. The Zenzanons and Nikkors are especially good.

Bronica ETR, ETRC, ETRS & ETRSi

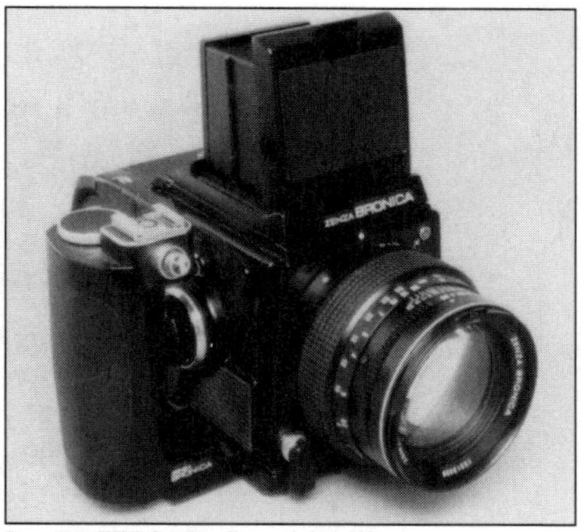

Bronica ETRS with Speed Grip E

Introduced in 1976, the ETR was Bronica's first leaf-shutter medium-format camera. It uses the 6x4.5 format and is a modular system, offering interchangeable lenses, finders and backs. Other than a few minor mechanical refinements in the ETRS, the ETR and ETRS are the same camera. Basic features include shutter speeds from 1 second to 1/500, plus T, with flash sync at all speeds.

The ETRSi is an ETRS with the following improvements: SCA/TTL flash capability with compatible strobes, mirror lock-up, a multiple exposure indicator visible within the viewfinder, and a bulb (B) setting. Also, Ei backs have an improved film transport/pressure plate system that keeps the film flatter during exposure, thereby insuring sharper images.

Lenses for the ETR/C/S/Si incorporate electronically-controlled leaf shutters. The shutters will fire at 1/500 and "T" only in the event of battery failure.

Bronica SQ, SQ-A, SQ-A/M & SQ-Ai

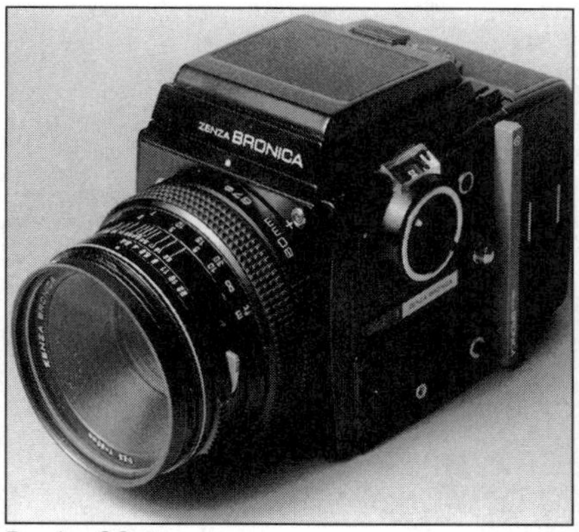

Bronica SQ-A

Bronica's SQ system is a modular 6 x 6 system featuring interchangeable lenses, finders and 120 or 220 backs. As with the ETR and its descendants, the system uses electronically-controlled leaf-shutter lenses with the standard range of speeds (1 second to 1/500) for flash sync at any setting. Mechanical speeds are 1/500 and "T" only.

In addition to the SQ's features, the SQ-A offers mirror lock-up, plus it has electrical contacts for the AE prism. The SQ-A/M is an SQ-A with a built-in 1 fps winder. The SQ-Ai is an SQ-A with TTL flash capability with the addition of the SCA 386 adapter and an SCA compatible flash unit.

Bronica GS-1

The GS-1 uses the popular 6X7 format, but is considerably lighter than its primary competitors, the Mamiya RB and RZ 67. As is true with other Bronicas, it is a fully modular system, accepting a full line of lenses, finders and backs. Like the SQA and ETR systems, the GS-1 also uses electronically-controlled leaf-shutter lenses with mechanical speeds of 1/500 and T only. The GS-1 is the only 6x7 camera that offers TTL flash metering (in fact, it was the first medium format camera to offer it). Unfortunately, its TTL system isn't SCA compatible, so you're locked into using Bronica's GS-1 Speedlite if you want to use TTL flash.

Bronica SLRs

New prices are for bodies with backs, but without finders. It's the only way Bronica will ship them into the U.S. Used prices are for bodies with waist level finders, but without backs.

Camera	Yrs. Made	New	Mint	Excellent	User
ETR	1976-80		275 250	250 190	190 150
ETRC	1978-?			220 150	
ETRS	1980-88		410 375	360 280	275 235
ETRSi	1988-	1350 1170	750 675	700 500	
GS-1		2200 1830	1100 1000	980 750	
SQ	c.1980-85			480 400	
SQ-A	c.1985-		565 500	520 450	460 400
SQ-A/M	1990-		790 720	750 635	
SQ-Ai	1991-	2150 1780		950 800	

Bronica Outfits

Camera	Yrs. Made	New	Mint	Excellent	User
S2, W/L, 75/2.8, 12/24				350 300	325 250
S2A, W/L, 75/2.8, 12/24				500 400	395 350
EC, W/L, 12/24, 75/2.8				500 425	400 350
EC-TL, W/L, 12/24, 75/2.8			725 650	650 525	500 400
ETR, W/L, 120, 75/2.8				575 500	
ETR, AE prism, 120, 75/2.8				950 825	
ETRS, W/L, 120, 75/2.8				800 695	
ETRS, AE prism, 120, 75/2.8II				1200 1000	
ETRS, AE II, 120, 75/2.8II			1495 1250		
ETRS, Std prism, 120, 75/2.8II			1150 975	995 900	
ETRSi, W/L, 120, 75/2.8		2200 1800	1600 1450	1400 1100	
GS-1, W/L, 120, 100/3.5		3350 2780	2320 1900	1800 1450	
GS-1, Std prism, 120, 100/3.5		3700 3190	2330 2100		
GS-1, AE prism, 120, 100/3.5		4400 3750	2995 2750		
SQ, W/L, 120, 80/2.8				900 850	
SQ, Std prism, 120, 80/2.8				975 900	
SQ-A, W/L, 120, 80/2.8			1225 1120	1145 995	
SQ-A, Std prism, 120, 80/2.8			1575 1440	1450 1275	
SQ-A, AE prism, 120, 80/2.8			1750 1600		
SQ-A, ME prism, 120, 80/2.8			1675 1580		
SQ-Ai, W/L, 120, 80/2.8		3050 2525			

Lenses for EC, EC-TL, S2 and S2A

Lens	Mint		Excellent		User	
40mm f/4 Nikkor			590	450		
40mm f/4 Zenzanon			450	390		
45mm f/4.5 Komura			275	225		
50mm f/2.8 Nikkor			325	270		
50mm f/2.8 Zenzanon			295	225		
50mm f/3.5 Komura			250	150		
50mm f/3.5 Nikkor			250	200	190	150
75mm f/2.8 Nikkor	100	75	60	55		
80mm f/2.4 Zenzanon			75	60		
100mm f/2.8 Komura			150	100		
100mm f/2.8 Zenzanon	185	150	165	125		
105mm f/3.5 LS Nikkor			425	300		
135mm f/2.3 Komura preset			150	100		
135mm f/2.8 Komura			125	90		
135mm f/3.5 Komura			100	80		
135mm f/3.5 Nikkor			275	200	190	120
150mm f/3.5 Komura			220	125		
150mm f/3.5 Zenzanon	300	220	250	190		
200mm f/3.5 Komura	240	180	150	110		
200mm f/3.5 Zenzanon	290	250				
200mm f/4 Komura			150	100		
200mm f/4 Nikkor			275	200	180	150
200mm f/4 Zenzanon			250	175		
300mm f/4.5 Zenzanon			490	380		
300mm f/5 Komura Preset			195	150		
300mm f/5.5 Meyer Tele-Megor			250	150		
300mm f/5.6 Nikkor			500	350		
400mm f/4.5 Nikkor			800	700		
400mm f/5.6 Nikkor			700	600		
400mm f/6.3 Komura			350	225		
500mm f/5.6 Zoomar Reflektar			500	400		
500mm f/7 Komura			350	250		
600mm f/5.6 Nikkor			850	750		
800mm f/8 Nikkor			1000	900		
1000mm f/8 Zoomar Reflektar			950	800		
1200mm f/11 Nikkor			1250	1000		
170-320 f/4 Zoomar			850	600		
2X (Vivitar or Komura)	150	125	100	80		

MEDIUM FORMAT

Zenzanon E Lenses (ETR, ETR-C, ETR-S, ETR-Si)

Lens	New		Mint		Excellent		User	
40mm f/4			600	570	550	490		
40mm f/4 PE	1500	1205						
50mm f/2.8			640	510	495	425		
50mm f/2.8 PE	1350	1080						
55mm f/4.5 PCS			3550	3200				
60mm f/2.8 PE	1370	1100						
75mm f/2.8 E, EII	870	690	550	500	510	400		
100mm f/4 Macro			685	580	600	500		
100mm f/4 Macro PE	1400	1135						
105mm f/3.5			450	400	390	350		
135mm f/4 PE	1370	1100						
150mm f/3.5 E, EII			575	525	540	425		
150mm f/3.5 PE	1350	1080						
150mm f/4			500	450	410	340		
180mm f/4.5 PE	1850	1500						
200mm f/4.5					675	500		
200mm f/4.5 PE	1490	1190						
250mm f/5.6			800	695	620	525		

Zenzanon E Lenses (ETR, ETR-C, ETR-S, ETR-Si)

Lens	New	Mint	Excellent	User
250mm f/5.6 PE	1590 1280			
500mm f/8 E, EII		1800 1650	1500 1000	
70-140 f/4.5		2000 1500	1500 1000	
125-250 f/5.6		2250 1700		
1.4X PE	890 750			
2X E	590 540	500 450	425 375	
2X PE	920 770			
2X Komura		200 150		

Zenzanon S & PS Lenses (SQ, SQ-A, SQ-Ai, SQ-A/M)

Lens	New	Mint	Excellent	User
40mm f/4		795 700	700 615	
40mm f/4 PS	1720 1490	1250 1125	1180 900	
50mm f/3.5		650 590	595 475	
50mm f/3.5 PS	1400 1285	1090 950	1000 820	
65mm f/4 PS	1300 1185	1000 900	950 725	
80mm f/2.8	500	400 350	325 250	
80mm f/2.8 PS	1100 915	800 720	680 500	
105mm f/3.5		500 440	450 350	
110mm f/4 Macro		750 650	700 580	
110mm f/4 Macro PS	1400 1285	1095 960	980 800	
135mm f/4 PS	1350 1235			
150mm f/3.5		750 650	650 550	
150mm f/4 PS	1400 1285	1050 950	1000 800	
180mm f/4.5 PS	1995 1700			
200mm f/4.5		800 650	695 550	
200mm f/4.5 PS	1700 1440		850 740	
250mm f/5.6		750 680	650 600	
250mm f/5.6 PS	1800 1545	1300 1185		
500mm f/8		1650 1450		
500mm f/8 PS	7800 7000			
75-150 f/4.5		2100 1695		
140-280 f/5.6		2250 1875		
1.4X PS	950 800			
2X PS	980 825	650 600	550 400	
2X Auto TC		450 400	385 300	

Zenzanon PG Lenses (GS-1)

Lens	New	Mint	Excellent	User
50mm f/4.5	1690 1550	1320 1100		
65mm f/4	1495 1390	1190 1090	1120 800	
100mm f/3.5	1125 1030	900 820	775 600	
110mm f/4 Macro	1640 1550	1320 1240		
150mm f/4	1480 1390	1175 1050	650 600	
200mm f/4.5	1560 1440	1195 1050	800 725	
250mm f/5.6	1720 1550	1300 1100		
500mm f/8	7800 7000			
1.4X Auto Teleconverter	980 875	780 700		
2X Auto Teleconverter	980 875	780 700		

Bronica S/S2/S2A Accessories

Item	New		Mint		Excellent		User	
Prism A or C			275	245	220	170		
Sport Finder					40	25		
Waist Level Finder					50	40		
Magnifier Hood					125	75		
12/24 back			125	110	120	80	90	70
120 back					70	50		
6X4.5 back					135	100		
Polaroid Back			395	350	360	325		
Bellows					135	100		
Bellows Model 2					275	185		
Ext. Tube Set (4 Piece)					90	70		
Helical Focusing Mount					70	50		
L Grip					45	25		
Pistol Grip T					50	35		

Bronica EC/EC-TL Accessories

Item	New		Mint		Excellent		User	
Waist Level Finder					90	80		
Prism A or C			275	235	225	180		
EC TTL Meter Finder					240	150		
TTL meter finder for EC, not EC-TL								
Magnifier Hood					105	75		
Deluxe Bellows					275	185		
Mini Bellows					125	100		
Ext. Tube Set (4 Piece)					90	70		
Helical Focusing Mount					70	50		
Pistol Grip					45	25		
12/24 Back					250	160		
Polaroid Back					360	310		

Bronica ETR/C/S/Si Accessories

Item	New		Mint		Excellent		User	
Waist Level Finder	140	115	100	80	75	45		
Prism Finder E	450	385	330	295	300	240		
AE Finder E			265	250	245	220		
AE-II Finder	980	875	750	690	650	500		
AE-III Finder.	1290	1030						
Rotary Finder	630	510	440	380	370	250		
High Eyepoint Finder	640	515	450	400				
Action Finder	520	410	350	300	300	250		
120 or 220 back			260	225	250	200	190	150
Ei 120 or 220 back	375	320	295	240	260	220		
135-N or W back	520	445	370	320	300	245		
Polaroid back E	425	360	300	250	270	220	200	150
NPC Polaroid Back	175	130			100	85		
Speed Grip E	290	235	200	160	170	125		
Motor Drive E			280	225	225	175		
Motor Winder Ei	520	410	350	300				
Auto Ext. Tube E14	440	370	300	250	250	190		
Auto Ext. Tube E28	440	320	300	255	260	200		
Auto Ext. Tube E42	440	370	300	260	250	210		
Auto Bellows E	1550	1400			800	725		
ETR Bellows					500	350		
Pro Lens Shade E	455	380	300	250	270	190		
ETRSi Flash Bracket			110	110				

Bronica SQ, SQ-A, SQ-A/M Accessories

Item	New	Mint	Excellent	User
Waist Level Finder S	160 130	110 90		
Prism Finder S	595 515	450 395	400 320	
High Eyepoint Finder	710 625			
AE Prism Finder (SQ-A,A/M,Ai)	1070 975	825 775	800 640	
AE Prism Finder (SQ)			525 400	
45 DS Prism Finder		560 550		
ME (TTL) Prism Finder	900 815	700 590	600 480	
MF (TTL) Chimney Finder	695 600	525 450	470 385	
120 or 220 Ai back	510 440		270 220	
120 or 220 back (SQ, A, A/M)		275 240	250 200	
120 or 220 6X4.5 back (SQ-J)	510 440	375 320	350 250	
135-N or W back	620 545	495 425	450 320	
Polaroid Back S	510 420	360 325	350 265	
NPC Polaroid Back	180 140			
Speed Grip S	340 270	225 200	300 150	
Pro Shade S	490 400	350 300	320 220	
Auto Ext. Tube S18	550 475		210 150	
Auto Ext. Tube S36	550 475	440 380	395 260	
Auto Bellows S	1740 1550		1000 695	
SQi Motor Drive.	810 670			

Bronica GS-1 Accessories

Item	New	Mint	Excellent	User
Waist Level Finder	170 145	120 100		
Prism Finder	690 555	495 450	460 350	
AE Prism Finder	1210 1030	900 840	870 685	
AE Rotary Prism Finder	1275 1080	950 895	900 725	
120 or 220 Back (6X6,6X7,6X4.5)	515 445	375 320	350 250	
Polaroid Back	535 460	395 340	380 295	
NPC Polaroid Back	200 175			
Speed Grip G	385 310	270 240	250 190	
G-1 Flash Unit	495 410		250 200	
Pro Shade G	420	350 325		
Auto Ext. Tube G18	570 485	425 350		
Auto Ext. Tube G36	570 485	425 350		
Auto Bellows	1750 1595			
20" Electro Cable Release	60 40			

Fuji

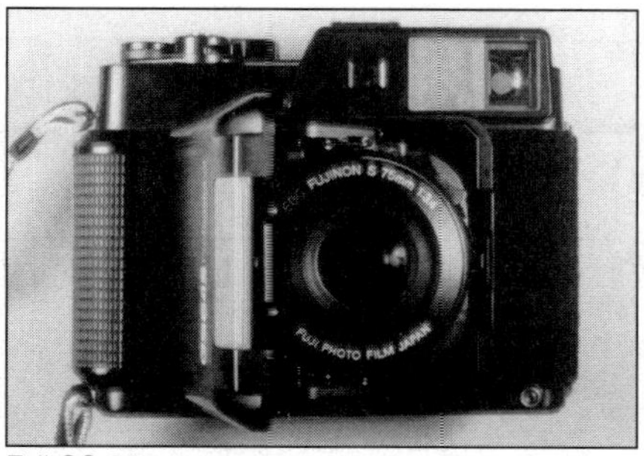

Fuji GS-645

Fuji's medium format rangefinder cameras are lightweight, well-made and have excellent optics. They have mechanical leaf shutters with speeds from 1 second to 1/500 and flash sync at all speeds. Model numbers refer to format size. For example, the GW-690 renders a 6cm x 9cm image. Prefixes (GS, GW, and GSW) indicate the focal lengths of lenses used with the various models: GS indicates a standard focal length, GW indicates a Wide angle focal length, and GSW indicates a Super Wide angle focal length. There are exceptions, however. To reduce confusion, the focal lengths are listed in parentheses following the camera model designations.

The 645 models have built-in meters. The original GS-645 has a retractable 75mm lens and was discontinued several years ago. It fits easily into a coat pocket and remains in high demand because of its size. Newer 645 models have fixed lenses.

The original G-690 and the GS-690 take interchangeable lenses. Available were a 65mm, 100mm, 150mm and 250mm. The cameras have built-in bright-line finders for the 100mm and 150mm focal lengths. The 65mm and 250mm came with auxiliary finders. Later model 690 and all 670s rangefinders all have fixed, non-interchangeable lenses.

The GX-680 is definitely a high-tech, computer-age looking camera, with lots of knobs and buttons and other cute gizmos — more than enough to satisfy the latent techie residing within most camera buffs. But to think of it as another gee-whiz camera is to miss the point entirely of this well-thought-out machine. This is a practical, easy-to-use studio view camera that just happens to take 120 film. It features a view camera-style front standard with most movements: tilt, shift, swing and rise. The lenses come mounted in their own lens boards, which are attached to the front standard. Fuji even makes an adapter that will allow the use of lenses in shutters mounted in Linhof Technica boards. Each lens has its own electronically-controlled shutter, which provides speeds from 8 seconds to 1/400, plus B. Flash sync is at all speeds. The backs rotate to vertical or horizontal, have ISO setting dials and integral motor drives that automatically advance the film to the first frame without having to align the arrows. The GX680 doesn't have a built-in exposure meter; it's an exposure monitor. It monitors illumination off the film, be it ambient or flash, and will issue a warning if the exposure exceeds the ±2EV range it allows. As this is a rather extreme exposure range, this feature is obviously meant as a back-up to an external meter. An AE prism is also available.

Fuji Medium Format Rangefinders

Camera	New		Mint		Excellent		User
GS-645 (folding 75mm lens)			650	575	590	450	
GS-645S (60mm lens)	825	685	595	550	570	480	
GS-645W (45mm lens)			425	400			
G-670 (100mm lens)					500	400	
GW-670II (90mm lens)			660	600			
GW-670III (90mm lens)	1010	880					
G-690 (w/100mm lens)					525	440	
GL-690 (100mm lens)					475	400	
GS-690 (w/100mm lens)					600	500	
GW-690 (90mm lens)					600	500	
GW-690II (90mm lens)			620	580	550	500	
GW-690III (90mm lens)	1010	880					
GSW-690II (65mm lens)			645	600			
GSW-690III (65mm lens)	1095	950					
G-617 (6x17cm Panorama)	3150	2800	2540	2200			
GX-617	2900	2485					

Lenses for G-690 and GS-690

Lens	Mint		Excellent		User
65mm			500	400	
100mm			400	300	
150mm			400	300	
250mm			500	400	

FUJI

The GX-680 System

Item	New		Mint		Excellent		User
GX-680 Body	2340	1920	1690	1500			
65mm f/5.6	1950	1785					
80mm f/5.6	1550	1410					
100mm f/4	1100	975					
125mm f/3.2	1525	1380					
125mm f/5.6	1060	900					
135mm f/5.6	1050	890					
150mm f/4.5	1125	990					
180mm f/3.2	1585	1450					
180mm f/5.6	1225	1050					
190mm f/8 Soft Focus	1350	1205					
210mm f/5.6	1200	1035					
250mm f/5.6	1250	1075					
300mm f/6.3	1690	1515					
120 Back	670	585			460	400	
220 Back	670	585			460	400	
Polaroid Back	385	290					
NPC Polaroid Back	215	195					
AE Finder	1350	1260					
Prism Finder					300	225	
Adj. Mag. Finder	375	295			200	200	
Angle Finder	510	425					
Battery Pack w/chgr	370	350					
Long Bellows	85	70					
Wide Bellows	85	70					
Bellows Lens Shade	410	360					
Focusing Rail Extension	75	65					
Strap GX	270	200					
RC Release (1 meter)	145	105					
RC Release (5 meter)	200	145					

Graflex

In the interest of providing the most complete and accurate information possible for the following Graflex cameras and accessories, this chapter was put together with the help of Roger Adams, past president of the now-defunct W.D. Service in Carson City, Nevada. Mr. Adams is an internationally recognized authority on the subject of Graflex, its history and its products. His company was devoted to the restoration, repair and sale of these fine photographic machines and had a clientele that reached around the globe.

If you're looking for that hard to find part for your old Graflex, don't despair. W.D. Service's entire inventory was acquired by Midwest Photo Exchange in Columbus, Ohio (pick up a copy of *Shutterbug* magazine to peruse one of their ads). Midwest's phone number is (614) 261-1264 and the fax number is (614) 261-1637.

Literally dozens of different models of Graflex-made cameras have been produced since the introduction of the original Graflex in 1902. The explanations and listings below are confined to the post-war Graphic models and the Graflex XL only. The pre-war models are fine cameras, also, but from an ease-of-use standpoint the post-war models are the more popular, especially models made after 1955.

Persons unfamiliar with these cameras often dismiss them as antiques, useful for little more than Hollywood props. Others think of them as heavy, awkward, unwieldy or inflexible. These folks couldn't be more wrong. In fact, most Graphic models are lighter than many medium format cameras once lenses, finders and backs have been attached.

Graphic cameras offer a variety of front movements for perspective control. They can achieve true 1:1 macro focusing with standard lenses. Many can take an enormous variety of backs and film holders, ranging in format sizes from 4x5 to 2¼ x 2¼ on 120 roll film. It's even possible to use some models as enlargers when fitted with Graflarger backs. Ever wished you could enlarge a photograph with the same lens you used to take the picture? You can with a Graphic camera.

Century Graphic

Compact and lightweight, the Century Graphic was made in the 2¼ film size only. Unique among Graflex cameras, the Century's body is constructed from an amazingly durable phenolic bakelite material that almost defies abuse.

Interchangeable lenses, ground glass focusing, front rise, tilt and shift with a drop bed, and a macro focusing capability down to 1:1 are just a few of its many features. A Graflok back is an integral part of the body to which roll film holders in 6cm x 6cm, 6cm x 7cm and 6cm x 8cm sizes can be attached.

The Century Graphic was available in the early-to-mid 1960's as an outfit that included an adjustable side grip, a side-mounted Kalart rangefinder, a 6x7 roll film holder and an 80mm f/2.8 Rodenstock Heligon lens in shutter. Prior to that, the Kalart rangefinder was an option. Other standard lenses available at the time were the 100mm f/3.5 Zeiss Tessar and the 101mm f/4.5 Graflex Graflar, although the Century is by no means limited to the use of just these lenses. Because of its drop-bed style, wide angles can be fitted and because of its long bellows draw, a variety of telephotos can be used as well.

Pacemaker Speed Graphic and Crown Graphic

The Speed Graphic and Crown Graphic are wooden-bodied cameras that were made in three film format sizes: 2¼ x 3¼, 3¼ x 4¼ and 4x5. Of all these sizes the 4x5 is, by far, the most versatile and the most popular. Because of this, only prices for the 4x5 models are listed below. Expect to pay somewhat less for cameras in the smaller format sizes.

Both Pacemaker cameras have view-camera-style between-the-lens shutters. The Speed Graphic also has a focal plane shutter that provides speeds up to 1/1000. Either design has a shutter release mounted on the body, called a "body release". Both cameras feature front standard movements of rise, tilt and shift, with a drop bed. Ground-glass focusing is possible on either model and the double-extension bellows allows close-focusing down to 1:1 macro size. Because of the long bellows draw, a variety of telephotos can be used. Because of the drop-bed style, wide angles can be fitted, also.

Early post-war Pacemakers are often found with Kalart side-mounted rangefinders. Pacemaker cameras made after 1955 have top-mounted optical rangefinders and optical viewfinders, which feature automatic parallax adjustments and interchangeable masks for different focal length lenses. Interchangeable rangefinder cams allow coupled-rangefinder focusing for a wide variety of lenses. A feature unique to the Pacemakers is Graflex's exclusive Rangelite, a built-in device that projects two beams of light on the subject. The focusing knob is turned to converge the two beams. When they converge, the subject is in focus. This eliminates guesswork in low-light situations or for those times when a photographer may be unable to bring the camera to his or her eye.

All three styles of backs (Graphic, Graflex and Graflok) will work on the Pacemaker series cameras, but because of its versatility is the Graflok back is the most desirable.

While these cameras will take a variety of lenses, the ones with which they are most often found are the 127mm f/4.5 Graflex Optar, 135mm f/4.7 Graflex Optar, or the 150mm f/4.5 Schneider Xenar. Some are also found with Kodak Ektars.

Super Graphic and Super Speed Graphic

Both the Super Graphic and Super Speed Graphic have all-metal (extruded aluminum) bodies and built-in coupled rangefinders. As is the case with the Pacemaker series, rangefinder cams can be interchanged as lenses are interchanged. The Supers feature front standard movements of tilt, shift, swing and rise with drop beds, ground glass focusing, macro focusing down to 1:1, revolving Graflok backs and electric shutter releases. The electric shutter release found on the Supers is somewhat prone to failure, especially after a camera has seen lots of use, but the shutter can still be tripped manually. Prices below are for cameras with working electric shutters.

The Super Speed Graphic differs only from the Super Graphic in that it was supplied with a 135mm f/4.5 Graflex Optar mounted in a Graflex 1000 shutter. (The 135mm f/4.5 is actually a Rodenstock. All other Optars were made by Wollensak.) This shutter is a unique Graflex design and is still the only commercially available between-the-lens shutter that offers a 1/1000 second top shutter speed.

Standard lenses available at the time were the 127mm f/4.5 Graflex Optar, the 135mm f/4.7 Graflex Optar or the 150mm f/4.5 Schneider Xenar.

Graflex XL

The Graflex XL was produced in three models, but the most common and most popular is the XL rangefinder model. It's also the only XL model listed below. Other models were the XL Super Wide Angle, which came with either a 47mm Schneider Super Angulon f/8 or f/5.6, and the XL Standard. Neither the XL Super Wide nor the Standard have rangefinders, but both allow ground glass focusing (as does the rangefinder model) and have range focusing scales. The rangefinder model bears a strong resemblance to the Mamiya Universal Press for good reason — Mamiya copied it.

The XL is a completely modular, medium format system, which accepts a large variety of lenses and film holders. While a wide selection of interchangeable lenses was produced in the XL lens mount, the camera is most often found with the 100mm f/3.5 Zeiss Tessar.

Graphic, Graflex and Graflok Backs

Graflex originated three different styles of backs over the years: the Graphic, the Graflex and the Graflok. Keeping track of the differences can be confusing, especially since the names are similar. Following is a brief explanation of their features.

The Graphic back, often called a "spring back", was designed for sheet film holders. It has two springs, one at the top and one at the bottom, which hold the ground glass in place and which also permit the ground glass to be drawn back when inserting a film holder. The ground glass and springs act as a pressure plate to keep the film holder firmly in place. Graphic backs will accept only Graphic-style accessories, which can be identified by the *raised rib* at the dark slide end. Although Graphic-style Grafmatic film magazines will work with a Graphic back, they are not recommended.

The Graflex back was designed to accept roll film holders, multiple film magazines, and sheet film holders. It has two sliding locks that hold the film accessory firmly in place. A ground glass focusing screen is held in place the same way, but must be removed before inserting the film holder. Graflex backs will accept only Graflex-style accessories. These can be identified by the *slot* at the dark slide end.

The Graflok back is the most recent style and has become something of an industry standard because of its flexibility. It is made up of three pieces: the back frame itself, a spring-loaded ground glass focusing panel and a viewing hood. With the focusing panel attached, standard Graphic-style sheet film holders can be used. The focusing panel is held in place by the back's built-in slide locks and can be removed easily, which will then allow the attachment of various Graphic-style film holding accessories (the ones with the raised rib). Graphic-style Polaroid and roll-film holders were designed specifically for use with the Graflok back and will not work on either the Graphic or Graflex back. The Graphic-style Grafmatic film magazine was also designed for use on the Graflok back and, while it can be used on a Graphic back, it is not recommended.

MEDIUM FORMAT

Graflex Cameras

The prices below include cameras with normal lenses and Graflok backs.

Camera	Mint	Excellent	User
Century Graphic	425	350	250
Crown Graphic 4x5 (side rangefinder)	550	400	300
Crown Graphic 4x5 (top rangefinder)	600	450	300
Speed Graphic 4x5 (top rfdr)	700	550	450
Speed Graphic 4x5 (side rfdr)	600	400	300
Super Graphic	700	550	450
Super Speed Graphic	750	600	475
XL (add $40-50 for grip)	650	500	350

Graflex XL Lenses

The 80mm Zeiss Planar, 95mm Rodenstock Heligon, 100mm Zeiss Planar and 150mm Rodenstock Ysarex have top shutter speeds to 1/400. All others have speeds to 1/500.

Lens	Mint	Excellent	User
58mm Rodenstock Grandagon f/5.6	500	325	275
80mm Rodenstock Heligon f/2.8	300	250	200
80mm Zeiss Planar f/2.8	300	240	200
95mm Rodenstock Heligon f/2.8	300	250	200
95mm Rodenstock Ysarex f/3.5	250	200	150
100mm Zeiss Planar f/2.8	300	300	250
100mm Zeiss Tessar f/3.5	175	120	80
150mm Rodenstock Ysarex f/4.5	300	250	200
180mm Zeiss Sonnar f/4.8	400	350	300
270mm Rodenstock Rotelar f/6.6	450	400	350

Graflex Accessories

Item	Mint	Excellent	User
Rapid Vance roll film holder	150	120	80
Knob Wind roll film holder	140	100	70
Grafmatic 4x5 film holder	125	130	60
Graphic sheet film holder	10	10	5
Type 5: for Graflok and Graphic backs			
Graphic Riteway film holder	15	15	10
Improved standard 4x5			
4x5 Graflok Back (complete)	150	125	75
4x5 Graflarger Back	100	125	75
XL Polaroid Back	125	160	100
XL Grip	50	50	40

Hasselblad

If you're thinking about taking the plunge and buying into a Hasselblad system, but are a bit confused over the differences among models, maybe this section will help a bit. First off, I haven't listed the 1000F and 1600F. It isn't that they aren't okay cameras — it's just that they're generally considered obsolete compared to modern Hasselblads. Besides, there is almost no interchangeability between the two systems.

HASSELBLAD 205TCC

The first truly new design from Hasselblad since the advent of the 2000FC, the 205TCC maintains the sense of tradition and backward compatibility for which Hasselblad has become world famous, yet it offers a host of new high-tech features sure to satisfy even the most jaded of die-hard technophiles.

Hasselblad has introduced a full line of TCC lenses and accessories to exploit the 205TCC's capabilities to the fullest, yet virtually all lenses and accessories made for the 500C and later cameras will operate as they were originally intended with the 205TCC.

The 205TCC is the first Hasselblad with an exposure meter built into the camera body. It provides TTL metering at full aperture with TCC lenses (stopped down metering with earlier ones), has an ISO 100 EV range of -1 to 20 with the 80mm f/2.8 lens, and meters the central 1% of the image, which is indicated by a 6mm central circle scribed onto the focusing screen. While some may grumble that Hasselblad didn't see fit to include a more sophisticated exposure measurement system into the meter's design, others who need critical exposure information will agree that if only one metering pattern is available, a tight spot pattern like the one found on this platform is the one to have.

Four different exposure modes and one programming mode are available by rotating a dial on the left side of the camera. Indicated on the dial by A, Pr, D, Z and M, the modes are Automatic, Programming, Differential, Zone and Manual.

The Automatic mode is an aperture-priority AE mode. You select the aperture, the 205TCC selects the shutter speed in 1/12 stop increments based on the scene's illumination. AE lock is available here by depressing the shutter release part way or by holding down the AE Lock button.

The next mode on the dial, Programming, is not an exposure mode at all (although if the dial is inadvertently left at this setting, the camera defaults to the A mode), but a mode in which three factory program settings can be changed to meet the user's requirements. The first setting is used for changing the default setting of a film's dynamic (contrast) range, the second can alter the self-timer's default setting from 10 seconds to anywhere from 2 seconds to 60 seconds, and the third setting is for selecting a default ISO value when non-TCC film backs are being used. When a TCC film back is used, its own ISO setting will override the default.

The Differential mode will measure the contrast range of a subject and compare it to the contrast range of the film being used. Used in conjunction with the AE Lock button, it amounts to a more sophisticated aperture-priority mode in which the photographer can verify that a scene's contrast range falls within that of the film by moving the metering spot around the subject area.

The LCD readout in the viewfinder enables the photographer to determine precisely where in the scene over or under-exposures may occur. Providing that the scene's contrast range is with acceptable limits, the exposure value (EV) can then be locked in and will remain so even if the photographer selects another aperture. The camera will automatically select a corresponding shutter speed to maintain the correct EV. If a scene's contrast range exceeds that of the film, the adjustment buttons are used to bring the exposure within the film's working range.

The Zone mode is, as you may have guessed, modeled after the Zone System pioneered by Ansel Adams. Tradition dictates the use of roman numerals when expressing Zone System values and without going into a detailed explanation of the Zone System here (entire books have been written on the subject), Zone 0 corresponds to absolute black while Zone X means absolute white.

In practice, the Zone mode works not unlike the Differential mode. The photographer meters a medium gray (18%) portion of the subject, which the camera records as Zone V. Then the photographer moves the metering spot to various portions of the subject and reads the Zone values from the LCD display. To vastly oversimplify the technique involved here, the idea is to get as much of the subject as one can to fall between Zones I and IX.

Finally, in the Manual mode, the meter is active and indicates exposure by means of a '+,' '-,' or '0' ('0' being correct exposure).

The 205TCC, like the 2000FC and its updates, has a focal-plane shutter with electronically controlled shutter speeds ranging from 16 seconds to 1/2000 second, plus B. Flash sync is available from B to 1/90 with the focal-plane shutter and at all speeds with leaf-shutter lenses.

Other features on the 205TCC include TTL/OTF flash exposure with SCA-compatible flash units, a self-timer, interchangeable backs and finders, motor drive capability, and compatibility with almost everything made for Hasselblads since 1957.

Hasselblad 500C, 500CM, 501C and 503CX

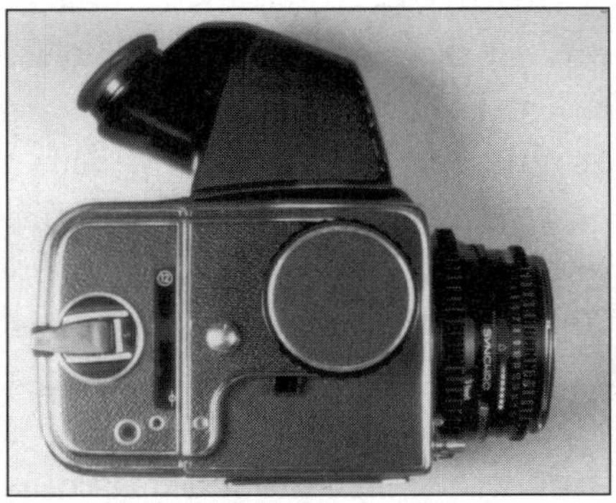

Hasselblad 500CM with 45° prism finder

The 500C is a modular system camera.. It has interchangeable lenses, finders and backs. You can lock up the mirror. The Zeiss lenses contain shutters, so flash sync is available at all speeds, from 1 second to 1/500. There have been so many accessories made for this camera that a complete listing with descriptions would fill a fair-sized book.

Next in the series is the 500CM. It differs chiefly from the 500C in the focusing screen mount. The 500C's screen is semi-permanently attached. The 500CM's is held in place by clips (see illustration). This minor difference in focusing screen mounts translates into a major difference in price, though. Just check the listings. Incidentally, some early 500CM's are labeled 500C. After the introduction of the 503CX, the 500CM was still produced for a couple of more years, available with the 500 Classic outfit, which consisted of the 500CM, an 80mm f/2.8 Planar, a waist-level finder, microprism screen and a 120 back.

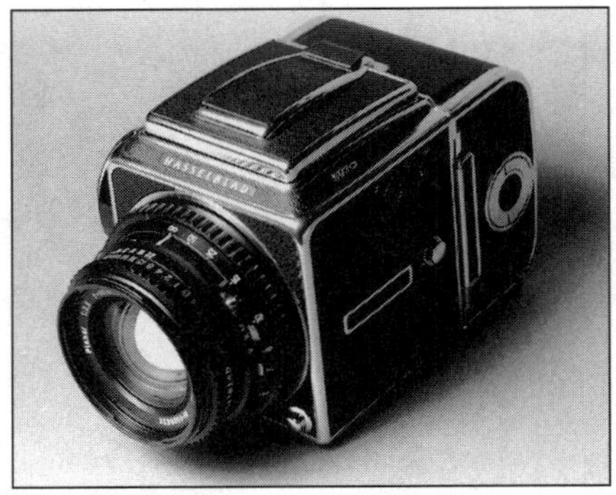

Hasselblad 503CX

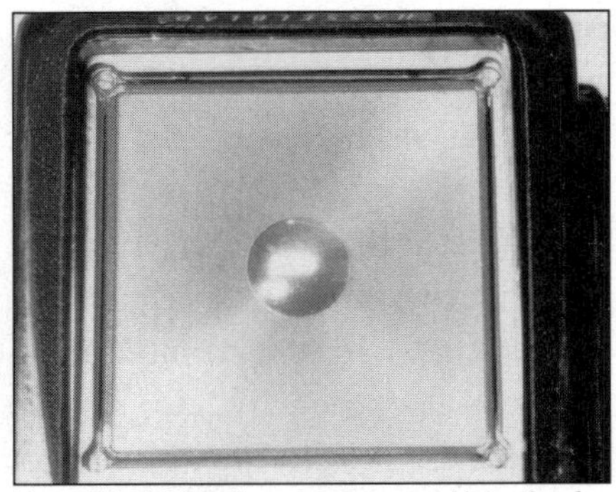

Hasselblad 500c focusing screen. Note the four mounting screws.

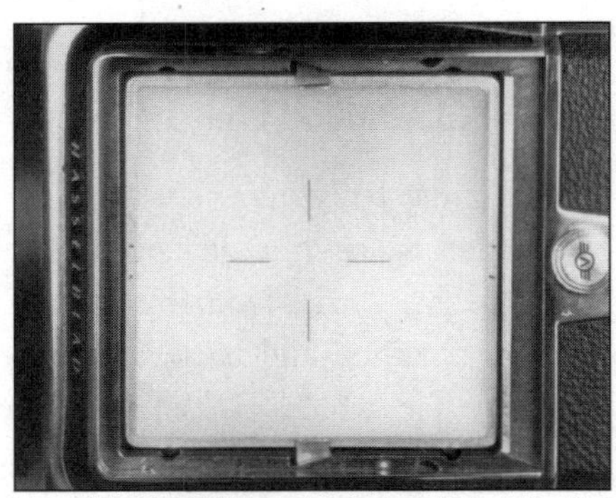

Hasselblad 500CM focusing screen. Note side clips.

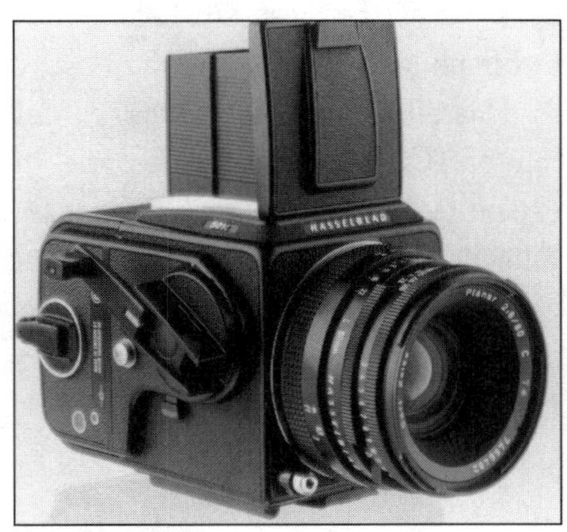

Hasselblad 501C

The 501C has replaced the 500 Classic. The body is essentially the same as the 500 CM, except there is no film confirmation window and it's only available in black. An 80mm f/2.8 C T* lens, which lacks the EV interlock found on the CF lenses, comes with the outfit. The 503CX is a 500CM with OTF (Off The Film plane) flash metering using SCA-compatible flash units, and an Acute Matte (extra-bright) focusing screen.

HASSELBLAD 500EL, 500ELM, 500ELX AND 553ELX

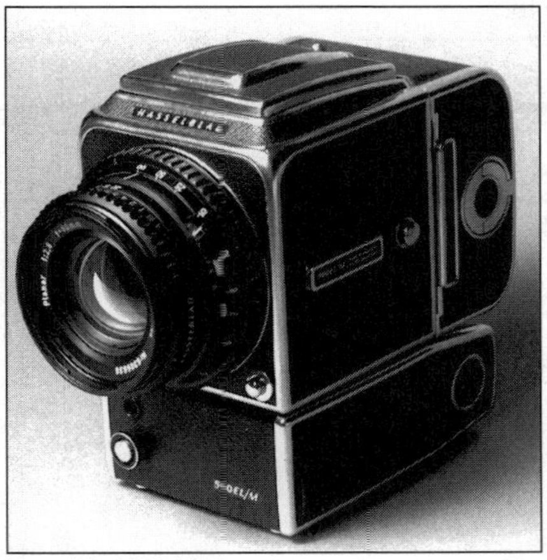

Hasselblad 500 ELM

The 500EL is essentially a 500C with an integral motor drive. The body should come with NiCad batteries and a charger. It's also quite a bit heavier than the 500C.

The 500ELM's focusing screen is held in place by clips. Other than that, it and the 500EL are the same.

The 500ELX has a larger mirror to eliminate vignetting that can occur in the viewfinder with some lenses. It also has TTL OTF flash capability with SCA compatible flash units.

The 553ELX is a 500ELX with an Acute Matte screen. The motor was also redesigned to take AA NiCads instead of the large NiCads used in the older style motor drives.

HASSELBLAD 2000FC, 2000FCM, 2000FCW, 2003FCW AND 201F

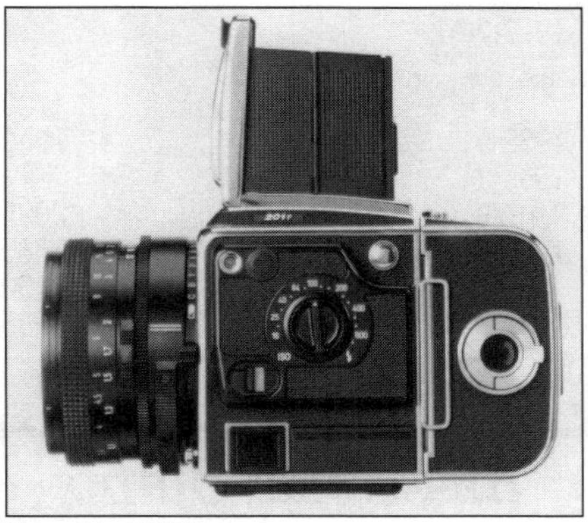

Hasselblad 201F

Hasselblad's 2000 series cameras incorporate focal plane shutters. The 2000 in the name represents the 1/2000 second top shutter speed, which is a nice feature, but the trade off is a slow flash sync. Zeiss F lenses (no shutter) are ordinarily used with these cameras, but the CF (shutter) lenses can be used also, giving the photographer flash sync at all lens shutter speeds.

The 2000FC and 2000FCM differ in one area: The 2000FCM has a provision for moving the shutter curtain out of the way when attaching or removing backs. The 2000FC doesn't. The 2000FCW is a 2000FCM that will take a winder. The 2003FCW is a 2000FCW with an Acute Matte screen. The current model, the 201F is a 2003 FCW with a self-timer.

HASSELBLAD SWC, SWC/M AND 903SWC

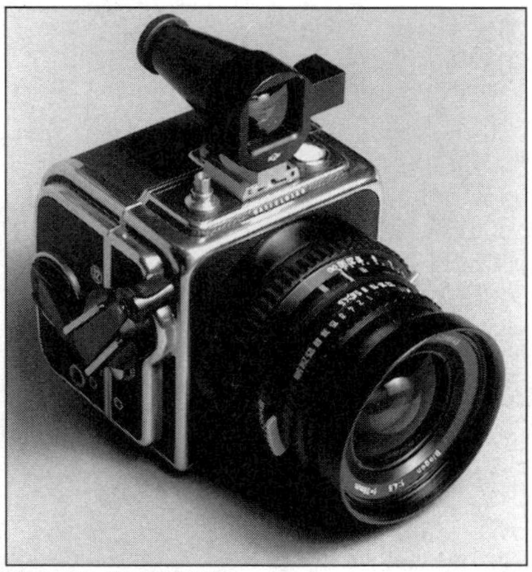

Hasselblad 903 SWC

The Hasselblad SWC has a non-removable 38mm f/4.5 Zeiss Biogon lens mounted in a leaf shutter, a matching, non-TTL viewfinder and takes interchangeable backs. The 38mm lens provides a distortion-free 90 degree angle of coverage.

The SWC/M differs primarily from the SWC in that it will accept Polaroid backs. SWC's can be modified to accept them also. Early SWC/M's came with T* lenses. Later models came with CF lenses.

The 903 SWC is essentially the same as a SWC/M camera with a built-in, bubble spirit level.

SPECIAL EDITION HASSELBLADS

Certain Hasselblad models, such as the 500 Gold, Moon Cameras and Anniversary Editions fetch quite a premium. These limited edition cameras are bought and sold exclusively as collectibles. Most are probably never used. And since they aren't used, they aren't listed.

Hasselblad Cameras

These camera prices are for bodies with waist level finders and do not include backs or lenses.

Camera	Yrs. Made	New		Mint		Excellent		User	
201F	1994-	3350	2995						
203 FE	1994-	5400	4890						
205TCC	1991-	7400	6450						
500C	1957-70			600	450	450	350	385	300
500CM	1970-		1000	750	590	650	500	560	460
503CX	1988-	1800	1570	1250	1095				
500EL w/NiCads, chgr	1965-70			600	585	595	450	485	395
500ELM w/NiCads, chgr	1970-?			1075	1000	850	695	650	550
500ELX w/NiCads, chgr	?-1988			1375	1150	1100	950		
553ELX w/NiCads, chgr	1988-	2650	2375	2095	1950	1890	1650		
2000FC	1977-?					600	550		
2000FCM						1200	950		
2000FCW				1700	1400				
2003FCW	1989-91			2050	1895				
SWC (early)	1959-?					1950	1375		
SWC (late)	?-1979			2095	1800	1875	1500	1375	1110
SWC/M (with T* lens)	1980-?			2660	2295	2195	1700		
SWC/M (with CF lens)				3150	2495	2570	2300		
903SWC	1989-	4900	4400	3295	3430				

Hasselblad Outfits

Outfit	New		Mint		Excellent		User	
205TCC, W/L,80/2.8TCC, A12TCC	10000	9550						
500 Classic Kit			2000	1700				
500C, W/L, 80 C, 12 back					1050	825	800	750
500C, W/L, 80 C, A12			1500	1095	1300	1000	950	850
500CM, W/L, 80 C, A12			1750	1500	1550	1345		
500CM, W/L, 80 CF, A12			1900	1595	1750	1350		
501C, W/L, 80 C, A12N	2325	2195						
503CX, W/L, 80 CF, A12	4150	3635	2995	2750				
500EL, W/L, 80 C, 12 back, chgr					1475	1250		
500ELM, W/L, 80 CF, A12, chgr			2100	1800	1750	1650		
500ELX, W/L, 80 CF, A12, chgr					2200	1800		
553ELX, W/L, 80 CF, A12, chgr	4900	4430						
2000FC, W/L, 80 F, A12					1450	1250		
2000FCM, W/L, 80 F, A12			1900	1795	1750	1450		
2000FCW, W/L, 80 F, A12			3000	2750				
2003FCW, W/L, 80 F, A12			3550	3250				

Zeiss C & CF Lenses

Lens	New		Mint		Excellent		User	
30mm f/3.5 Distagon C T*			2695	2420	2350	2200		
30mm f/3.5 Distagon CF T*	5120	4880	4250	3880				
40mm f/4 Distagon C			1850	1550	1500	1320		
40mm f/4 Distagon C T*			2575	1995	2100	1595		
40mm f/4 Distagon CF T*			3100	2950	2885	2450		
40mm f/4 Distagon CF FLE	3950	3595						
50mm f/4 Distagon C			1250	980	1050	795		
50mm f/4 Distagon C T*			1500	1375	1400	1100	1050	900
50mm f/4 Distagon CF T*			1950	1380	1430	1200		
50mm f/4 Distagon CF FLE	2550	2270	2050	1725				
60mm f/3.5 Distagon C			1285	795				
60mm f/3.5 Distagon C T*					1300	1100		
60mm f/3.5 Distagon CF T*	2380	2025	1750	1595	1400	1300		

Zeiss C & CF Lenses

Lens	New	Mint	Excellent	User
60mm f/4 Distagon C			800 675	
60mm f/4 Distagon C T*			950 730	
60mm f/5.6 Distagon C			700 500	
80mm f/2.8 Planar C		590 450	485 350	385 325
80mm f/2.8 Planar C T*		725 625	650 525	535 480
80mm f/2.8 Planar CF T*	1575 1450	1250 1050	1000 750	
100mm f/3.5 Planar C		1085 1000	950 795	780 700
100mm f/3.5 Planar C T*		1300 1215	1195 1035	
100mm f/3.5 Planar CF T*	2350 2075	1850 1560	1490 1285	
105mm f/4.5 UV Sonnar CF	13500 12060			
120mm f/4 Macro Planar CF	2550 2350	2100 1895	1780 1540	
120mm f/5.6 S-Planar C			1195 950	
120mm f/5.6 S-Planar C T*			1350 1175	
135mm f/5.6 S-Planar C (Bellows)		1060 895	795 650	
135mm f/5.6 S-Planar C T* (Bellows)			890 800	
135mm f/5.6 Macro Planar CF T* (Bellows)	2285 2065	1800 1550		
150mm f/4 Sonnar C		1250 1095	1175 950	
150mm f/4 Sonnar C T*			1450 1275	
150mm f/4 Sonnar CF T*	2550 2320	2080 1950	1895 1500	
180mm f/4 Sonnar CF T*	2820 2560			
250mm f/5.6 Sonnar C		1150 945	950 800	790 695
250mm f/5.6 Sonnar C T*		1535 1425	1350 1080	
250mm f/5.6 Sonnar CF T*	2950 2650	2200 2080	1995 1495	
250mm f/5.6 Sonnar Super Achr		2495 2100		
250mm f/5.6 Sonnar Super Achr CF T*	4480 4230	3850 3670	3450 2995	
350mm f/5.6 Tele-Tessar C		2150 1895	1795 1495	
350mm f/5.6 Tele-Tessar C T*			2450 2200	
350mm f/5.6 Tele-Tessar CF T*	3950 3635	3250 2995	2850 2400	
500mm f/8 Tele-Tessar C		1500 1350	1350 1195	
500mm f/8 Tele-Tessar C T*		2100 1950	1900 1550	
500mm f/8 Tele-Tessar CF T*		3295 2850	2795 2500	
500mm f/8 Tele-Apotessar CF T*	5050 4775	4390 4050		
140-280 f/5.6 Variogon C		3600 3000	2950 2600	
140-280 f/5.6 Variogon CF	5890 5420	4600 4150	3895 3450	
1.4X Mutar Shift Converter	3050 2840			
2X Mutar		1095 1025	950 850	
2XE Converter	1250 1120			
2X Vivitar, Kenko or Komura	350 230	175 150	150 125	

MEDIUM FORMAT

Zeiss F Lenses (No shutter)

Lens	Mint	Excellent	User
50mm f/2.8 Distagon T*	1575 1400	1350 1200	
80mm f/2.8 Planar T*	550 440	425 390	
110mm f/2 Planar T*	1525 1150		
150mm f/2.8 Sonnar T*	1700 1450	1450 1325	
250mm f/4 Tele-Tessar T*	1675 1625	1600 1450	
350mm f/4 Tele-Tessar T*		3500 3000	

Zeiss TCC Lenses (205TCC)

Lens	New	Mint	Excellent	User
50mm f/2.8 Distagon T*	3780 3450			
80mm f/2.8 Planar T*	2120 1750			
110mm f/2 Planar T*	3720 3400			
150mm f/2.8 Sonar T*	3350 3080			
250mm f/4 Tele-Tessar T*	3550 3200			
350mm f/4 Tele-Tessar T*	7890 7200			

Hasselblad Accessory Film Magazines

Item	New	Mint	Excellent	User
12 Film Mag		300 240	285 195	
16 Film Mag			275 200	
16S Film Mag		245 195	180 125	
A12 Film Mag	640 615	580 495	450 375	355 290
A12 TCC Film Mag	1250 1130			
A16 Film Mag	750 685	595 450	400 350	
A16S Film Mag		300 230	240 200	
A16 TCC Film Mag	1310 1130			
A24 Film Mag	750 690	625 540	500 380	
A24 TCC Film Mag	1225 1125			
70mm 70 Exp Film Mag	1140 1000	570 495	450 350	
70mm 500 Exp Mag			2250 1700	
Polaroid 80 Back			190 120	95 80
Polaroid 100 Back	470 420	350 310	295 240	260 180
NPC Polaroid Back MF-1	250 210		140 100	
NPC Polaroid Back MF-2	345 300			

HASSELBLAD

Hasselblad Viewfinders and Prisms

Item	New	Mint	Excellent	User
HC-1 Prism (90°)		465 380	375 325	
HC-3 Prism (90°)		440 415	380 325	
HC-4 Prism (90°)			550 450	
Meter Prism (45°)			495 425	430 225
NC-2 Prism (45°)		550 500	500 390	350 250
PM Prism (45°)		770 700	650 500	
PME Prism (45°)		1050 880	820 650	
PME-3 Prism (45°)		1150 1030		
PM-5 Prism (45°)	995 880			
PME-5 Prism (45°)		1200 1150		
PME-51 Prism (45°)	1590 1440			
PM-90 Prism (90°)	650 570			
RM-2 Reflex finder (90°)	1230 1070	850 825		
Meter Knob	330 265	100 80	75 50	
Magnifying Hood (early)		150 120	125 90	
Magnifying Hood (52094)		225 200	190 150	
Magnifying Hood (52096)	440 365			
Waist Level Finder (early)		100 80	85 50	
Waist Level Finder	250 205	185 150		
SWC Finder		315 275	250 225	240 200
SWC/M Finder	775 675			
Sportfinder		50 30	40 20	
Petersen 6x6 Mag w/ Adapter	150 120			

Hasselblad Close-up Accessories

Item	New	Mint	Excellent	User
Auto Bellows	1480 1350	1100 975	850 725	
Round Bellows		395 345	350 290	
Square Bellows			250 200	
Lens Shade for Bellows	395 330			
Ext Tube 8mm	350 290	225 190	180 150	
Ext Tube 10mm			160 130	
Ext Tube 16mm	320 270	225 190	180 130	
Ext Tube 16mm TCC	475 400			
Ext Tube 21mm		220 200	185 150	
Ext Tube 32mm	350 290	225 190	180 150	

Hasselblad Close-up Accessories

Item	New	Mint	Excellent	User
Ext Tube 32mm TCC	495 400			
Ext Tube 55mm			150 105	
Ext Tube 56mm	395 330	270 225	215 150	
Ext Tube 56mm TCC	540 490			
Variable Ext Tube 64mm-85mm	795 725	540 450		

Other Accessories

Item	New	Mint	Excellent	User
Double Hand Grip (ELM/ELX)			150 120	
Hasselblad Pro Flash #4504		500 400		
Flashgun Bracket (C/CM)			90 65	
Flashgun Bracket #46329 (ELM)		230 175		
Flashgun Bracket #45071		200 175	170 140	
Flash Bracket #45072 (CM,CX,2000)	395 335	240 210		
Flash Bracket #46330 (ELM,ELX)	415 350	250 220		
Macro Flash Set (flash & bracket)	1250 1055	900 750		
Macro Flash Bracket		150 100		
Pistol Grip #45047 (C/CM)	95 85	50 45	50 25	
Pistol Grip #46221 (ELM/ELX)	95 85	60 50	45 25	
Pro Shade #40676	350 300	280 220		
Pro Shade (early)		220 200	150 100	
Winder for 205TCC	940 800			
Winder for 500C/CM (NPC)	490 445		390 325	
Winder for 2000FCW	650 635	570 500		

MEDIUM FORMAT

Mamiya

Over the past couple of decades, Mamiya's medium format cameras have earned solid reputations as reliable workhorses, especially the C and RB series. The company has never shown signs of complacency once it hit on a good thing, however, and has produced a wider spectrum of medium format designs over the years than anyone else. From the now-discontinued Universal Press to the classic C series interchangeable-lens TLRs to the 645 and 67 SLRs to the Mamiya 6 interchangeable-lens rangefinder, Mamiya has addressed almost the entire realm of medium format photography.

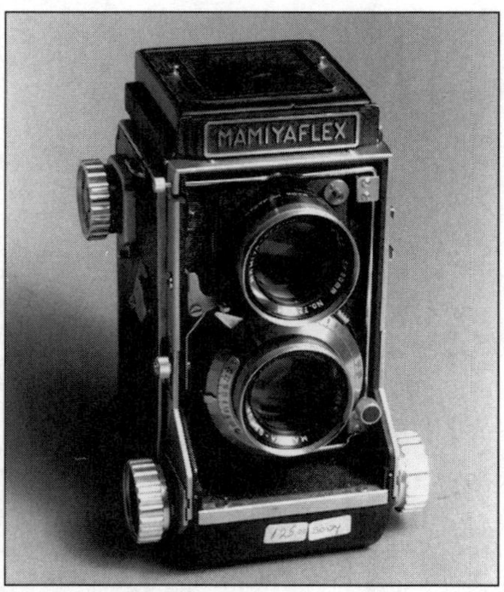

Mamiyaflex: Mamiya's first interchangeable-lens TLR

Mamiya M645, M645J, M645 1000S, M645 Super & M645 PRO

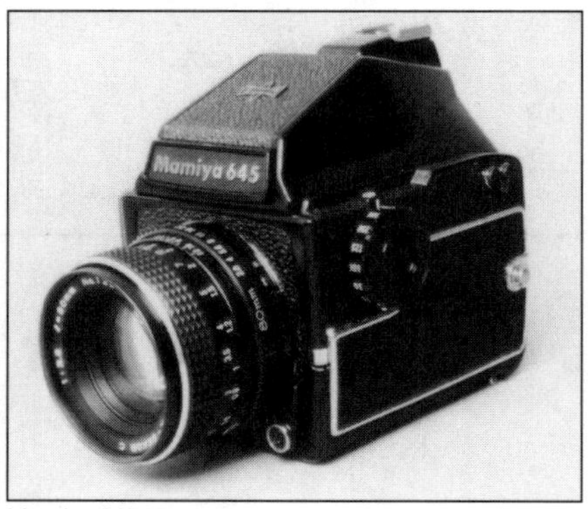

Mamiya M645

The original Mamiya M645 was introduced in 1976 and remains very popular among those who prefer the flexibility and ease-of-use of a 35mm system, but who also prefer the almost 3 times larger image size that this camera provides.

The M645 is a modular camera that will accept a variety of finders and lenses, plus a motor drive. It has an electronic focal-plane shutter, offering speeds up to 1/500 second with X sync at 1/60. Other features include interchangeable focusing screens, mirror lock-up and multiple exposure capability.

The M645J is an economy model: the J stands for Junior. It is less rugged in construction, but the biggest difference between the J and its more full-featured sibling is the elimination of the mirror lock-up feature.

The M645 1000S is the same camera as the original M645, with the addition of a quartz-controlled shutter that provides a top speed of 1/1000 second. Its shutter speed settings lock in place to prevent inadvertent changes.

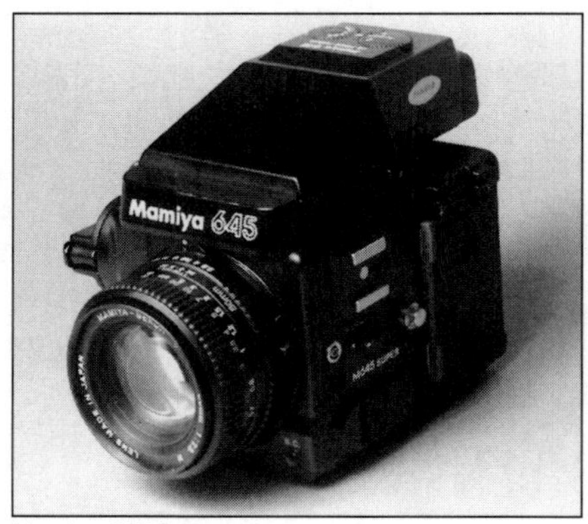

Mamiya 645 Super

The M645 Super is a completely redesigned camera. It's the only M645 that uses interchangeable backs. A new style motor drive, called the Power Drive Grip, is available as an option. It shares the 1000S' shutter and other features.

The 645 PRO is Mamiya's most recent refinement of this workhorse of the format. But the refinements don't come without a price. As I write this, the street price of the PRO is more than double that of the Super. Is it worth it? Mamiya seems to think so. Let's take a look at its features and see for ourselves.

Introduced with the PRO is an optional new finder, called the 645 PRO AE Prism Finder. On the A-S setting this new metered prism finder determines exposure by evaluating the entire scene and then selecting an appropriate pattern. It will shift the pattern from average to spot or will calculate a centerweighted average somewhere between the two extremes. This metering mode functions with either the aperture-priority or manual exposure mode engaged. Exposure compensation is available in ± ⅓ stop increments also. The Average or Spot settings can be selected manually, as well. By the way, this new prism will also work on the 645 Super.

The 645 PRO's electronically controlled focal plane shutter offers speeds from 8 seconds to 1/1000 second. The new electronic self-timer now has a mirror-up feature, obviating the need for a cable release in some situations. The camera's B setting has also been improved, allowing for unlimited time exposures without having to worry about battery drain.

Mamiya RB67, RB67 Pro S & RB67 Pro SD

The RB67 is a monster of a camera that, with everything attached, is about the same size and weight as a car battery. Okay, so I exaggerate...a little. It is an all-mechanical, reliable workhorse. As its name indicates, it uses the 6X7 format and features a revolving, Graflok-style back (RB stands for Revolving Back) that enables the photographer to switch from horizontal to vertical shots easily. This is one reason why the camera is so large; it needs a mirror box and viewing area that is at least 7 centimeters square to accommodate this feature. A wide array of accessory finders, backs and lenses are available for this camera. The lenses incorporate leaf shutters, so flash sync is available at all speeds, from 1 second to 1/400.

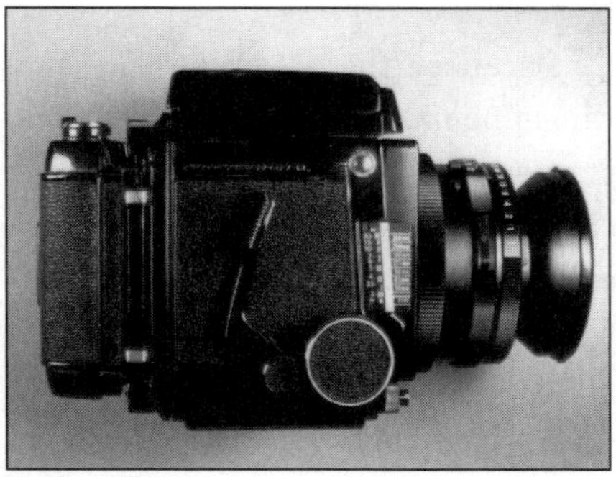

Mamiya RB67

The RB67 Pro S has been the current model since 1974. We aren't talking high-tech here, folks, but it gets the job done well. Features added to the Pro S include a focus lock, an accessory shoe and red horizontal cropping lines visible in the viewfinder when the back is horizontal. When using a Pro S back, there is also a double-exposure prevention feature that can be overridden.

The latest model of the venerable RB67 line, the Pro SD, has a few improvements over its predecessors. Perhaps most significant is its more heavily reinforced lens mount — a mount which enables the use of the new APO lenses. These lenses can be used only on the SD and the RZ67; they cannot be used on earlier RB models.

Mamiya RZ67

The RZ67 might best be described as an electronic RB67. It retains the revolving back of the RB, but offers such up-to-date options as a motor winder and an AE Prism, which will transform the RZ into an aperture-priority AE camera. RZ lenses have electronic shutters, providing speeds from 8 seconds to 1/400 and flash sync at all speeds. Lenses for the RB can be used on the RZ, but not vice-versa.

Mamiya RZ67 Pro II

According to Mamiya, the recently-introduced RZ67 Pro II is not a replacement to the tried-and-true RZ67, but should instead be regarded as a deluxe model. (Translation: Mamiya still has a large inventory of RZ67's, so please buy these first.) While the difference in the street price between the two models is significant (some $300 and change as I write this), the features found on the Pro II may be worthwhile enough that many, if not most, buyers will opt for it over the original model.

Several things are new on the Pro II. Starting with the camera body, the focusing system has been improved. The Pro II still has right and left side focusing knobs, but the right one has been changed from a single knob to a coaxial pair of knobs, larger in diameter than the old one. The outer knob operates the RZ67 Pro II's rack-and-pinion focusing mechanism in the traditional manner. The inner knob is a fine-focus control, which should ease critical focusing tasks greatly.

Shutter speeds can now be set in half-stop increments from 1/200 second to 4 seconds.

The Pro II has an improved focusing screen with three LED displays that render the following information: the first will remind you if the camera hasn't been cocked when you try to take a picture, the second reminds you to remove the dark slide (doubles as a battery indicator), and the third indicates when a Pro II-dedicated flash is ready to fire (there are no Pro II-dedicated flashes available yet, though).

A new AE Prism Finder is also being produced for the Pro II. Its shape is more rounded than predecessors and its control layout is reminiscent of that found on the Mamiya M645 Pro. The finder has a shutter speed control, ±3 EV of exposure compensation in ⅓ stop increments, and a meter pattern selector. The available patterns are Spot, Averaging and an automatic switching mode, which evaluates the contrast in a scene and which will switch between Spot or Averaging as the situation dictates.

Also new for the Pro II is a redesigned film magazine. It's basically the same as earlier RZ67 film magazines, but for one very handy feature: there are now two film counter windows, which means that one is always visible from the top of the camera, no matter what position the back happens to be in.

MAMIYA 6

Not to be confused with the folding-bed Mamiya 6 of the 1940's and 1950's, this latest generation Mamiya 6 has caused quite a stir since its release. Shaped like an oversized 35mm rangefinder, its sleek, contoured polycarbonate body is light, comfortable and a joy to use. It provides 6cm x 6cm exposures on either 120 or 220 film.

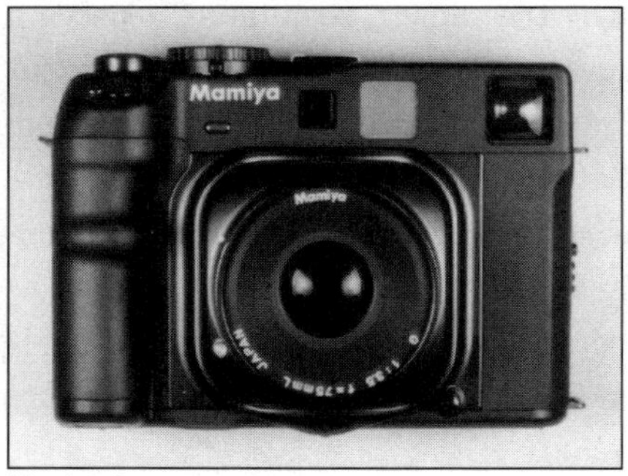

Mamiya 6

Because the Mamiya 6 is a rangefinder camera that takes leaf shutter lenses, its operation is almost silent. The lenses incorporate electronically-controlled shutters for speeds from 4 seconds to 1/500, plus B. The large, bright viewfinder contains the LED meter display.

Other features are as follows: Film winding is done with the single-stroke advance lever, the lens mount retracts part way into the body for added compactness when the camera isn't in use, and it has a top-mounted hot shoe.

MAMIYA TWIN LENS CAMERAS

The three models of the C330, the C330S, the C330f and the original C330, differ only in minor areas. All cameras offer interchangeable finders, focusing screens and lenses.

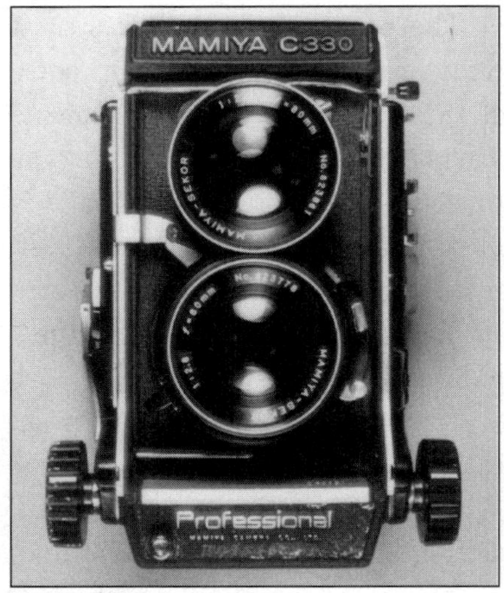

Mamiya C330

The C220 series cameras are essentially scaled down versions of the C330. Made in two models, the original C220 and the C220f, the most notable differences between them and the 330 series are that the lenses' shutters must be cocked manually.

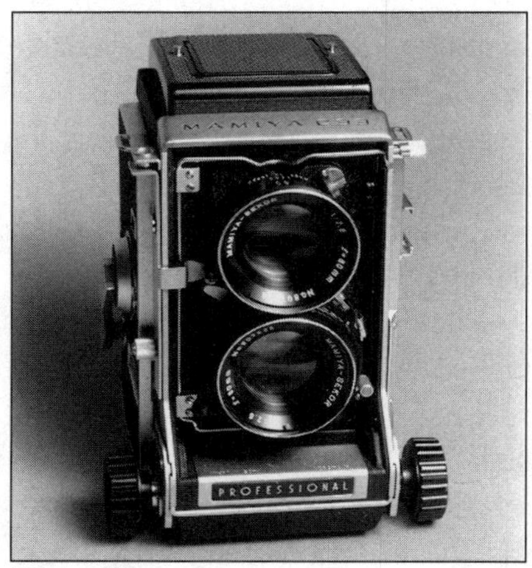

Mamiya C33

Earlier models, such as the C2, C22, C3 and C33 all accept interchangeable lenses and differ only slightly in features.

Mamiya Medium Format SLRs

Prices for the following camera bodies include waist level finders.

Camera	New		Mint		Excellent		User	
M645			375	350	360	250		
M645J					300	200	195	170
M645 1000S			550	490	475	360	350	320
M645 PRO	1645	1500						
M645 Super			725	615	650	470		

Mamiya Medium Format SLRs

Prices for the following camera bodies include waist level finders.

Camera	New		Mint		Excellent		User	
RB67 Pro					350	275	250	170
RB67 Pro S			600	535	545	400	410	325
RB67 Pro SD	1820	1540						
RZ67	1695	1430			1075	800		
RZ67 PRO II	2085	1830						

Mamiya Medium Format SLR Outfits

Outfit	New		Mint		Excellent		User	
M645, W/L, 80/2.8					550	490		
M645, Std Prism, 80/2.8					650	600		
M645, AE Prism, 80/2.8					850	700		
M645J, W/L, 80/2.8					550	450		
M645J, CDS Prism, 80/2.8					690	550		
M645 1000S, W/L, 80/2.8, Insert					675	625		
M645 1000S, Std Prism, 80/2.8, Insert			775	700	725	650		
M645 1000S, PDS Prism, 80/2.8, Insert			850	750	770	670		
M645 1000S, AE Prism, 80/2.8, Insert			950	900				
M645 PRO, AE Prism, 80/2.8, 120 back	3350	2995						
M645 Super, AE Prism, 80/2.8, 120 back			1800	1450				
RB67, W/L, 90/3.5, 120 back					850	700		
RB67 Pro S, W/L, 90/3.5, 120 back					1100	950		
RZ67, W/L, 90/3.5, 120 back	3780	3300			1900	1650		
RZ67, W/L, 110/2.8, 120 back	3820	3350			1795	1595		
RZ67, PD Prism, 110/2.8, 120 back					2100	1800		

Mamiya-Sekor C Lenses

The following listings are for Mamiya-Sekor C lenses only. The older, non-C lenses should be 10% to 20% less. Some recent lenses have a W suffix, which indicates an improved mechanical design. The latest lenses for the M645 have an N suffix (meaning New). Like the W lenses, these have mechanical improvements as well. There seems to be almost no difference in used prices between the new-and-improved versions versus the older ones. The abbreviation L.S. following several of the following lens' descriptions stands for Leaf Shutter.

Mamiya-Sekor C Lenses - M645

Lens	New		Mint		Excellent		User	
24mm f/4 ULD	2350	1995	1750	1500	1500	1000		
35mm f/3.5					500	370		
35mm f/3.5 N	1295	975	780	650				
45mm f/2.8			450	400	425	315		
45mm f/2.8 N or S	950	795	625	580	600	450		
50mm f/4 Shift	1600	1325	1100	900				
55mm f/2.8			370	330	350	290		
55mm f/2.8 N	745	625	540	470				
55mm f/2.8 L.S.	1165	850						
70mm f/2.8 L.S.			450	350	390	300		
80mm f/1.9			295	250	275	220		
80mm f/1.9 N	735	600	520	460	475	380		
80mm f/2.8			230	200	200	150		

Mamiya-Sekor C Lenses - M645

Lens	New	Mint	Excellent	User
80mm f/2.8 N	580 450	390 320	350 270	
80mm f/2.8 L.S.	825 660			
80mm f/4 Macro	1150 995	850 800	820 650	
Macro Spacer for 80mm f/4 Macro	125 110			
110mm f/2.8			370 265	
110mm f/2.8 N	895 700			
145mm f/4 Soft Focus	1320 1150	1025 950	975 695	
150mm f/2.8	1625 1400			
150mm f/3.5		350 330	315 275	
150mm f/3.5 N	720 575	500 450	450 340	
150mm f/3.8 L.S.	1025 840			
150mm f/4		380 350	330 250	
210 f/4		420 380	350 275	
210mm f/4 N	795 660	580 500		
250mm f/5		500 470		
300mm f/2.8 APO IF	13000 11540			
300mm f/5.6	1400 1255	1100 1000	975 700	
300mm f/5.6 N				
500mm f/5.6	2450 2260	1850 1795	1800 1450	
500mm f/8 Mirror		500 390	420 350	
55-110 f/4.5	1985 1730	1550 1400	1380 1200	
75-150 f/4.5		1025 900	850 770	
105-210 f/4.5 ULD	1875 1630	1470 1300	1325 1050	
2X Teleconverter	850 700			
2X Vivitar, Kenko, Komura	210 170	150 125	120 90	

Mamiya-Sekor C Lenses - RB67

The KL lenses are for the RB67 Pro SD

Lens	New	Mint	Excellent	User
37mm f/4.5	2800 2560	2195 2000	2100 1600	
50mm f/4.5	1725 1550	1400 1250	1300 900	
65mm f/4 KL	1995 1770			
65mm f/4.5		870 750	750 620	600 500
75mm f/3.5 KL	1995 1770			
75mm f/4.5 KL Shift	3100 2890			
90mm f/3.5 KL	1700 1520			
90mm f/3.8		565 500	500 360	
127mm f/3.5 KL	1610 1370			
127mm f/3.8		770 575	550 420	
140mm f/4.5 Macro	1690 1500	1350 1200	1275 980	
140mm f/4.5 KL	2000 1780			
150mm f/3.5 KL	1640 1400			
150mm f/4.5 Soft Focus	1720 1530	840 795	750 640	
180mm f/4.5		860 795	800 650	
180mm f/4.5 KL	1625 1430			
210mm f/4.5 KL APO	3440 3150			
250mm f/4.5	1095 900	790 750	775 630	
250mm f/4.5 KL	2025 1830			
250mm f/4.5 KL APO	3995 3630			
350mm f/5.6 KL APO	4495 4050			
360mm f/6 KL	2295 2080			
360mm f/6.3	2050 1850	1500 1400	1440 1100	
500mm f/6 KL APO	6395 5870			
500mm f/8	4450 4100	3550 3300	3150 2500	
100-200 f/5.2	3995 3660	3100 2890		
2X (Kenko or Vivitar)	270 220	180 150	150 100	
37mm f/4.5	2800 2560			
50mm f/4.5	1725 1530	1400 1250	1300 900	
65mm f/4		1035 825	750 675	
65mm f/4 LA	1995 1770			
75mm f/3.5 L	1995 1770			

Mamiya-Sekor C Lenses - RZ67

Lens	New	Mint	Excellent	User
75mm f/4.5 Shift	3195 2990		2550 1700	
90mm f/3.5	1485 1300	1125 1000	945 720	
110 f/2.8	1525 1330	1150 1000	960 750	
127mm f/3.8	1610 1370		1000 750	
140mm f/4.5 Macro	1690 1150		750 600	
150mm f/3.5	1640 1400			
180mm f/4.5	1360 1070	875 750	790 650	
210mm f/4.5 APO Z	3440 3150			
250mm f/4.5	2025 1830	1550 1400	1495 1200	
250mm f/4.5 APO Z	3995 3630			
350 f/5.6 APO Z	4495 4050			
360mm f/6	2300 2100	1625 1500	1550 1250	
500mm f/6 APO Z	6395 5870			
500mm f/8	4560 4200		1950 1640	
100-200 f/5.2	3970 3570	2950 2800		
1.4X	950 840			
2X (Kenko or Vivitar)	275 225	200 175	150 120	

Mamiya M645 Accessories

Item	New	Mint	Excellent	User
Waist Level Finder		80 65	60 50	
Waist Level Finder, Super/PRO	195 150	120 100	100 75	
AE Prism	690 635	400 325	350 270	
AE Prism, Super	730 680	560 500	525 440	
AE Prism, PRO	1050 940			
CDS Prism		310 250	240 190	
PD Prism		335 260	260 225	
PDS Prism	495 400	360 300	280 230	
Standard Prism		215 180	190 130	
Standard Prism, Super	365 335	270 250	240 200	
Standard Prism, PRO	625 500			
Right Angle Finder			75 60	
Right Angle Finder Model 2	285 230		110 90	
2X Magnifier	120 90	75 60		
120 or 220 Insert	90 80	60 50	50 40	
120 or 220 Back, PRO	510 420			
120 or 220 Back, Super	275 245	200 175	190 140	
35mm Back, Super/PRO	420 295	265 250	250 200	
35mm Back w/Panorama Adapter, Super PRO	650 520			
Polaroid Back, Super/PRO	510 420	370 345		
L Grip, Deluxe	120 100	70 55	50 40	
L Grip Super	235 185	150 120	125 90	
Left Hand Grip, PRO	250 210			
Vari-Angle Grip			80 60	
Pistol Grip	120 90	75 60	55 40	
Motor Drive w/hand grip	395 350		250 170	
Power Drive Grip		220 175	200 150	
Power Drive Grip, Super/PRO	540 400	325 250	270 195	
Power Drive 2, Super/PRO	610 520			
Auto Bellows w/cable release		650 590	550 400	
Auto Bellows Super/ PRO	1350 1185			
Auto Macro Spacer	170 130			
Slide Duplicator	100 90	80 70		
Revolving Camera Stage	640 515			
Auto Ext Tube 1	130 100			
Auto Ext Tube 2 or 3	160 125			
Auto Ext Tube Set		200 170	150 120	
Bellows Lens Hood	185 160	135 115	100 80	
Infrared Remote Control, PRO	610 495			

Mamiya RB67 Accessories

Item	New	Mint	Excellent	User
Waist Level Finder	135 115	90 80	75 65	
CDS Prism		550 480	500 400	
PD Prism (also fits RZ)	1310 1140	950 875	840 600	
Prism Finder		390 350	360 300	285 260
Prism Finder 2 (also fits RZ)	945 790		375 330	
Adjustable Diopter Magnifier	260 190			
Magnifier Hood		110 100	90 70	
CDS Magnifier Hood		250 180	175 140	
PD Magnifier Hood	510 480		360 300	
Universal Sports Finder		120 80	95 50	
120 or 220 Back		200 180	180 140	150 120
120 or 220 Pro S Back	350 310	265 220	215 160	225 180
120 or 220 Pro SD Back	660 525			
120 6x4.5 Back	450 390	320 250	225 180	
70mm Back		310 260	250 230	
120 or 220 6x4.5 Pro SD Back	725 580			
Polaroid Back w/adapter		245 175	185 150	
Polaroid Back N (w/built-in adptr)	385 330			
Polaroid Back SD	550 440			
NPC Polaroid Back	240 170	140 125		
NPC SX70 Polaroid Back	295 240			
Quadra 72 Sheet Film Back (7.2cm square)	725 540			
Power Drive w/control pack *Takes 120 or 220 film*			345 250	
Power Drive Back (6X7 or 6X8) *Takes 120 or 220 film*	650 680	465 420	350 280	
Grip Holder	90 80		40 30	
Deluxe Grip w/flash swivel			90 55	
Flash Gun Bracket	95 65			
Pistol Grip			45 35	
Pistol Grip 2	160 120	100 80		
Multi-Angle Grip	375 270	240 200	210 150	
Auto Ext Tube 1	375 270	240 200	210 150	
Auto Ext Tube 2	410 300	260 220	235 180	
Auto Ext Tube 1 KL	540 420			
Auto Ext Tube 2 KL	590 460			
Bellows Lens Hood G2	270 190	160 150	150 100	
Bellows Lens Hood G3	620 490		300 200	

Mamiya RZ67 Accessories

Item	New	Mint	Excellent	User
Waist Level Finder	170 150	125 95	100 70	
AE Prism	1340 1160	1000 940	875 650	
AE Prism Finder 2	1340 1160			
PD Prism (also fits RB)	1340 1140	980 900	850 600	625 400
Prism Finder 2 (also fits RB)	1050 790	600 500		
AE Magnifier Hood	810	650 575	495 400	
120 or 220 Magazine	610 500	450 420	425 350	300 250
120 or 220 Pro II Magazine	720 600			
6x4.5 Magazine	695 550	490 395		
6x4.5 Pro II Magazine	720 600			
6x6 Magazine	695 580		275 200	
Polaroid Back	585 460	395 350	350 225	
NPC Polaroid Back	225 170			
Quadra 72 Sheet Film Back (7.2cm square)	665 540			
G Adapter *Allows use of RB film magazines and Polaroid backs on RZ*	130 100	80 65		
Motor Winder			250 150	
Power Winder 2	645 520			
L Grip RZ	250 200		150 100	
Multi-Angle Grip	375 270	240 200	200 150	

Mamiya RZ67 Accessories

Item	New	Mint	Excellent	User
Auto Ext Tube #1	550 410	350 300	325 220	
Auto Ext Tube #2	575 450	395 350		
Bellows Lens Hood G2	240 190	150 125	135 100	
Bellows Lens Hood G3	625 490		395 240	

Mamiya 6 System

Item	New	Mint	Excellent	User
Mamiya 6 Body	1840 1680	1450 1250		
50mm f/4	1800 1570	1390 1200		
75mm f/3.5	1400 1230	1000 850		
150mm f/4.5	2000 1750	1500 1300		
Close-up Attachment	575 470			
NPC Polaroid Back	900			
35mm Panoramic Adapter Set	250 190			
Stroboframe Flash Bracket	120 75			

Mamiya Twin Lens Cameras

Prices are for cameras without lenses, but with waist level finders.

Camera	New	Mint	Excellent	User
C2			100 80	
C22			120 95	
C220		250 180	215 150	140 90
C220f		295 245	260 225	
C3			125 100	
C33			150 125	
C330			275 180	230 150
C330f		575 500	370 300	270 230
C330s	1150 900	750 700	650 500	

Mamiya TLR Lenses

Lens	New	Mint	Excellent	User
55mm f/4.5	995 800	675 600	550 400	375 300
65mm f/3.5		275 230	225 150	170 85
80mm f/2.8	610 495	425 380	400 270	250 200
80mm f/2.8 chr		180 150	170 125	
105mm f/3.5		300 220	245 150	
105mm f/4.5			220 200	
105mm f/4.5 chr			165 125	
135mm f/4.5	640 550	475 420	400 270	
180mm f/4.5 chr			225 150	135 100
180mm f/4.5	870 700	600 550	540 375	350 280
180mm f/8 chr			140 120	
250mm f/6.3	750 600	520 470	450 325	

Mamiya TLR Accessories

Item	New	Mint	Excellent	User
Waist Level Finder	210 140		50 35	
CDS Magnifier Hood		225 200	190 145	
CDS Finder			200 150	
Chimney Finder			100 90	

Mamiya TLR Accessories

Item	New		Mint		Excellent		User	
Magnifier Hood					70	40		
Porroflex Finder					100	50		
CDS Porrofinder			175	150	150	110		
Prism Finder	550	400	360	330	280	250	235	200
Paramender					70	40		
Paramender 2	160	120			75	50		
Grip Holder C220					40	25		
Grip Holder C330	120	75						
L-Grip					50	25		
Pistol Grip					35	20		
Pistol Grip Model 2	160	120						

Mamiya Press Cameras

Camera	Mint		Excellent		User	
23			170	85	70	
23, 90/3.5, back			220	150		
Super 23			250	100		
Super 23, 100/3.5, back, grip			325	200		
Universal			290	200		
Universal, 90/3.5, back, grip			400	350		
Universal, 100/3.5, back, grip	595	485	450	400		

Mamiya Press Lenses

Lens	New		Mint		Excellent		User	
50mm f/6.3 w/finder	1100	850			580	350		
65mm f/6.3 w/finder					230	180		
75mm f/5.6 w/finder	650	530			475	300		
90mm f/3.5					100	80		
100mm f/2.8	575	490			300	260		
100mm f/3.5			245	200	210	125	100	90
127mm f/4.7	495	410	300	250	280	180		
150mm f/4.5							195	170
150mm f/5.6					275	200		
250mm f/5	1345	1050			600	400		

Mamiya Press Accessories

Item	New		Mint		Excellent		User	
Sports Finder					75	50		
Polaroid Back					200	110		
Film Holder, Knob Wind (6x7 or 6x9)	250	200			95	80	70	45
Film Holder, Lever Wind (6x7 or 6x9)	290	240			150	100	115	75
Model 3 Film Holder (6x7 or 6x9)					150	100		
G or M Adapter Back					60	45		
Focusing Screen Holder	130	90						
Right Angle Back w/screen					140	90		
Magnifying Focus Back w/screen & hood					120	75		
Duophot Adapter				230	60	50		
Tetra Photo Adapter	475	390						
Focusing Hood					75	50		
Extension Ring Set	200	150						
Spacer Set	215	160						

MAMIYA

Pentax Medium Format

Pentax 6x7

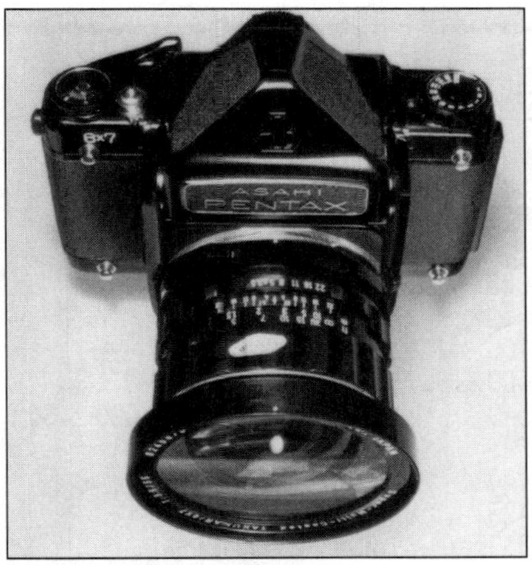

Pentax 6x7 with 55mm f/3.5 lens

One of the best values on the market in medium format SLRs is the Pentax 6x7. Dubbed a "Spotmatic on steroids," it looks like a giant-sized 35mm SLR and features interchangeable viewfinders and a wide array of very fine lenses. It accepts both 120 and 220 film. The electronically-controlled, horizontal focal plane shutter provides speeds from 1 second to 1/1000 plus B, with a slow 1/30 flash sync. The camera is not without its drawbacks, however: In the event of battery failure, X sync and B are the only available shutter speeds. With a standard lens and meterless prism, the 6x7 weighs about the same as a Nikon F2 or Canon F-1 with motor drive attached — heavy, but easily hand-held. Another drawback is its lack of interchangeable film backs (although NPC makes a polaroid back for the camera). Early 6x7s lack a mirror lock-up provision whereas later models have it — a nice feature with such a large mirror.

Pentax 645

The Pentax 645 is a sophisticated, all-in-one 6cm x 4.5cm medium format SLR. It has a non-interchangeable meter prism and a built-in 1.5 fps motor drive. The electronically-controlled, focal-plane shutter delivers speeds from 15 seconds to 1/1000, with a top flash sync of 1/60. Mechanical speeds are B and 1/60. Available exposure modes are program, aperture or shutter priority AE, metered manual and TTL OTF flash with dedicated strobe units. New prices for the 645 do not include the film insert.

Pentax Medium Format SLRs

Camera	New		Mint		Excellent		User	
645	1650	1300	1150	1000	1050	900		
645, 75/2.8, 120 insert	1950	1600	1400	1250	1300	950		
6x7 (early - no finder)					500	450	400	350
6x7 (late - no finder)	1200	900	845	800	780	690		
6x7 (late - std prism)	1380	1080			650	600		
6x7 (late - TTL prism)					880	750		
6x7 (early), std prism, 105/2.4					750	670		
6x7 (late), std prism, 105/2.4	1850	1490			850	750		
6x7 (late), TTL prism, 105/2.4	1995	1670	1350	1100	1145	950		

Pentax 645 Lenses

645 and 6x7 lenses followed by LS incorporate leaf shutters. If you need flash sync at higher speeds than either of the cameras normally allows, a leaf-shutter lens is the solution. They provide flash sync at all lens shutter speeds (1 second to 1/500).

Lens	New		Mint		Excellent		User	
35mm f/3.5	795	660	595	540	325	425		
45mm f/2.8	745	590	525	480	300	400		
55mm f/2.8	630	510	450	400	290	300		
75mm f/2.8	420	300	250	175	150	350		
75mm f/2.8 LS	745	590	500	450	350	410		
120mm f/4 Macro	770	620	550	525	395	460		
135mm f/4 LS	870	700	650	595	455	300		
150mm f/3.5	620	480	420	575	265	350		
200mm f/4	685	540	490	450	325	250		
300mm f/4 EDIF	2695	2200			1500	1200		
600mm f/5.6 EDIF	4995	4400						
80-160 f/4.5	1350	1130	995	900	650	750		
1.4X Rear Converter A	450	330	285	250	245	225		
2X Rear Converter A	520	365	300	275				

Pentax 6x7 Lenses

Lens	New		Mint		Excellent		User	
35mm f/4.5	1295	1000	895	850	865	700		
45mm f/4	995	730	650	600	615	470		
55mm f/3.5					480	350		
55mm f/4	1010	740	680	645	620	490		
75mm f/4.5	625	495	425	380	375	280		
75mm f/4.5 Shift	1750	1400	1250	1100	1050	995		
90mm f/2.8	640	520	450	400				
90mm f/2.8 LS			575	540	560	400	400	300
105mm f/2.4	520	410	350	325	300	225		
120mm f/3.5 Soft Focus	695	560	485	440				
135mm f/4 Macro	690	530	470	425	435	320		
150mm f/2.8			375	350	325	265		
165mm f/2.8	750	600	540	500	480	325		
165mm f/4 LS	830	670	595	550				
200mm f/4	840	680	600	550	560	450		
300mm f/4	1325	1020	900	850	820	685		
400mm f/4			1500	1350	1400	1180	1000	850
400mm f/4 EDIF	4995	4400	3885	3700	3550	3190		
500mm f/5.6	2395	2000	1750	1680	1650	1475		
600mm f/4	3495	3000	2680	2500	2435	2200		
800mm f/4	6150	5600			4100	3450		
800mm f/6.7 EDIF	10500	9000			6500	5650		
1000mm f/8	5925	5350			3950	3345		
1.4X Teleconverter	575	460						
2X Teleconverter	645	510			350	285		
2X T6 Teleconverter					300	250		
Kenko or Vivitar 2X Teleconverter	270	220	190	170	150	125		

Pentax 645 Accessories

Item	New		Mint		Excellent		User	
120 or 220 Insert	195	150	125	100	110	80		
70mm film holder (w/eyepiece)	960	650						
Right Angle Ref converter	255	195	165	130				
2X Magnifier	120	80						
Auto Bellows	1035	850						

Pentax 645 Accessories

Item	New	Mint	Excellent	User
Auto Ext Tube Set	410 290	245 200		
Helicoid Ext Tube	260 185		140 110	
Reverse Adapter Set	140 100			
645 to 6X7 Lens Adapter	150 105	95 80	80 70	
AF-280T Strobe (TTL)	210 155	120 100	90 70	
AF-400T Strobe set (TTL)	475 380	320 260		
510v Power Pack (AF-400T)	180 130			
Transistor Power Pack (AF400T)	165 120			
Remote Battery Pack	80 55			
NPC Polaroid Back	1500 1300			

Pentax 6x7 Accessories

Item	New	Mint	Excellent	User
Waist Level Finder	135 95	75 60	65 40	
Pentaprism Finder	220 175	170 150	150 125	115 100
TTL Prism Finder	445 360	315 240	245 210	
Rigid Mag Hood	225 155	120 100		
Right Angle Finder	315 220	175 150		
2X Magnifier	140 80	65 50		
NPC Polaroid Back	845 750			
Hand Grip	110 75	65 50		
Auto Bellows	1100	950 850	775 600	500 400
Ext Tube Inner	240 180			
Ext Tube Outer		75 50		
Slide Copier	785 670			
Helicoid Ext Tube	160 130		90 70	
Reverse Adapter (67mm)	70 50			

Rollei Medium Format TLRs

Rolleiflex Twin Lens Reflex Cameras

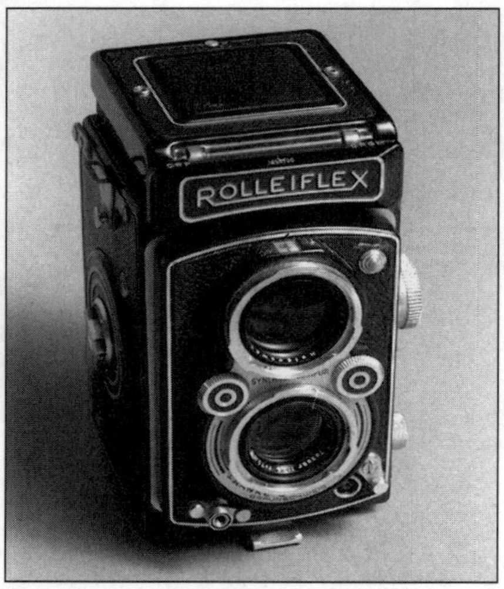

Rolleiflex Automat w/Tessar lens and MX sync

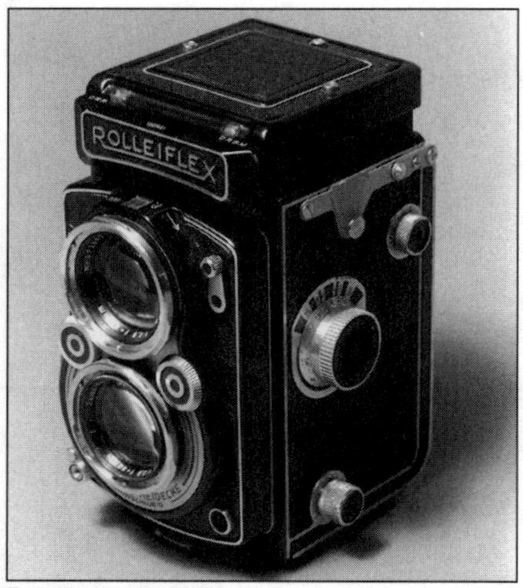

Rolleiflex 2.8A with Tessar lens

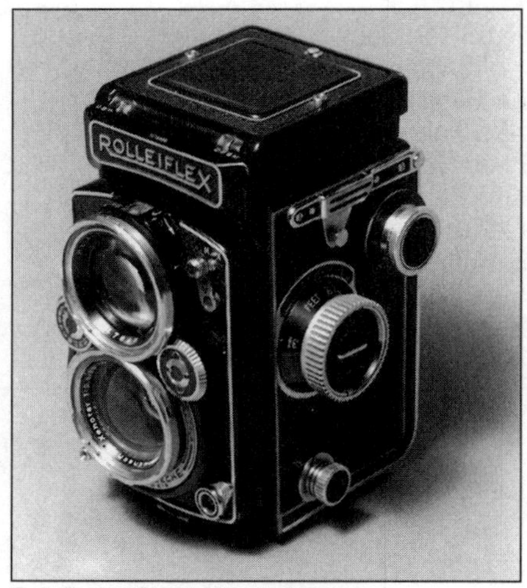

Rolleiflex 2.8D with Xenotar lens

Most Rollei TLRs, while certainly not modern cameras in terms of dates of manufacture, are quite modern when one considers their capabilities. Thirty and forty year-old Rolleis still see daily use world-wide, undoubtedly due to their almost bullet-proof construction and excellent optics. I've talked to many people who still use the earliest models and swear by the excellent photos these antiques provide.

During the past few years, the used market prices of certain models of Rolleiflexes have risen to almost ridiculous levels because of the demand caused by overseas collectors. Even so, most "ordinary" models, especially those in user condition, still represent a very cost-effective way for one to move into medium format. Because something like fifty different models of Rolleiflex cameras have been made since the Rolleiflex I of 1929, space does not permit my explaining each model's features. (The exception is the 2.8GX, Rollei's only current TLR camera. Its pertinent data is listed below.)

The Tessar and Planar lenses are made by Zeiss. Xenar and Xenotar lenses are made by Schneider. Collectors prefer the Zeiss lenses, especially the Planars. I've heard different stories about why this is so. One claim I often hear from collectors is that the Zeiss lenses are contrastier than the Schneiders. But I've heard others, who were mostly users, say just the opposite. Gene Lester, a well-known Hollywood photographer and the President of the American Society of Camera Collectors, explained to me that Rollei conducted rigorous quality-control tests on the Zeiss lenses, rejecting fully sixty percent of the ones they received, and that they didn't subject the Schneider lenses to these same tests. Collectors may be inclined to believe that the Zeiss optics are better because of this. But it sounds to me as if Rollei had a lot more confidence in Schneider's quality control process than Zeiss'. Furthermore, Rollei made no distinction between the two makes of lenses when they priced their cameras. From personal experience, I can tell you this: I've used Rolleiflexes with Schneider and Zeiss lenses, both 3.5's and 2.8's. And I'm here to tell you, they're all so darn sharp and contrasty that I think these folks are splitting hairs. So, if you're looking for a budget medium format camera, get a Rolleiflex with a Schneider 3.5 lens and rest easy with the knowledge that you have acquired one of the finest photographic tools ever made. Take care of it and you'll be passing it on to your grandchildren.

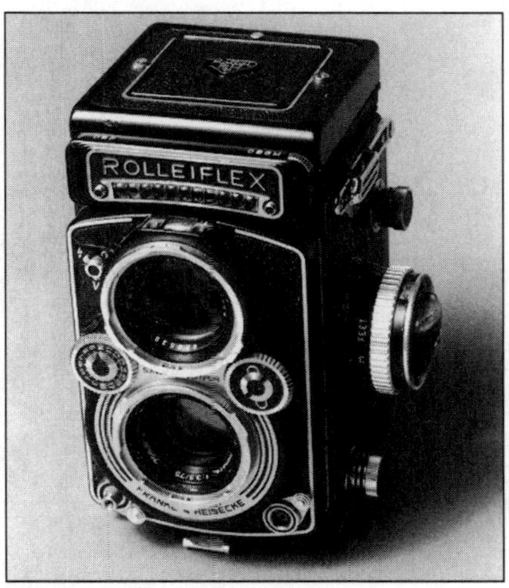

Rolleiflex 3.5E3 with Xenotar lens and meter

Rolleiflex 2.8GX

Continuing the grand tradition of Rolleiflex TLRs, the 2.8GX has such niceties as a Planar 80mm f/2.8 taking lens (manufactured by Rollei under license from Zeiss) mounted in a Synchro Compur between-the-lens leaf shutter, which provides speeds from 1 second to 1/500, plus B, with X sync at all speeds. The 2.8GX uses 120 film only. It offers TTL match-diode metering (through the viewing lens), using a centerweighted pattern. When using SCA-compatible flash units, TTL flash via the dedicated hot shoe is available. Auto film advance to the first frame (an ancient Rollei tradition) was retained, as was multiple-exposure capability.

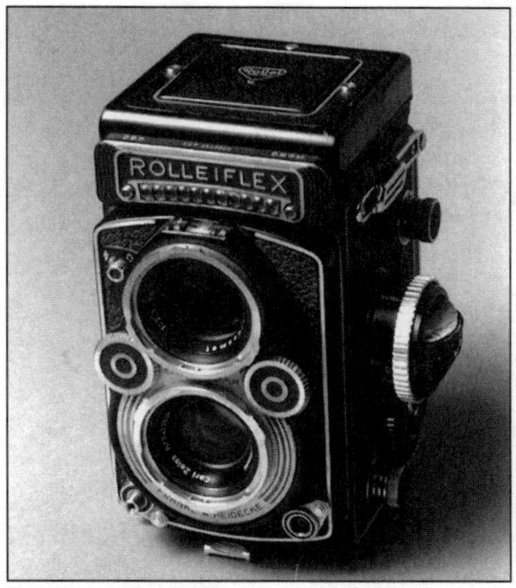

Rolleiflex 3.5F with Planar lens and meter

There is no question that the 2.8GX is expensive, but if one wants the very best, one must be prepared to pay for it.

In the TLR listings below, letters or numbers in parentheses indicate the following: (m) = m-type flash bulb sync only. (mx) = both m-type bulb and electronic strobe sync. (mx-evs), also called mx-lvs, means the cameras have the above-mentioned flash capabilities, plus Rollei's Automat feature.

The evs, or lvs, stands for "exposure (or light) value setting." It's a system common to a number of different cameras, where the shutter speeds and apertures are cross-coupled: when one changes the shutter speed, the aperture will change automatically in an inverse-proportional manner ensuring correct exposure. (12/24) refers to an option that was available on certain later model Rolleiflexes that allows the use of either 120 or 220 film.

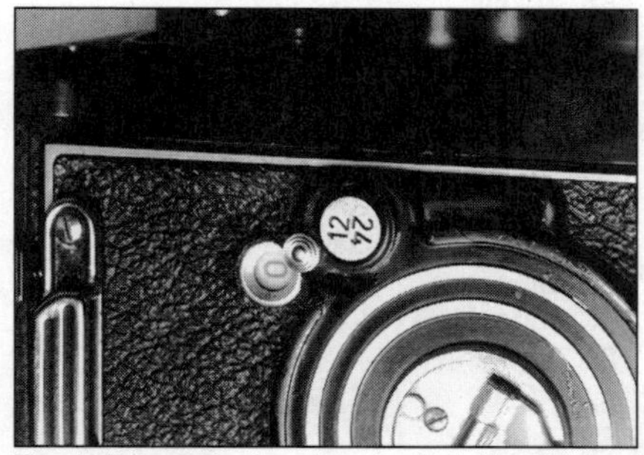

The 12/24 selector found on the Rolleiflex 2.8F and 3.5F12/24 models.

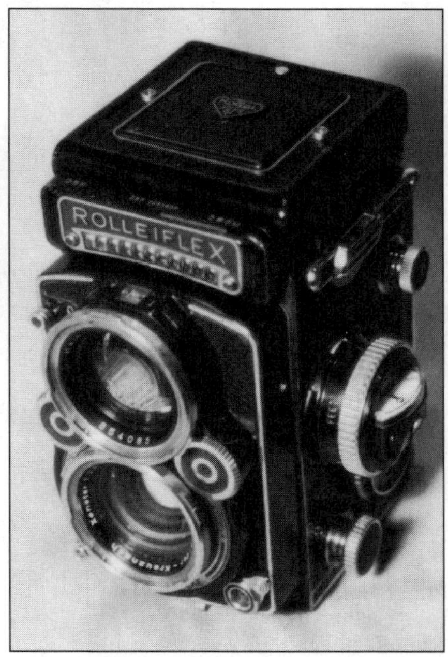

Rolleiflex 2.8F with Schneider Xenotar lens and meter

The Rolleiflex TLRs are arranged in approximate chronological order. You'll note that several listings have no prices. If you have verifiable pricing info for these cameras, I'd appreciate your input.

Rolleiflex TLRs

Camera	Yrs. Made	New		Mint		Excellent		User	
I (orig), Tessar 75/4.5	1929					180	140		
I, Tessar 75/3.8	1929-32					200	160		
Original, Tessar 60/2.8	1931-38								
Original, Tessar 75/3.5	1931-38								
Std, Tessar 75/3.8	1932-41							190	140
Std, Tessar 75/3.5	1932-41								
Std, Tessar 75/4.5	1932-41								
Sports, Tessar 60/2.8	1938-41								
3.5A, Tessar	1937-49					105	90		
3.5A, Xenar	1939-49					110	90		
2.8A, Tessar	1950-51					375	250		
3.5A, Xenar (m)	1949-51					150	120		
3.5A, Tessar (m)	1949-51					150	120		
3.5A, Tessar (mx)	1951-54			240	225	220	150	120	90
3.5A, Xenar (mx)	1951-54					220	130		
3.5A, Tessar (mx-evs)	1954-56			320	250	245	220		
3.5A, Xenar (mx-evs)	1954-56			300	220	240	220		
2.8B, Biometar	1952-53								
2.8C, Planar	1953-55					430	320		
2.8C, Xenotar	1953-55					390	275		
2.8D, Planar	1955-56					400	295	250	200
2.8D, Xenotar	1955-56			525	375	295	220	230	200
2.8E, Planar	1956-59					425	300		
2.8E, Xenotar	1956-59					400	295		
3.5E, Planar	1956-59					350	280	260	185
3.5E, Xenotar	1956-59					330	270	250	170
2.8E2, Planar	1959-62					480	400	300	200
2.8E2, Xenotar	1959-62					425	350		
3.5E2, Planar	1959-60					400	350		
3.5E2, Xenotar	1959-60					390	295	255	140
2.8E3, Planar	1962-65					500	410		
2.8E3, Xenotar	1962-65					470	380		
3.5E3, Planar	1962-65					400	300		
3.5E3, Xenotar	1962-65					380	295		
2.8F, Planar	1965-?					750	520	550	450
2.8F, Planar (12/24)	1965-?			1250	1000	895	725	575	475
2.8F, Xenotar	1965-?					575	420	410	300
2.8F, Xenotar (12/24)	1965-?			1100	950	825	550		
3.5F, Planar	1965-?			810	595	540	470	445	290
3.5F, Planar (12/24)	1965-?			900	650	645	550	480	350
3.5F, Xenotar	1965-?			580	525	500	350	320	240
3.5F, Xenotar (12/24)	1965-?			820	625	575	500	480	415
3.5T, Tessar	1958-75			450	350	390	275		
2.8GX	1986-	2400	2095	1795	1530				
Rolleimagic I	1960-63			200	180	160	120	105	95
Rolleimagic II	1962-67			290	220				
Tele, Sonnar 135/4	1959-?					1265	900		
Wide, Distagon 55/4	1961-67			2995	2590	2495	1450		

Rolleicord TLRs

Camera	Yrs. Made	New	Mint	Excellent	User
I (art deco)	1933-36		175 ... 150	135 ... 100	
I (leather)	1934-36			90 ... 80	
Ia	1936-47			100 ... 90	
II	1936-50			120 ... 80	90 ... 60
III	1950-53			150 ... 90	90 ... 60
IV	1953-54			170 ... 110	140 ... 70
V	1954-57			180 ... 120	100 ... 90
Va	1957-61			170 ... 120	
Vb	1962-70			295 ... 200	

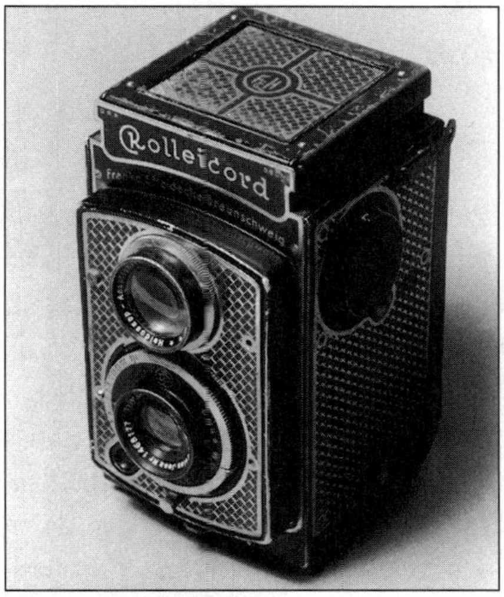

Rolleicord 1 with Art Deco trim

Rollei TLR Accessories

Rollei has made many, many different accessories for their TLRs over the last several decades. Many of these have become as collectible as the cameras. It's beyond the scope of this book to attempt anything near a complete listing, so I've listed some of the most common.

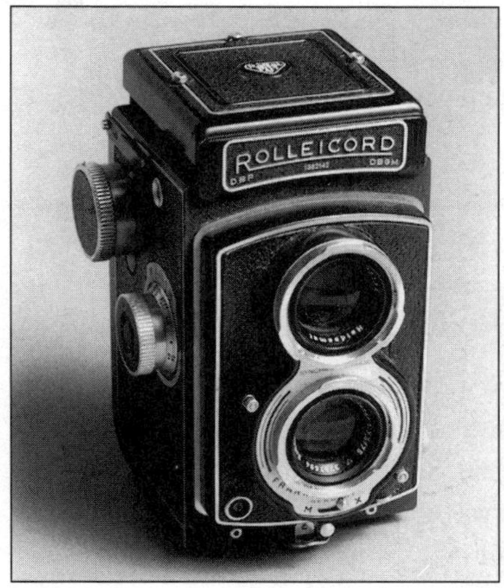

Rolleicord IV

Rollei TLR Accessories

Item	New	Mint	Excellent	User
Rolleiflex W/L Finder			60 ... 50	
Rolleiprism		350 ... 275	300 ... 175	150 ... 100
Binocular Magnifier		150 ... 100	100 ... 85	
Rolleimeter (3.5 or 2.8)		75 ... 60	60 ... 50	
Rolleifix			50 ... 40	35 ... 30
Rolleigrip			80 ... 50	
Rolleikin			80 ... 60	
Rolleimarine U/W Housing			500 ... 450	
Panorama Head		70 ... 40	50 ... 40	
Rolleicord 24 exp kit		25 ... 20		
Rolleinar Close Up Lens Set			125 ... 70	

Rollei Medium Format SLRs

Rollei SL66 Series SLRs

Rolleiflex SL66

The SL66 was Rollei's first medium format SLR. It's a mechanical camera and has no built-in meter. The SL66 system is, in the tradition of medium format SLRs, a totally modular one, accepting a wide array of interchangeable finders, focusing screens, lenses and backs. It also has a focal plane shutter, with shutter speeds ranging from 1 second to 1/1000, plus B and with X sync at 1/30 second. Instead of using the more traditional integral focusing helicals, lenses on the SL66 are focused by racking a bellows in and out of the body. Such a system allows for greater close-up focusing flexibility than would otherwise be possible. Another nice feature, one which remains unique to the SL66 line, is Rollei's Retromounting®, which allows some lenses to be reverse-mounted without the use of accessory adapters, giving the photographer easy access to the world of high-magnification photography without having to incur a lot of additional expense. And, in its effort to add even further control to the final image, Rollei decided to give the SL66 a tilt feature, allowing for ±8 degrees of movement. The SL66 also has a PC connector, a hot shoe, a cable release socket, multiple exposure capability and a mirror pre-release.

Rolleiflex SL66E

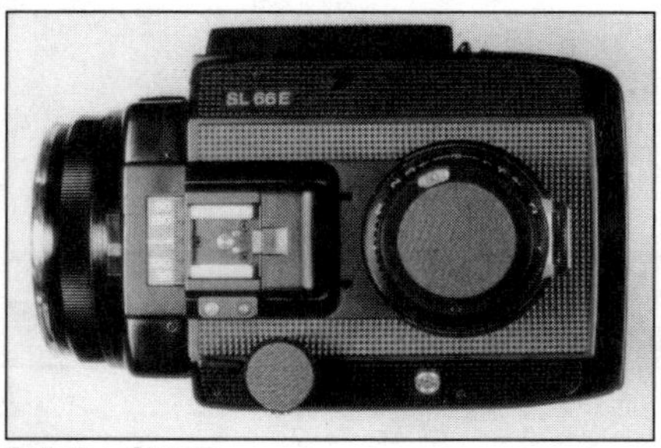

Rolleiflex SL66E

The SL66E is an SL66 with a few nice improvements. It has a TTL meter using a centerweighted pattern. The meter readout in the viewfinder is provided by a 5 LED array. Exposure compensation (±1.5 EV) is also available. The SL66E provides TTL auto flash exposure and metering with SCA 356-compatible units. Film emulsion speeds are set on the backs with the SL66E. This information is communicated to the camera's meter via three electrical contacts on the E-type back.

Rolleiflex SL66SE

Despite rumors to the contrary, SL66-style cameras are still being made, but the SL66SE is the only surviving model. And it is an expensive one, justifiably living up to its SE (Special Edition) designation.

The SL66SE is similar to the SL66E, with significant improvements. It has three TTL metering patterns: a bottom-centerweighted multi-zone averaging pattern, a spot pattern, and TTL flash metering with SCA 356-compatible flash units. Exposure options include metered manual, shutter-priority AE, aperture-priority AE and TTL auto flash.

Rolleiflex SL66X

The SL66X is an SL66 with slight cosmetic alterations, updated to include the TTL flash technology found on the SL66E and SL66SE.

Rollei SLX & 6000 Series SLRs

All the following cameras have several things in common: They all accept the electronic leaf-shutter lenses (in other words, they will not accept lenses for the SL66 series). All cameras have a 14-pole universal socket for external control units and accessories (such as the ME-1 or RC-120). They accept interchangeable finders and focusing screens. They have integral motor drives which allow single and continuous film advance at speeds up to 1.5 fps (2 fps with the 6003, 6008 and 6008 SRC 1000), as well as first-frame prewind and auto film rewind. They are battery-dependent, but the batteries are rechargeable NiCads and can be interchanged in seconds. Each battery provides more than 500 exposures between charges.

Rolleiflex SLX

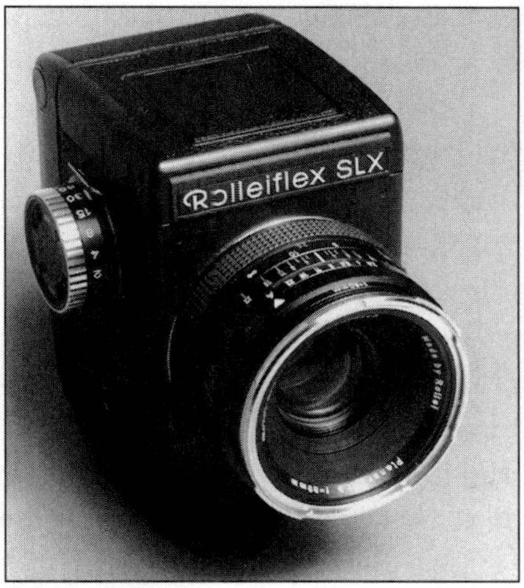

Rolleiflex SLX

Introduced in 1977, the SLX was the first model of the new-look Rollei medium format SLRs. Its exposure modes are shutter-priority AE and non-metered manual. In the shutter-priority mode, a centerweighted metering pattern is used. The SLX does not have a provision for mid-roll film back interchangeability. Instead, it uses a fixed (but removable) back into which one pops a pre-loaded film insert. In addition to the above features, the SLX also has a PC socket and a depth-of-field preview button that doubles as a AE lock.

Rolleiflex 6002

The 6002 was introduced after the 6006 as a more economical model. Like the SLX, it does not have a provision for changing backs mid-roll.

Three exposure modes are available: shutter-priority AE, non-metered manual and TTL auto flash with SCA-356 compatible flash units. For metering, a centerweighted pattern is used. The 6002 also has a PC socket in addition to the dedicated hot shoe and a depth-of-field preview button that doubles as an AE lock.

Rolleiflex 6003 SRC 1000

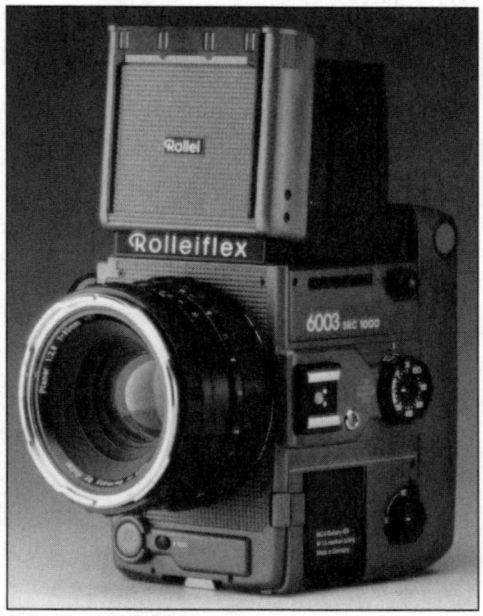

Rolleiflex 6003 SRC 1000

The whole philosophy behind the Rollei 6003 is that you should only have to pay for the features you need, but if you should need more features at a later date, you shouldn't be denied them. The 6003 SRC 1000 is a little smaller and a little lighter than the 6008 SRC 1000, but is very similar to it in terms of its capabilities, so only the points where it differs from the more full-featured model will be addressed here. For starters, the multi-spot metering function is not supported with the 6003. Also, the Action Grip that comes standard with the 6008 is available as an option for the 6003. Mirror prerelease is done using the RC-120 remote control unit; there is no prerelease button built into the body. The dark slide built into the 6008 is available as an accessory for the 6003. All other features are shared by the two cameras.

Rolleiflex 6006 & 6006-II

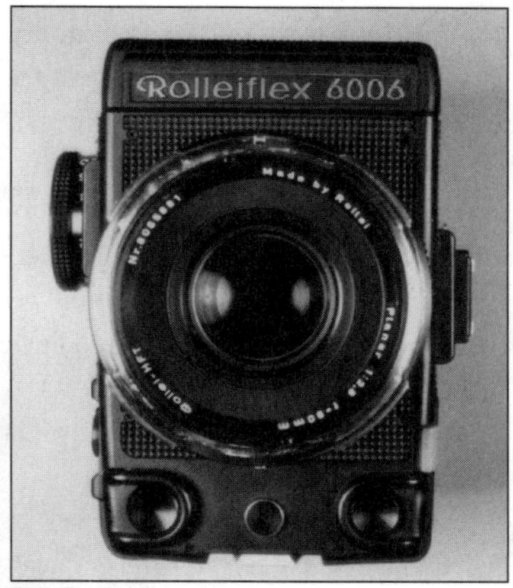

Rolleiflex 6006

The 6006 has three exposure modes: shutter-priority AE, non-metered manual and TTL auto flash with SCA-356 compatible flash units. For metering, a centerweighted pattern is used.

The 6006 was the first in this series of Rollei SLRs to offer fully interchangeable film backs. Other features include single and continuous film-advance settings (up to 1.5 fps in continuous mode), a PC socket in addition to the dedicated hot shoe, a button that doubles as a depth-of-field preview selector and AE lock, a cable release socket, and a mirror prerelease (the SLX and 6002 require the use of the RC-120 electric remote control release to access this feature).

The 6006-II is, as its name implies, an improved 6006. The major difference is the addition of a two-position switch for single or multiple exposures. The two positions are labeled SE and ME. Prior models (the 6006 and 6002) could take multiple exposures only by using the expensive ME-1 multi-exposure control unit or the MRC-120 electric multi-exposure remote release.

Rolleiflex 6008 & 6008 SRC 1000

The 6008 has all the features of the 6006-II, plus the following: it supports the 1/1000 top shutter speed on the new PQS lenses. The exposure system has two metering patterns: a multi-zone, bottom-centerweighted pattern, and a 1% spot pattern. Up to five spot readings can be stored and averaged for critical exposure situations. Exposure modes are program, shutter- and aperture-priority AE, metered manual (a first for this series), and TTL auto flash using SCA 356-dedicated flash units. A three-shot auto-bracketing feature is also available.

New film backs (Rollei prefers to call them magazines) were also developed for the 6008. Instead of setting the film speeds on the camera, as is done with previous models, the film speeds are set on the backs. For the photographer who often shoots using a variety of emulsions and speeds, this is a welcome feature. The older, 6006-style backs will still work on the 6008, but the camera will default to ISO 100. Not to worry, though: the 6008 has such an extreme EV adjustment range available (-4$\frac{2}{3}$ to +2 EV, which is equivalent to ISO 2500 to ISO 25) that the camera's meter and exposure options can still be used. Rollei will convert the older backs to the newer style if one prefers. Also new to the 6008 is the Action Grip. The grip is fitted to the hub of the shutter speed dial on the right side of the camera and has a built-in meter-activation/AE lock switch and a shutter release.

The 6008 SRC 1000 differs from the 6008 in only a couple of areas. The SRC, by the way, stands for Scanning Remote Control — we'll get to that shortly. As you may have guessed the "1000" in its name refers to its top shutter speed. The SRC 1000 has the 1/1000 second shutter speed indicated on the shutter speed dial. The older 6008 has two marked (but unlabeled) detents above 1/500, one for 1/750 and the other for 1/1000. They were not labeled on the original 6008 because the high speed leaf shutters were still in development when the camera was ready for release. The 1/750 detent was dropped from the SRC 1000's dial.

The other difference came about as a result of a new accessory for the 6008 and the 6003: Rollei's Digital ScanPack. The Digital ScanPack allows the Rollei 6008 SRC 1000 to interface directly with a Macintosh II or IBM-compatible 80386 or higher with a minimum of 8 MB RAM and 100 MB of free hard disk storage space, and converts it to a state-of-the-art ultra high-resolution digital imaging scanner. Because the Digital ScanPack requires relatively long exposure times (3 seconds and up), the shutter was redesigned so that it is not held open by an electromagnet on the B setting, eliminating battery drain during long exposures. This feature will not only be of interest to those working with digital imaging, but to other photographers who regularly use long exposure times in their work.

Rollei Medium Format SLRs

Camera	New	Mint	Excellent	User
SL66			525 480	370 320
SL66E			850 700	
SL66SE		4895 4500		
SL66X		1995 1750		
SLX			600 350	
6002		1295 1250		
6003 SRC 1000	1795			
6006		1825 1500	1100 800	
6006-II		2895 2350		
6008		3200 2750		
6008 SRC 1000	4050 3695			

Rollei Medium Format SLR Outfits

Outfit	New	Mint	Excellent	User
SL66, W/L, 80 Planar, back		1200 895	950 800	
SL66E, W/L, 80 Planar, back		2895 2250	2320 1850	
SL66SE, W/L, 80 Planar, back	9995 9225			
SL66X, W/L, 80 Planar, back		3750 2995		
SLX, 80 Planar, back, chgr		980 895	895 740	
6002, 80 Rolleigon, chgr		1150 970	900 800	
6003 SRC, 80 Planar, back, chgr	3895 3395			
6006, 80 Planar, back, chgr		1795 1700	1695 1275	
6006-II, 80 Planar, back, chgr		3000 2495	1995 1650	
6008, 80 Planar, back, chgr		3695 3000		
6008 SRC, 80 Planar, back, chgr	5995 5595			

Lenses for Rollei SL66

Lens	New	Mint	Excellent	User
30mm f/3.5 Distagon HFT	6100 5175		3000 2500	
40mm f/4 Distagon HFT	7200 6100		3300 2780	
50mm f/4 Distagon			860 695	
50mm f/4 Distagon HFT	3680 3100		1425 1095	
75mm f/4.5 Rolleigon PC		4500 4000		
80mm f/2.8 Planar			280 190	
80mm f/2.8 Planar HFT	1970 1675	1500 1450	1295 1100	
80mm f/4 Distagon w/shutter			860 650	
120mm f/4 Makro Planar HFT	5235 4450			
120mm f/5.6 S Planar			920 750	
120mm f/5.6 Opton		760 700	690 500	
150mm f/4 Sonnar			700 510	
150mm f/4 Sonnar HFT	3750 3190	1950 1500	1200 800	
150mm f/4 Sonnar w/shutter		850 670	550 400	
250mm f/5.6 Opton		780 650		
250mm f/5.6 Sonnar			930 750	
250mm f/5.6 Sonnar HFT	4990 4240	2850 1750		
300mm f/5.6 Tele-APO Kilar			500 460	
350mm f/5.6 Tele-Tessar			800 650	
2X Teleconverter	1265 1075			
2X Teleconverter (E/SE)	1500 1275			

Lenses for Rollei SLX and 6000 Series

Lens	New	Mint	Excellent	User
30mm f/4 Distagon HFT PQ "fisheye"	7250 6780			
40mm f/3.5 Super Angulon PQ	6300 5845			
40mm f/4 Distagon HFT		2500 2200	2300 1950	
40mm f/4 Distagon HFT PQ	5595 5330			
50mm f/2.8 Super Angulon HFT PQS	5295 4995			
50mm f/4 Distagon HFT		1195 1100	1000 875	
50mm f/4 Distagon HFT PQ	3470 2815			
50mm f/4 Rolleigon HFT		750 650		
55mm f/4.5 PCS Super Angulon HFT PQ	11500 9550			
60mm f/3.5 Curtagon HFT PQ	3300 2885			
60mm f/3.5 Distagon HFT		1450 1300		
60mm f/3.5 Distagon HFT PQ	3450 2995			
80mm f/2 Xenotar HFT PQ	4970 4360			
80mm f/2.8 Planar HFT			400 250	
80mm f/2.8 Planar HFT PQ	2250 1900			
80mm f/2.8 Planar HFT PQS	2550 2190			
80mm f/2.8 Rolleigon HFT		300 260		
80mm f/2.8 Xenotar HFT PQ	1720 1360			
90mm f/4 APO Symmar Macro HFT PQS	5025 4795			
120mm f/4 Makro Planar HFT		2250 1900		
120mm f/4 Makro Planar HFT PQ	3750 3440			
120mm f/5.6 S Planar HFT			1250 950	
150mm f/4 Rolleigon			1095 950	
150mm f/4 Rolleigon HFT			800 750	
150mm f/4 Sonnar HFT		1395 1250	1195 995	
150mm f/4 Sonnar HFT PQ	3650 2995			
150mm f/4 Sonnar HFT PQS	4500 3800			
150mm f/4 Tele-Xenar HFT PQ	3900 3400	2900 2700		
150mm f/4 Tele-Xenar HFT PQS		3500 3300		
150mm f/4.6 APO Symmar	4700 4150			
180mm f/2.8 Tele-Xenar	5985 5200			
250mm f/5.6 Sonnar HFT		1750 1450	1250 900	
250mm f/5.6 Sonnar HFT PQ	3940 3500			
250mm f/5.6 Sonnar HFT PQS	4695 4220			
300mm f/4 APO Tele-Xenar HFT PQ	6500 6000	5600 5200		
350mm f/5.6 Tele-Tessar HFT		2250 1700	1650 1375	
350mm f/5.6 Tele-Tessar HFT PQ	5495 4995			

Lenses for Rollei SLX and 6000 Series

Lens	New	Mint	Excellent	User
500mm f/8 Tele-Tessar HFT PQ	6890 6350			
1000mm f/8 Tele-Tessar	38900 34900		4000 3500	
1000mm f/5.6 Mirotar	66000 56600			
75-140 f/4.5 Variogon HFT PQ	8450 7500			
75-150 f/4.5 Variogon HFT		3500 2500		
140-280 f/5.6 Variogon HFT		3700 2800		
140-280 f/5.6 Variogon HFT PQ	8900 8100			
1.4X Teleconverter	1835 1580			
2X Teleconverter	1835 1580		925 695	

Rollei SL66 Accessories

Item	New	Mint	Excellent	User
6x6 12/24 back		400 340	350 280	250 190
6x4.5 16/32 back			450 330	
6x6 120 Back	1495 1270			
6x6 220 Back	1675 1425			
6x4.5 120 Back	1675 1425			
6x4.5 220 Back	1675 1425			
Polaroid back	1480 1250	425 395		
Arca-Swiss Polaroid Back			570 525	
45° Rotating Prism	1290 1095	700 650	450 350	
90° Rotating Prism	1290 1095			
TTL Magnifying Hood			280 250	

Rollei SLX and 6000 Series Accessories

Item	New	Mint	Excellent	User
6x6 120 or 220 back (6002/SLX)	390 330	260 200		
6x4.5 120 or 220 back (6002)	390 330			
6x6 120 or 220 back (6006)	740 630	450 390	385 250	
6x4.5 120 or 220 back (6006)	865 730		400 330	
6x6 120 back (6008)	1500 900	700 600		
6x6 220 back (6008)	1150 1030	850 700		
6x4.5 120 back (6008)	1070 910			
6x4.5 220 back (6008)	1070 910			
70mm Bulk Film Magazine	4390 3730	2450 1900		
70mm Vacuum back		2700 2500		
70mm Vacuum Data back	5500 4680			
Polaroid Magazine (SLX: no dark slide)		250 200	180 120	
Polaroid Magazine (6006/2/SLX: dark slide)	650 550	425 400	350	
Polaroid Magazine (6008)	900 770			
Film Insert (6006/2/SLX)	90 75	50 40		
45° Rotating Prism (6006/2/SLX)	1250 1170	925 770	690 550	
90° Rotating Prism (6006/2/SLX)	1250 1170		650 520	
Magnifying Hood (6006/2/SLX)	550 400	290 220	250 200	
W/L Hood (6006/2/SLX)	160 140			
Pistol Grip (latest)	295 250	190 145	160 130	
Pistol Grip (SLX)			100 75	
Nicad Battery	175 150			
ME-1 Multi-Exp Control Unit (6006/2/SLX)	1290 1100		450 300	
Compendium Shade (Bay VI)	650 550	475	280 250	
9mm Ext Tube	500 425	260 240	250 200	
17mm Ext Tube	570 485	295 240	250 200	
34mm Ext Tube	650 550	325 290	280 225	
68mm Ext Tube	690 585	400 295		
Ext Bellows	1430 1430			
Tripod Quick Rel	125 125			
Auto Bellows	600 600			

Miscellaneous Medium Format Cameras

MEDIUM FORMAT

The point of this section is to provide listings for medium format cameras whose company isn't in business anymore, or that are somewhat obscure, or that are just plain old -- but cameras that a lot of folks still use and love. Invariably, I'll be leaving out somebody's favorite, since so many good medium format cameras have been made over the years. These are the ones I know about, either through personal use or through testimonials from those whose views I can rely upon. I'd be interested in hearing from you if I've made some obvious, unconscionable omissions.

Exakta 66 / Practisix / Pentacon 6 / Kiev 6

While the evolution of these cameras can be traced back better than fifty years, it's a twisted path to follow involving war and the rise and fall of nations and political systems. Such a convoluted history is quite beyond the scope of this book. Thus, we will concentrate instead on a more important subject to the practicing photographer: functionality. In this respect, the following models are quite capable picture takers: rugged, no-frills cameras that share a common lens mount and accept an assortment of excellent lenses.

The **Exakta 66 Model 1** is a large, 35mm-SLR-looking thing with absolutely no bells or whistles. Basically, what you're buying is a light tight box with mechanical shutter speeds and either a prism or waist level finder that will couple to an array of top-notch Schneider optics and render 6x6 exposures on 120 film. The mechanical, horizontal, cloth focal plane shutter provides speeds from 1 second to 1/1000, plus B. X sync occurs at 1/30. A TTL meter prism was made for the Model 1, but it will not fit the Model 2. The TTL meter prism finder for the Model 2 is not available as this is being written.

Of the four marques listed, the **Exakta 66 Model 2** is the only one still in production. The differences between it and the Model 1 are few, but significant. The Model 2 has a larger viewfinder (showing about 85% of the actual image area), a brighter viewing screen, an improved back catch and a redesigned film advance lever.

The **Practisix** and **Pentacon 6** are basically the same camera—the Pentacon 6 being the later model. Both have the same basic features found on the Exakta 66 Model 1; in fact the Pentacon 6 was the immediate predecessor of the Exakta 66.

The **Kiev 6** was produced in Ukraine, but was based on the Praktisix / Pentacon 6 design. The Kiev also shares similar features to these other models.

Exakta 66 / Practisix / Pentacon 6 / Kiev 6

Item	New		Mint		Excellent		User
Exakta 66 Mod. 1, W/L			775	650	575		
Exakta 66 Mod. 1, W/L, 80/2.8			1095	880			
Exakta 66 Mod. 2, W/L	1250	925					
Exakta 66 Mod. 2, W/L, 80/2.8	1400	1150					
Kiev 6, W/L					295	200	
Kiev 6, W/L, 80/2.8					430	340	
Pentacon 6 / Praktisix, W/L, 80/2.8					250	200	
Pentacon 6 / Praktisix, Prism, 80/2.8					375	250	
30mm f/4.5			600	500			
50mm f/4 Flectogon					750	250	
60mm f/3.5 Schneider	1695	1580					
65mm f/3.5 Kiev					250	200	
80mm f/2.8 Biometar					165	80	
80mm f/2.8 Schneider	850	775			600		
120mm f/2.8 Biometar					225	150	
150mm f/4 Schneider	1675	1595					
180mm f/2.8 Auto Sonnar					350	250	
250mm f/5.6 Schneider	1975	1850					
300mm f/4 Preset					120	80	
300mm f/4 Zeiss					380	250	
500mm f/5.6					775	600	
75-150 Schneider	4395	4050					
140-280 Schneider	4550	4150					
Exakta 66 Prism (Mod 1/Praktisix/Pentacon)			400	350			
Exakta 66 Prism (Mod 2)	650	500					
Exakta 66 TTL Prism (Mod. 1)	1295	1050					
(Mod 1/Praktisix/Pentacon)	800	650					
Pentacon/Praktisix Prism (fits Exakta Mod 1)					90	60	
Pentacon/Praktisix Meter Prism (fits Exakta Mod 1)					150	100	
Waist Level Finder					45	30	
Waist Level Finder (Hi-Magnification)					95	70	
Auto Bellows					250	150	
Auto Extension Tube Set					80	50	

MISCELLANEOUS

KIEV 88 / SALYUT

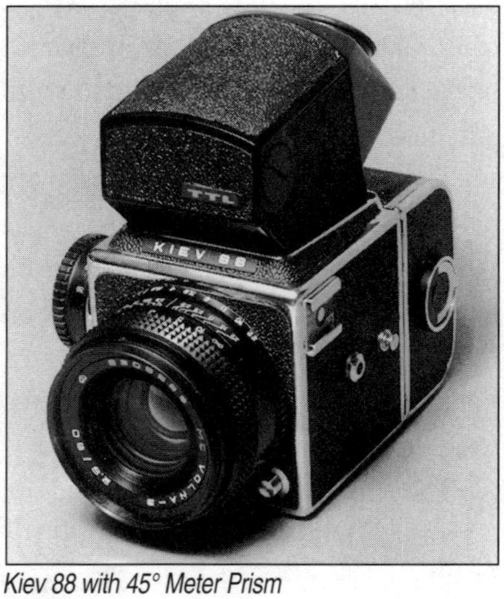

Kiev 88 with 45° Meter Prism

No, the Kiev is not a Soviet or Russian made camera (not anymore, at least). It's made in Ukraine and, with the Cold War thawed to room temperature and the various former Soviet republics being left to fend for themselves, it is no wonder, one would think, that a solid medium-format SLR like the Kiev with its great low price should become more common in the West. Older Kievs are sometimes found under other brand names, at least one being in Cyrillic — the Salyut.

The Kiev is a mechanical, square-format SLR — a very close copy of the venerable Hasselblad 1000F. It has a metal focal-plane shutter, interchangeable lenses, finders and backs. The lenses, finders and backs will interchange with those designed for the 1000F. Unlike the Hasselblad, no accessory contact shoe is required for flash photography; the Kiev uses a standard PC connector. Shutter speeds range from 1 second to 1/1000, plus B, with X sync at 1/60. The Kiev optics are reported to be excellent and represent an outstanding value.

The basic Kiev outfit, until recently, came with a body, an 80mm f/2.8 lens, *two* 12-exposure backs and a leather carrying case. Because of the various and sundry means by which these cameras were exported, however, don't expect to be able to find this same configuration when searching for an outfit. The current Kiev outfit, as supplied by the factory for export, consists of a Kiev 88 body, a 12 exposure back, a Polaroid back, an 80mm f/2.8 Volna lens, a lens hood, two filters, a strap, cable release and a case.

Kiev 88 / Salyut

Item	New	Mint	Excellent	User
Kiev 88 Body	400 .. 300			
Kiev 88 Outfit	700 .. 600	550 .. 450	395 .. 350	
30mm f/3.5 Zodiak	870 .. 695	600 .. 500	475 .. 370	
45mm f/3.5 Mir	600 .. 475		325 .. 250	
65mm f/3.5 Mir	540 .. 395		295 .. 220	
80mm f/2.8 Volna (included in outfit)			150 .. 100	
120mm f/2.8 Vega	500 .. 395	295 .. 250	250 .. 200	
150mm f/2.8 Kaleinar	540 .. 450	400 .. 340	320 .. 250	
250mm f/3.5 Jupiter	620 .. 495		300 .. 245	
300mm f/4.5			420 .. 350	
2x Teleconverter	220 .. 150	140 .. 120		
45° Prism	395 .. 285	250 .. 200	200 .. 125	
45° Meter Prism	540 .. 395		250 .. 175	
90° Prism	470 .. 350	275 .. 240		
120 Back	250 .. 195	90 .. 70		
6x4.5cm Back	300 .. 230			
Polaroid Back	300 .. 200			
NPC Polaroid Back	280 .. 220			
Pistol Grip	80 .. 60			
Waist-level Finder	170 .. 140			

KONI OMEGA

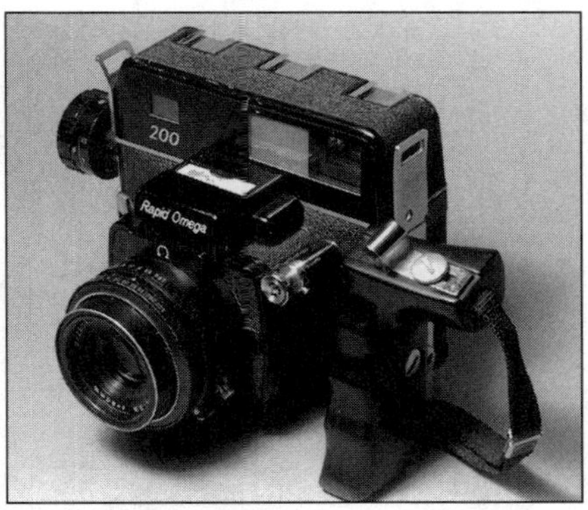

Koni Rapid Omega 200

The different Koni Omega models all bear strong resemblance to the Graflex XL and the Mamiya Universal Press: they are boxy rangefinder cameras that take interchangeable lenses and backs. The optics for these cameras are first rate.

The Koni Omega M and Rapid Omega 100 take interchangeable film holders. The Rapid Omega 200 takes interchangeable film magazines, to which the film holders are attached.

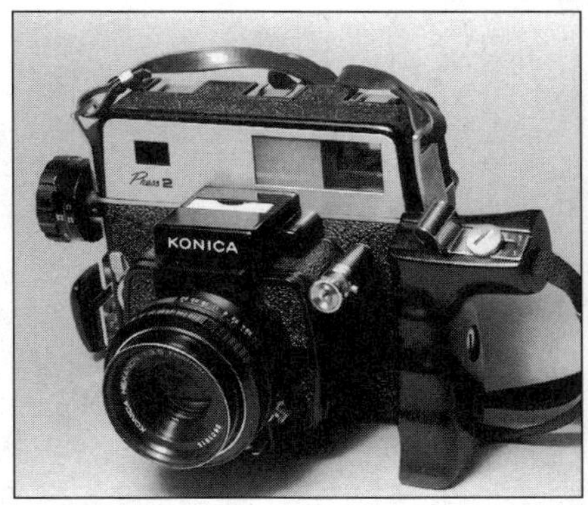

Konica Press 2

Koni Omega

Item	Mint	Excellent	User
Konica Press 2, 90/3.5, 120 back		400 .. 325	
Omega M, 120 Back, Grip		250 .. 185	
Omega M, 90/3.5, 120 Back		350 .. 250	
Rapid Omega 100 120 Back		150 .. 100	
Rapid Omega 100 90/3.5, 120 Back		260 .. 200	
Rapid Omega 200 120 Back		250 .. 185	
Rapid Omega 200 90/3.5, 120 Back		320 .. 200	190 .. 150
58mm f/5.6 w/finder		310 .. 220	
60mm f/5.6 w/finder		260 .. 170	
90mm f/3.5		100 .. 80	
135mm f/3.5		200 .. 150	
180mm f/4.5	330 .. 280	260 .. 220	
120 or 220 Film Holder		70 .. 55	
120 or 220 Magazine		100 .. 65	

Kowa

Although Kowa has been out of business for several years, a lot of loyal Kowa users are still around. The Kowa Super 66 is the model Kowa aficionados prefer. It has interchangeable lenses, finders and backs. The Kowa 6 takes the same lenses and finders, but film is loaded the same as in a TLR—hence no interchangeable backs. Both cameras have multiple-exposure capability and will take either 120 or 220 film.

Kowa lenses have depth-of-field preview levers, self-timers and mechanical leaf shutters, which provide shutter speeds from 1 second to 1/500, plus B, with M and X sync at all speeds. Finders made for the cameras are the standard waist level finder, a horizontal prism finder, a 45°meter prism and a chimney-style meter finder. Both metered finders have CdS cells to provide TTL metering.

Kowa

Item	Mint	Excellent	User
Kowa 6, W/L, 85/2.8		325 250	
Kowa Super 66, W/L, 12/24, 85/2.8		480 350	
35mm f/4.5		650 550	
40mm f/4		500 425	
55mm f/3.5		280 200	
85mm f/2.8		125 80	
110mm f/5.6 Macro		380 290	
150mm f/3.5		295 250	
200mm f/4.5		375 250	
250mm f/5.6		350 260	
2X Teleconverter		225 150	
Extension Tube T1, T2 or T3		125 75	
Meter Finder		250 175	
Meter Prism		350 250	
45° Prism		180 125	
90° Prism		200 140	
Sports Finder		40 25	
120 Back		80 60	
12/24 Back		180 140	
Polaroid Back		225 175	
L Grip		50 30	
Pistol Grip		40 25	

Plaubel Makina

Plaubel has been producing cameras since the early 1900's. But the image that most frequently comes to mind for a photographer, as opposed to a collector, is that of the lens-shutter medium format rangefinders Plaubel has produced since the mid-1970's. Undoubtedly, the Plaubel Makina 67 is the camera that gave Fuji the inspiration for its rangefinder cameras. Importation of these cameras into the U.S. ceased a few years ago, but recently the 69W Pro-Shift model has reappeared. All are highly sought after, and clean examples are pricey.

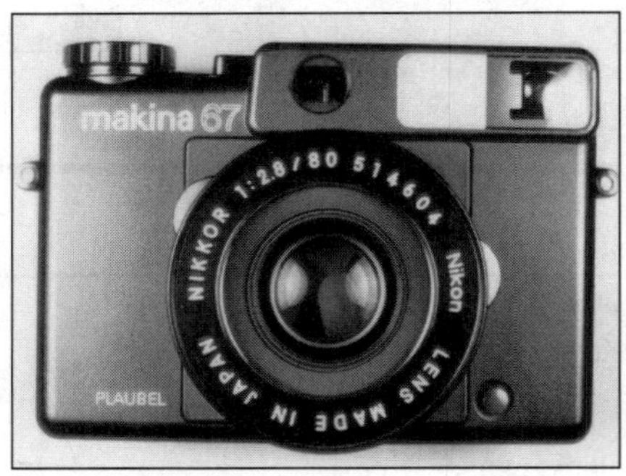

Plaubel Makina 67

Plaubel Makina

Camera	New	Mint	Excellent	User
Plaubel Makina 67 (80mm f/3.5 Nikkor)		1695 1290	1295 1050	
Plaubel Makina 67W (55mm f/4 Nikkor)			1450 1195	
Plaubel Makina 69W Pro-Shift *47mm f/5.6 Schneider Super Angulon*	3600 3300		2800 2400	

YASHICA MEDIUM FORMAT TLRS

Yashica's Medium Format TLRs have long been regarded as providing some of the most economical avenues available to enter medium format photography. The optics, especially those found in the more recent models, are quite sharp with good color and contrast. The 124G has been a popular seller on the used market ever since it was discontinued in 1988.

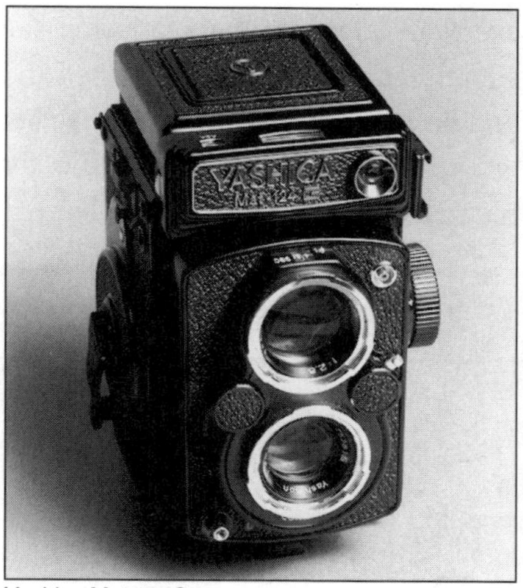

Yashica Mat 124G

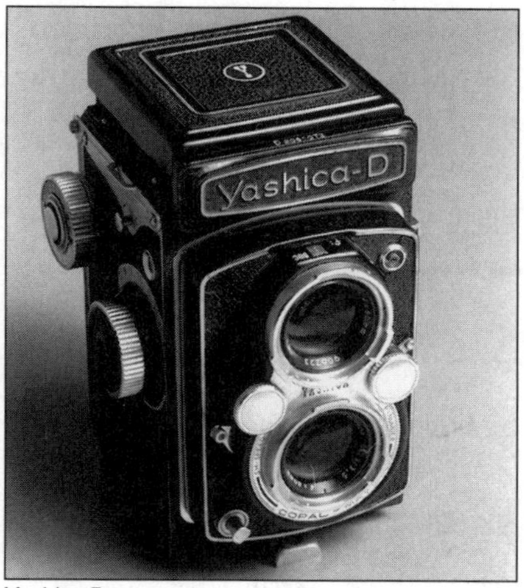

Yashica D

Yashica Medium Format TLRs

Camera	Mint	Excellent	User
Yashica 24 (220 film only)		160 .. 150	
Yashica 635 (120/35mm)		125 .. 80	
Yashica A		85 .. 50	
Yashica C		80 .. 65	
Yashica D		75 .. 50	
Yashica LM		95 .. 60	
Yashica Mat		120 .. 80	
Yashica Mat 124		210 .. 150	
Yashica Mat 124G	300 .. 260	240 .. 160	

ZEISS SUPER IKONTA

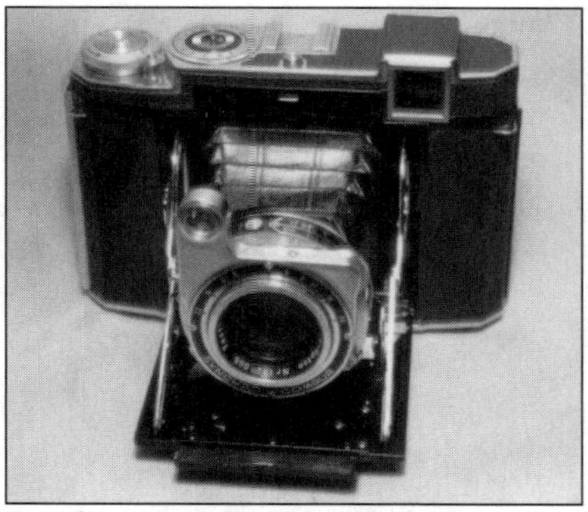
Zeiss Super Ikonta B with Synchro-Compur shutter

Although Zeiss has made many great cameras over the past several decades, this listing is confined to the Super Ikonta models only, mostly because they are such fine user cameras. When folded, most models are quite compact, easily fitting into a coat pocket. The lenses are superb in sharpness, color and contrast.

All Super Ikontas are folding-bed, medium-format, rangefinder cameras. They were produced from 1934 to about 1970 in six principle variations: the A, B, C, D, III and IV. Super Ikontas exist in a variety of film format sizes, from 6cm x 4.5cm to 6cm x 9cm and each model exists in several sub-variations. The Super Ikonta A, the smallest of the family, is the sole 6cm x 4.5cm model. The Super Ikonta C is the 6cm x 9cm model. The Super Ikonta B is a 6cm x 6cm model, as are the Super Ikonta BX, III and IV. These four cameras differ in the following areas: The BX differs from the B in that it has an uncoupled selenium exposure meter built in to the top plate. The III is essentially a late B with a redesigned rangefinder. The IV resembles the III, but has a built-in selenium meter and uses the EVS system for cross-coupling shutter speeds and apertures. The model D was made for now-obsolete film and is not included in the following listings.

As was stated previously, within each model classification variations exist. Rather than go into deep detail, only the distinctions shown in the following listings will be addressed. The model number (e.g., 532/16) can be found somewhere on the camera body, usually on the back. This is often the only indication on the camera as to which specific model it is.

The Compur Rapid is an earlier shutter style than the Synchro Compur. Some Compur Rapids have flash sync. All Synchro Compurs do. Early model Super Ikontas usually have uncoated lenses, while the later models' lenses are coated.

Because Super Ikontas are highly collectible, these variations and others, when combined with a camera's condition, can greatly affect price. Examples in mint or near-mint condition are much more expensive than those in user condition now, because overseas collectors have depleted the supplies of clean examples in the U.S., and because many domestic collectors are still willing to pay top dollar for them. Even examples in clean, but not mint condition can be subject to more price volatility than other makes of cameras. Thus, the following prices will be more useful as guidelines, and should be interpreted as such.

Zeiss Super Ikonta

Camera	Mint	Excellent	User
Super Ikonta A (530 w/Compur Rapid, uncoated)		200	150
Super Ikonta A (530 w/Compur Rapid, coated)		400	250
Super Ikonta A (531 w/Synchro-Compur, coated)		650	500
Super Ikonta B (532/16 w/Compur Rapid, uncoated)		250	150
Super Ikonta B (532/16 w/Compur Rapid, coated)		400	300
Super Ikonta B (532/16 w/Synchro-Compur, coated)		600	400
Super Ikonta BX (532/16 w/Compur Rapid, uncoated)		200	150
Super Ikonta BX (532/16 w/Compur Rapid, coated)		400	300
Super Ikonta BX (532/16 w/Synchro Compur, coated)		600	400
Super Ikonta C (531/2 w/Compur Rapid, uncoated)		200	150
Super Ikonta C (531/2 w/Compur Rapid, coated)		400	280
Super Ikonta C (531/2 w/Synchro-Compur, coated)		700	550
Super Ikonta III		550	350
Super Ikonta IV		550	350

MISCELLANEOUS

Large Format Cameras & Equipment

Large format cameras have been around as long as the art of photography has — over one-hundred-fifty years. Many models still seeing frequent use date back almost that long. This longevity can be attributed to one basic trait: the simple elegance of a large format camera's design. This attribute can be deceptive, however, because it allows the photographer an extraordinary amount of freedom to manipulate ordinary reality and to transform it into the image his mind's eye sees. The dichotomy to large format photography is this: the tools are simple and straightforward, yet flexible and exceedingly complex in their capabilities. In the hands of an expert, these simple, flexible tools are exploited to their fullest and render images that would not be possible with any other film format.

Because of the underlying complexity of large format, it will be assumed in this next section that the reader already has a good understanding of large format photography and has more than a casual familiarity with many of the cameras and lenses available. The explanatory text prefacing each manufacturer's products will be accordingly brief.

If you're just starting out with large format and are planning to use this section as a reference to help you formulate an equipment list, but are not yet familiar with all the format has to offer, follow the advice given by most large format users: start out with a modestly-priced 4x5 outfit. Make sure the camera is well made and in good repair, and buy the best lenses you can afford.

And don't sell your 35mm stuff just yet. Let's face it, large format is not for everybody. After the newness has worn off, you may decide that all the hassle involved in taking a photograph just isn't worth it. That's fine. That's why medium format and 35mm cameras exist. But, you're better off finding out your true interests before you sink large sums of money into an outfit than after the fact. On the other hand, you may discover that you've found your artistic tool at last—that large format was everything you hoped it would be, and more. If the latter case sounds like you, then welcome to the small, select family of dedicated large-format users.

Large Format Cameras

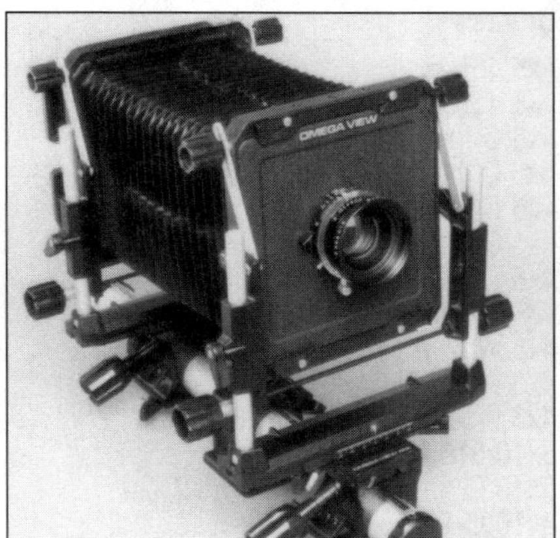

Omega 4x5 monorail view camera

The following prices are for camera bodies without lenses, optional backs or film holders.

Agfa/Ansco

Agfa and Ansco joined forces in the late 1920's and marketed a series of capable view cameras up until the mid-1940's. The prices are for Agfa/Ansco models, but should not differ substantially from prices for cameras made before the merger.

Camera	Mint	Excellent	User
4x5 View			
5x7 Commercial Field		400 .. 300	
5x7 Flat Bed View			
5x7 Portrait View		300 .. 200	
8x10 View	1200	345	
8x10 View (Cherrywood)		825	
8x10 Commercial Field		650 .. 550	
8x10 Flat Bed Universal View	800	600	

Burke & James

Burke & James large format cameras have long been regarded as large-format workhorses. They remain popular among amateurs and professionals alike for their sturdiness, reliability and relatively low cost.

Camera	Mint	Excellent	User
4x5 Commercial Field	475 .. 400	350 .. 250	225 .. 150
4x5 monorail (Grover/Orbit/Saturn)		325 .. 250	175
4x5 View	475	295	
5x7 Commercial Field		350 .. 250	170
5x7 monorail (Grover/Orbit/Saturn)		330 .. 250	130
5x7 View		350	
8x10 Commercial Field		675 .. 550	395 .. 325
8x10 monorail (Grover/Orbit/Saturn)		525	

Busch

Camera	Mint	Excellent	User
4x5 Pressman w/lens		250 .. 150	

Calumet

Camera	Mint	Excellent	User
4x5 45N	450 .. 375	380 .. 330	295 .. 250
4x5 45NX	550 .. 500	480 .. 400	
4x5 C (gray)		250 .. 150	
4x5 C (black)	400 .. 350	325 .. 275	
4x5 CC-400		330 .. 280	195 .. 150
4x5 CC-401		350 .. 300	
4x5 CC-402		350 .. 300	
4X5 CC-403		275 .. 275	
4x5 Wide Angle		350 .. 250	
4x5 Wood Field		350 .. 300	
4x5 Wood Field XM			
8x10 810 N		895	
8x10 C		430 .. 320	250 .. 190
8x10 C-1		750 .. 650	
8x10 C-2 (green)		925 .. 850	
8x10 M (black)		695 .. 600	

LARGE FORMAT

Cambo

Camera	Mint		Excellent		User	
4x5	300	245	250	220	190	170
4x5 45N			330	300		
4x5 45NX	600	550	490	420		
4x5 45SR			690			
4x5 45SRX						
4x5 Legend PC	1550	850	750			
4x5 SC	400	350	340	305		
4x5 SC-II	490	450	470	350		
4x5 SC-II RS						
4x5 SCX			810			
4x5 Pro						
8x10			1270	750		
8x10 810SRX						
8x10 Legend			1500	1250		
8x10 SC			895			
8x10 SC-II			1095	895		
8x10 SCX			1595	1195		
Cambo Wide 75	1750					
Cambo Wide 650	2255					

Canham

Camera	New	Mint	Excellent	User
4X5	2500			
4x10 Panorama	2990			
5x7	2500			
8x10	3500			

Conley

Camera	New	Mint		Excellent		User
8x10 w/5x7 Reducing Back				550	450	

Deardorff

Without question, the most revered name in American-made view cameras is Deardorff. Known world-wide for their excellence of design and craftsmanship, and for their ability to stand up to hard use, Deardorff cameras continue to be some of the most highly sought-after large format cameras available anywhere, for any price. The only models currently available new are the 8x10 and 11x14 Field.

Camera	New	Mint		Excellent		User	
4x5 Baby Deardorff				1550	1395		
4x5 Original Style				1095	600		
4x5 Special (front swings)		2250	1950	2175	1695		
5x7 Original Style				1050	620		
5x7 Later Model (front swings)				1895	1575		
8x10 Original Style				1850	1400		
8x10 Later Model (front swings)		2495	2290	2100	1450	1400	1250
8x10 New Model	2800	2495	2000	1895			
8x10 Commercial				995	700		
11x14 Field	3795						

LARGE FORMAT

Gandolfi

Gandolfi cameras are not as well known in the U.S. as they are in Europe — Great Britain in particular. The Gandolfi family, based in London, has produced a large variety of high-quality large format cameras for over one hundred years, but the ones most often seen as user cameras are the post-war 4x5 and 8x10 models (listed).

Camera	New	Mint	Excellent	User
4x5 Field		1295 .. 850		
8x10 Field		1750 .. 1395		

Gowland

Peter Gowland made a name for himself back in the 1960's and 1970's as a glamour photographer and is still active in the field. He's expanded his business to include a unique array of specialized large-format equipment. Most of the cameras he offers are listed below.

Camera	New	Mint	Excellent	User
Pocket View 4x5 (vert/horiz)	495			370
Pocket View 5x7	950			
Pocket View 8x10	795			
Pocket View 8x10 (vert/horiz)	950			
Aerial-Scenic Cameras:				
4x5 Fixed Focus	595			
4x5 Variable Focus	695			
4x5 Interchangeable Lenses	795			
5x7 Variable Focus	695			
8x10 Variable Focus	895			
Gowlandflex Cameras (large-format twin-lens reflex):				
4x5 (90-210)	795			
4x5 (180-250)	995			
4x5 (300)	1055			
5x7 (240-300)	1095			
8x10 (360-500)	3500			

Graflex

Only the monorail Graflexes, the Graphic View and the Graphic View II are listed below. See the Graflex chapter for more information on Graflex and the folding-bed Graphic cameras.

Camera	Mint	Excellent	User
Graphic View		280 .. 225	190 .. 130
Graphic View II		400 .. 270	250 .. 170

Hoffman

Camera	New	Mint	Excellent	User
4x5 Master View	2395			
5x7 Master View	2395			
8x10 Master View	3495			

Horseman

Camera	New	Mint	Excellent	User
450	1830	1350	1000 880	
450B	1250 1050			
450EM		1370		
450EMB	1675	1475 1400	1370 1285	
45FA	2895 2350			
810N	3230	2300		
ER-1	2100			
L 45 EX	1600	1275 1000		
L 810		2000		
LB	2250 2045			
LB 4X5	1770			
LS 4X5	2715			
LM	2770 2165			
LMC	2800 2650			
LMX	3870			
LMX-C	4760			
LS	3500 3150			
LX	3750 3100			
LX-C	4800 4285			
VH	2450 2350			
VHR	3550 3185		1900 1250	

Ikeda

Camera	New	Mint	Excellent	User
4x5 Field			275 250	
5x7 Field			450 350	

Iston (Chinese)

Camera	New	Mint	Excellent	User
4x5 WF45 Special	500			

Kodak

These old Kodaks have been around a long time and, judging by their longevity and steady popularity, they'll be around for a while longer. Of the following cameras, the 8x10 2D is by far the most popular.

Camera	Mint	Excellent	User
5x7 2D		350 250	
8x10 Century		500 400	
8x10 Commercial		615 490	
8x10 2D	650 550	400 300	330 225
8x10 Master		920 695	

Korona (Gundlach)

Camera	Mint	Excellent	User
4x5		260 195	
5x7		270 190	
7x17 Panoramic View		895 695	
8x10 View		500 350	
8x20 Panoramic View			700 600
12x20 Panoramic View		2000 1600	

Nagaoka

Camera	New	Mint	Excellent	User
4x5 Field			400 350	

New Vue (Newton Photo Products)

Camera	New	Mint	Excellent	User
4x5 New Vue bi-rail			225 175	

Omega (Toyo)

Camera	New	Mint	Excellent	User
45C			550 450	
45D		450 375	355 310	260 220
45E		500 450	425 330	290 250
45F		585 495	475 385	
45G		710 580		
450			330 250	

Osaka

Camera	New	Mint	Excellent	User
4x5 Field	650 585			
8x10 Field	1750 1625	1300 900	850 690	

Rajah (Protech)

Camera	New	Mint	Excellent	User
4x5 Wood Field	350 295			
5x7 Wood Field			350 300	
8x10 Wood Field	500 400			

Sinar

Camera	New	Mint	Excellent	User
4x5 A1	850		795 700	
4x5 A1 Image Kit (150mm Lens)	1795			
4x5 F1 Image Kit (210mm Lens)	1995			
4x5 Alpina		625	495 430	
4x5 C			1750 1650	
4x5 C Expert Kit		2995		
4x5 F		1050 970	900 730	
4x5 F+		950	800 650	
4x5 F1	1395	1100		
4x5 F1 Image Kit (150mm Lens)	2650			
4x5 F1 Image Kit (210mm Lens)	2895			
4x5 F2	1990		1675 1450	
4x5 F2 Image Kit (150mm Lens)	3095	2450 1975		
4x5 F2 Image Kit (210mm Lens)	3395			
4x5 Norma			1950 1100	
4x5 P			2880 2150	
4x5 P Expert Kit			5750 4800	

Sinar

Camera	New		Mint		Excellent		User
4x5 P2	6895	4980			4870	4495	
4x5 P2 Expert Kit	10450	7750					
4x5 P2 Pro Kit	11850	9295					
5x7 P			3300	2800			
8x10					2195	1750	
8x10 C			2500				
8x10 F					2450	1800	
8x10 F1	3575	2750	2500		1950		
8x10 F2					4140	3500	
8x10 P			6200	5700	4000	2450	2150
8x10 P2	10190	7590	7200	6500			
8x10 P2 Expert Kit	13765	10750					
8x10 P2 Pro Kit	15650	13830					

Tachihara

Camera	New		Mint		Excellent		User
4x5 Field			500	450			
8x10 Field			1200	1050	900	750	

Toyo

Camera	New		Mint		Excellent		User
4x5 45A Field			1250	1100	1010	880	
4x5 45A II Field		1500					
4x5 45AR Field					950	730	
4x5 45C		950	650	545			
4x5 45D	620	530	400	350	350	300	
4x5 45E					295	250	
4x5 45F					565	475	
4x5 45G			1450	995	950	845	
4x5 45GB		1500					
4x5 45GX		2900					
4x5 Robos		3175	2900	2700	2650		
8x10 810G	3850	3695	2895	2615	2425	1900	
8x10 810GB		2995					
8x10 810M Field	3325	2700			2395	1900	
VX-125		5700					

Wisner

Wisner cameras are widely regarded as the finest wooden view cameras made. Models with "(aluminum/brass)" following their name use brass-plated aluminum hardware to save weight. The Panorama cameras are built to order.

Camera	New		Mint		Excellent		User
4x5 Technical Field		1795			1475		
4x5 S Traditional		1400					
4x10 Panorama		2195					
5x7 Classic Convertible			1750	1400			
5x7 Technical Field		2675					
8x10 Classic Convertible			2150	1800			
8x10 Expedition		4195					
8x10 Technical Field		3495					
8x10 Tech (aluminum/brass)		3400					
8x10 Traditional S Field		2395					
8x20 Panorama		4000					
11x14 Technical Field		4495					
11x14 Tech (aluminum/brass)		4400					
12x20 Panorama		5000					

LARGE FORMAT

Wista

Camera	New		Mint		Excellent		User	
4x5 45 DX Field (Cherrywood)	1040	990	850	780	750	650		
4x5 45 DX Field (Rosewood)	1140	1065						
4x5 45 DX Field (Ebony)	1645	1550						
4x5 45 DX II (Cherrywood)	980	1060						
4x5 45 DX II (Cherrywood) w/shift		1120						
4x5 45 DX II (Rosewood)	1080	1400						
4x5 45 DX II (Rosewood) w/shift		1430						
4x5 45 DX III-W (Rosewood)		1650						
4x5 M-450	1200	1145						
4x5 Tech 45 RF		2750			1900	1560		
4x5 Tech 45 SP	1950	1830			1290	900		
4x5 Tech 45 VX		1800	1095	945				
8x10 Field Double (26")	1750	1630						
8x10 Field Triple (30")	2575	2400	2050	1900				
8x10 M Wood Field	1270							
8x10 Wood Field (Early)	950							

Zone VI

Camera	New		Mint		Excellent		User	
4x5 Field	795		650	525				
4x5 Field Classic	1195		1050	1000	900	625		
4x5 Walnut.	1335	1095						
4x5 Mahogany	995							
8x10 Field	1995		1740	1600	1670	1450		
Wood Field (Early)	1695	1250						
Wood Field (Current Style)	1675							

Large Format Lenses

Many of the lens makers who have produced lenses for the larger film formats recorded their lenses' focal lengths in either inches or millimeters and, in a few cases, both. Nowadays, most everybody uses millimeters.

However, some older lenses indicate only the format they cover (Bausch & Lomb 8x10 Protar, for example). Thus, in order to make it as easy as possible for you to locate a particular optic when a manufacturer has used both inches and millimeters to measure a lens' focal length, lenses are listed in a combined format [e.g.: (Goerz) 210mm (8¼") f/6.8 Gold Dot Dagor]. If a lens was made with its focal length marked in inches only, it will be found at the end of the manufacturer's listing.

Another method of grouping the lenses was used in addition to the above. Where applicable, each manufacturer's lenses in shutters are listed first, followed by lenses in barrels. In the case of lenses in shutters, the prices take into account shutters of good quality that are also in good mechanical condition.

Bausch & Lomb Lenses in Shutters

Lens	Mint	Excellent	User
72mm B&L Macro Tessar		125	
88mm f/6.8 Wide Angle	410	250	115
158mm B&L Macro Tessar		140	
185mm f/6.3 B&L Tessar			100
190mm f/4.5 B&L Tessar		160	
210mm f/4.5 B&L Tessar			140
250mm f/4.5 B&L Zeiss Tessar		190	
4 7/16" f/18 Protar Series V		295	250
5"/8 3/4" B&L Zeiss Protar Series VII		450	
6" f/4.5 B&L Zeiss Tessar Series Ic			90
8"/16" B&L Convertible		300	
11" f/4.5 B&L Zeiss Tessar Series Ic			130
12"/18"/36" B&L Triple Convertible		270	
13"/16" B&L Protar Convertible	495		
19" f/4 Portrait		300	
20" f/5.6 B&L Anastigmat		675	
8x10 f/12.5 B&L Series IV		200	

Bausch & Lomb Lenses in Barrels

Lens	Mint	Excellent	User
100mm f/2.3 B&L Anastigmat			70
102mm f/18 B&L Zeiss Protar V		70	
210mm f/4.5 B&L Tessar		100	
260mm f/4.5 B&L (Zeiss) Tessar (coated)	250	95	
300mm f/4.5 B&L Zeiss Tessar		100	
6½"/8" f/18 B&L Zeiss Protar Series V		150	
8"/16" B&L Series VII		300	
9"/14"/19" B&L Zeiss Convertible Anastigmat		300	
10" f/6.3 B&L Tessar IIc		95	
13" f/10 B&L Process Anastigmat		150	
16" f/10 B&L Process Anastigmat		195	
19" B&L APO Tessar		200	
5x7 f/18 B&L Zeiss Protar Series V		150	125
5x8 B&L Tessar Ic	95		
8x10 f/18 B&L Protar Series V		150	
8x10 f/12.5 B&L Zeiss Protar Series IV		185	
11x14 f/18 B&L Zeiss Protar Series V		225	
12x15 B&L Protar Series IV		375	
32x36 B&L Zeiss APO Tessar Series VIII	795		

LARGE FORMAT

Calumet

Lens	Mint		Excellent		User
65mm f/4.5 Caltar II					
65mm f/4.5 Caltar II-N MC	695	650			
65mm f/4.5 Caltar Professional	550		400		
75mm f/4.5 Caltar II			365		
75mm f/6.8 Caltar II			230		
75mm f/6.8 Caltar II-N MC			550		
90mm f/4.5 Caltar II-N MC	750				
90mm f/5.6 Caltar Professional MC			660		
90mm f/6.8 Caltar II			355		
90mm f/6.8 Caltar II-N MC	590	485			
90mm f/8 Caltar II	550	395	290		
90mm f/8 Ilex-Calumet			360	250	
90mm f/8 Caltar HR			720		
90mm f/8 Caltar W			360	265	
90mm f/8 Caltar W II			650	600	
135mm f/5.6 Caltar II	380		275		
135mm f/5.6 Caltar II-N MC	250				
150mm f/5.6 Caltar-S			275	240	
150mm f/5.6 Caltar II	225		260		
150mm f/5.6 Caltar II-N	425	320	295	225	
150mm f/5.6 Caltar-S II	380	350	325	280	
150mm f/5.6 Caltar HR	450	295			
165mm f/6.3 Caltar			250	150	
180mm f/5.6 Caltar II			275		
180mm f/5.6 Caltar II-N	590	485	425	300	
210mm f/5.6 Caltar II	375		365		
210mm f/5.6 Caltar II-E			450	325	
210mm f/5.6 Caltar II-N	550	475	475	370	
210mm f/5.6 Caltar-S II	465	435	385	320	
210mm f/5.6 Caltar HR	695	495	445		
210mm f/5.6 Caltar-S			285		
210mm f/5.6 Caltar Professional	400				
210mm f/6.8 Caltar	295				
210mm f/6.8 Caltar II	340	240	360		
210mm f/6.8 Caltar II-E			325	250	
210mm f/6.8 Caltar HR			350		
210mm f/6.8 Caltar-S					
240mm f/5.6 Caltar Professional			450		
240mm f/5.6 Caltar-S II			650	550	
240mm f/5.6 Caltar-S			600		
240mm f/6.8 Caltar Y			440		
300mm f/5.6 Caltar Professional			600		
300mm f/5.6 Caltar II			700	590	
300mm f/5.6 Caltar II-N MC	795		780	700	
300mm f/5.6 Caltar-S II			850	825	600
300mm f/5.6 Caltar HR			700		
305mm (12") f/6.3 Ilex-Calumet			395	300	
355mm f/? Ilex-Calumet			375		
360mm f/6.8 Caltar II			845		
360mm f/6.8 Caltar II-N MC	1160	1050	995	795	
360mm f/6.8 Caltar-S II	1195	900	865		
375mm f/6.3 Ilex-Caltar			600		
8 1/4" f/6.1 Caltar Pro			280		
8 1/2" f/6.3 Caltar			225	170	
8 1/2"/14" f/4.8-10 Caltar-S	350	315	185	165	
10" f/6.3 Ilex-Calumet			280	200	
14 1/2" f/6.3 Ilex-Calumet			570		
14 3/4" f/6.3 Ilex-Calumet			570		460
14 3/4" f/6.3 Caltar Acutar	460	395	475	425	
20" f/7 Ilex-Calumet			575	500	425

Fuji

At the time of this writing, Fuji does not directly distribute its large format lenses in the U.S. A handful of dealers buy direct from Fuji and import the lenses themselves. Del's in Santa Barbara, California has the best advertised inventory.

Lens	New	Mint	Excellent	User
65mm f/5.6 SW EBC	780	675 650		
65mm f/5.6 SWD			725	
65mm f/8 SW			325	
75mm f/5.6 EBC		695	440	
75mm f/5.6 SWD	995	1075 795		
75mm f/8 EBC		440 380		
75mm f/8 SW		385 350	325 265	
90mm f/5.6 SW	1130 870			
90mm f/5.6 SWD		850	790	
90mm f/8 NWS		500		
90mm f/8 SW	660	585 525	450 395	
105mm f/5.6 NWS	465	300	300	
105mm f/5.6 W	350			
105mm f/8 SW	985	800		
125mm f/5.6 NWS	485			
125mm f/5.6 W		830	625	415
135mm f/5.6 NWS	485			
135mm f/5.6 W			295 250	
150mm f/5.6 NWS	465	410 385	360 290	
150mm f/5.6 W		395 275	275 240	
150mm f/6.8			335	
180mm f/4.5			230	
180mm f/5.6 A or AS			225	
180mm f/5.6 W	585			
180mm f/9 AS	750 600			
210mm f/5.6 W		520 425	410 370	
240mm f/9 A or AS	750		475 415	395 350
250mm f/5.6 SF		660 525	495	
250mm f/6.3 NWS			480	
250mm f/6.3 W	955	850 725	685 565	
250mm f/6.7 WS		625	600	
300mm f/5.6 L		740	710 535	
300mm f/5.6 W	1340	945 895	775 650	
300mm f/5.6 SW	1120			
300mm f/8 T	1190			
300mm f/8.5 CS APO	1035			
360mm f/6.3 W		995 925	850	
360mm f/6.3 WS	1725		850	
360mm f/9 A or AS			895 775	
360mm f/10 A or AS		950	750	
400mm f/8 T	1590	900	865	
420mm f/5.6 SF (bbl)		325		
420mm f/8 L			950 750	700 600
450mm f/12.5 CS APO	1185			
600mm f/11.5 CS APO	2295			
600mm f/12 T	2385		1325	

Goerz Lenses

With Goerz lenses, as with most other German-made lenses, the name denotes a lens formula. The following listings have been alphabetized according to lens formula, e.g. Artar or Dagor, even though there may be a prefix to the name that would seem to put it out of alphabetical sequence.

The most widely known and widely used Goerz lenses are the Artars and Dagors. The Artar formula is an APO formula, even though not all Artar lenses will be inscribed "APO Artar". Red Dot Artars are supposedly premium versions of the Artar formula, but the consensus among Goerz cognoscenti is that the Red Dot designation was largely a marketing ploy. This same reasoning largely applies to the Gold Ring and Gold Dot Dagors. In both cases, however, you'll note that the premium versions command higher prices than the standard ones.

Goerz Lenses in Shutters

Lens	New	Mint	Excellent	User
35mm f/8 Wide Angle Dagor			295	
75mm f/9 Dagor			280	
90mm f/6.8 Dagor			650 495	
90mm (3 5/8") f/8 Wide Angle Dagor			375 250	
130mm f/6.8 Dagor Double Anastigmat			300	
150mm f/5.6 Gold Ring Dagor			690	
150mm f/6.3 Dagor			320	
150mm (6") f/6.8 Dagor			550 350	
150mm f/9 Red Dot Artar			400	
150mm f/9 Dagor			675	
165mm f/8 WA Gold Dot Dago	1450			
180mm f/9 Dagor	1800			
180mm f/? American Dagor			325	
190mm (7½") f/4.5 Dagor			275	
203mm (8") f/6.8 Dagor			510 450	
203mm (8") f/6.8 Gold Dagor		750	650	
210mm f/? American Dagor			575	
210mm f/5.6 Dagor Series V			350	
210mm (8¼") f/6.8 Dagor			650 550	
210mm (8¼") f/6.8 Gold Dot Dagor		950 795		
210mm (8¼") f/9 APO Red Dot Artar		500 375	400 325	
240mm (9½") f/6.8 Dagor			400 375	275 230
240mm f/6.8 Gold Dot Dagor				395
240mm (9½") f/6.8 Red Dot Artar			375 310	
240mm f/9 APO Red Dot Artar			575 390	
260mm f/9.5 APO Red Dot Artar			380	
270mm f/6.8 American Dagor			775	300
270mm f/7.7 Berlin Dagor			625 570	
270mm f/9.5 APO Artar			325	
276mm/480mm Pantar Convertible			500	
300mm f/9.5 APO Artar			375	
300mm f/9.5 Red Dot Artar			475	
300mm (30cm) f/6.8 Dagor			325 250	
300mm f/6.8 Gold Dagor			650 495	
305mm (12") f/6.8 Double Anastigmat			140	
305mm (12") f/6.8 Dagor			575 475	
305mm (12") f/9 APO Red Dot Artar		650 550	475 400	
355mm (14") f/8 Gold Dot Dagor		895 795		
355mm (14") f/9 Red Dot Artar		595	475	
360mm f/7.7 American Dagor			1000 850	
360mm f/11 APO Artar			450	
360mm f/11 Red Dot Artar			375	
360mm f/8 Gold Dot Dagor			500	
420mm f/? American Dagor			850	
420mm (16½") f/7.7 Dagor			1250 920	
420mm (16½") f/9.5 APO Red Dot Artar			950 880	700
420mm f/11 Red Dot Artar			850	
420mm f/11 APO Artar			775	
480mm (19") f/11 Red Dot Artar (APO)		975 615		
600mm f/? Red Dot Artar			1750 1500	
3" f/4.5 Hycon			2500 1800	
43/8" f/8 Wide Angle Dagor			795 625	
5" f/4.5 Dogmar			250	
5¼" f/4.5 Dogmar			155	
6" f/6.3 Planigon		775	700	
6" f/6.8 Dagor (uncoated)			250 225	
6" f/9 APO Red Dot Artar			360 280	
6" f/9 Red Dot Artar			350 240	
6¼" f/6.8 Dagor			125	
6½" f/6.8 Dagor			650	
6 ½" f/8 Golden Dagor			1195 1000	
7" f/6.8 Dagor		480	375	
9½" f/9 Red Dot Artar		550		
10¼" f/6.8 APO Red Dot Artar			490 400	

LARGE FORMAT

Goerz Lenses in Shutters

Lens	Mint	Excellent	User
10¾" f/? Dagor			170
12" f/6.8 Golden Dagor		900	
12" f/9 APO Artar		375 325	
14" f/5.5 Celor		190	
14" f/7.7 Dagor		395	
14" f/9 APO Red Dot		425	
30" f/12.5 Red Dot Artar		2000	
42" f/14.5 Red Dot Artar		2050	
47" f/15 APO Artar		350	

Goerz Lenses in Barrels

Most of the Goerz lenses listed here are uncoated. Their prices are pretty good indicators.

Lens	Mint	Excellent	User
90mm f/4.5 Goerz Berlin		85	
210mm f/5.6 Dagor Series V		350	
240mm f/6.8 Dagor		200	
270mm f/9.5 Red Dot Artar		175	
300mm f/9.5 APO Artar		175	
360mm f/11 APO Artar		175	
420mm f/11 APO Artar		125	
480mm f/11 APO Artar		275 175	
480mm (19") f/5.5 Dogmar		300	
600mm f/7.7 Berlin Dagor		430	
875mm f? APO Artar		900	
6¼" f/6.8 Dagor		125	
6.5" f/6.8 Dagor	325		
7½" F/4.5 Dogmar			75
8¼" f/6.8 Dagor		160	
10¼" f/9.5 APO Artar	225 190		
10¼" Dagor		250	
12" f/4.5 Dogmar		125	
12" f/5 Goerz Portrait		250	
12" f/9 APO Red Dot Artar	495	385 285	
12" f/10 Gotar		80	
14" f/5.5 Celor			70
14" f/? Ross Goerz Double Anastigmat		150	
14" f/8 Gotar		200	
14" f/9 APO Artar	335		
14" f/9 Red Dot Artar		425 350	
16½" f/9.5 APO Red Dot Artar			350 280
19" f/5.5 Dogmar		300	
19" f/11 APO Artar		275 200	
19" f/11 Red Dot Artar	625 500	450 315	
24" f/11 APO Artar		625	
24" f/11 APO Red Dot Artar		700	345 280
30" f/12.5 APO Artar	650	625	
35" f/12.5 APO Artar	1250	695	
42" f/14.5 APO Artar	800	750	
47½" f/15 APO Artar		750	

Graflex

Lens	Mint	Excellent	User
90mm f/6.8 Wide Angle Optar		225 160	130
101mm f/4.5 Graflar or Optar		100 60	
135mm f/4.7 Optar		110 80	
162mm f/4.5 Optar	175	165	
202mm (8") f/5.6 Tele-Optar		275 200	
203mm f/7.5 Tele-Optar			250 170
250mm f/5.6 Tele-Optar		250 175	
380mm f/5.6 Tele-Optar		225 195	

LARGE FORMAT

Horseman

Lens		Mint		Excellent		User	
65mm f/7 Super	1100	550		400	285		
75mm f/3.5 Pro		475					
75mm f/5.6 Pro	900	350		230			
75mm f/5.6 VHR		425		380			
90mm f/5.6	890			320			
105mm f/3.5		395	365	325			
105mm f/4.5 Super				445	330		
150mm f/5.6 Super				340	300		
180mm f/5.6 Pro	1000			270	260		
180mm f/5.6 VHR		475					

Ilex

Lens	Mint		Excellent		User	
65mm f/8 Wide Angle Acugon			340	250		
75mm f/1.9 Oscillo-Paragon			65	50		
90mm f/8 Wide Angle	250					
140mm (5½") f/4.5 Paragon Anastigmat			100	80		
162mm f/4.5 Paragon			120			
165mm (6½") f/4.5 Paragon			100			40
165mm f/6.3 Acutar		215	175			
180mm f/4.5 Acutar			175			
180mm/247mm f/4.8 Acugon Convertible			225			
190mm (7½") f/4.5 Paragon	275		225	180		
190mm (7½") f/5.6 Pargon			165			
210mm f/6.3 Acutar		250	215			
215mm (8½") f/4.5 Paragon			270	200		
215mm (8½") f/6.3 Acutar			300	230		
229mm (9") f/5.6 Paragon	100	80				
240mm (9½") f/? Dago-Ilex (uncoated)		250				
250mm f/6.3 Paragon			400			
254mm (10") f/6.3 Acutar			240			
305mm (12") f/4.5 Paragon Anastigmat			400			
305mm f/6.3			400	250		
305mm (12") f/6.8 Ilex Bruning Wide Angle (bbl)	195					
305mm (12") f/9 Ilex Copy Paragon (bbl)				165		
375mm f/6.3 Acutar			500	350		
375mm (14¾") f/6.3 Paragon	595					

Kodak Lenses in Shutters

Lens	Mint		Excellent		User	
80mm f/6.3 Wide Field Ektar			295	200		
100mm f/6.3 Wide Field Ektar			285	270	235	190
101mm f/4.5 Ektar			180	125	70	60
105mm f/3.7 Ektar			140			
107mm f/3.7 Anastigmat			100			
127mm f/4.7 Ektar	195	130	135	85	95	60
135mm f/6.3 Wide Field Ektar			325	245	225	
152mm f/4.5 Ektar			180	150		
178mm (7") Zeiss Kodak Anastigmat			80			
190mm (7½") f/4.5 Ektar	325	240	240	195		
190mm (7½") f/6.3 Ektar	315		350			
190mm (7½") f/6.3 Commercial Ektar			315			
190mm (7½") f/6.3 Wide Field Ektar	435		395	325		
203mm (8") f/7.7 Ektar (coated)		350	325	250	200	175
210mm (8¼") f/6.3 Commercial Ektar			325	275	235	
210mm (8¼") f/6.3 Wide Field Ektar			290			
250mm f/6.3 Wide Field Ektar			750	600	550	

LARGE FORMAT

Kodak Lenses in Shutters

Lens	Mint	Excellent	User
250mm f/6.3 Commercial Ektar		450 400	
300mm f/6.3 Commercial Ektar		650	
360mm f/6.3 Commercial Ektar		575	
360mm f/6.3 Ektar		300	
405mm (14") f/4.5 Portrait		270	
6⅜" f/4.5 Anastigmat #32	175		
8" f/6.3 Commercial Ektar	350		
8½" f/4.5 Anastigmat		195	
8½" f/6.3 Commercial Ektar	650	365 270	250
10" f/6.3 Ektar			
10" f/6.3 Commercial Ektar	550 450	375	300 250
10" f/6.3 Wide Field Ektar	845	745 625	
12" f/4.5 Ektar		395	295
12" f/4.5 Commercial Ektar		460 395	330
12" f/4.8 Portrait Ektar		475 330	
12" f/6.3 Ektar			375 300
12" f/6.3 Commercial Ektar		575 495	390 300
14" f/6.3 Ektar		415	
14" f/6.3 Commercial Ektar	675 595	590 485	450 425

Kodak Lenses in Barrels

Lens	New	Mint	Excellent	User
4⅜" f/1.5 Fluro Ektar			95	
5½" f/4.5 Anastigmat			50	
6⅜" f/4.5 Anastigmat			55 40	
7" f/2.5 Aero Ektar			125 100	
7½" f/4.5 Anastigmat		110 95		
7½" f/4.5 Ektar		120		
10" f/4.5 Anastigmat				90
12" f/10 Copying Ektanon		295		
17" f/10 Copying Ektanon		225		
18½" f/10 Copying Ektanon		225		
18½" f/10 Anastigmat			125 95	
19¾" f/10 Anastigmat			150	
21¼" f/10 Anastigmat			175	

Komura

Lens	New	Mint	Excellent	User
47mm f/6.8 W			245	
75mm f/5.6 Super W			350	
90mm f/5.6		450		
90mm f/6.3 Super W			315 300	
152mm f/2.8			350	
210mm f/6.3 Commercial			225	
300mm f/5			240	
400mm f/8 Komuranon			400	

Nikon

Lens	New	Mint	Excellent	User
65mm f/4 SW	1150 970	900 825		
70mm f/5 Micro-Nikkor			240	
75mm f/4.5 SW	1320 1100			
90mm f/4.5 SW	1420 1190	1050 1000	995 850	
90mm f/8 SW	875 750	675 600		
105mm f5.6 W	565 455	395 350	360 250	

LARGE FORMAT

Nikon

Lens	New		Mint		Excellent		User	
120mm f/5.6 AM-ED Macro	1020	900	840	780	750	640		
120mm f/8 SW	1200	1050	940	875	850	700		
135mm f/5.6 W	675	525	450	400	390	320		
150mm f/5.6 W	650	500	425	375	350	290		
150mm f/8 SW	2165	2000	1745	1650	1580	1300		
180mm f/5.6 W	695	580	500	450	455	350		
200mm f/8 M	680	545	480	425	450	325		
210mm f/5.6 AM-ED Macro	2250	2020			1650	1400		
210mm f/5.6 W	750	600	525	460	495	350		
240mm f/5.6 W	1140	1060	850	725				
270mm f/6.3 ED T	1525	1340						
300mm f/5.6 W	1560	1390	1050	995				
300mm f/9 M	765	630	435		375			
360mm f/6.5 W	1640	1480	1230	1070	1000	800		
360mm f/8 ED T	1900	1695	1500	1420	1375	1100		
360mm f/9 APO			850	700				
Rear Unit 360	550	425						
420mm f/9 APO-Nikkor				850				
450mm f/9 M	1235	1080	850	765	650			
480mm f/9 APO-Nikkor					460			
500mm f/11 ED T	1720	1500						
Rear Unit 500	660	510						
600mm f/9 ED T	2810	2400	2090	1995	1850	1640		
Rear Unit 600	710	560						
610mm f/9 APO-Nikkor			1280	880				
720mm f/16 ED T	2295	1900			1400	1200		
Rear Unit 720	755	625						
800mm f/12 ED T	2945	2640						
Rear Unit 800	775	650						
1200mm f/18 ED T	2995	2700						
Rear Unit 1200	985	830						

Rodenstock

Lens	New		Mint		Excellent		User	
45mm f/5.6 Grandagon	1480	1330						
55mm f/5.6 Grandagon	1625	1410						
58mm f/5.6 Grandagon			475		350	300		
65mm f/4.5 Grandagon-N	1250	1060	895	750	695			
75mm f/4.5 Grandagon-N	1220	1150	1050	975				
75mm f/6.8 Grandagon	795	700	695	625	600	550		
90mm f/4.5 Grandagon-N	1375	1250			880	760		
90mm f/6.8 Grandagon	915	790	675	640	610	550		
90mm f/6.8 Sironar					850			
90mm f/8 WA Geronar					410	360		
90mm f/8 Grandagon					495			
100mm f/5.6 Sironar			350	300				
100mm f/5.6 Sironar-N	475	420	365	320	290	230		
105mm f/5.6 APO Sironar-N	615	465						
115mm f/6.8 Grandagon-N	1495	1345	1200	995	895			
120mm f/5.6 Sironar-N	595	540						
127mm f/4.7 Ysarex			95	80				
135mm f/5.6 Sironar-N	515	445	415	375	360	275		
135mm f/5.6 APO Sironar-N	675	500						
135mm f/5.6 APO Sironar-S ED	780	640						
150mm f/4.5 Ysarex					225	195		
150mm f/5.6 APO-Sironar			900	800				
150mm f/5.6 APO Sironar-N	715	540						
150mm f/5.6 APO Sironar-S ED	795	700						
135mm f/5.6 APO Sironar-W ED	1295	1050						
150mm f/5.6 Sironar-N	565	480	350	460	375	325	300	240
150mm f/6.3 Geronar	345	245	250	225	290			

LARGE FORMAT

Rodenstock

Lens	New	Mint	Excellent	User
150mm f/9 APO-Ronar	820 730	695	500 380	
155mm f/6.8 Grandagon	3135 3025	2450 2000		
180mm f/5.6 Sironar		350	290	
180mm f/5.6 Sironar-N	725 650	600 475	425 365	
180mm f/5.6 APO Sironar-N	840 700			
135mm f/5.6 APO Sironar-S ED	975 840			
200mm f/5.8 Imagon		675 570	600 490	
200mm f/6.8 Grandagon	4725 4555	3800 3400	2900 2400	
210mm f/5.6 APO-Sironar		1425 1250		
210mm f/5.6 APO Sironar-N	900 780			
210mm f/5.6 APO Sironar-S ED	1180 990			
135mm f/5.6 APO Sironar-W ED	1940 1630			
210mm f/5.6 Sironar		450 370		190
210mm f/5.6 Sironar-N	795 690	625 550	475 525	
210mm f/5.6 Macro Sironar-N	1515 1430	935	875	
210mm f/6.3 Ysarex			220	125
210mm f/6.8 Geronar	485 430	350 300	290 250	
240mm f/5.6 Sironar-N	1320 1150	1000 775		
240mm f/5.6 APO Sironar-N	1460 1290			
240mm f/5.6 APO Sironar-S ED	1850 1600			
240mm f/9 APO-Ronar	900 825	750 620	560 350	
250mm f/6.8 Imagon		750 665		
250mm f/8 Imagon			480	
270mm f/5.6 Rotelar		440 350	325 280	
300mm f/5.6 Imagon		650 600	585	500
300mm f/5.6 APO Sironar		2500 2000		
300mm f/5.6 APO Sironar-N	2085 1750			
300mm f/6.8 APO Sironar-S ED	2485 2190			
135mm f/5.6 APO Sironar-W ED	3695 3300			
300mm f/5.6 Sironar-N	1785 1635	1525 1250	1100 995	
300mm f/5.6 Macro Sironar-N	3000 2875		1450	
300mm f/6.8 Imagon			490 400	
300mm f/9 APO-Gerogon		400	215 200	
300mm f/9 APO-Ronar	1080 975	900 820	750 675	
300mm f/9 Geronar	655 600	525 460		
360mm f/5.8 Imagon		500		
360mm f/6.8 Sironar-N	1925 1845	1575 1450	1275	900
360mm f/6.8 APO Sironar-N	2295 2000			
360mm f/9 APO-Gerogon			400	
360mm f/9 APO-Ronar	1520 1400	1250 980	1050 800	
420mm f/5.8 Imagon			750	
420mm f/9 APO-Ronar	1750 1625			
480mm f/8.4 Sironar-N	2780 2520		1595	
480mm f/9 APO-Ronar	1825 1700	1450 1230		
600mm f/9 APO-Ronar			995	

Schneider

Lens	New	Mint	Excellent	User
47mm f/5.6 Super Angulon MC	840 805			
47mm f/5.6 XL Super-Angulon MC	1275			
47mm f/5.6 Super-Angulon		550 445		
47mm f/8 Super-Angulon		325 305		
58mm f/5.6 Super-Angulon MC	1045 940			
58mm f/5.6 XL Super-Angulon MC	1195 1050			
65mm f/5.6 Super-Angulon		650 525	500	
65mm f/5.6 Super-Angulon MC	1195 1050	925 850		530
65mm f/6.8 Angulon		295 250	275 200	
65mm f/8 Super Angulon		475 420	425 325	
72mm f/5.6 XL Super-Angulon MC	1375			

Schneider

Lens	New	Mint	Excellent	User
75mm f/5.6 Super Angulon MC	1395 1200	1095 980	950 800	
75mm f/8 Super-Angulon		550 450	475 375	
80mm f/2.8 Xenotar		450	230 170	
90mm f/5.6 Super-Angulon		890 720	755	
90mm f/5.6 Super-Angulon MC	1290 1125	1050 925	825	
90mm f/5.6 Super-Angulon XT	1575 1420			
90mm f/6.8 Angulon		325 250	275 150	
90mm f/8 Angulon			240 125	
90mm f/8 Super-Angulon		600 525	500 395	345 300
90mm f/8 Super-Angulon MC	910 795	700 600	650 520	375
100mm f/5.6 Symmar Convertible			195	
100mm f/5.6 Symmar S		300	285	
100mm f/5.6 Symmar-S MC		400	270	
100mm f/5.6 APO-Symmar MC	675 580		385	
105mm f/3.5 Xenar			230 150	
105mm f/4.5 Xenar		250 200	165	
120mm f/5.6 Symmar-S			215 175	
120mm f/5.6 APO-Symmar MC	675 580	520 475		
120mm f/5.6 Macro Symmar MC	1100	1000 925		
120mm f/5.6 Super Symmar-HM MC	1100	1000 925	750	
120mm f/6.8 Angulon		650 475	395 245	
120mm f/8 Super-Angulon		795 725	715 650	
120mm f/8 Super-Angulon MC	1395 1265	1180 1045		
127mm f/4.7 Press-Xenar			180 120	
135mm f/3.5 Xenotar			335 250	
135mm f/3.8 Press-Xenar			225 200	185 175
135mm f/4.5 Zecanar			60	
135mm f/4.7 Xenar		200 175	170 125	85 80
135mm f/5.6 Symmar Convertible			300 280	170
135mm f/5.6 Symmar-S			325 245	
135mm f/5.6 Symmar-S MC		355 320	325 260	
135mm f/5.6 APO-Symmar MC	675 580	525 510		
135mm f/8 Repro Claron			540 325	250
150mm f/2.8 Xenotar		595 480	450 300	
150mm f/3.5 Xenar			80	
150mm f/4.5 Xenar		265 200	180 150	
150mm/265mm f/5.6 Symmar Convertible			350 300	275 225
150mm f/5.6 Symmar			300 225	
150mm f/5.6 Symmar-S		395 375	350 300	
150mm f/5.6 Symmar-S MC		395 365	350 290	
150mm f/5.6 Super Symmar-HM MC	1795 1575	1420 1300	1250 925	
150mm f/5.6 APO-Symmar MC	645 580	515 395	450 320	
150mm f/5.6 Xenar	415 335	240 210	220 170	
150mm f/9 G-Claron	510 420	385 320	325 235	
165mm f/6.8 Angulon			450 375	
165mm f/8 Angulon				125
165mm f/8 Super-Angulon		1700 1575	1600 1250	975
165mm f/8 Super-Angulon MC	3350 3025		2150 1600	
180mm f/3.5 Xenar (bbl)			80	
180mm f/4 Tele-Arton			495 300	
180mm f/5.5 Tele-Arton		455	300	
180mm f/5.5 Tele-Xenar		365	325 275	240
180mm/315mm f/5.6/12 Symmar Convertible			350 285	
180mm f/5.6 Symmar			350	
180mm f/5.6 Symmar-S			400 300	
180mm f/5.6 Symmar-S MC		550 525	480 400	
180mm f/5.6 APO-Symmar MC	795 710	650 585		
180mm f/5.6 Macro-Symmar MC	1425 1250			
210mm f/3.5 Xenar			160 120	

LARGE FORMAT

Schneider

Lens	New		Mint		Excellent		User	
210mm f/4.5 Xenar			265	220				
210mm/370mm f/5.6/12 Symmar Convertible			475	450	450	330	325	310
210mm f/5.6 Symmar			500	440	380	325		
210mm f/5.6 Symmar-S			430	395				
210mm f/5.6 Symmar-S MC	650	620	525	480	455	380		
210mm f/5.6 Super-Symmar HM MC	2685	2410	1850		1650			
210mm f/5.6 APO-Symmar MC	880	790	650	570				
210mm f/6.1 Xenar	630	510			285			
210mm f/6.8 Angulon			1250		750	725	550	
210mm/325mm/405mm f/6.8/12/13 Symmar Triple Conv					310	250		
210mm f/8 Super-Angulon			2900	2650	2750	2400		
210mm f/8 Super-Angulon MC	5180	4390						
210mm f/9 G-Claron	675	585	520	395				
210mm f/9 Repro-Claron					390	340		
240mm f/4.5 Tele-Arton					450	370		
240mm f/4.5 Xenar					340	300		
240mm f/5.5 Tele-Arton					350	300		
240mm f/5.5 Tele-Xenar					275	240		
240mm/420mm f/5.6/12 Symmar Convertible			695	530	575	540	325	
240mm f/5.6 Symmar					540	465	425	
240mm f/5.6 Symmar-S					750	640		
240mm f/5.6 Symmar-S MC	1125	990	870	750				
240mm f/5.6 APO-Symmar MC	1575	1330	1150	1000	940	780		
240mm f/9 APO-Artar	1350	1160						
240mm f/9 G-Claron	750	630	570	525	475	400		
240mm f/9 Repro-Claron					375	300		
250mm f/5.6 Tele-Arton			840	795	765	640		
250mm f/5.6 Tele-Arton MC	1550	1310			940	900		
270mm f/5.5 Tele-Arton					450	330		
270mm f/5.5 Tele-Xenar					395	320		
270mm f/9 G-Claron	970	820						
270mm f/11 G-Claron Wide Angle					630			
300mm f/5.5 Tele-Xenar					365	300		
300mm f/5.6 APO-Symmar MC	2200	1840						
300mm/500mm f/5.6/12 Symmar Convertible			795	750	560	495		
300mm f/5.6 Symmar					625	495		
300mm f/5.6 Symmar-S			1095	985	970	850		
300mm f/5.6 Symmar-S MC			1245	1200	1215	900		
300mm f/5.6 Xenar	920	795			500	440		
300mm f/6.8 Symmar Double Anastigmat						350		
305mm/560mm (12"/22") f/6.8 Symmar Convertible					350			
305mm f/9 G-Claron	950	820	750	675				
305mm f/9 Repro-Claron			650	600	575	450		
355mm f/9 G-Claron	1285	1230	1125	850	785	600		
360mm f/5.5 Tele-Xenar			1100	750	645	500		
360mm/640mm f/5.6/12 Symmar Convertible			895	795	745	580		
360mm f/5.6 Symmar					575	550		
360mm f/6.8 Symmar-S					1250	1000		
360mm f/6.8 Symmar-S MC	2040	1780	1550	1425	1350	1100		
360mm f/6.8 APO-Symmar MC	2295	2080						
360mm f/9 APO-Artar	1840	1660	1300					
400mm f/5.6 APO Tele-Xenar	5095	4510						
420mm f/9 Repro-Claron					630			
480mm f/8.4 Symmar-S MC					1650			
480mm f/8.4 APO-Symmar MC	2990	2720						
480mm f/9 Repro-Claron					700	550		
480mm f/11 APO-Artar	2230	2040	1400					
800mm f/12 APO Tele-Xenar	7920	7590						

LARGE FORMAT

Sinar

Lens	Mint		Excellent		User	
90mm f/6.8 Sinaron W		650				
135mm f/5.6	385					
150mm f/5.6 Sinaron	400					
210mm f/5.6 Sinaron	525	400				
240mm f/5.6 Sinaron	550					
300mm f/5.6	1075					

Turner-Reich

Lens	Mint		Excellent		User	
7½"/12"/18" Triple Convertible	395	300	250	185		
10"/14"/20" Triple Convertible		120				
10½" f/8.8 Triple Convertible			270			
12"/18"/24" Triple Convertible			295			
12"/21"/28" Triple Convertible			400		320	
12¼"/19"/25" Triple Convertible			395	300		

Wollensak

Lens	Mint		Excellent		User	
75mm f/1.9 Oscilo-Raptar			130			
83mm f/3.5 Raptar	200					
90mm f/6.8 Wide Angle Raptar			190	125	100	80
103mm f/4.5 Graftar			55	45		
108mm (4½") f/6.8 Wide Angle Raptar			275	200		
135mm f/4.7 Raptar			95	75		
159mm f/12.5 Extreme Wide Angle		400	320	250		
162mm f/4.5 Raptar			200	125		
165mm (6½") f/4.5 Series II			125			
190mm f/4.5 Raptar			190			
190mm f/4.5 Velostigmat (bbl)			75			
203mm (8") f/5.6 Raptar			200			
210mm f/5.6 Pro Raptar			495			
210mm f/6.8 Raptar Triple Convertible			550			
240mm (9½") f/4.5 Velostigmat			250			
254mm (10") f/4.5 Raptar			140			
254mm (10") f/5.6 Tele-Optar			225	200		
300mm f/4.5 Velostigmat Series II			300			
302mm f/4.5 Raptar			225			
305mm (12") f/4.5 Velostigmat			300	225		
330mm (13") f/6.8 Raptar			300			
360mm f/6 Veritar/Alphax		325				
380mm (15") f/5.6 Raptar (bbl)			150	100		
380mm f/5.6 Tele-Optar			195			
380mm (15") f/8 Process Anastigmat			175			
405mm f/4.5 Velostigmat			200			
3½" f/12.5 Extra Wide Angle Series IIIA (bbl)			80	50		
4" f/12.5 Wide Angle Raptar					150	
4 5/16" f/12.5 Series III			385			
5¾"/8¼"/12¾" f/7.7 Raptar Triple Convertible		190				
6" f/12.5 Wide Angle Raptar			395			
6½" f/4.5 Velostigmat Series II			70	65		
7" f/9.5 Velostigmat Wide Angle Series III			150			
7¼" f/4.5 Velostigmat Series II			160	125		
7½" f/4.5 Velostigmat Series II			100	85		
9½" f/4.5 Velostigmat Series II			250			
10" f/5.6 Raptar			200			
11½" f/4 Verito (bbl)			330	275		

LARGE FORMAT

Wollensak

Lens	Mint		Excellent		User	
11½"/20" f/6.3 Convertible					300	
12" f/12.5 Wide Angle Series III			325			
12½" f/6.3 Velostigmat Triple Convertible Series I			225	180		
13"/20"/25½" f/6.8/12.5/16 Raptar Triple Convertible IA			350			
14½" Verito Soft Focus			400	275		
15" f/5.6 Tele (bbl)			160	100		
15" f/6 Versar (bbl)				110		
15" f/8 Process Anastigmat (coated) (bbl)			175			
15" f/10 APO Raptar			150	100		
16" f/3.8 Vitax (variable soft focus)			225	170		
18" f/4 Verito			250	180		
19" f/10 Process Velostigmat					200	
20" f/6 Rapid Rectilinear			475	330		

Zeiss

Lens	Mint		Excellent		User	
53mm f/? Biogor			1950			
80mm f/2.8 Planar			200	160		
80mm f/2.8 Tessar			285			
100mm f/2.8 Planar			425			
105mm f/3.5 Tessar			200			
130mm/220mm/290mm Protarlinse (bbl)			225			
135mm f/3.5 Tessar			155	110		
135mm f/4.5 Tessar			150	100		
150mm f/3.5 Tessar			170	120		
150mm f/4.5 Tessar			150	100		
165mm f/4.5 Tessar			175	125		
165mm f/6.3 Tessar			135	75		
170mm f/9 Protar (coated)			450			
180mm f/4.5 Tessar	235	200				
180mm f/4.8 Sonnar			450			
180mm f/6.3 Tessar	125					
210mm f/3.5 Tessar				200		
210mm f/4.5 Tessar			300	225		
210mm f/6.3 Tessar			270	200		
210mm f/6.3 Commercial Astigon Tessar			350			
240mm f/9 APO Tessar			275	200		
300mm f/9 APO Tessar (bbl)			175			
310mm/480mm/590mm Protar Series VII			700	650		
350mm f/5 Protar Series IV (uncoated)			200			
360mm f/9 APO Tessar (bbl)			225			
400mm f/4.5 Tessar			350			
450mm f/9 APO Tessar			350	250		

LARGE FORMAT

Miscellaneous Large Format Lenses

Lens	New	Mint		Excellent		User	
80mm f/2.8 Heligon				125			
90mm f/6.3 Leitmeyer				310			
105mm f/4.5 APO-Lanthar				1100			
105mm f/6.8 Leitmeyer Wide Angle				60			
120mm f/6.3 Chromar				200			
120mm f/6.3 Osaka				275			
127mm f/4 Ross Wide Angle (bbl)						120	
135mm f/4.2 Plaubel Anticomar				150			
135mm f/4.5 Astragon				170	110		
135mm f/4.5 Laack				80			

Miscellaneous Large Format Lenses

Lens	New	Mint	Excellent	User
135mm f/4.5 Leitmeyer			100	
135mm f/9 Meyer-Goerlitz Wide Angle Aristostigmat (bbl)			55	
135mm/200mm/279mm Dallmeyer Stigmatic (bbl)			100	
149mm f/4.5 Milles Griot			350	300
150mm f/5.6 Osaka Commercial			235	
150mm f/6.3 Computar			200	
150mm f/6.3 Prinz Astragon			100	
180mm f/4.5 Plaubel Anticomar				160
197mm/321mm Hugo Meyer Double Plasmat			250	
210mm f/4.5 APO-Lanthar			680	
210mm f/6.3 Commercial Astragon			170	
210mm f/6.3 Computar Symmetrigon			375	250
210mm f/8 Kern Repro-Kilar (bbl)			100	
210mm f/9 Computar			300	
215mm f/4.8 Acuton			200	
215mm f/5.6 Orbit (Sch. Symmar Conv.)			295	
250mm f/8 Dallmeyer (bbl)			100	
259mm f/3.5 Elgeet Navitar (bbl)			100	
260mm f/4.5 Boyer Paris Saphir (bbl)			80	
260mm f/5.6 E. Krauss Paris Tessar (bbl)				230
270mm f/8 Carl Meyer Apochromat-Orthox (coated)			265	
280mm/360mm/430mm Steinheil Orthostigmat (bbl)			600	
300mm f/4.5 Astragon			100	
300mm f/5.6 Tele-Astragon			240	
300mm f/6.3 Commercial Astragon			350	
300mm f/6.3 Prinz Telephoto			270	
300mm f/7.7 Collinear			350	
305mm f/6.3 Orbit	320			
360mm f/4 Steinheil Cassar (bbl)			150	
360mm f/4.5 Astragon (bbl)	360	300		
400mm f/4.5 Steinheil Unifocal Doppel			200	
5" f/4 Ross Wide Angle Express (bbl)			95	
7" f/8 Gundlach Manhattan Triple Convertible			275	
7"/12"/18" f/8/16/22 Gundlach 5x7 Rapid Convertible			150	
8" f/2.9 Dallmeyer Pentac (bbl)			95	
8½" f/4.5 Taylor & Hobson (bbl)			150	
10" f/4.5 Elgeet Anastigmat (bbl)			150	
10"/12" Carl Meyer Convertible			430	
12" f/4.5 Dallmeyer Adon Series XI (bbl)			150	
12" f/6.3 Carl Meyer Anastigmat (coated)			430	350
12" f/6.3 Carl Meyer Wide Field			385	340
12" f/6.3 Ross Homocentric (bbl)			200	
12" f/7.7 Dallmeyer Dallon Tele-Anastigmat	300			95
12" f/10 Wray London Process Lustrar APO			275	
13" f/10 Taylor & Hobson Cooke Series IX Process (bbl)	195	100		
14" f/4.5 Voigtlander Heliar (bbl)			130	
14" f/5.6 Dallmeyer Tele-Anastigmat			250	
14" f/12.5 Dallmeyer Tele-Anastigmat			250	
16" f/10 Taylor & Hobson Cooke Series IX Process (bbl)		195	100	
18" (12x15) Taylor & Hobson			140	
18" f/10 Wray London Process Lustrar APO			420	
25" f/11 Hunter Penrose Penray Hilite (bbl)			550	
32¼" f/8 Ross (Zeiss patent) (bbl)			595	
40" f/5 Perkins-Elmer				2800
5x7 f/16 Gundlach Radar Extreme Wide Angle				
8x10 f/18 Gundlach Radar Wide Angle				

LARGE FORMAT

Aftermarket Strobes

This listing has been confined to somewhat recent vintages of the three most popular makes of camera-mount or hand-held strobes: Metz, Sunpak and Vivitar. There are other good ones around, but they aren't as common as the three makes listed here. Because of the relatively small market the makers of studio strobes cater to, their high-end professional models haven't been included in this listing, either.

Metz

Item	New		Mint		Excellent		User
30 BCT-4	105	80					
32 BCT-4	170	150					
32 CT-3	130	115	110	70			
32 CT-4			125	100			
32 CT-7	220	170	125	105			
32 Z-1		110					
32 Z-2		130					
32 MZ-3		155					
36 CT-3	265	215	175	150			
40 MZ-2		315					
45 CL-1/CT-1	260	205	160	135			
45 CL-1/CT-1 w/NiCads	300	245					
45 CL-3/CT-3	320	265			180	160	
45 CL-3/CT-3 w/NiCads	395	310					
45 CL-4/CT-4	365	300	225	200	200	150	
45 CL-4/CT-4 w/NiCads	425	345					
45 CT-5			285	260			
50 M25		540					
50 M25 (w/controller)		725					
60 CT-1	525	465			295	280	
60 CT-1 w/NiCads	545	485					
60 CT-2			350	300	280	250	
60 CT-2 w/NiCads			380	325			
60 CT-4	675	580	470	450	460	385	
60 CT-4 w/NiCads	695	600					

Sunpak

Item	New		Mint		Excellent		User	
30DX w/module			70	60	50	40		
120J Pro	325	275						
144			35	25				
144D			40	30				
144PC			40	30				
211					40	30		
220					50	40		
221D					40	30		
266D			50	40				
321					25	20		
322			50	40				
333					35	30		
333AZ			60	50				
344D			60	50	50	40		
383 Super	85	70						
388			50	40				
411			85	80				
421					25	20		
422D w/module					70	60		
433D w/module	100	75			65	60		
433AF	110	85						
444D w/module	150	125	100	70				
511					100	90		
522					100	90		
544	185	135	125	85				
555	210	160						
611 w/remote sensor, A/C adapt			160	145				
622 w/std head	330	220			160	140		
622 w/zoom head	360	250						
622 Super Zoom Kit	395	285						
993			70	65	60	50		
1600A			25	20				
2000DZ			40	30				
DX 8R Ring Flash	220	150						
DX 12R Ring Flash	260	225						

Vivitar

Item	New		Mint		Excellent		User	
252					25	20		
265					35	30		
273					65	50		
275					45	40		
283	80	65			50	45		
285					70	60		
285 HV	95	80			70	65		
292					50	40		
365 w/vari-sensor & bracket					200	150		
550 FD	60	45						
600 Series 1	100	75						
628 AF	70	50						
636 AF	110	85						
728 AF	65	50						
736 AF	100	75						
836 AF Zoom	240	180						
1900	25	15						
2000	30	25						
2600	30	25						
2600 D	35	30						
2800	35	30						
2800 D	50	40	30	25				
3500 w/module	70	60			35	30		
3700 w/module	105	70			50	30		
3900 w/bracket	145	115			100	75		
4600					70	60		
5000 Ring Light Macro Flash	100	65						
5200 w/module	115	100	85	75	65	60		
5600 w/module			120	110	115	75		

STROBES

Exposure Meters

Calcu-Light (Quantum)

Item	New	Mint	Excellent	User
Calcu-Flash			75 65	
Calcu-Flash II	215 185	125 100	110 75	
Calcu-Flash S	130 115		75 65	
Calcu-Light X	145 120	80 75		
Calcu-Light XP	170 135	90 80		
Photometer 1 and Lux	185 165			
Photometer 2	210 180			

Gossen

Item	New	Mint	Excellent	User
Color Pro 2F	535 490			
Color Pro 3F	810 735			
Flash Meter			80 60	
Flash Meter II			120 100	
Luna Lux	150 130		85 70	
Luna Pro		130 110	110 90	
Luna Pro Digital	190 155			
Luna Pro F	325 250	220 180	175 150	
Luna Pro S	210 175			
Luna Pro SBC	260 220	180 150	140 120	
Luna Six 3 (European Luna Pro)			90 70	
Luna Star F		220 200		
Luna Star F II	345 275			
Multi Pro	385 325	285 260		
N100	120 95	70 60		
Panlux	495 430			
Pilot II	75 60			
Scout II	55 40			
SixtiColor			150 125	
Super Pilot			50 40	
Ultra Pro	650 570	475 420	430 350	
Ultra Spot 1°	470 425			
Enlarging Attachment**	55 45			
Fiber Optics Probe**	200 195	150 135		
Luna Color Attachment***	315 250			
Luna Flash Attachment*	240 215		170 100	
Luna Micro Attachment***	60 50			
Luna Probe Attachment***	240 215	160 140		
Luna Sphere Attachment***	190 145	110 95	90 75	

** Can be used with Luna Pro SBC only*
*** Can be used with Luna Six 3, Luna Pro, Luna Pro SBC, Luna Pro F, Luna Lux, Multi Pro, Ultra Pro*
**** Can be used with Luna Pro SBC and Ultra Pro only*
***** Can be used with Luna Six 3 and Luna Pro only*

Gossen

Item	New	Mint	Excellent	User
Luna Star 5° Attachment (Star F only)	100 85			
Microscope Attachment**	45 40		25 20	
Multi-Beam (Spot) Attachment***	450 390	250 225	200 175	
Repro-Copy Attachment**	55 45			
Vari-Angle Attachment**	80 65	50 40	40 30	
Vari-Angle Attachment (early)****			35 25	

** Can be used with Luna Pro SBC only*
*** Can be used with Luna Six 3, Luna Pro, Luna Pro SBC, Luna Pro F, Luna Lux, Multi Pro, Ultra Pro*
**** Can be used with Luna Pro SBC and Ultra Pro only*
***** Can be used with Luna Six 3 and Luna Pro only*

Minolta

Item	New	Mint	Excellent	User
Autometer Pro			80 70	
Autometer			80 65	
Autometer II			80 65	
Autometer III	210 165	130 120	120 95	
Autometer IIIF		200 180		
Autometer IVF	310 260			
Auto Spot 2°			150 115	
Auto Spot II			175 125	
Colormeter I		200 180		
Colormeter II	640 550	495 475		
Colormeter IIIF	940 850			
Flashmeter				150 125
Flashmeter II			195 140	
Flashmeter III		395 375	375 325	
Flashmeter IV	520 440	420 385	380 340	
Spotmeter F	445 380	340 300		
Spotmeter M		320 300	270 235	
5° Viewfinder	120 95			
10° Viewfinder	95 80			
Booster II Set	270 220			
Data Receiver DR1000	290 240			
Flash Color Receptor	430 360			
IR Receiver Trigger	235 190			
Mini Receptor	140 110			

Pentax

Item	New	Mint	Excellent	User
Spotmeter V	325 250		150 100	
Spotmeter V FL	335 260			
Digital Spot	395 330		230 200	

Sekonic

Item	New	Mint	Excellent	User
L158 Auto-Lumi	40 35			
L164 Marine	270 230			
L188 Auto-Leader	60 45	30 20		
L228 Zoom Meter		100 90	75 60	
L246 Foot Candle Meter	95 75			
L248 Multi-Lumi		60 50		
L256 Flash Meter		140 100		

Sekonic

Item	New	Mint	Excellent	User
L308	245 ... 195			
L318 Digi-Light	235 ... 155	130 ... 100		
L318B w/Viewfinder	210 ... 170			
L328 Digi-Lite F	310 ... 250			
L398 (Gold)		100 ... 90		
L398 Studio	160 ... 125	90 ... 85	80 ... 65	
L398 II	120 ... 90			
L428 System Meter		120 ... 90	110 ... 90	
L438 View Spot			175 ... 130	
L448 Studio		265 ... 240		
L458 Digi-Flash		160 ... 140	130 ... 100	
L488 Digi-Spot (w/flash)	385 ... 300	300 ... 200		
L518 Digi-Pro		320 ... 295		
L718 Digi-Pro	495 ... 430			
L778 Dual Spot F (1°/3°)	640 ... 370			
Viewfinder for L518/L718	90 ... 70			
Viewfinder for L428	35 ... 25			

Shephard

Item	New	Mint	Excellent	User
DM-170	105 ... 95			
FM-800		65 ... 50		
FM-880	100 ... 85			
FM-900		80 ... 65		
FM-990	120 ... 100			
FM-1000	165 ... 145			

Soligor

Item	New	Mint	Excellent	User
Spot Sensor			75 ... 50	
Spot Sensor II	240 ... 190	120 ... 105	100 ... 85	
Digital Spot	285 ... 230	150 ... 125		
Flash Meter			55 ... 45	

Vivitar

Item	New	Mint	Excellent	User
Flash Meter			80 ... 70	
Flash Meter 2	125 ... 100			

Wein

Item	New	Mint	Excellent	User
WP-500B	90 ... 65			
WP-1000	125 ... 95			

Glossary

Action Finder: An accessory viewfinder with a large eyepiece for interchangeable-finder camera systems that allows an eye-relief of up to several inches, while still allowing total visibility of the viewing area. Popular for sports photography and other situations in which the photographer may need to observe action outside the viewfinder frame.

AE: Auto Exposure. A system in which the camera determines a scene's exposure based on lighting conditions and selects the correct aperture for a user-selected shutter speed, or the correct shutter speed for a user-selected aperture, or, with Program AE, both.

AE Lock: Auto Exposure Lock. Usually a button that locks in the selected AE setting. Most useful for holding an AE reading when recomposing a scene in unusual lighting situations.

AF: Auto Focus.

Angle Finder: An viewfinder accessory that attaches to the eyepiece of a camera, which projects the image at a 90 degree angle. Useful for copy work and other instances in which straight-on viewing may be awkward.

Aperture: The interior opening of a lens. Usually the aperture size can be varied by an iris diaphragm mechanism to control the amount of light reaching the film plane. Some lenses have fixed apertures; that is, they cannot be varied in size.

Aperture Numbers: (See *F/stop*)

Aperture-Priority AE: An auto exposure mode in which the camera determines the shutter speed based on a scene's light conditions and the lens aperture the user has selected.

Auto Bracketing: A feature on many modern cameras that will automatically vary exposure for a series of frames, usually in ½ stop increments. This slight variation in exposure between successive shots is called bracketing and is often used to insure that at least one frame in a series is properly exposed.

Auto Diaphragm: A lens diaphragm that is coupled by means of a mechanical or electronic link to a camera body such that it will close down to a pre-selected opening size just prior to and during exposure.

Auto Film Loading: A system on many modern cameras in which the camera secures the film to the film take-up spool and automatically winds the film to the first frame.

Auto Film Rewind: A system in which the camera will rewind the film automatically once the last frame has been exposed.

ASA: American Standards Association. Former standard used to determine film speed and, for all practical purposes, synonymous with the current designation, ISO. See ISO, Film Speed.

Auto Winder: Also called a winder, an auto winder is a film winding accessory that is usually attached to the bottom of a camera. Typical settings on a winder are S for Single frame and C for Continuous. A winder will usually advance film at rates up to 2 frames per second when on the continuous setting. Not all winders have a Continuous setting. Not all cameras will accept winders.

Averaging Meter: An exposure meter which reads and averages all light values within its range of acceptance, and which recommends exposure based on the lighting situation.

B: Bulb. A manual setting on a camera in which the shutter will remain open for as long as the shutter release is depressed.

BLC: Back Light Control. Usually a button on auto exposure cameras that, when depressed, will overexpose the frame by 1 ½ to 2 stops. Used in situations where the subject is close to a bright light source, such as a window. Often this sort of lighting situation will fool a camera's meter and cause the subject to be underexposed.

Bottom-Centerweighted Metering: Centerweighted metering that has a stronger emphasis toward the bottom of the image area. The idea behind this is to reduce the influence a bright sky may have on outdoor subjects.

CdS: Cadmium Sulfide. The first substance used in metering cells for battery-powered light meters. It offers better low-light sensitivity and more accurate response to light temperature than Selenium meters.

Continuous AF: An autofocus selection in which a camera will autofocus continually on a subject, especially a moving one, and will allow exposures to be taken whether or not the subject is in focus. Also called Servo AF.

Data Back: An accessory camera back that will imprint data on the film emulsion, usually within the frame. A typical databack will imprint the current date, but little else. Databacks with advanced features, usually available only for cameras with advanced features, may offer such additional options as printing information between frames, printing exposure information, an intervalometer and film-rewind options.

Depth-of-Field Preview: A feature on many cameras, usually a button or a lever, that allows the user to examine the actual depth of focus at a given aperture. The smaller the aperture (the larger the aperture number), the greater the depth of focus.

DX Film Coding: On cameras supporting it, a feature that will automatically set a film's ISO (ASA) speed based on coded information on the film cassette. Some cameras allow users to override this feature and select their own ISO settings.

EI: Exposure Index. A user-assigned film speed that differs from that recommended by the film manufacturer.

EV: Exposure Value. EV is a light measurement method in which a given exposure ratio between apertures and shutter speeds is assigned a number independent of film speed. For example: 1/60 @ f/8 = 1/125 @ f/5.6 = 1/250 @ f/4 and so on. These settings represent equivalent exposure values and have the same EV number. In the above example, that number is EV 12 and will always be EV 12, no matter what the film speed is. Each successively higher whole number on the EV scale represents a doubling of the amount of light or exposure a subject receives, just as each successively lower number represents a decrease in exposure by one-half. When metering a scene at different ISO settings, however, the EV number will change. A scene metered at EV 12 at ISO 100 will need an exposure of 1/60 @ f/8 (or its equivalent). This same scene, when metered at ISO 400, will have an EV of 14, requiring an exposure of 1/60 @ f/16 (or equivalent). The difference of 2 steps on the EV scale corresponds to a 2x2, or a four-fold increase in light or light sensitivity, which is exactly the difference between that of ISO 100 and ISO 400. If it sounds confusing, just think about it for a minute. It makes sense. The handy thing about the EV system, once one gets the hang of it, is that one can think in simplified terms when calculating exposure.

Exposure Compensation: A feature on most auto-exposure cameras that allows the user to bias exposure, typically in ⅓ or ½ stop increments, usually over a 2-stop range. Useful for unusual lighting situations that may otherwise fool a camera's meter.

Extension Tube: Often available as a set with three to four different lengths. An extension tube placed between lens and camera, will reduce the minimum focusing distance, while increasing the magnification. Auto extension tubes retain the coupling mechanism between lens and camera, allowing auto diaphragm operation.

Film Speed: The "speed" of a film's emulsion is determined by its relative sensitivity to light. A "fast" film is one that is sensitive to small amounts of light, enabling shorter exposure times in low-light situations. A "slow" film, on the other hand, is better able to handle extremely bright situations. The trade-offs are: a fast film's inherent grainy structure will reduce a photograph's sharpness whereas a slow film has a much smaller grain size, hence much better sharpness; a slow film is inconvenient to use in low or subdued-light situations because of the longer exposure times involved.

Fish Eye: A very short focal length lens (typically in the range from 6mm to 8mm for 35mm cameras) with a 180° or more field view. Fish eye lenses cause extreme distortion of perspective and make a circular image. Straight lines that pass through the center of the image area remain straight; all others become progressively more distorted as they are located closer to the edge of the image area.

Flash Sync: The fastest shutter speed setting at which a flash can be used. See M sync and X sync.

FPS: Frames Per Second.

F/ratio: Theoretically, the mathematical ratio of a lens' focal length to the diameter of its front element. For example, (100mm focal length)÷(50mm front element diameter) = 2, so this lens would be considered a 100mm f/2. The larger the maximum aperture, the lower the f/ratio and the more light an optic gathers. Lenses with low f/ratios are frequently referred to as "fast" lenses because they allow faster shutter speeds than lenses with smaller maximum apertures.

F/stop: A ratio of a lens' focal length to the size of the opening of its interior diaphragm. With adjustable diaphragms, this ratio can change and is expressed as a logarithmic scale on the lens' aperture ring. The higher the number, the smaller the opening. See F/ratio.

Focus Priority AF: An autofocus feature in which the camera will not allow an exposure to be made until the subject is in focus.

Focusing Screen: The ground glass or fresnel panel, made from either glass or plastic, on which the image actually appears for viewing. Some 35mm and medium format cameras have interchangeable focusing screens, which provide the user with a greater variety of composition or viewing options.

Full-Frame Fish Eye: An apparent contradiction in terms, a full-frame fish eye lens has a focal length typically in the range of 15mm to 16mm for 35mm cameras. The image is distorted as is the case with a fish eye lens, but the image is not circular, hence the designation "full-frame." A full-frame fish eye lens has a 180° field of view measured on the diagonal.

GN or Guide Number: A measurement of a strobe's light output that can be used to determine exposure according to the following formula: (Camera to Subject Distance) x (Lens Aperture) = Guide Number. In the U.S., the Distance to Subject is expressed in feet (elsewhere, it's expressed in meters) and the Lens Aperture is expressed in f/stops. The guide number of a strobe is always given in terms of feet or meters at a particular ISO number. When a guide number is cited in this book, it is given in feet at ISO 100.

ISO: International Standards Organization. In photography, the letters ISO are most often associated with film emulsion speeds. To the casual observer ISO may seem synonymous with the older film-speed rating, ASA (and it is treated the same in this book), but that isn't quite the case. When used as a film-speed rating, ISO incorporates both the ASA rating used in the U.S. and the DIN rating used in Europe. Using the former standards, a film emulsion rated at ASA 100, for example, carried the equivalent DIN rating of 21°. The ISO rating of this same film emulsion is now expressed as 100/21°

Macro: In photography, a term denoting higher than normal magnification and usually expressed as a ratio. For example, a macro ratio of 1:2 means that the image size on the film is ½ its actual size. Generally, "true" macro magnification is considered to begin at a ratio of 1:2. Macro is also a setting found on many zoom lenses that allows a degree of close focus. Most zoom lenses with a macro setting do not offer true macro focusing, in that they cannot focus down to a minimum of a 1:2 ratio.

Macro Lens: Also called a Micro lens. Macro lenses are specially designed, flat-field optics with close-focusing capabilities and maximum macro ratios of usually either 1:2 or 1:1 (½ or full life size at the film plane), depending upon make and model. Macro lenses (except some bellows lenses) retain infinity focus and work well for regular photography. Some macro lenses are designed especially for use with bellows and cannot be focused without them.

Macrophoto Lens: A special, high-magnification lens that must be used in conjunction with a bellows. Image magnifications from 2x to 20x life size are possible with sufficient extension.

Manual Diaphragm: A variable, iris-bladed mechanism inside a lens that is coupled to an aperture ring, but has no coupling linkage to the camera. When using a lens with a manual diaphragm on cameras with TTL meters, metering must be done at the lens' taking aperture using either stop-down metering or aperture priority AE.

Manual Exposure Mode: An exposure method in which the user selects both the aperture and shutter speed according to either the camera's built-in meter or an external source.

Micro Lens: See Macro Lens.

Mid-Roll Rewind: A feature on many modern SLRs with built-in motordrives that allows the user to rewind a roll of film before it is totally exposed. This is a useful feature when the photographer wishes to change film emulsion types before the existing roll is finished. Most cameras that offer this feature wind the film back into the cassette, leaving no film leader protruding. Some cameras allow the user to select an option which stops rewinding just short of sucking the leader back into the cassette, which makes it much easier to reload the roll at a later time.

Mirror Lock-Up: A feature on many professional-oriented SLRs in which the camera's mirror can be raised and locked manually. Its main purpose is to minimize mirror-induced vibration when taking high magnification photos, or when using slow shutter speeds, or both. Most 35mm SLRs that have vertical focal-plane shutters offer a pseudo mirror lock-up capability, which can be employed by using the self-timer. After charging the self-timer mechanism (or selecting the self-timer option on an electronic SLR), when the shutter is released the mirror raises immediately. In most cases the ensuing delay is sufficient to eliminate fuzzy photos caused by mirror-induced vibration.

Motor Drive: A high-speed film winding accessory that attaches to the base of a camera and that typically offers continuous film winding speeds which may range anywhere from 3 frames per second to over 6 frames per second (depending on the model, the camera, and the shutter speeds selected). Most motor drives offer a single-frame setting and many offer two or more continuous speeds. Some motor drives have motorized rewind.

M sync: The flash sync setting or switch for M-class flashbulbs.

Multiple Exposure Capability: The ability to take more than one exposure on a single frame. Many cameras that offer this feature have a separate switch for this. Others require that the film-rewind button on the bottom of the camera be depressed prior to each additional exposure. Still other cameras don't support this feature at all.

OTF: Off The Film plane. This refers to a method of either TTL exposure metering or TTL flash metering in which the reflectance of the film is used to calculate correct exposure. See TTL.

Partial Metering: Also called Selective Metering. A metering system in which only a specified central area within the viewfinder meters a scene. This system is more useful in critical exposure situations than the various averaging methods, since extraneous light in a scene will not affect a camera's meter as long as it remains outside the metering area.

PC Lens: A *Perspective Control*, or Shift lens. Allows the front element of the lens to be shifted away from the centerline. Most common in focal lengths ranging from 24mm to 35mm. A PC lens is used mostly for architectural photography and other situations in which converging lines are undesirable.

PC Socket: Push Connector Socket. A receptacle for standard flash cords, enabling a flash to be used off the camera.

Pentaprism: A solid, five sided, aluminized prism used to reflect the image from a camera's focusing screen to the eyepiece.

Polycarbonate: Marketing jargon for plastic. To be fair, though, polycarbonate is a general term which includes a variety of plastics, all of which are noted for durability and a high melting temperature. When reinforced with carbon fibers or fiberglass, the resulting composite's strength and durability rivals and, in some cases, surpasses that of many metals.

Porroprism: A series of mirrors used to reflect an image from the focusing screen to the eyepiece.

Predictive Focus: A feature on some of the latest-generation autofocus cameras that, when engaged, will track a moving subject and predict its location and correct focus at the instant of exposure.

Preset: This term applies to certain manual-diaphragm lenses that have an additional ring adjacent to the aperture ring. When rotated one way, this additional ring will open the aperture to its maximum, facilitating ease of focus. The ring is then rotated in the opposite direction to close the iris down to the preselected taking aperture.

Program: An auto exposure mode in which the camera selects both the aperture and shutter speed according to a scene's lighting conditions.

Program Shift: An adjustment to the program setting that allows the user to bias toward higher or lower shutter speeds, or greater or smaller apertures, while maintaining the inversely proportional relationship between the two values.

Rangefinder: A term used to indicate a camera design, but which is more precisely a component of a camera design. An optical rangefinder is a system of prisms or mirrors or both that use a parallax method of measurement to determine distance and correct focus. Focus is obtained by bringing a double image visible in the center of the viewfinder frame into coincidence. A big advantage to a rangefinder camera is the lenses it can use. Lenses for rangefinder cameras often exhibit superior sharpness and contrast because of their less complex design. (A general rule in optics is that the more elements a lens has, the greater the image degradation it will experience.) Another plus is that because a rangefinder camera does not have a reflex mirror it is much quieter than an SLR and produces much less vibration. Its disadvantages include an inability to see exactly that which the lens sees (although most rangefinders have parallax correction) and a limited lens selection, especially in focal lengths greater than 135 millimeters.

SBC: Silicon Blue Cell. A recent-technology metering cell that offers improved sensitivity over silicon photo cells.

SCA: Sync Cord Adapter. A system of compatibility for flash photography that has become the standard in Europe and is slowly gaining in popularity elsewhere.

Selective Metering: See Partial Metering.

Servo AF: See Continuous AF.

Shift: See Program Shift.

Shift Lens: See PC Lens.

Shutter-Priority AE: An auto exposure mode in which the camera determines the lens aperture based on the scene's light conditions and the shutter speed selected by the user.

Shutter Speed: The time that a shutter remains open. Typically expressed in whole numbers on a shutter speed dial or display, the numbers above 1 are actually reciprocals (i.e. 250 is actually 1/250 second). The numbers below 1 on certain electronic SLRs are multiples of seconds (i.e. 8 = 8 seconds).

Single Shot AF: Usually coupled with a camera's focus priority feature, this system allows only one exposure at a time, and then only after the subject is in focus.

SLR: Single Lens Reflex. The design of most interchangeable-lens 35mm and medium format cameras. Most SLRs have a mirror located directly behind the lens, which projects the image onto a focusing screen, then through a pentaprism (or in some cases a porroprism), which provides the user with a right-side-up, left-to-right corrected image. In a typical SLR the mirror swings up immediately before exposure, allowing the image to be projected directly onto the film plane. Advantages to the SLR design include: most SLRs have TTL metering and many have TTL flash metering; what you see is what you get because you're observing the scene through the lens; a wide range of accessories and lenses. Disadvantages include: the user cannot see the image at the moment of exposure because the mirror rises, momentarily blanking out the scene visible from within the viewfinder (Exceptions to this include a handful of SLR's that have fixed, pellicle mirrors. Their main disadvantage, however, is an inherently dimmer viewfinder.); a higher noise and vibration level due to the mirror assembly's operation.

SPD: Silicon Photo Diode. A widely-used type of metering cell that has all but replaced its CdS predecessors. Its advantages over CdS is a faster response, increased light sensitivity range, and no "memory," an affliction of CdS meters in which the meter will "remember' a bright scene for a while after being exposed to it.

Sport Finder: See Action Finder.

Spot Meter: A light meter that is either hand-held or, in some cameras, built in to the camera. A true spot meter features a 1° angle of acceptance, thereby allowing the photographer to make critical exposure measurements of a scene. A built-in spot meter meters the central area of the viewfinder only, typically from 1% to 3% of the viewfinder image.

Stop: Sometimes synonymous to f/stop, "stop" also means a single gradation of exposure value (see EV). When a photographer says, for example, that a scene has a three-stop range between highlight and shadow, he or she is referring to a three step range in exposure values, or to put it another way, that the highlight area is receiving eight times the light that the shadow area is.

Stop-Down Metering: A metering method that measures exposure at a lens' taking aperture. Used nowadays primarily with lenses that have manual or fixed apertures. Many early SLRs with TTL meters use this method for determining exposure. Modern full-featured SLRs retain this capability.

Strobe: Electronic Flash.

T: Time. When making an exposure with a camera set on "T," the shutter will remain open until the T setting is disengaged. Seen now mostly on older cameras, the T setting is essentially "B" with a built-in lock.

Teleconverter: This device fits between the lens and the camera. It is an economical method of increasing a lens' focal length without affecting its minimum focusing distance. The most popular configuration is the 2x teleconverter, which doubles a lens' focal length. Other magnifications are, however, available: most common being 1.4x and 3x. But you never get something for nothing. The increase in power also corresponds to the amount of light lost when using one; e.g. a 2X increase in focal length results in a two-stop loss of light. However, if your camera has a TTL meter, it will automatically take into account this light loss and display the resulting correct exposure.

TLR: Twin Lens Reflex. A camera with separate taking and viewing lenses. A mirror is used in conjunction with the viewing lens to reflect the image onto a focusing screen. The image is right-side-up, but uncorrected from right to left (i.e. backwards).

Trap Focus: A feature on some latest-generation autofocus cameras in which the camera will automatically take a photograph once a subject enters a pre-determined area of focus.

TTL: Through The Lens. This acronym is often used when referring to viewing an image, a meter design, or a flash metering method. All have the same thing in common in that they refer to the ability to evaluate a scene as the lens sees it, or Through The Lens.

Variable Aperture: A design common to modern zoom lenses in which the aperture setting changes as the focal length is changed. Usually as much as one stop of light is lost when zooming from the shortest focal length to the longest. This presents little problem when using a camera in an auto exposure mode, but can be annoying when using it in manual or when using it with a manual strobe, especially at intermediate focal lengths.

Varifocal Lens: Often mis-categorized as a zoom lens, a varifocal "zoom" requires refocusing after a shift in focal length, except at infinity focus. Advantages to the varifocal design include fewer lens elements than a true zoom of the same focal length, and a more compact size.

Waist Level Finder: A collapsible hood, which, when opened, gives the photographer a direct view of the camera's focusing screen. Called a waist level finder due to the fact that the focusing screen is corrected for best viewing from that distance. Often, a waist level finder will have a magnifier incorporated into its design, which can be moved into position above the focusing screen, and which enables the photographer to examine a magnified image for critical focus. The view through a waist level finder is not corrected from right to left (i.e., images seen are backwards).

Winder: See Auto Winder.

X sync: The fastest shutter speed setting at which an electronic flash can be used. Often symbolized by a lightning bolt.

Zoom Lens: Available in two basic designs, known as either two-ring or one-touch, zoom lenses provide photographers with continuously variable focal lengths throughout their range. Many two-ring, or two-touch, zooms are older vintage lenses, whereas most newer zooms are of the one-touch style. Exceptions to this are autofocus zooms, which are two-touch. Each style has its advantages and disadvantages: The two-ring style allows zooming without accidentally shifting focus, but because it has separate rings for focus and zoom control, it is a little slower to use (not a problem with autofocus cameras, however). The one-touch style is quicker to use, since the single collar allows simultaneous focusing and zooming, but the focus can be shifted inadvertently when zooming from one focal length to another.

Index

See Page 238 for Ordering & Sales Information

Other Books from Amherst Media

Basic 35mm Photo Guide

Craig Alesse **110,000 In Print!**

For beginning photographer! Designed to teach 35mm basics step-by-step—completely illustrated. Features the latest cameras. Includes: 35mm automatic and semi-automatic cameras, camera handling, f-stops, shutter speeds, composition, and lens & camera care. $12.95 list, 9 x 8, 112 p, 178 photos, order no. 1051.

The Art of Infrared Photography

Joseph Paduano

A complete, straightforward approach to B&W infrared photography for the beginner and professional. Includes a beautifully printed portfolio. Features: infrared theory, precautions, use of filters, focusing, film speed, exposure, night & flash photography, developing, printing and toning. $17.95 list, 9 x 9, 76 p, 50 duotone prints, order no. 1052.

Infrared Nude Photography

Joseph Paduano

A stunning collection of natural images with wonderful how-to text. Over 50 rich duotone infrared images. Photographed on location in the natural settings of the Grand Canyon, Bryce Canyon and the New Jersey Shore. $18.95 list, 9 x 9, 80 p, over 50 photos, order no. 1080.

Build Your Own Home Darkroom

Lista Duren & Will McDonald

This classic book shows how to build a high quality, inexpensive darkroom in your basement, spare room, closet, bathroom, garage, attic or almost anywhere. Full information on: darkroom design, woodworking, tools, building techniques, lightproofing, ventilation, work tables, enlargers, lightboxes, darkroom sinks, water supply panels & print drying racks. $17.95 list, 8 1/2 x 11, 160 p, order no. 1092.

Into Your Darkroom Step-by-Step

Dennis P. Curtin

The ideal beginning darkroom guide. Easy to follow and fully illustrated each step of the way. From developing black & white negatives to making your own enlargements. Full information on: equipment you'll need, setting up the darkroom, making proof sheets & enlargements, and special techniques for fine prints. $17.95 list, 8 1/2 x 11, 90 p, hundreds of photos, order no. 1093.

Big Bucks Selling Your Photography/Revised Edition

Cliff Hollenbeck

A must reference for any pro or beginner. Packed with information from a successful pro. Features: setting up a profitable business, targeting the kind of photography that sells, creating successful portfolios, shooting stock images, planning your business, and computerizing in your business,. Includes: samples of agreements, contracts, releases, and more. $14.95 list, 6 x 9, 336 p, order no. 1177.

The Wildlife Photographer's Field Manual

Joe McDonald

The classic, inclusive reference for every wildlife photographer. Complete technical how-to, including: lenses, lighting, blinds, exposure in the field, focusing techniques, and more. Tips and special sections on: sneaking up on animals, close-up macro photography, studio and aquarium shots, photographing insects, birds, reptiles, amphibians and mammals., and more. Joe McDonald is one of the world's most accomplished wildlife photographers and a trained biologist. $14.95 list, 6 x 9, 208 p. order no. 1005.

The Freelance Photographer's Handbook

Fredrik D. Bodin

A complete and comprehensive handbook for the working freelancer (or anyone who wants to become one). Full of how-to info & examples, along with tips, techniques and strategies both tried & true and new & innovative. Chapters on marketing, customer relations, inventory systems and procedures for stock photography, portfolios, plus special camera techniques to increase the marketability of your work. $19.95 list, 8 1/2 x 11, 160 p, order no. 1075

Camera Maintenance & Repair

Thomas Tomosy

A step-by-step, fully illustrated guide by a master camera repair technician. Sections include: general maintenance, testing camera functions, basic tools needed and where to get them, basic repairs for accessories, camera electronics, plus "quick tips" for maintenance and repair of specific models. $24.95 list, 8 1/2 x 11, 176 p, order no. 1158

Camcorder Tricks & Special Effects

Michael Stavros

Turn you camcorder into a toy! Over 40 tricks and effects show you how. With only a camcorder and simple props, you can simulate effects used by Hollywood pros. It's so easy, the whole family can join in the fun — even Rover! Enjoy creating video fun, and make your videos an adventure to watch. $12.95 list, 7x10, 128 p, order no. 1482

Basic Camcorder Guide/ Revised Edition

Steve Bryant

For everyone with a camcorder, or those who want one. Easy and fun to read. Packed with up-to-date info you need to know. Includes: selecting a camcorder, how to give your videos a professional look, camcorder care tips, advanced video shooting techniques, and more. $12.95 list, 6 x 9, 96 p, order no. 1239.

Underwater Videographer's Handbook

Lynn Laymon

Accomplished diver, instructor and underwater videographer, Lynn Laymon, will show you how to get started and have fun shooting your own professional-quality underwater videos. Fully illustrated and packed with step-by-step instruction on: evaluating & purchasing equipment, basic & advanced underwater techniques, video dive planning strategies, underwater composition & lighting, video editing & post production techniques, shooting underwater video at night, marketing your underwater video skills, and much more. $19.95 list, 8 1/2 x 11, 128 p, over 100 photos, order no. 1266.

Write Amherst Media for a free catalog of over 200 books and videos about photography and videography.

ORDERING & SALES INFORMATION:

Dealers, distributors & colleges: Write, call or fax to place orders. For price information, contact Amherst Media or an Amherst Media sales representative. Net 30 days.

Individuals: If possible, purchase books from an Amherst Media retailer. To order direct, send a check or money order with a note listing the books you want and your shipping address. U.S. & overseas freight charges are $3.00 first book and $1.00 for each additional book. Visa and Master Card accepted. New York state residents add 8% sales tax.

Prices are in U.S. dollars. Payment in U.S. funds only.

All prices, publication dates and specifications are subject to change without notice.

AMHERST MEDIA, INC.
PO Box 586
Amherst, NY 14226 USA

Fax: 716-874-4508
Phone: 716-874-4450

McBroom's Camera Bluebook Registration Form

Please fill out this sheet and send or fax to receive free information about future Bluebook editions and other photo books.

CUSTOMER INFORMATION

DATE

NAME

STREET OR BOX #

CITY STATE

ZIP CODE

PHONE (   )

OPTIONAL INFORMATION

I BOUGHT *MCBROOM'S BLUEBOOK* BECAUSE

I FOUND THESE CHAPTERS TO BE MOST USEFUL

I PURCHASED THE BOOK FROM

CITY STATE

I WOULD LIKE TO SEE MORE BOOKS ABOUT

I PURCHASE BOOKS PER YEAR

ADDITIONAL COMMENTS

FAX to: 1-800-622-3298

CUT ALONG DOTTED LINE

IF MAILING, FOLD IN NUMBER ORDER ALONG DASHED LINES.

①

②

Name________________________________
Address______________________________
City________________________State_____
Zip__________________ — __________

Place
Postage
Here

Amherst Media, Inc.
PO Box 586
Amherst, NY 14226

③

IF MAILING, PASTE UNDERSIDE OF FLAP, OR TAPE HERE.